W9-CCJ-738

INTRODUCTION TO DOCUMENTARY

INTRODUCTION TO
DOCUMENTARY

Second Edition

Bill Nichols

INDIANA UNIVERSITY PRESS

Bloomington & Indianapolis

To Pascale Menconi—as loving and beautiful
a spirit as anyone could hope to know

This book is a publication of

Indiana University Press
601 North Morton Street
Bloomington, Indiana 47404-3797 USA

www.iupress.indiana.edu

Telephone orders　800-842-6796
Fax orders　812-855-7931
Orders by e-mail　iuporder@indiana.edu

© 2001, 2010 by Bill Nichols
1st edition 2001, 2nd edition 2010
All rights reserved

No part of this book may be reproduced
or utilized in any form or by any means,
electronic or mechanical, including
photocopying and recording, or by
any information storage and retrieval
system, without permission in writing
from the publisher. The Association
of American University Presses'
Resolution on Permissions constitutes
the only exception to this prohibition.

∞ The paper used in this publication
meets the minimum requirements of
the American National Standard for
Information Sciences—Permanence
of Paper for Printed Library
Materials, ANSI Z39.48-1992.

Manufactured in the United
States of America

Library of Congress Cataloging-
in-Publication Data

Nichols, Bill, [date]-
  Introduction to documentary
/ Bill Nichols. — 2nd ed.
    p. cm.
  Includes bibliographical
references and index.
  Includes filmography.
  ISBN 978-0-253-35556-0 (cloth : alk.
paper) — ISBN 978-0-253-22260-2
(pbk. : alk. paper) 1. Documentary
films—History and criticism. I. Title.
  PN1995.9.D6N539 2010
  070.1'8—dc22

                    2010017294

1　2　3　4　5　15　14　13　12　11　10

Contents

· *Acknowledgments* · *ix*

· Introduction · *xi*

1 How Can We Define Documentary Film? · *1*

2 Why Are Ethical Issues Central to
Documentary Filmmaking? · *42*

3 What Gives Documentary Films a
Voice of Their Own? · *67*

4 What Makes Documentaries
Engaging and Persuasive? · *94*

5 How Did Documentary Filmmaking
Get Started? · *120*

6 How Can We Differentiate among Documentaries?
Categories, Models, and the Expository and
Poetic Modes of Documentary Film · *142*

7 How Can We Describe the Observational,
Participatory, Reflexive, and Performative
Modes of Documentary Film? · *172*

8   How Have Documentaries Addressed
    Social and Political Issues? · 212

9   How Can We Write Effectively about
    Documentary? · 253

·   *Notes on Source Material* · *273*
·   *Filmography* · *289*
·   *List of Distributors, Internet Distribution
    Venues, Internet Search Engines, and
    International Distributors* · *301*
·   *Index* · *323*

Acknowledgments

My greatest debt of gratitude goes to the students who have studied documentary film with me over the years. Their curiosity and questions have provided the motivation for this book. I am also greatly indebted to those who have gathered at the Visible Evidence conferences since their inception in 1993 to exchange ideas and pursue debates about documentary film. These conferences, initiated by Jane Gaines and Michael Renov, have proven invaluable to the promotion of a lively dialogue about documentary film in the broadest possible terms.

Without the assistance of the filmmakers who so generously provided still images of their work, this book would be greatly impoverished. I thank them for their willingness to provide superb illustrations, often on short notice.

Michael Wilson initiated and Victoria Gamburg updated and completed the research for the original list of distributors. Their assistance was timely and indispensable to the completion of the first edition. Tori Palmatier performed a comparable role for the second edition. Her search of websites, most of which were not functional at the time of the first edition's publication, greatly enriches this resource list. David Gray took on the task of obtaining the stills I needed and carried it out superbly. I am greatly indebted to Tori and David for their invaluable help.

Jane Behnken has served as my editor at Indiana University Press for the preparation of the second edition. Her support and enthusiasm for the idea of a second edition has proven indispensable. Jamison Cockerham did the layout and design for the book and designed the cover.

Introduction

Organized into chapters by a series of questions, the second edition of *Introduction to Documentary* examines this fascinating type of film-making in detail. The questions involve issues of definition, ethics, content, form, modes, and politics. Because documentaries address *the* world in which we live rather than *a* world imagined by the filmmaker, they differ from the various genres of fiction (science fiction, horror, adventure, melodrama, and so on) in significant ways. They are made with different assumptions about purpose, they involve a different quality of relationship between filmmaker and subject, and they prompt different sorts of expectations from audiences.

These differences, as we shall see, guarantee no absolute separation between fiction and documentary. Some documentaries make strong use of practices such as scripting, staging, reenactment, rehearsal, and performance that we associate with fiction. Some adopt familiar conventions such as the individual hero who undergoes a challenge or embarks on a quest, building suspense, emotional crescendos, and climactic resolutions. Some fiction makes strong use of conventions that we typically associate with nonfiction or documentary such as location shooting, nonactors, hand-held cameras, improvisation, found footage (footage not shot by the filmmaker), voice-over commentary, and natural lighting. The boundary between the two realms is highly fluid but, in most cases, still perceptible.

Since notions about what is distinct to documentary, and what is not, change over time, specific films may well spark debate about the boundaries of fiction and nonfiction. At one point Eric von Stroheim's *Greed* (1925) and Sergei Eisenstein's *Strike* (1925) were praised for the high degree of realism or verisimilitude they brought to their stories. They possessed a documentary appeal. At another point Roberto Rossellini's *Rome, Open City* (1945) and John Cassavetes's *Shadows* (1960) seemed to bring lived reality to the screen in ways not previously experienced. Although all these works have been normally treated as fiction, a case could be made for the power of their documentary dimensions and their ability to stimulate documentary as well as fiction filmmakers to rethink their assumptions. Reality TV shows like *Cops, American Idol,* and *Survivor* have heightened the degree to which television can exploit a sense of documentary authenticity and melodramatic spectacle simultaneously. And films such as *Forrest Gump* (1994), *The Truman Show* (1998), *The Blair Witch Project* (1999), and *The Road to Guantanamo* (2006) build their narratives around the underlying premise of documentary: we feel a distinct fascination when we witness the lives of others who seem to belong to the same historical world that we do.

In *The Blair Witch Project*, this fascination not only relies on combining documentary conventions with the gritty realism of camcorder technology to impart historical credibility to a fictional situation, it also makes full use of promotional and publicity channels that surround the film proper and help prepare us for it. These included a website with background information about the Blair witch, expert testimony, and references to "actual" people and events, all designed to market the film not as fiction, and not even simply as a documentary, but as the raw footage of three filmmakers who tragically disappeared.

If nothing else, *The Blair Witch Project* should remind us that our own idea of whether a film is or is not a documentary is highly susceptible to suggestion. (Susan Stewart's July 10–16, 1999, *TV Guide* review of a Sci-Fi Channel program, "Curse of the Blair Witch," treats it as a bad but authentic attempt to document the story of an actual witch rather than as a promotional tie-in to this clever fiction story.) Film, video, and now digitally based images can bear witness to what took place in front of the camera with extraordinary fidelity. Painting and drawing seem a pale imitation of reality compared to the sharp, highly defined, precise representations available on film, video, or computer monitors. Yet this fidelity serves the needs of fiction filmmaking as much as it facilitates the work of medical imaging through the use of X-rays, MRIs, or CAT scans. The fidelity of the image may be as crucial to a close-up of Tom Cruise or Catherine Deneuve as it is to an X-ray of a lung, but the uses of that fidelity are vastly different. We may know that both offer evidence about the world around us, but we treat the former as evidence highly filtered through the eyes of the filmmaker and the latter as an almost direct, untampered transcription of specific properties found in the world. We believe what we see at our own risk.

As digital media make all too apparent, fidelity lies in the mind of the beholder as much as it lies in the relationship between a camera and what comes before it. (With digitally produced images there may be no camera and nothing that ever came before it, even if the resulting image bears an extraordinary fidelity to familiar people, places, and things.) Whether what we see is exactly what we would have seen had we been present alongside the camera cannot be guaranteed.

Certain technologies and styles encourage us to believe in a tight, if not perfect, correspondence between image and reality, and the effect of lenses, focus, contrast, depth of field, color, and high-resolution media (such as fine grain film or digital images with over 300 pixels per square inch) seem to guarantee the authenticity of what we see. They can all be used, however, to give the *impression* of authenticity to what has actually been fabricated or constructed. And once images are selected and arranged into patterns or sequences, into scenes or entire films, the interpretation and meaning of what we see will hinge on many more factors than whether the image is a faithful representation of what, if anything, appeared before the camera.

The documentary tradition relies heavily on being able to convey an impression of authenticity. It is a powerful impression, made possible by some basic qualities of moving images in any medium. It begins with the appearance of movement: no matter how poor the image and how different from the thing photographed, the *appearance* of movement is perceptually indistinguishable from actual movement. (Each frame of a film is a still image; apparent motion relies on the effect produced when the frames are projected in rapid succession.) When that movement is the movement of social actors (people) not performing for the camera and not playing a role in a fiction film, it appears to attest to the authenticity of the film. Coupled with more

Palace of Delights (Jon Else and Steve Longstreth, 1982). A documentary film crew on location. Most of the components of a feature film are replicated on a documentary production, though usually on a smaller scale. The "crew" can be as small as a single camera-sound operator/director. For many documentaries, the ability to respond to events that do not unfold entirely as the director intends, to, that is, "real life," plays a central role in the organization of the crew and in its working methods. In this case, Jon Else does the filming, with a 16mm camera, and Steve Longstreth records the sound with a Nagra tape recorder designed to keep the sound synchronized to the image. They are shooting a scene about the "Momentum Machine" at the San Francisco Exploratorium. *Photo by Nancy Roger, courtesy of Jon Else.*

specific documentary conventions—such as voice-over commentary, location shooting, the use of nonactors engaged in their daily lives as people, and the exploration of social issues like global warming or social justice—the sense of an authentic representation of the world we share can be powerful indeed.

Digital forms of representation add to the number of media that fulfill this criteria. The emergence of these new digital forms typically represents something akin to a process of cross-pollination with the documentary tradition. Related media trade conventions and borrow techniques from one another. Websites such as YouTube and Facebook, like photography before them, will soon deserve a history and theory of their own. For now we can treat all these related forms of production, distribution, and exhibition as significant contributors to an ongoing documentary tradition.

When we believe that what we see bears witness to the way the world is, it can form the basis for our orientation to or our action within the world. This is obviously true in science, where medical imaging plays a vital diagnostic role in almost all branches of medicine. Decisions are made and treatments commenced based on what images reveal. Propaganda, like advertising, also relies on our belief in a bond between what we see and the way the world is and how we might act within it. So do many documentaries when they set out to persuade us to adopt a given perspective or point of view about the world. Through the course of this book we will explore how the issues involved in representing reality have tested the resourcefulness and inventiveness of documentary filmmakers.

Introduction to Documentary covers elements of documentary film history since the issues and practices examined here arise in history (both social history and film history) and cannot be discussed entirely free from it. The book does not, however, attempt to provide comprehensive and balanced coverage of the various key filmmakers, movements, and national characteristics of the documentary genre over the course of its history. The topics and films discussed here are indicative of specific questions or exemplify important approaches to certain issues. They are illustrative more than definitive.

Selecting some films for discussion immediately suggests the idea of a canon, a list of films that constitute the best of the tradition. I have tried to avoid constructing a canon. Such an approach carries implications about how history works (great artists, great works lead the way). My own view is that certain artists, while extremely influential, are but one part of a larger stew of ideas, values, issues, technologies, institutional frameworks, sponsorship, and shared forms of expression that all contribute to the history of documentary or any other medium. This book, therefore, tries to indicate that the works chosen, while often extraordinary accomplishments artistically and socially, have little standing as uncontested monuments or icons. It is *how* they solve problems and exemplify solutions, how they suggest trends, practices, styles, and issues rather than any absolute sense of intrinsic value that takes priority.

Many of the works referred to in *Introduction to Documentary* are already part of a canon in that they are works frequently cited in other commentaries and frequently included in courses. It seems more useful to develop the conceptual tools proposed here by referring to familiar works rather than less accessible ones. This book may therefore reinforce the sense of a canon, but wherever possible I have chosen at least two films to use as examples for a given point. In this way I hope to give a fuller sense of how different films find at least slightly different solutions to common problems and to suggest that no one film deserves the status of best or greatest, certainly not in any timeless, ahistorical sense.

This book assumes that the bond between photographic, video, or digital images and what they represent can be extraordinarily powerful even if it can also be entirely fabricated. The questions pursued in this introduction are not intended to allow us to decide whether or to what degree fabrication has taken place so that we can determine what the referent is "really" like or what "really happened." They are designed more to ask how is it that we are willing to trust in the representations made by moving images, whether such trust is more, or less, warranted, and what might be the consequences for our relation to the historical world in which we live?

Introduction to Documentary pursues the following questions: "How Can We Define Documentary Film?" in chapter 1. This chapter explores some of the ways in which commonsense definitions of documentary can be refined. It also sets the stage for the issues posed in the remaining chapters by considering the distinct assumptions and expectations of the filmmaker, institutions that support documentary, and the audience. In chapter 2 we ask, "Why Are Ethical Issues Central to Documentary Filmmaking?" The chapter explores issues involving power, trust, and responsibility and how their formulation may differ from similar issues in fiction film.

Chapter 3 asks, "What Gives Documentary Films a Voice of Their Own?" This question introduces concepts from the art of rhetoric to show how documentary remains indebted to the rhetorical tradition and how the documentary filmmaker often resembles the orator of old in his or her efforts to address issues or problems that call for social consensus or solution. Chapter 4 wants to know, "What Makes Documentaries Engaging and Persuasive?" It looks at some characteristics of those issues that tend to provide the content or subject matter for documentary, especially the degree to which the issues taken up by documentary evade scientific or purely logical solution. These issues revolve around values and beliefs, which, since they vary, then call on representations such as documentaries to persuade us of the worthiness of one approach over others. Chapter 5 asks, "How Did Documentary Filmmaking Get Started?" It challenges prevailing assumptions about documentary being synonymous either with early cinema of the sort Louis Lumière promoted, such as *Workers Leaving the Lumière Factory* (1895), or with nonfiction film generally. The chapter identifies four different contributing practices that combined into the distinct form of a documentary film practice by the late 1920s.

Chapter 6 proposes to answer the question, "How Can We Differentiate among Documentaries?" Previously part of a single chapter on the six modes of documentary film, chapter 6 gives extra attention to how the modes differ from models, developed in other media but adapted to documentary film, and looks closely at two specific modes: expository and poetic. Each mode has its exemplary filmmakers, its paradigmatic films, and its own forms of institutional support and audience expectation. Chapters 6 and 7 explore these topics in some detail.

Chapter 7 raises the question, "How Can We Describe the Observational, Participatory, Reflexive, and Performative Modes of Documentary Film?" Like chapters 4 and 5, chapters 6 and 7 also have a historical dimension as they look at how the central issue of interpersonal relationship, or community, finds representation in documentary: How do documentaries intensify or disrupt the bonds we have with others, and how do they testify to the nature and quality of the filmmaker's relation to the historical world he or she chose to address? The four modes discussed in this chapter often place the filmmaker into direct encounter with others in a way the expository and poetic modes may not, and therefore they sharpen this question to a considerable degree. Chapter 8 addresses the question, "How Have Documentaries Addressed Social and Political Issues?" The chapter considers the close ties between the rise of the documentary film and the needs of the nation-state. To this day, many documentaries address issues of national and, increasingly, international significance. Historically, they have done so on behalf of the government of the day or in direct opposition to it. The chapter looks at various options for taking up social issues and compares the personal portrait film, which may raise broader social questions obliquely, to the social issue documentary, which tackles them directly.

Chapter 9 explores the question, "How Can We Write Effectively about Documentary?" Answering this question involves walking through some of the basic steps in constructing an essay, using a hypothetical writing assignment and two possible responses to it. By providing two model essays that take very different views of a classic documentary film, Robert Flaherty's *Nanook of the North* (1922), the chapter tries to indicate how the student's own perspective becomes a central part of a written response to a given film. This edition includes a discussion of how to use various on-line and library resources to support the thesis of an essay.

Behind *Introduction to Documentary* lies the assumption that awareness of the central concepts in documentary film practice, along with a sense of the history of documentary filmmaking, provides extremely valuable tools to the filmmaker as well as the critic. A strong link between production and study has been characteristic of much documentary filmmaking in the past. My hope is that it will remain a vital link in the future and that the concepts discussed here will nourish that vitality.

INTRODUCTION TO **DOCUMENTARY**

1 How Can We Define Documentary Film?

This introduction to the ways in which documentary engages with the world as we know it takes up the series of questions indicated by the chapter titles. These questions are the commonsense sort of questions we might ask ourselves if we want to understand documentary film. Each question takes us a bit further into the domain of documentary; each question helps us understand how a documentary tradition arose and evolved and what it has to offer us today.

The current Golden Age of documentaries began in the 1980s. It continues unabated. An abundance of films has breathed new life into an old form and prompted serious thought about how to define this type of filmmaking. These films challenge assumptions and alter perceptions. They see the world anew and do so in inventive ways. Often structured as stories, they are stories with a difference: they speak about the world we all share and do so with clarity and engagement. Anyone who has come of age since the 1980s doesn't need to be convinced of this, but older generations may have to adjust their assumptions about the power of nonfiction relative to fiction. In a time when the major media recycle the same stories on the same subjects over and over, when they risk little in formal innovation, when they remain beholden to powerful sponsors with their own political agendas and restrictive demands, it is the independent documentary film that has brought a fresh eye to the events of the world and told stories, with

The Times of Harvey Milk (Robert Epstein and Richard Schmeichen, 1984). A significant influence on the acclaimed 2008 feature film, *Milk*, with Sean Penn as Harvey Milk, this documentary traces the career of the first openly gay political figure. *Courtesy of Rob Epstein/Telling Pictures, Inc.*

verve and imagination, that broaden limited horizons and awaken new possibilities.

Documentary has become the flagship for a cinema of social engagement and distinctive vision. The documentary impulse has rippled outward to the internet and to sites like YouTube and Facebook, where mock-, quasi-, semi-, pseudo- and bona fide documentaries, embracing new forms and tackling fresh topics, proliferate. Still one of many routes that aspiring directors take en route to their first feature film, documentary filmmaking is now, more than ever, an end in itself. The cable channels, low-cost digital production and easy-to-distribute DVDs, the internet and its next-to-nothing costs of dissemination, along with its unique forms of word of mouth enthusiasm, together with the hunger of many for fresh perspectives and alternative visions, give the documentary form a bright and vibrant future.

The Oscars from the mid-eighties onward mark the ascendancy of the documentary as a popular and compelling form. Never known for its bold preferences, often sentimental in its affections, the Academy of

Eyes on the Prize (Henry Hampton, 1987). The film depends heavily on historical footage to recapture the feel and tone of the civil rights movement of the early 1960s. The capacity of historical images to lend authenticity to what interviewees tell us makes their testimony all the more compelling. *Courtesy of Blackside Inc./Photofest.*

Motion Picture Arts and Sciences has nonetheless been unable to help itself when it comes to acknowledging many of the most outstanding documentaries of the current Golden Age. Consider the Oscar winners and some of the runners-up from the 1980s:

- *The Times of Harvey Milk* (1984), about the pioneering gay activist and politician Harvey Milk
- *Broken Rainbow* (1985), about the eviction of 10,000 Navajo from their ancestral lands in the 1970s, and Lourdes Portillo and Susana Muñoz's *Las Madres de la Plaza de Mayo* (1985), about the mothers who protested the illegal "disappearance" of their sons and daughters by the Argentine government, along with runner-up Ken Burns's first Oscar-nominated film, *The Statue of Liberty*
- *Artie Shaw: Time Is All You've Got* (1985), about the great jazz musician, and

- *Down and Out in America* (1986), about those most affected by the mid-eighties recession; the co-Oscar winners in 1986
- Runner-ups *Radio Bikini* (1987), about the atomic bomb blast that resulted in radiation death and injury to many, and *Eyes on the Prize* (1987), the epic story of the civil rights movement
- *Hotel Terminus* (1988), about the search for the infamous Nazi Klaus Barbie, and runner-up Christine Choy and Renee Tajima-Peña's *Who Killed Vincent Chin?* (1988), about the murder of a young Chinese-American man whom an unemployed Detroit autoworker attacked, partly out of irrational rage at the success of the Japanese auto industry in their competition with domestic car makers
- The AIDS-related tale of the Quilts Project, *Common Threads: Stories from the Quilt* (1989)
- *American Dream* (1990), Barbara Kopple's penetrating study of a prolonged, complex labor strike, and runner-up *Berkeley in the Sixties* (1990), a rousing history of the rise of the free speech and the anti–Vietnam War movements.

Conspicuous by their absence from this list are some of the first major box office successes of the late 1980s and early 1990s: Errol Morris's brilliant *The Thin Blue Line* (1988), about an innocent man awaiting execution in Dallas, Texas; Michael Moore's *Roger and Me* (1989), about his mock-heroic attempt to ask the head of General Motors, Roger Smith, what he planned to do about all the folks left unemployed when he closed a factory in Flint, Michigan; and the extraordinary chronicle of 4 years in the lives of two high school basketball players whose ambition it is to play in the NBA: *Hoop Dreams* (1994).

These films, like dozens of others that have found national and international audiences at festivals, in theaters, and on cable and websites, attest to the resounding appeal of the voice of the filmmaker. This is not simply a voice-over commentary—although it is striking how many recent films rely on the actual voice of the filmmaker, speaking directly and personally of what he or she has experienced and learned. It is a voice that issues from the entirety of each film's audio-visual pres-

Who Killed Vincent Chin? (Renee Tajima-Peña and Christine Choy, 1988).
Throughout the film, the directors draw on footage taken by local television
stations as well as their own footage to explore what led to Vincent Chin's
murder. This shot is a still camera shot taken by the filmmakers as television
crews jockeyed to cover the event as well. The victim's mother is speaking at a
rally with the Reverend Jesse Jackson in attendance. *Courtesy of the filmmaker.*

ence: the selection of shots, the framing of subjects, the juxtaposition
of scenes, the mixing of sounds, the use of titles and inter-titles—from
all the techniques by which a filmmaker speaks from a distinct perspective on a given subject and seeks to persuade viewers to adopt this perspective as their own. The spoken voices of filmmakers like Jonathan
Caouette (*Tarnation*, 2003), Morgan Spurlock (*Super Size Me*, 2004),
Zana Briski (*Born into Brothels*, 2004), and, of course, Michael Moore
(*Fahrenheit 9/11* [2004] and *Sicko* [2007]) remind us that these filmmakers maintain their distance from the authoritative tone of corporate
media in order to speak to power rather than embrace it. Their stylistic
daring—the urge to stand in intimate relation to a historical moment
and those who populate it—confounds the omniscient commentary

of conventional documentary and the detached coolness of television news. Seeking to find a voice in which to speak about subjects that attract them, filmmakers, like all great orators, must speak from the heart in ways that both fit the occasion and issue from it.

THE SEARCH FOR COMMON GROUND: DEFINING DOCUMENTARY FILM

Given the vitality of expression, range of voices, and dramatic popularity of documentary film, we might well wonder what, if anything, all these films have in common. Have they broadened the appeal of documentary by becoming more like feature fiction films in their use of compelling music, reenactments and staged encounters, sequences or entire films based on animation, portrayals of fascinating characters and the creation of compelling stories? Or do they remain a fiction unlike any other? That is, do they tell stories that, although similar to feature fiction, remain distinct from it? This book will answer in the affirmative, that documentaries are a distinct form of cinema but perhaps not as completely distinct as we at first imagine.

A concise, overarching definition is possible but not fundamentally crucial. It will conceal as much as it will reveal. More important is how every film we consider a documentary contributes to an ongoing dialogue that draws on common characteristics that take on new and distinct form, like an ever-changing chameleon. We will, however, begin with some common characteristics of documentary film in order to have a general sense of the territory within which most discussion occurs.

It is certainly possible to argue that documentary film has never had a very precise definition. It remains common today to revert to some version of John Grierson's definition of documentary, first proposed in the 1930s, as the "creative treatment of actuality." This view acknowledges that documentaries are creative endeavors. It also leaves unresolved the obvious tension between "creative treatment" and "actuality." "Creative treatment" suggests the license of fiction, whereas "actuality" reminds us of the responsibilities of the journalist and historian. That neither term has full sway, that the documentary form balances creative vision with a respect for the historical world, identifies, in fact, one source of documentary appeal. Neither a fictional invention nor a factual reproduction, documentary draws on and refers to historical reality while representing it from a distinct perspective.

Commonsense ideas about documentary prove a useful starting point. As typically formulated they are both genuinely helpful and unintentionally misleading. The three commonsense assumptions about documentary discussed here, with qualifications, add to our understanding of documentary filmmaking but do not exhaust it.

1. Documentaries are about reality; they're about something that actually happened.

Though correct, and although built into Grierson's idea of the "creative treatment of actuality," it is important to say a bit more about how documentaries are "about something that actually happened." We must note, for example, that many fiction films also address aspects of reality. *Do the Right Thing* (1989) deals with the very real issue of racism; *Schindler's List* (1993) tells the true story of Oscar Schindler, a Nazi Party member who saved the lives of over a thousand Jews, and *JFK* (1991) reexamines the actual assassination of President John F. Kennedy, using Abraham Zapruder's documentary footage of the president as the rifle shots struck him.

We might, therefore, modify this definition of documentary by saying, "Documentary films speak about actual situations or events and honor known facts; they do not introduce new, unverifiable ones. They speak directly about the historical world rather than allegorically." Fictional narratives are fundamentally allegories. They create one world to stand in for another, historical world. (In an allegory or parable everything has a second meaning; the surface meanings therefore may constitute a disguised commentary on actual people, situations, and events.) Within an alternative fictional world a story unfolds. As it does so it offers insights and generates themes about the world we already inhabit. This is why we turn to fiction to understand the human condition.

Documentary films, though, refer directly to the historical world. The images, and many of the sounds, they present stem from the historical world directly. Although this statement will receive qualification later, documentary images generally capture people and events that belong to the world we share rather than present characters and actions invented to tell a story that refers back to our world obliquely or allegorically. One important way in which they do so is by respecting known facts and providing verifiable evidence. They do much more than this, but a documentary that distorts facts, alters reality, or fabricates evidence jeopardizes its own status as a documentary. (For some mockumentaries and for some provocative filmmakers this may well be exactly what they set out to do: as we will see, *Land without Bread* (1932) is a prime example of this possibility.)

2. Documentaries are about real people.

This statement, although true, also needs modification. Fiction films also focus on real people, except that these people are usually trained actors playing assigned roles (characters). Viewers often go to fiction films to see their favorite stars, even if the film itself seems mediocre. In fiction real people assume roles and become known as the characters who populate a fictional world.

A more accurate statement might be, "Documentaries are about real people who do not play or perform roles." Instead, they "play" or present themselves. They draw on prior experience and habits to be themselves in the face of a camera. They may be acutely aware of the camera's presence, which, in interviews and other interactions, they address directly. (Direct address occurs when individuals speak directly to the camera or audience; it is rare in fiction where the camera functions as an invisible onlooker most of the time.)

The presentation of self in front of a camera in documentary might be called a performance, as it is in fiction, but this term may confuse as much as clarify. What happens in a documentary differs from a stage or screen performance in the usual sense. Real people, or social actors, as Erving Goffmann pointed out several decades ago in his book, *The Presentation of Self in Everyday Life* (1959), present themselves in everyday life in ways that differ from a consciously adopted role or fictional performance. A stage or screen performance calls on the actor to subordinate his or her own traits as an individual to represent a specified character and to provide evidence through his or her acting of what changes or transformations that character undergoes. The actor remains relatively unchanged and goes on to other roles, but the character he or she plays may change dramatically. All of this requires training and relies on conventions and techniques.

The presentation of self in everyday life involves how a person goes about expressing his or her personality, character, and individual traits, rather than suppressing them to adopt a role. It is how people undergo change as people, rather than how they represent change in fictional characters. There is no specific training for self-presentation other than the experience of becoming a member of society.

Instead of a gap between the presentation of self and the actual person, the "front" a person presents serves as a way to negotiate with others about the nature and quality of an interaction as it unfolds. Self-presentation allows the individual to reveal more or less of him- or herself, to be frank or guarded, emotional or reserved, inquisitive or distant, all in accord with how an interaction unfolds moment by moment. The presentation of self is less an adopted mask than a flexible means of adaptation. It suggests that individual identity develops in response to others and is not a permanent, indelible feature. Some have even argued that gender identity (how a person understands his or her masculine or feminine nature) possesses a fluid, adaptable quality. The presentation of self comes into full play when people come before the camera and interact with filmmakers. It is not the same as adhering to a predetermined role.

In other words, a person does not present in exactly the same way to a companion on a date, a doctor in a hospital, his or her children at home, and a filmmaker in an interview. Nor do people continue to present the same way as an interaction develops; they modify their behavior as the situation evolves. Friendliness prompts a friendly presentation, but the introduction of a sarcastic remark may prompt guardedness. In documentaries, we expect social actors to present themselves in this sense, not perform the role of a character of the filmmaker's devising, even if the act of filming has a definite influence on how they present themselves. Fiction films such as *Battleship Potemkin* (1925), *Bicycle Thieves* (1948), *Salt of the Earth* (1954), and *Shadows* (1960) and TV shows like *Real World* or *Survivor* give us untrained social actors playing roles so strongly shaped by the filmmaker or producers

Monster (Patty Jenkins, 2003). Charlize Theron, a former model, dramatically altered her appearance to play the down-and-out Aileen Wuornos. We learn very little about Ms. Theron as an individual apart from her acting skill as the film dwells on the character she plays. *Copyright Media 8 Entertainment. Courtesy of Film Look Studios.*

that these works are usually treated as fictions even though their style locates them very close to the documentary tradition.

3. Documentaries tell stories about what happens in the real world.

This commonsense notion refers to the story-telling power of documentaries. They tell us what leads up to actual events or real changes, be they the experiences of an individual or an entire society. Documentaries tell us about how things change and who produces these changes.

This notion also needs refinement. The basic question is, When documentaries tell a story whose story is it? The filmmaker's or the subject's? Does the story clearly derive from the events and people involved or is it primarily the work of the filmmaker, even if based on reality? We need to add to this commonsense notion something like, "To the extent a documentary tells a story, the story is a plausible representation

Aileen Wuornos: The Selling of a Serial Killer (Nick Broomfield, 1992). In this documentary we see and hear Aileen Wuornos herself talk about her life. We learn a great deal from how she presents herself to the filmmaker as well as from what others say about her. Broomfield openly acknowledges the complex negotiations, and payments, involved in making the film. *Courtesy of Nick Broomfield.*

of what happened rather than an imaginative interpretation of what might have happened."

In most fiction films the story is essentially the filmmaker's even if based on actual events. "This is a true story" can easily be the introduction to a fiction film that draws from historical events for its plot. *Schindler's List* is not the story as told by Oscar Schindler himself or by the people he saved but an imaginative, allegorical representation of his story as told by Steven Spielberg, even though it is heavily based on historical facts. *Monster* (2003) is likewise a fictional account of the life of Aileen Wuornos, a female serial killer, but with Charlize Theron playing Ms. Wuornos. By contrast, *Aileen Wuornos: The Selling of a Serial Killer* (1992) is a documentary by Nick Broomfield that features Aileen Wuornos herself and addresses her life directly.

The "creative treatment of actuality," to loop back to Grierson's definition, allows "treatment" to include story telling, but such stories must meet certain criteria to qualify as documentaries. This is akin to the criteria of factual accuracy and interpretative coherence that governs history writing. The division of documentary from fiction, like the division of historiography from fiction, rests on the degree to which the story fundamentally corresponds to actual situations, events, and people versus the degree to which it is primarily a product of the filmmaker's invention. There is always some of each. The story a documentary tells stems from the historical world but it is still told from the filmmaker's perspective and in the filmmaker's voice. This is a matter of degree, not a black-and-white division.

A surprising number of documentaries, just like fiction films, tell stories—from how migrant farmworkers experience abject poverty as they move from Florida to New York harvesting the nation's bountiful crops in Edward R. Murrow's trenchant television documentary, *Harvest of Shame* (1960), to how, in 1974, Philippe Petit managed to walk from the top of one World Trade Center tower to the other in *Man on Wire* (2008). In these cases the stories told speak about the actual events directly, not allegorically, and the film adheres to the known historical facts. Social actors, people, present themselves in fluid, negotiated, revealing ways. They don't play roles or characters of someone else's invention.

Nanook of the North (1922), discussed in some detail in chapter 9, where it serves as a model for how to write about documentary films, is a vivid case in point. Whose story is it? The story is ostensibly that of Nanook, an intrepid Inuit leader and great hunter. But Nanook is to a large degree Robert Flaherty's invention. His nuclear family matches European and American family structure more than Inuit extended families. His hunting methods belong to a period some 30 or more years prior to the time that film was made. The story is of a bygone way of life that Nanook embodies in what amounts to a role and character performance more than a presentation of self in everyday life at the time of filming. The film could be labeled either fiction or documentary. Its classification as documentary usually hinges on two things: (1) the degree to which the story Flaherty tells so carefully matches the ways of the Inuit, even if these ways are revived from the past, and (2) on the way Allakariallak, the man who plays Nanook, embodies a spirit and sensibility that seems as much in harmony with a distinct way of Inuit life as with any Western conception of it. The story can be understood as both a plausible representation of Inuit life and of Flaherty's distinct vision of it.

Were documentary a *reproduction* of reality, these problems would be far less acute. We would then simply have a replica or copy of something that already existed. But documentary is not a reproduction of reality, it is a *representation* of the world we already occupy. Such films are not documents as much as expressive representations that may be based on documents. Documentary films stand for a particular view of the world, one we may never have encountered before even if the factual aspects of this world are familiar to us. We judge a reproduction by its fidelity to the original—its capacity to reproduce visible features of the original precisely and to serve purposes that require precise reproduction as in police mug shots, passport photos, or medical X-rays. We judge a representation more by the nature of the pleasure it offers, the value of the insight it provides, and the quality of the perspective it instills. We ask different things of representations and reproductions, documentaries and documents.

The question of whose story is it leaves considerable room for ambiguity. Documentary reenactments are a prime example of this. Here the filmmaker must imaginatively recreate events in order to film them at all. All of *Nanook of the North* can be said to be one gigantic reenactment, but it retains significant documentary qualities. (John Grierson said *Nanook* possessed "documentary value." This is apparently how the term documentary film gained prominent use.) What the reenactment creates, however, needs to correspond to known historical fact if it is to remain plausible.

Reeanctments need not be highly realistic recreations, as they usually are in fiction films. Some documentaries recreate past events in clearly stylized ways. For example, in *Waltz with Bashir* (2008), the recreation of actual battles from the 1982 Israeli invasion of Lebanon, the experiences of traumatized soldiers, and the grizzly massacre of

Lebanese Muslims involves animated and highly stylized representations (except for the film's final scene). These animated sequences clearly possess a strongly subjective, even expressionistic, quality. They attempt to see war as the disoriented, confused Israeli soldiers, including the filmmaker, saw it. Their memories of the war come across in a series of actual interviews, represented by animation, as well. As a representation of subjective states of mind, the film achieves a high degree of plausibility even as it departs from any standard sense of documentary realism.

The idea that what we see and hear offers a plausible perspective also allows us to acknowledge that for any given event, more than one story exists to represent and interpret it. *Enron: The Smartest Guys in the Room* (2005), for example, does not support the story of Enron's failure as told by its own executives who claim it was a result of innocent mistakes or someone else's wrongdoing, and not their own actions. Instead the film tells the story uncovered by investigative journalists Peter Elkind and Bethany MacLean: it was the result of deliberate deception and greed by these very same executives.

Modifying the three commonsense definitions we have just examined into one somewhat more precise definition yields something like this:

Documentary film speaks about situations and events involving real people (social actors) who present themselves to us as themselves in stories that convey a plausible proposal about, or perspective on, the lives, situations, and events portrayed. The distinct point of view of the filmmaker shapes this story into a way of seeing the historical world directly rather than into a fictional allegory.

FUZZY CONCEPTS AND THE PROCESS OF CHANGE

The definition above is a useful first step but it leaves considerable room for "creative interpretation." It is quite a mouthful, too. The temptation remains to resort to shorter, simpler definitions such as, "Documentaries address reality" or "Documentaries deal with real people being themselves." Such shorthand definitions have their usefulness as long as we remember that their brevity conceals complexity.

The more elaborate definition has another notable flaw: it does not differentiate among different types of documentary. (This task will fall to chapters 6 and 7.) Documentaries tend to cluster into different types or modes. They do not all address the historical world in the same way and do not adopt the same cinematic techniques. Voice-over commentary, once taken for granted, became anathema to the observational filmmakers of the 1960s, for example. Filmmakers are not beholden to definitions and rules to govern what they do. They delight in subverting conventions, challenging viewers, provoking debate. Definitions of documentary are always playing catch-up, trying to adapt to changes in what counts as a documentary and why.

Documentaries adopt no fixed inventory of techniques, address no one set of issues, display no single set of forms or styles. Documentary film practice is an arena in which things change. Alternative approaches are constantly attempted and then adopted or abandoned. Prototypical works stand out that others emulate without ever being able to copy or reproduce entirely. Test cases appear that challenge the conventions defining the boundaries of documentary film. They push the limits and sometimes change them.

More than upholding a definition that fixes once and for all what is and is not a documentary, we need to look to examples and prototypes, test cases and innovations as evidence of the broad arena within which documentary operates and evolves. The usefulness of prototypes to a definition is that they propose generally exemplary qualities or features without requiring every documentary to exhibit all of them. *Nanook of the North* stands as a prototypical documentary even though many films that share its reliance on a simple quest narrative to organize events, its exemplary, photogenic main character, and its implication that we can understand larger cultural qualities by understanding individual behavior also reject the romanticism, the challenges of the natural environment, and patronizing elements of *Nanook.* Indeed, some fiction films, like Vittorio De Sica's *Bicycle Thieves,* can also share these qualities with *Nanook* without being considered a documentary at all.

Changes in an understanding of what a documentary is come about in different ways. Most change, however, occurs because of what goes on in one or more of the following four arenas: (1) institutions that support documentary production and reception, (2) the creative efforts of filmmakers, (3) the lasting influence of specific films, and (4) the expectations of audiences. In fact, these four factors—institutions, filmmakers, films, and audiences—deserve more extended discussion. They are the four fundamental factors that both uphold a sense of what a documentary is at a given time and place and promote the continual transformation of what a documentary is over time and in different places. We can get more of a handle on how to understand documentary film by considering these four factors in greater detail.

AN INSTITUTIONAL FRAMEWORK

It may seem circular, but another way to define documentary is to say, "Documentaries are what the organizations and institutions that produce them make." This is similar to saying that the Hollywood feature film is what the Hollywood studio system produces. If John Grierson calls *Night Mail* (1936) a documentary or if the Discovery Channel calls a program a documentary, then these items come labeled as documentary before any work on the part of the viewer or critic begins. This labeling, despite its circularity, functions as an initial cue that a given work can be considered a documentary. The context provides the cue; we would be foolish to ignore it even if this form of definition is less than conclusive.

The segments that make up the CBS news program *60 Minutes*, for example, are normally considered examples of journalistic reporting first and foremost simply because that is the kind of program *60 Minutes* is. We assume that the segments refer to actual people and events, that the standards of journalistic reporting will be met, that we can rely on each story to be both entertaining and informative, and that any claims made will be backed up by a credible display of evidence. Shown in another setting, these episodes might seem more like melodramas or docudramas, based on the emotional intensities achieved and the high degree of constructedness to the encounters that take place, but these alternatives dim when the entire institutional framework functions to assure us that they are, in fact, journalistic reportage.

The classic mockumentary *This Is Spinal Tap* (Rob Reiner, 1984) builds this type of institutional framing into the film itself in a mischievous or ironic way: the film announces itself to be a documentary, only to prove to be a fabrication or simulation of a documentary. Much of its ironic impact depends on its ability to coax at least partial belief from us that what we see is a documentary because that is what we are told we see. (Mockumentaries adopt documentary conventions but are staged, scripted, and acted to create the appearance of a genuine documentary as well as leaving clues that they are not. Part of the pleasure they provide lies in how they let a knowledgeable audience in on the joke: we can enjoy the film as a parody and gain new insight into taken-for-granted conventions.) If we take *This Is Spinal Tap's* self-description seriously, we will believe that the group Spinal Tap is an actual rock group. In fact, one had to be created for the film, just as a "Blair witch" had to be invented for *The Blair Witch Project* (1999). The band members are real in the same way the actors who play characters in a film are real: they are real people but they are playing roles rather than presenting themselves.

An institutional framework also imposes an institutional way of seeing and speaking, which functions as a set of limits, or conventions, for the filmmaker and audience alike. To say "it goes without saying" that a documentary will have a voice-over commentary or "everyone knows" that a documentary must present both sides of the question is to say what is usually the case within a specific institutional framework. Voice-over commentary, sometimes poetic, sometimes factual, was a strong convention within the government-sponsored film production units headed by John Grierson in 1930s Britain, and reportorial balance, in the sense of not openly taking sides, prevails among the news divisions of network television companies today.

This "it goes without saying" quality also serves to leave documentary conventions unquestioned. For a long time, it was taken for granted that documentaries could talk about anything in the world except themselves. Reflexive strategies that call the very act of representation into question unsettle the assumption that documentary builds on the ability of film to capture reality. To remind viewers of the construction of the reality we behold, of the *creative* element in John Grierson's famous definition of documentary as "the creative treatment of actuality," undercuts the very claim to truth and authenticity on which the documentary depends. If we cannot take its images as visible evidence of the particular nature of the historical world, of what can we

Always for Pleasure (Les Blank, 1978). Les Blank's films are difficult to place. Books on documentary and ethnographic film sometimes neglect his work even though films such as this one, on aspects of Mardi Gras in New Orleans, exhibit important characteristics of each of these types of filmmaking. Blank, like most accomplished documentary filmmakers, does not follow rules or protocols; he does not concern himself with where and how his films fit into categories. His avoidance of voice-over commentary, political perspectives, identifiable problems, and potential solutions follows from an emphasis on affirmative, often exuberant, forms of experience. *Photo courtesy of Les Blank and Flower Films.*

take them? By suppressing this question, the institutional framework for documentary suppresses much of the complexity in the relationship between representation and reality, but it also achieves a clarity that implies documentaries achieve direct, truthful access to the real. This functions as one of the prime attractions of the form, even if it is a claim we must assess with care.

Along with sponsoring agencies for the production of documentary work, a distinct circuit of distributors and exhibitors function to support the circulation of these films. These agencies supplement the dominant movie theater chains and video/DVD rental stores that emphasize mainstream fiction films over documentaries. Sometimes one organization, such as the National Geographic or Discovery channels, produces, distributes, and exhibits documentary work. Some distributors are distinct entities, such as specialty film distributors Women Make Movies, New Day Films, Facets, Third World Newsreel, or Netflix, or websites like YouTube that make documentaries produced by others available for viewing. (Netflix now combines both viewing on demand over the internet and film rental via DVD sent by mail.) Other agencies, such as the Corporation for Public Broadcasting and the British Film Institute, provide financial support for documentary production. Still others agencies, such as the Foundation for Independent Film and Video, the European Documentary Film Institute, or the International Documentary Association, provide professional support for documentary filmmakers themselves, much as the Academy of Motion Picture Arts and Sciences does for Hollywood filmmakers. Whatever its role, these institutions contribute to the reality of what gets made and how it looks. They often impose standards and conventions on the work they support, and their goals and criteria change over time. Without them far fewer documentaries would reach their intended audience.

A COMMUNITY OF PRACTITIONERS

Those who make documentary films, like the institutions that support them, hold certain assumptions and expectations about what they do. Although every institutional framework imposes limits and conventions, individual filmmakers need not accept them. The tension between established expectations and individual innovation proves a frequent source of change.

Documentary filmmakers share a common, self-chosen mandate to represent the historical world rather than to imaginatively invent alternative ones. They gather at specialized film festivals such as the Hot Springs Documentary Film Festival (United States), the Yamagata Documentary Film Festival (Japan), or the Amsterdam International Documentary Film Festival (the Netherlands), and they, along with critics, contribute articles and interviews to journals such as *Documentary*, *Dox*, and *Studies in Documentary Film* or to on-line forums such as that of In Media Res, part of the mediaCommons.futureofthebook. org website. They debate social issues such as the effects of pollution and the nature of sexual identity and explore technical concerns such as the authenticity of archival footage and the consequences of digital technology.

Documentary practitioners speak a common language regarding what they do. Like other professionals, documentary filmmakers have a vocabulary, or jargon, of their own. It may range from the suitability of various digital cameras for different situations to the techniques of recording location sound, and from the challenges of observing social actors effectively to the pragmatics of finding distribution and negotiating contracts for their work. Documentary practitioners share distinct but common problems—from developing ethically sound relationships with their subjects to reaching a specific audience, for example—that distinguish them from other filmmakers.

These commonalities give documentary filmmakers a shared sense of purpose despite the ways in which they may also compete for the same funding or distributors. Individual practitioners will shape or transform the traditions they inherit, but they do so in dialogue with others who share their sense of mission. These efforts contribute to the fuzzy but distinguishable outline of documentary film and to the historical variability of the form: our understanding of what is a documentary changes as those who make documentaries change their idea of what they want to make. What might begin as a test case or apparent anomaly, such as early observational films like *Les Racquetteurs* (1958), *Chronicle of a Summer* (1960), or *Primary* (1960), may fade away as a failed deviation or, as in this example, come to be regarded as transformative innovations leading to a new standard of accepted practice. Documentary has never been only one thing. For now we can use this history of a changing sense of what counts as a documentary as a sign of the variable, open-ended, dynamic quality of the form itself. Practitioners, through their engagement with issues, institutions, subjects, and audiences, contribute significantly to this sense of dynamic change.

A CORPUS OF TEXTS: CONVENTIONS, PERIODS, MOVEMENTS, AND MODES

The diversity of the films that make up the documentary tradition also contributes to its fluidity. Though different, *Nanook of the North*, *Man with a Movie Camera* (1929), *Land without Bread, Hoop Dreams, Dont Look Back* (1967), *Koyaanisqatsi* (1983), and *Roger and Me* all represent landmarks in documentary film production. They all adopt and modify conventions associated with documentary. They offer us alternative ways of seeing the world, from the caustic but double-edged voice-over commentary on a seemingly doomed culture in *Land without Bread* to the unobtrusive, sync sound portrait of a great musician (Bob Dylan) in *Dont Look Back.* In looking at this wide array of films, we can consider documentary a genre like the western or the science-fiction film. To belong to the genre a film has to exhibit conventions shared by films already regarded as documentaries or westerns. These conventions help distinguish one genre from another: the use of a voice-of-God commentary, interviews, location sound recording, cutaways from a given scene to provide images that illustrate or complicate stated points, and a reliance on social actors, or people, who present themselves in their everyday roles and activities, are among the conventions common to many documentaries.

Another convention is the prevalence of an informing logic that organizes the film in relation to the representations it makes about the historical world. A typical form of organization is that of problem solving. This structure can resemble a story, particularly a detective story: the film begins by establishing a problem or issue, then conveys something of the background to the issue, and then, like a good detective, follows up with an examination of its severity or complexity. This examination leads to a recommendation or solution that the film encourages the viewer to endorse or adopt personally.

The City (Ralph Steiner and Willard Van Dyke, 1939) exhibits a prototypical approach to the idea of a documentary logic. It establishes, through a montage of scenes that include fast motion clips of frenzied city living and shots of extreme poverty, the proposal that urban existence has become a burden more than a joy. Modern city life saps people of their energy and zest for life. (The film also ignores related issues such as whether urban misery correlates with class.) What is the solution?

The film's final section provides one: carefully planned, "green" communities where everyone lives in harmony and the workplace is just a walk away. The terrible din of massive machinery and the billowing smoke of heavy industry are nowhere to be seen. Poverty appears to vanish. Everyone is happy. While a labor-saving device (the 1930s version of a washing machine) takes care of the laundry, a group of women sit in the warn sunlight, chatting with one another.

The contentment of traditional small town life, buttressed by worker-friendly factories and plants, is suddenly available to all. The film's solution is a fascinating mix of visionary planning quite different from the cookie-cutter suburbia of the postwar years and a wishful evasion of hard economic realities. The film makes no reference to race and gives no hint how the urban down and out pick up and move to an idyllic new Shangri-la. What it does do is create a compelling vision of both a problem and a solution. It lets the viewer appreciate what it feels like to experience the joyful contentment of green communities as well the stress and misery of the traditional city. A classic in the documentary film genre, *The City*'s main sponsor was the American Institute of City Planners. This group had a real stake in the transformation of the American city. The federal government also sponsored several key films of the 1930s, especially *The Plow That Broke the Plains* (1936) and *The River* (1937), a film that championed the efforts of the Tennessee Valley Authority to prevent flooding and produce electricity, a federal initiative that ran into conservative opposition.

A variation on the problem/solution style of logic occurs in *Triumph of the Will* (1935). Speeches by Nazi Party leaders refer to Germany's disarray following World War I while these same leaders nominate themselves, their party, and, above all, Adolf Hitler as the solution to the problems of national humiliation and economic collapse. The film glosses over the problem. It could assume viewers were well aware of inflation and political unrest. Instead it devotes the great bulk of its energy to the solution: the Nazi Party and its leader, Adolf Hitler. This man and this party would redeem Germany and put it on the path to recovery, prosperity, and power. More crucial to Leni Riefenstahl than archival footage of Germany's defeat in World War I, a review of the humiliating terms imposed by the Treaty of Versailles, or evidence of the hardships worked by skyrocketing inflation was a vivid, compelling portrait of the Nazi Party, and Hitler, at their carefully choreographed best.

The Cove (2009) takes up a very different dual problem: the slaughter of massive numbers of dolphins in a secret cove near the city of

Taijii, Japan, since the Japanese see the dolphin as annoying competitors to their fishing industry, on the one hand, and how to document this slaughter in the face of organized government efforts to thwart them, on the other. The film weaves a compelling tale that oscillates between detailing the scope of the slaughter and the exploits that allow them to secretly make their way to the forbidden cove. The film makes clear that the solution to the problem lies beyond its scope: it will require concerted action by any and all concerned parties to convince the Japanese government to put an end to the slaughter. Former dolphin trainer Ric O'Barry, now a fierce defender of dolphins, is the film's main protagonist, but his efforts are presented more as a model for others than an end in themselves.

The logic organizing a documentary film supports an underlying proposal, assertion, or claim about the historical world. With documentaries, we expect to engage with films that engage the world. This engagement and logic frees the documentary from some of the conventions relied upon to establish an imaginary world. Continuity editing, for example, which works to make the cuts between shots in a typical fiction film scene invisible, has a lower priority. What is achieved by continuity editing in fiction is achieved by history in documentary film: things share relationships in time and space not because of the editing but because of actual, historical linkages. Editing in documentary demonstrates these linkages. The demonstration may be convincing or implausible, accurate or distorted, but it occurs in relation to situations and events with which we are already familiar, or for which external sources of verifiable information exist. Documentary is therefore much less reliant on continuity editing to establish the credibility of the world it refers to than is fiction.

Documentary films, in fact, often display a wider array of shots and scenes than fiction films, an array yoked together less by a narrative organized around a central character than by a rhetoric organized around a controlling perspective. Characters, or social actors, may come and go, offering information, giving testimony, providing evidence. Places and things may appear and disappear as they are brought forward in support of the film's point of view or perspective. A logic of implication bridges these leaps from one person or place to another.

If, for example, we jump from a woman sitting in her home describing what it was like to work as a welder during World War II to a

The City (Ralph Steiner and Willard Van Dyke, 1939). Images of vast numbers of similar objects, and people, help make *The City*'s point: urban design has fallen behind human need. *Photo courtesy of National Archives.*

shot from a 1940s newsreel of a shipyard, the cut implies that the second shot illustrates the type of workplace and the kind of work the woman in the first shot describes. The cut hardly seems disruptive at all even though there is no literal spatial or temporal continuity between the two shots.

Cuts like this occur over and over in Connie Field's *The Life and Times of Rosie the Riveter* (1980); the leaps of time and space do not confuse us because they support an evolving story and consistent argument about how women were first actively recruited to fill jobs left vacant by men called into the military and then, when the men returned, actively discouraged from remaining in the workforce. The shots fall into place in relation to what the women Field interviews have to say. We attend

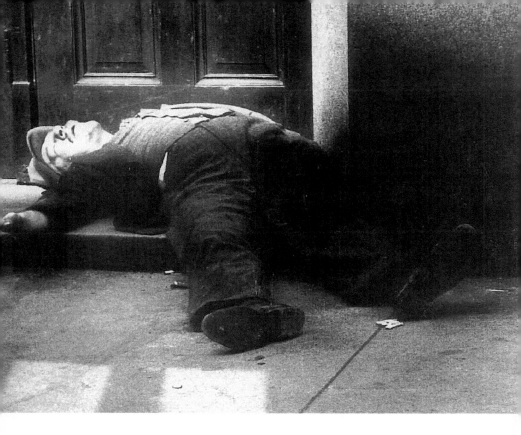

The City (Ralph Steiner and Willard Van Dyke, 1939). Images of individuals such as this one disassociate the rise of the city with the rise of civilization: human triumph succumbs to a congested, frenzied environment. Such images illustrate the film's theme that the traditional city defeats the human spirit; they help prepare us for the film's solution: planned, green belt communities. *Photo courtesy of National Archives.*

to what they say; what we see serves to support, amplify, illustrate, or otherwise relate to the stories they tell and the line of argument Field follows in relation to what they say.

Instead of continuity editing, we might call this form of documentary editing evidentiary. Instead of organizing cuts within a scene to present a sense of a single, unified time and space in which we follow the actions of central characters, evidentiary editing organizes cuts within a scene to present the impression of a single, convincing proposal supported by a logic. Rather than cutting from one shot of a character approaching a door to a second shot of the same character entering the room on the far side of the door, a more typical documentary edit would be from a close-up of a bottle of champagne being broken across the bow of ship to a long shot of a ship, perhaps an entirely different ship, being launched into the sea. The two shots may have been made years or continents apart, but they contribute to the representation of a single process rather than the development of an individual character.

Pursuing the example provided by *The Life and Times of Rosie the Riveter*, some specific choices for structuring a documentary about a topic such as shipbuilding can be sketched out. A film might

- Poetically or evocatively describe the process, capturing some of its mystery and wonder through camera angles, editing, and music.
- Offer a proposal or make an argument via commentary about shipbuilding—that women were urged to take up work during and then discouraged from continuing it after World War II, for example.
- Interact with actual shipbuilders by either simply observing them as they go about their work or by actively engaging with them, perhaps through interviews.
- Explain how to build a ship with details and information about specific parts of the process that would be of use to those who do the work. This might amount to an informational or "how to" film more than a documentary, although there is room for hybrid approaches.

In each of these cases editing serves an evidentiary function. It not only furthers our involvement in the unfolding of the film but supports the kinds of proposals or assertions the film makes about the world. We tend to assess the organization of a documentary in terms of the persuasiveness or convincingness of its representations rather than the plausibility or fascination of its fabrications.

In documentary, a great deal of this persuasiveness stems from the sound track. Ever since the end of the 1920s documentary filmmaking has relied heavily on sound in all its aspects: spoken commentary, synchronous speech, acoustic effects, and music. Arguments call for a

The Life and Times of Rosie the Riveter (Connie Field, 1980). Women welders at the Landers, Frary and Clark Plant, Connecticut, 1943. *Rosie the Riveter* is a brilliant example of a film that uses archival film material not to confirm the truth of a situation but to demonstrate how truth claims can serve political goals. In this case the historical footage was designed to encourage women to enter the workforce during World War II and was then redesigned to urge them to leave the workforce when men returned from the war. Thanks to Field's editing, the contortions of logic required for this task are often hilariously blatant. (Few of the government's propaganda films even acknowledged the presence of African American women in the work force, giving this particular photo by Gordon Parks extra value.) *Photograph by Gordon Parks.*

logic that words are better able to convey than are images. Images lack tense and a negative form, for example. We can make a sign that says, "No Smoking," but we typically convey this requirement in images by the convention of putting a slash through an image of a cigarette. To decide to *not* show an image of a cigarette at all would not in any way communicate the same meaning as a sign declaring the injunction, "No Smoking." The convention of a slash mark through an image to mean "No" or "Not" is very hard to adapt to filmmaking. Whether it is through what we hear a commentator tell us about the film's subject, what social actors tell us directly via interviews, or what we overhear social actors say among themselves as the camera observes them, documentaries depend heavily on the spoken word. Speech fleshes out our sense of the world. An event recounted becomes history reclaimed.

Like other genres, documentaries go through phases or periods. Different countries and regions have different documentary traditions and styles of their own. European and Latin American documentary filmmakers, for example, favor subjective and openly rhetorical forms such as Luis Buñuel's *Land without Bread* or Chris Marker's *Sans Soleil* (1982), whereas British and North American filmmakers place more emphasis on objective and observational forms such as the "two sides of every argument" tone to much journalistic reporting and the highly noninterventionist approach of Frederick Wiseman in *High School* (1968), *Hospital* (1970), and *La Danse* (2009), among others.

Documentary, like fiction film, has also had its movements. Among them we could include the documentary work by Dziga Vertov, Esther Shub, Mikhail Kalatazov, Victor Turin, and others working in the Soviet Union in the 1920s and early 1930s. These filmmakers pioneered the development of the documentary form as a way of seeing the world afresh; they drew heavily on avant-garde practices and techniques. The British Documentary movement of the 1930s joined documentary filmmaking to the needs of the state and launched the careers of numerous filmmakers like Basil Wright, Harry Watt, Alberto Cavalcanti, Paul Rotha, and Humphrey Jennings under the leadership of John Grierson. The Free Cinema of 1950s Britain established another movement when Lindsay Anderson, Karel Reisz, Tony Richardson, and others took a fresh, unadorned look at contemporary British life in films such as *Every Day except Christmas* (1957), *Momma Don't*

Allow (1956), and *We Are the Lambeth Boys* (1958). The observational filmmaking of Frederick Wiseman, the Maysles brothers, and Drew Associates (principally Richard Drew, D. A. Pennebaker, and Richard Leacock) in early 1960s America married a journalistic tone of apparent neutrality with a strongly observational style.

Film movements arise when a group of individuals who share a common outlook or approach join together formally or informally. Manifestoes and other statements such as Dziga Vertov's "WE: Variant of a Manifesto" and "Kino Eye," which declared open warfare on scripted and acted films, often accompany movements. Vertov's essays defined the principles and goals to which films like *The Man with a Movie Camera* and *Enthusiasm* (1930) gave tangible expression. Lindsay Anderson's essay in *Sight and Sound* magazine in 1956, "Stand Up! Stand Up!" urged a vivid sense of social commitment for documentary filmmaking. He defined the principles and goals of a poetic but gritty representation of everyday, working-class reality freed from the sense of civic obligation to provide "solutions" that had made work produced by John Grierson in the 1930s a handmaiden of the British government's policies of social amelioration.

Free Cinema advocates and practitioners sought a cinema free of a government's propaganda needs, a sponsor's purse strings, or a genre's conventions. Their movement helped stimulate the revival of the British feature film built around similar principles of the unvarnished representation of working people and an irreverent attitude toward social and cinematic conventions. The "angry young men" of 1950s Britain gave us *Saturday Night and Sunday Morning* (Karel Reisz, 1960), *The Loneliness of the Long Distance Runner* (Tony Richardson, 1962), and *This Sporting Life* (Lindsay Anderson, 1963) in a spirit that drew on sensibilities quite similar to the Free Cinema of the time. Many of those who began in documentary production in fact went on to make the "kitchen sink" feature films that dramatized working-class life.

Documentary falls into periods as well as movements. A period identifies a specific stretch of time during which films display common characteristics. Periods help define the history of documentary film and differentiate it from other types of films with different movements and periods. The period of the 1930s, for example, saw much documentary work address contemporary issues with an assembly of images held together by a voice-over commentary. Such films shared a Depression-era sensibility that reached across media, including a strong emphasis on social and economic issues. The 1960s saw the introduction of lightweight, hand-held cameras that could be used together with synchronous sound. Filmmakers acquired the mobility and responsiveness that allowed them to follow social actors in their everyday routines. The options to observe intimate or crisis-laden behavior at a distance or to interact in a more directly participatory manner with their subjects both became possible. The 1960s were thus a period in which the ideas of a rigorously observational and of a far more participatory cinema gained prominence over the use of voice-over commentary. These modes signaled a radical break with dominant documentary styles from the 1930s to the 1950s.

In the 1970s and 1980s, documentary frequently returned to the past through the use of archival film material and contemporary interviews to give a new perspective to past events or current issues. (Historical perspective was generally missing from observational and participatory filmmaking.) Emile de Antonio's *In the Year of the Pig* (1969) provided the model or prototype that many emulated. De Antonio combined a rich variety of archival source material with trenchant interviews to recount the background to the Vietnam War in a way radically at odds with the American government's official version. *With Babies and Banners* (1979), about a 1930s automobile factory strike but told from the women's point of view; *Union Maids* (1976), about union-organizing struggles in different industries; and *The Life and Times of Rosie the Riveter,* about women's role in the workforce during and after World War II, are but three examples that draw on de Antonio's example. They inflect his model to address issues of women's history. As such they were also part of a broad tendency in the 1960s and 1970s to tell history from below, history as lived and experienced by ordinary people, rather than history from above, based on the deeds of leaders and the knowledge of experts.

Periods and movements characterize documentary, but so does a series of modes of documentary film production that represent viable ways of using the resources of the cinema to make documentary films. Each mode emphasizes different cinematic resources or techniques.

Each mode also displays considerable variation based on how individual filmmakers, national emphases, and period tendencies affect it. Expository documentaries initially relied heavily on omniscient voice overs by professional male commentators. The mode remains in great use today but many voice overs are by females rather than males and a great many are by the filmmaker him- or herself rather than a trained professional. Observational filmmaking began in the 1960s but it remains an important resource today, although it is now frequently mixed with other modes to produce more hybrid documentaries.

The six principal modes of documentary filmmaking are

- *Poetic mode*: emphasizes visual associations, tonal or rhythmic qualities, descriptive passages, and formal organization. Examples: *The Bridge* (1928); *Song of Ceylon* (1934); *Listen to Britain* (1941); *Night and Fog* (1955); and *Koyaanisqatsi*. This mode bears a close proximity to experimental, personal, and avant-garde filmmaking.
- *Expository mode*: emphasizes verbal commentary and an argumentative logic. Examples: *The Plow That Broke the Plains*; *Spanish Earth* (1937); *Trance and Dance in Bali* (1952); *Les Maîtres Fous* (1955); and television news. This is the mode that most people associate with documentary in general.
- *Observational mode*: emphasizes a direct engagement with the everyday life of subjects as observed by an unobtrusive camera. Examples: *Primary*; *High School*; *Salesman* (1969); *The War Room* (1993); and *Metallica: Some Kind of Monster* (2004).
- *Participatory mode*: emphasizes the interaction between filmmaker and subject. Filming takes place by means of interviews or other forms of even more direct involvement from conversations to provocations. Often coupled with archival footage to examine historical issues. Examples: *Chronicle of a Summer*; *Solovky Power* (1988); *Shoah* (1985); *The Fog of War: Eleven Lessons from the Life of Robert McNamara* (2003); and *Enron: The Smartest Guys in the Room*.
- *Reflexive mode*: calls attention to the assumptions and conventions that govern documentary filmmaking.

Increases our awareness of the constructedness of the film's representation of reality. Examples: *The Man with a Movie Camera*; *Land without Bread*; *The Ax Fight* (1975); *The War Game* (1966); and *Reassemblage* (1982).

- *Performative mode*: emphasizes the subjective or expressive aspect of the filmmaker's own involvement with a subject; it strives to heighten the audience's responsiveness to this involvement. Rejects notions of objectivity in favor of evocation and affect. Examples: *The Act of Seeing with One's Own Eyes* (1971); *History and Memory* (1991); *Tongues Untied* (1989); *Chile, Obstinate Memory* (1997); *Waltz with Bashir*; and reality TV shows such as *Cops* (as a degraded example of the mode). The films in this mode all share qualities with the experimental, personal, and avant-garde, but with a strong emphasis on their emotional and social impact on an audience.

Modes come into prominence at a given time and place, but they persist and become more pervasive than movements. Each mode may arise partly as a response by filmmakers to perceived limitations in other modes, partly as a response to technological possibilities and institutional constraints or incentives, partly as an adaptation to particularly impressive (prototypical) films, and partly as a response to a changing social context, including audience expectations. Once established, though, modes overlap and intermingle. Individual films often reveal one mode that seems most influential to their organization, but individual films can also "mix and match" modes as the occasion demands.

A striking example of this mix and match phenomenon is the *Battle 360* series on the History Channel. It chronicles the history of World War II from different perspectives such as that of one ship: the USS *Enterprise*, an aircraft carrier. The series uses voice-over commentary and archival footage (expository mode) predominantly but couples this with interviews (participatory mode) and animated sequences of battle (performative mode). The animation has the look and feel of a video game: planes dive-bomb ships and gunfire streaks through the sky; close-up shots track alongside steel-cased bombs as they plummet to their target; torpedoes streak beneath the sea and pound into the flanks of enemy ships. Most of the animated attack sequences have no human figures in them: battle becomes removed from its human element and cost. These animated elements can also have a reflexive effect on some viewers, prompting them to question the assumption that a documentary must support its proposals or perspective with historically authentic footage. But the series' sponsor does even more. The History Channel website allows viewers to chat about the series online or to shop for DVDs of the different shows in the series. Although anchored in the expository mode, the series spills beyond not only that mode but the traditional frame within which documentary film production has taken place.

A CONSTITUENCY OF VIEWERS: ASSUMPTIONS, EXPECTATIONS, EVIDENCE, AND THE INDEXICAL QUALITY OF THE IMAGE

The final way to consider the fluidity of the documentary film involves the audience. The institutions that support documentary may also support fiction films; the practitioners of documentary may also make experimental or fiction films; the characteristics of the films themselves can be simulated in a fictional context, as works like *No Lies* (1973), *The Blair Witch Project,* and *Best in Show* (2000) make clear. In other words, what we have taken some pains to sketch out as the domain of documentary exhibits permeable borders and a chameleon-like appearance. The sense that a film is a documentary lies in the mind of the beholder as much as it lies in the film's context or structure.

What assumptions and expectations characterize our sense that a film is a documentary? What do we bring to the viewing experience that is different when we encounter a documentary rather than some other genre of film? The commonsense assumptions with which we began reveal some basic assumptions. Documentaries are

- About reality
- About real people
- Tell stories about what really happened.

Although we went on to qualify and elaborate on these points in important ways, they remain common starting points for audiences. These assumptions often turn out to rely heavily on the indexical capacity of the photographic image, and of sound recording, to replicate what we take to be the distinctive visual or acoustic qualities of what they record. This is an *assumption*, encouraged by specific properties of lenses, emulsions, optics, sound recorders, and styles, such as realism: the sounds we hear and the images we behold seem to bear the tangible trace of what produced them. Digital, computer graphic techniques can be used to achieve a similar effect even though they create the sound or image they appear to reproduce.

Some notes about the indexical image: recording instruments (cameras and sound recorders) register the imprint of things (sights and sounds) with great fidelity. It gives these imprints value as documents in the same way fingerprints have value as documents. This uncanny sense of a document, or image that bears a strict correspondence to what it refers to, is called its indexical quality. The indexical quality of an image refers to the way in which its appearance is shaped or determined by what it records: a photo of a boy holding his dog will exhibit, in two dimensions, an exact analogy of the spatial relationship between the boy and his dog in three dimensions; a fingerprint will show exactly the same pattern of whorls as the finger that produced it; a photocopy replicates an original precisely; markings on a fired bullet will bear an indexical relationship to the specific gun barrel through which it passed. The bullet's surface "records" the passage of that bullet through the gun barrel with a precision that allows forensic science to use it as documentary evidence in a given case.

Similarly, cinematic sounds and images, like photographic images, enjoy an indexical relationship to what they record. They capture precisely certain aspects of what stood before the camera, which is sometimes called the pro-filmic event. This quality is what makes the documentary image appear as a vital source of evidence about the world. Though true, it is immediately crucial to clarify this point. A document and an indexical sound recording or an indexical photo are documents; they provide evidence. But a documentary is more than evidence: it is also a particular way of seeing the world, making proposals about it, or offering perspectives on it. It is, in this sense, a way of *interpreting* the world. It will use evidence to do so.

What we need to keep in mind, therefore, is the difference between the indexical image as evidence and the argument, perspective, explanation, or interpretation it supports. Evidence is put to use. It serves the film's overall purpose. The same evidence can serve as raw material for multiple proposals and perspectives, as virtually every court trial demonstrates. The prosecution and defense refer to the same evidence but draw opposing conclusions. Similarly, the indexical image can appear to be proof of a given interpretation, but the interpretation cannot be assessed simply in terms of whether it uses valid evidence. Other interpretations, using the same evidence, will dispute its underlying assumptions.

This does not mean all interpretations are equally valid, however. Some may well make more convincing use of the available evidence and some may willfully misrepresent or suppress aspects of the same evidence. What is clear, in any case, is that the indexical image possesses a strong evidentiary power that has strongly contributed to the appeal of the documentary film. Who is not excited to see future President John F. Kennedy wind his way through labyrinthian backstage spaces only to emerge before a live audience during his 1960 Wisconsin primary battle with Hubert Humphrey in *Primary*? Who doesn't shudder to see the solitary Timothy Treadwell share the frame with looming grizzly bears in the remote reaches of the Alaskan wilderness in *Grizzly Man* (2005)? The indexical power of these images has a unique, compelling power.

The shots of concentration camp victims and survivors in Alain Resnais's haunting documentary *Night and Fog* bear the same appearance as what we would have seen had we been there because the cinematic image is a document of how these individuals appeared at the moment when they were filmed during and at the end of World War II. The perspective of the film on these events, however, differs considerably from Donald Brittain and John Spotton's *Memorandum* (1965), Claude Lanzmann's *Shoah*, or James Moll's *The Last Days* (1998). Even if we rule out special effects, digital manipulation, or other forms of alteration that could allow a photographic image to give false evidence, the authenticity of the image does not necessarily make one argument or perspective conclusive and another not. The internal logic and external verification of what a documentary claims to be true must be rigorously assessed: the inclusion of indexical images as evidence cannot do that job for us.

The weight we grant to the indexical quality of sound and image, the assumption we adopt that a documentary provides documentary evidence at the level of the shot, or spoken word, does not automatically extend to the entire film. We usually understand and acknowledge that a documentary is a *creative treatment* of actuality, not a faithful transcription of it. Transcriptions or strict records have their value, as in surveillance footage or records of specific events such as the launching of a rocket, the progress of a therapeutic session, or the performance of a particular play or sports event. We tend, however, to regard such records strictly as documents or "mere footage," rather than as documentaries. Documentaries marshal evidence and then use it to construct their own perspective or proposal about the world. We expect this process to take place. We are disappointed if it does not.

Among the assumptions we bring to documentary, then, is that individual shots and sounds, perhaps even scenes and sequences, will bear a highly indexical relationship to the events they represent, but that the film as a whole will go beyond being a mere document or record of these events to offer a perspective on them. As an audience we expect to be able both to trust to the indexical linkage between what we see and what occurred before the camera *and* to assess the poetic or rhetorical transformation of this linkage into a commentary or perspective on the world we occupy. We anticipate an oscillation between the recognition of historical reality and the recognition of a representation about it. This expectation distinguishes our involvement with documentary from our involvement with other film genres.

This expectation often characterizes what we might call the "discourses of sobriety." These are the ways we have of speaking directly about social and historical reality such as science, economics, medicine, military strategy, foreign policy, and educational policy. Inside an institutional framework that supports these ways of speaking, what we say and decide can affect the course of real events and entail real

Hoop Dreams (Steve James, Frederick Marx, Peter Gilbert, 1994). William Gates is one of the two young men we follow in *Hoop Dreams*. These publicity shots of him, which offer an indexical record of his appearance as a young man, promise a "coming of age" narrative in which we will witness how he and Arthur Agee, the other main character, develop as basketball players and mature as men. The distributor of *Hoop Dreams*, in fact, mounted a campaign to have the Academy of Motion Picture Arts and Sciences nominate the film not for Best Documentary but for Best Picture. The campaign failed, but it underscored the permeable and often arbitrary nature of sharp distinctions between fiction and documentary film. *Photos courtesy of Fine Line Features.*

consequences. These are ways of seeing and speaking that are also ways of doing and acting. Power runs through them. An air of sobriety surrounds these discourses because they are seldom receptive to whim or fantasy, to "make-believe" characters or imaginary worlds (unless they serve as useful simulations of the real world, such as in-flight simulators or econometric models of business behavior). They are the vehicles of action and intervention, power and knowledge, desire and will, directed toward the world we physically inhabit and share.

Like these other discourses, documentary claims to address the historical world and to possess the capacity to intervene by shaping how we regard it. Even though documentary filmmaking may not be accepted as the equal partner in scientific inquiry or foreign policy initiatives (largely because, as an image-based medium, documentaries lack important qualities of spoken and written discourse, such as the immediacy and spontaneity of dialogue or the rigorous logic of the written essay), this genre still shares a tradition of sobriety in its determination to make a difference in how we regard the world and proceed within it. Not all documentaries, of course, are sober-minded, stodgy affairs any more than all political speeches or all scientific reports are dull. Wit, imagination, and persuasive rhetorical skills come into play in many cases. The history of documentary demonstrates just how true this is with its remarkable array of persuasive, compelling, even poetic representations of the historical world.

In viewing documentary films we expect to learn or be moved, to discover or be persuaded of possibilities that pertain to the historical world. Documentaries draw on evidence to make a claim something like, "This is so," coupled to a tacit, "Isn't it?" This claim is conveyed by the persuasive or rhetorical force of the representation. *The Battle of San Pietro* (1945), for example, makes a case that "war is hell" and persuades us of this with evidence such as close-ups of a series of dead soldiers rather than, say, a single long shot of a battlefield that would diminish the horror and perhaps increase the nobility of battle. The impact of such a sight, in close-up, carries an impact, or "indexical whammy," that is quite different from the staged deaths in fiction films, such as *The Thin Red Line* (Terrence Malick, 1998) or *Saving Private Ryan* (Steven Spielberg, 1998), that also ponder the human price of waging war. The representations may be similar, but the emotional impact of close-up images of the dead and dying changes considerably when we know that there is no point at which the director can say, "Cut" and lives can be resumed. Like many documentaries, *The Battle of San Pietro* has a sober-minded purpose, but it uses emotionally compelling means of achieving it.

Audiences, then, encounter documentaries with an expectation that their desire to know more about the world will find gratification during the course of the film. Documentaries activate this desire to

American Teen (Nanette Burstein, 2008). Nanette Burstein's documentary uses many fictional techniques to heighten the sense of what it feels like to be a high school teen (continuity editing, point-of-view shots, cross cutting, and so on). As this poster illustrates, the film pointedly marketed itself as a portrait of five classic high school types, or stereotypes, and it develops each of its main characters to reinforce how they embody a given type. The strategy resembles genre film marketing and caused debate about the film's status as a documentary. *Courtesy of Paramount Vantage/Photofest.*

know when they invoke a historical subject and propose their individual variation on the history lesson. How did a given state of affairs come to pass (poverty among migrant farmworkers in *Harvest of Shame*, the degradation of farm land in *The Plow That Broke the Plains*)? What's it feel like to be a high school student (in *High School* or *American Teen* [2008])? How do people conduct themselves in situations of stress (female army recruits during basic training in *Soldier Girls* [1980], subjects undergoing tests of obedience that might cause harm to others in *Obedience* [1965])? What kind of interpersonal dynamics takes place in a concrete historical context (among family members all trying to make a go of a marginal pizza parlor in *Family Business* [1982] or trying to cope with charges of pedophilia against the father and one of the sons in *Capturing the Friedmans* [2003])? What is the source of a given problem and how might we address it (inadequate housing for working people in *Housing Problems* [1935] or colonial history and exploitation in Argentina in *The Hour of the Furnaces* [1968])? For what reasons should men fight (the *Why We Fight* series [1942–1945] on the reasons for the United States' entry into World War II, or Eugene Jarecki's more recent *Why We Fight* (2005), on the power of the military-industrial complex to fuel a need for wars)? How do members of a different culture organize their lives and express their social values (among the Dani of the New Guinea Highlands in *Dead Birds* [1963], among the Turkana of Kenya in *Wedding Camels* [1980])? What happens when one culture encounters another, notably when Western, colonial powers encounter so-called primitive people (for the first time in 1930s New Guinea in *First Contact* [1984], or on a recurring basis along the Sepic River in New Guinea as tourists meet indigenous people in *Cannibal Tours* [1988])?

Documentaries stimulate epistephilia (a desire to know) in their audiences. At their best, they convey an informing logic, a persuasive rhetoric, and a moving poetics that promises information and knowledge, insight and awareness. Documentaries propose to their audiences that the gratification of this desire to know will be their common business. He-Who-Knows (the agent has traditionally been masculine) will share knowledge with those who wish to know. We, too, can occupy the position of The-One-Who-Knows. *They speak about them to us* and we gain a sense of pleasure, satisfaction, and knowledge as a result.

This dynamic may pose questions as well as resolve them. We may ask, Who are we that we may come to know something? What kind of knowledge is the knowledge documentaries provide? To what kind of use do we put the knowledge a film provides? What we know, and how we come to believe in what we know, are matters of social importance. Power *and* responsibility reside in knowing; the use we make of what we learn extends beyond our engagement with documentary films to our engagement with the historical world represented by such films.

Why Are Ethical Issues Central to Documentary Filmmaking?

The bond between documentary and the historical world is deep and profound. Documentary adds a new dimension to popular memory and social history. Documentary engages with the world by representing it. It does so in three ways.

First, documentaries offer us a likeness or depiction of the world that bears a recognizable familiarity. Through the capacity of audio and visual recording devices to record situations and events with great fidelity, we see in documentaries people, places, and things that we might also see for ourselves, outside the cinema. This quality alone often provides a basis for belief: we see what was there before the camera; it must be real (it really existed or happened). This remarkable power of the photographic image cannot be underestimated, even though it is subject to qualification because

- An image cannot tell everything we want to know about what happened
- Images can be altered both during and after the fact by both conventional and digital techniques
- A verifiable, authentic image does not necessarily guarantee the validity of larger claims made about what the image represents or means.

In documentaries we find stories and proposals, evocations or descriptions that help us see the world anew. The ability of the photographic image to reproduce the likeness of what is set before it, its indexical quality, compels us to believe that it is reality itself re-presented before us, while the story or proposal presents a distinct way of regarding this reality. We may be familiar with the problems of corporate downsizing, plant shutdowns, and global assembly lines, but Michael Moore's *Roger and Me* (1989) views these issues in a fresh, distinctive way. We may know about cosmetic surgery and the debates surrounding efforts to regain lost youth by these means, but Michael Rubbo's *Daisy: The Story of a Facelift* (1982) adds his own personal perspective to our knowledge.

Second, documentaries also stand for or represent the interests of others. In a participatory democracy, each individual participates actively in political decision making rather than relying on a representative. Representative democracy, however, relies on elected individuals to represent the interests of their constituency. Documentary filmmakers often take on the role of public representatives. They speak for the interests of others, both for the individuals whom they represent in the film and for the institution or agency that supports their filmmaking activity. *The Selling of the Pentagon* (1971), a CBS News production on the ways in which the American military markets itself and ensures itself a substantial slice of the federal tax dollar, presents itself as a representative of the American people, investigating the use and abuse of political power in Washington. It also represents the interests of CBS News in marketing itself as an institution independent from government pressure and committed to a well-established tradition of investigative journalism.

Similarly, *Nanook of the North* (1922), Robert Flaherty's great story of an Inuit family's struggle for survival in the Arctic, represents Inuit culture in ways that the Inuit were not yet prepared to do for themselves. It also represents the interests of Revillon Freres, Flaherty's sponsor, at least to the extent of depicting fur hunting as a practice that benefits the Inuit as well as consumers.

Third, documentaries may represent the world in the same way a lawyer may represent a client's interests: they make a case for a par-

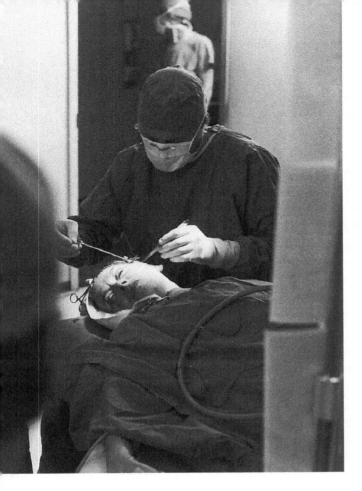

Daisy: The Story of a Facelift (Michael Rubbo, National Film Board of Canada, 1982). Michael Rubbo does not spare us the clinical details. His own voice-over commentary tries to grasp the complexity of the issues while his images detail the realities of the process.

ticular interpretation of the evidence before us. In this sense documentaries do not simply stand for others, representing them in ways they could not do for themselves, but rather they more actively make a case or propose an interpretation to win consent or influence opinion. *The Selling of the Pentagon* represents the case that the U.S. military aggressively fuels the perception of its own indispensability and its enormous need for continued, preferably increased funding. *Nanook of the North* represents the struggle for survival in a harsh, unforgiving climate as the test of a man's mettle and a family's resilience. Through the valor and courage of this family unit, with its familiar gender roles and untroubled relationships, we gain a sense of the dignity of an entire people. *Daisy: The Story of a Facelift* represents the case for the social construction of an individual's image in novel and disturbing ways that include the effects of social conditioning, medical procedures, and documentary filmmaking practices.

THE ETHICS OF REPRESENTING OTHERS

Documentaries, then, offer aural and visual likenesses or representations of some part of the historical world. They stand for or represent the views of individuals, groups, and institutions. They also convey impressions, make proposals, mount arguments, or offer perspectives of their own, setting out to persuade us to accept their views.

The concept of representation is what compels us to ask the question, "Why are ethical issues central to documentary filmmaking?" This question could also be phrased as, "What do we do with people when we make a documentary?" How do we treat the people we film; what do we owe them as well as our audience? Should they receive compensation? Should they have a right to block the inclusion of events that prove incriminating? Is it all right to have people repeat actions or conversations for the sake of the camera? Does this compromise the integrity of their actions and the film's claim to represent a reality that exists autonomously from its filming?

For fiction films the answer to the question of what to do with people is simple: we ask them to do what we need them to do. "People" are treated as actors who are working in their professional capacity. Their social role in the filmmaking process is defined by their professional role as actors. Trained actors agree to contractual terms to portray a given character in a film in exchange for compensation. The director has the right, and obligation, to obtain a suitable performance. The actor is valued for the quality of performance delivered, not for fidelity to his or her own everyday behavior and personality. Using nonactors begins to complicate the issue. Stories that rely on nonactors, such as many of the Italian neo-realist films or some of the New Iranian cinema, often occupy part of the fuzzy territory between fiction and nonfiction. Such work has often had an influence on both documentary and fiction filmmakers.

For nonfiction, or documentary, film, the answer is not quite so simple. "People" are treated as social actors rather than professional actors. Social actors continue to conduct their lives more or less as they would have done without the presence of a camera. They remain cultural participants rather than theatrical performers. Their value to the filmmaker consists not in what a contractual relationship requires but in what their own lives embody. Their value resides not in the ways in which they disguise or transform their everyday behavior and personality but in the ways in which their everyday behavior and personality serve the needs of the filmmaker.

That said, documentary filmmakers often favor individuals whose unschooled behavior before a camera conveys a sense of complexity and depth similar to what we value in a trained actor's performance. These individuals possess charisma: they attract our attention, they hold our interest, they fascinate. Nanook may well have been the first "star" of documentary film but many have followed, from Timothy Treadwell, the central character in Werner Herzog's remarkable documentary, *Grizzly Man* (2005), to Becky Fischer, the riveting Christian fundamentalist who leads young boys and girls to Christ in Heidi Ewing and Rachel Grady's *Jesus Camp* (2006).

The director's right to a performance is a "right" that, if exercised, threatens the sense of authenticity that surrounds the social actor. Social actors present themselves as they are, not as a director conceives a role. Too much direction and the sense that we behold an authentic self-presentation may waver. Nanette Burstein's *American Teen* (2008) received criticism from some reviewers on this score since it actively shaped its five principal characters, a set of high school seniors, into relatively stereotypic roles (handsome jock, artistic misfit, etc.), but the students claimed the film represented them fairly.

On the other hand, self-consciousness and modifications in behavior can document the ways in which the act of filmmaking alters the reality it sets out to represent. As mentioned in chapter 1, people modify how they present themselves to others over the course of their interaction, depending on the feedback they receive. The famous 12-hour documentary series on the Loud family televised on PBS, *An American Family* (Craig Gilbert, 1972), for example, raised considerable debate about whether the Louds' behavior and their own family relationships were altered by the act of filmmaking or were simply "captured" on film. The parents divorced and their son declared himself gay. These acts figured heavily in the overall drama of the series. If these events

Jesus Camp (Heidi Ewing, Rachel Grady, 2006). Becky Fisher, seen in close-up, ministers to young children. Her charismatic personality has a powerful effect on them. *Jesus Camp* shows her at work and lets the viewer decide how to judge the impact of her fundamentalist views. *Courtesy of Loki Films and Magnolia Pictures.*

came about because of the watchful eye of the camera and the presence of the filmmakers, were these changes encouraged, even if inadvertently, because they added to the dramatic intensity of the series?

Documentary filmmakers typically obtain a release from anyone they film. A release grants full decision-making power to the filmmaker. The individual forfeits any and all control over the use of his or her likeness and therefore over the final outcome. Nonetheless, some participants in financially successful documentaries may end up feeling used. As individuals who are central to the success of a film, they may feel entitled to compensation commensurate with the compensation an actor would receive. After all, their "performance" drew people to the film. In separate cases, both Randal Adams, the central figure in Errol Morris's powerful documentary, *The Thin Blue Line*

(1988), and Georges Lopez, the hero of Nicolas Philibert's remarkable study of a teacher in a one-room school in rural France, *Etre et avoir* (*To Be and to Have*) (2002) sued the directors for a fair share of the considerable box office revenue the films generated. Both filmmakers' lawyers rebutted that they were prepared to offer some compensation but that they balked at the idea that individuals had a right to be paid for being themselves, even in front of a camera. Doing so would destroy the documentary tradition, they argued. The American and French courts that heard the cases upheld the filmmakers' basic position, even though the men did receive compensation as part of the settlement.

What to do with people? Another way to put the question is, "What responsibility do filmmakers have for the effect of their acts on the lives of those filmed?" Most of us think of the invitation to act in a film as a desirable, even enviable, opportunity. But what if the invitation is not to act in a film but to *be* in a film, to be yourself in a film? What will others think of you; how will they judge you? What aspects of your life may stand revealed that you had not anticipated? What pressures, subtly implied or bluntly asserted, come into play to modify your conduct, and with what consequences? These questions have various answers, according to the situation, but they are of a different order from those posed by most fictions. They place a different burden of responsibility on filmmakers who set out to represent others rather than to portray characters of their own invention. These issues add a level of ethical consideration to documentary that is much less prominent in fiction filmmaking.

Consider Luis Buñuel's *Land without Bread* (1932). In it, Buñuel represents the lives of the citizens of Las Hurdes, a remote, impoverished region of Spain, and he does so with an outrageously judgmental, if not ethnocentric, voice-over commentary. "Here is another type of idiot," the narrator tells us at one moment as a Hurdano man raises his head into the frame. At another moment we see a tiny mountain stream as the narrator informs us, "During the summer there is no water other than this, and the inhabitants use it despite the disgusting filth it carries." Taken at face value, this abusive representation of people takes our breath away. How profoundly disrespectful; how contemptuous! How little regard for the hardships and difficulties of those who confront an inhospitable environment and whom the filmmaker does not

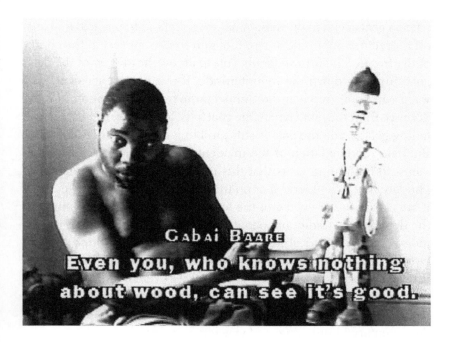

In and Out of Africa (Ilisa Barbash and Lucien Taylor, 1992). This film adopts a radically different attitude from *Land without Bread*. A high degree of collaboration occurred between filmmakers and subject. Their interaction gives the viewer a sense of "inside" or "behind-the-scenes" knowledge rather than the impression of parody, or possibly disrespect. Middleman and merchant Gabai Barré assures the filmmakers that this piece of "wood," as he calls it, is a good sculpture. The leap in value that an object takes when it goes from "wood" to "art" is the source of Barré's livelihood and of his clients' sense of aesthetic pleasure. *Photos courtesy of Lucien Taylor.*

choose to nominate for the myth of noble savage, as Robert Flaherty did with Nanook.

On the surface of it, *Land without Bread* seems to be an example of the most callous form of reporting, worse even than the hounding of celebrities by paparazzi or the gross misrepresentations of others in "mondo" films such as *Mondo Cane* (Gualtiero Jacopetti and Franco E. Prosperi, 1962). But Luis Buñuel's film gradually suggests a level of self-awareness and calculated effect that might prompt us to wonder if Buñuel is not the insensitive cad we initially thought. In one scene, for example, we are told the Hurdanos eat goat meat only when a goat accidentally dies. What we see, though, is a goat that falls off a steep mountainside as a puff of gun smoke appears in the corner of the frame. The film suddenly cuts to an overhead view of the dead goat tumbling down the mountainside. If this was an accident, why was a gun fired? And how did Buñuel jump from one position, at some distance from the point where the goat falls, to another, right above the falling goat, while the goat is still tumbling down the mountainside? Buñuel's representation of the incident seems to contain a wink: he seems to be hinting to us that this is *not* a factual representation of Hurdano life as he found it or an unthinkingly offensive judgment of it but a *criticism* or exposé of the forms of representation common to the depiction of traditional people. Perhaps the film's comments and judgments are a caricature of the kind of comments found both in typical travelogues and among many potential viewers. Perhaps Buñuel is satirizing a form of representation that uses documentary evidence to reinforce preexisting stereotypes. *Land without Bread*, from this perspective, might be a highly political film that calls the ethics of documentary filmmaking, and viewing, into question.

Seen from this perspective, Buñuel sounds, in 1932, an early and important cautionary note against our own tendency to believe literally what we see and hear. We risk missing the irony of a Buñuel or the manipulations of a Riefenstahl if we think seeing is believing in all cases. Leni Riefenstahl constructs as flattering a portrait of the National Socialist Party and its leader, Adolf Hitler, at their 1934 Nuremberg rally in *Triumph of the Will* (1935) as Buñuel constructs an unflattering portrait of the Hurdanos in *Land without Bread*. We accept either film as a "truthful" representation at our own peril. Buñuel may be among the first filmmakers to explicitly raise the issue of the ethics of documentary filmmaking, but he is hardly the last.

THE PURPOSE OF ETHICS

Ethics exist to govern the conduct of groups regarding matters for which hard and fast rules, or laws, will not suffice. Should we tell someone we film that they risk making a fool of themselves or that there will be many who will judge their conduct negatively? Should Ross McElwee have explained to the women he films in *Sherman's March*

In and Out of Africa (1992). Art gallery owner Wendy Engel assesses Gabai Barré's wares to choose items for her shop. Much of this film's emphasis is on how objects take on new meanings and values when they cross cultural boundaries. Barré plays a vital but customarily unnoticed role in this process. His willingness to let the filmmakers create new meanings and values of their own from his activity led them to give Barré a credit as a co-creator of the film.

(1985), as they interact with him during his journey through the South, that many viewers will see them as examples of coquettish, heterosexually obsessed Southern "belles"? Should Michael Moore have told the people of Flint, Michigan, he interviews in *Roger and Me* that he may make them look foolish in order to make General Motors look even worse? Should Jean Rouch have warned the Hausa tribesmen whom he films performing an elaborate possession ceremony in *Les Maîtres Fous* (1955) that their actions may seem bizarre, if not barbaric, to those not familiar with their customs and practices, despite the illuminating interpretation his voice-over commentary provides? Should Tanya Ballantyne have warned the husband of the down-and-out family she portrays in *The Things I Cannot Change* (1966) that her record of his

Triumph of the Will (Leni Riefenstahl, 1935). In contrast to *The City, Triumph of the Will* celebrates the power of the assembled, choreographed masses. The coordinated *movement* of the troops and the cadence of the sound track's music make it clear that these city dwellers experience not alienation but ecstasy.

behavior could serve as legal evidence against him (when he gets into a street fight, for example)?

These questions all point to the unforeseen effects a documentary film can have on those represented in it. Ethical considerations attempt to minimize harmful effects. Ethics becomes a measure of the ways in which negotiations about the nature of the relationship between filmmaker and subject have consequences for subjects and viewers alike. Filmmakers who set out to represent people whom they do not initially know but who typify or possess special knowledge of a problem or issue run the risk of exploiting them. Filmmakers who choose to observe others but not to intervene overtly in their affairs run the risk of altering behavior and events and of having their own human responsiveness called into question. Filmmakers who choose to work with people already familiar to them face the challenge of represent-

Two Laws (Caroline Strachan and Alessandro Cavadini, 1981). The camera height, the wide angle lens that shows the spatial relation between individuals, and the visible presence of the sound recorder (one of the social actors) are all decisions that were made in consultation between the filmmakers and their subjects. *Courtesy of Facets Multimedia.*

ing common ground responsibly, even if it means sacrificing their own voice or point of view for that of others. Carolyn Strachan and Alessandro Cavadini consciously adopt precisely such a collaborative, self-effacing position in *Two Laws* (1981), as they go about making decisions about everything from subject matter to camera lenses through dialogue with the Aboriginal people whose case to regain title to their ancestral land provides the core of their film.

A common litmus test for many of these ethical issues is the principle of "informed consent." This principle, relied on heavily in anthropology, sociology, medical experimentation, and elsewhere, states that participants in a study should be told of the possible consequences of their participation. To invite someone to join in a medical experiment involving a new drug without telling him or her that the drug has potentially dangerous side effects, may not prove an effective treatment, and may or may not be, in fact, a placebo breaches medical ethics. The individual may consent to participate because he or she cannot afford the standard drug treatment, for example, but cannot consent on an informed basis without a conscientious explanation of the design and risks of the experiment itself.

To invite someone to participate in a film about his or her family, unemployment, the possibilities of romance in the nuclear age (as Ross McElwee describes his goal in *Sherman's March*), or to follow someone through the process of obtaining a facelift as Michael Rubbo does with *Daisy: The Story of a Facelift*, poses a less clear-cut issue. Of exactly what consequences or risks should filmmakers inform their subjects? To what extent can the filmmaker honestly reveal his or her intentions or foretell the actual effects of a film when some intentions are unconscious and many effects are unpredictable?

A striking exception to this perspective is Stanley Milgram's extraordinary film, *Obedience* (1965). It is an expository summary of the experiments he conducted at Yale in which unwitting subjects agreed to "test" the memory of other subjects. If the "student" failed the memory test the target subject had to administer a shock. Each failure led to a stronger shock, up to and including levels marked "Danger Severe Shock" and "Fatal." After each subject either administered the most severe shock or refused to continue before reaching this point, the experimenters disclosed to them that the shocks never reached the student and that the other subject was in on the deception. It was not, in fact, a test of memory but of people's willingness to obey commands in a given context.

Milgram himself was shocked by how many people displayed full compliance with the command to continue giving the electrical jolts. His results have led to considerable debate about obedience. Less discussion has gone to noting that his experiment required that the target subjects not know the true purpose of the experiment. The experiment's design required that truly informed consent be withheld. Milgram himself did not seek to defend this choice in later discussions—he didn't think so many would go so far and therefore did not think informed consent would loom as an issue. The experiment and subsequent film made of it stand as a cautionary example of what can be at stake in matters of ethics. In 2002, Alex Gibney revisited Milgram's work, the 1970s Stanford prison experiment that divided students into prisoners and guards only to see brutality and sadism erupt

Obedience (© 1968 by Stanley Milgram, copyright renewed 1993 by
Alexandra Milgram, and distributed by Penn State Media Sales). This
image presents an unsuspecting subject who thinks he is giving powerful
shocks to a "student." The shocks never arrive but the subject does not know
this. The body language of many subjects suggests extreme discomfort
or anguish even though many of them deny being strongly affected by
what they had to do. *Permission granted by Alexandra Milgram.*

to a shocking degree, and other similar experiments in *The Human
Behavior Experiments* (2006). He links their findings to recent events
such as the torture carried out at Abu Ghraib prison in 2004 by military
police and the CIA and to the callous conduct of Enron corporation
when it deliberately manipulated the electrical power supply in the
state of California in his *Enron: The Smartest Guys in the Room* (2005).
Errol Morris, in *Standard Operating Procedure* (2008), also explores the
ramifications of obedience to authority through a series of interviews
with some of the military police who "softened up" prisoners for their
interrogations. These MPs, but not the actual interrogators or higher
officials, were prosecuted and given jail sentences.

The issue of whether informed consent can be withheld moves us
toward questions of deception. What is a deceptive practice in documentary filmmaking? Is it acceptable to feign interest in a company's

achievements to gain evidence of unsafe labor practices? Is it appropriate to film illegal acts (using cocaine or stealing cars, say) to make a documentary about a successful but severely stressed businessman or an urban gang? What obligation do documentarians have to their subjects relative to their audience or their conception of the truth? Is it all right to make Miss Michigan look foolish by asking for her opinion about local economic conditions in order to mock the irrelevance of beauty pageants to the damage caused by automotive plant shutdowns in Flint, as Michael Moore does in one scene from *Roger and Me?*

Another concrete example of such issues involves a scene from *Hoop Dreams* (1994) in which the filmmakers go with Arthur Agee to a local playground. Arthur is one of the two young men whose hopes of making it to the NBA (National Basketball Association) form the basis of the film. But as Arthur practices his game in the foreground, the camera records his father engaged in a drug deal in the background. Should the filmmakers have included this scene in the final film? Did it compromise Mr. Agee or risk providing legal evidence against him? To answer these questions, the filmmakers consulted their lawyers, who judged the degree of detail in the image was insufficient to serve as evidence in court, and they discussed the matter with the Agee family itself. They were prepared to remove the scene if anyone in the family wanted it removed. In fact, the family, including Mr. Agee, felt it should stay in. Mr. Agee was subsequently arrested on a drug charge, an event that transformed him, on his release, into a far more responsible father. He felt that the scene would help dramatize his own growth as a parent over the course of time.

Given that most filmmakers act as representatives of those they film or of the institution sponsoring them rather than as community members, tensions often arise between the filmmaker's desire to make a compelling film and the individual's desire to have his or her social rights and personal dignity respected. Mitchell Block's film *No Lies* (1973) makes this point exceptionally clear. The film takes place entirely inside the apartment of a young woman whom the filmmaker visits with his hand-held camera. He nonchalantly chats with her as he films, seemingly to practice his shooting skills, until a casual question reveals a traumatic event: the young woman was recently raped. What should the filmmaker do? Stop shooting and console her as a friend?

No Lies (Mitchell Block, 1973). The "production crew" in action. In *No Lies* a single person with a camera shoots the film we see. In this case we may end up wondering if we have been deceived when we learn that the cameraman is not Mitchell Block, the actual filmmaker. On the other hand, we may decide that Mitchell Block has made a wise decision to employ actors to play the role of a filmmaker and his subject, given the highly intrusive nature of the filmmaker's questioning.

Continue shooting and make a film that might aid our understanding of the effects of this form of criminal behavior? Exploit the moment to capture something much more sensational than he anticipated? The filmmaker opts to continue shooting. His questions become increasingly probing and personal. He expresses doubt about whether the rape happened at all, causing the woman considerable distress. Finally, as the short film comes to a close, he seems to realize he has pushed too hard and agrees to stop filming.

What do we make of the young man's conduct? Block's film would seem grotesquely callous if Mitchell were himself the filmmaker and the events we see entirely authentic. But *No Lies* functions something like *Land without Bread* and the harrowing Belgian film *Man Bites Dog* (1992), in which a documentary film crew appears to become complicit with the criminal acts of a thug whose life they set out to document: the films work to call into question audience assumptions about documentary representation. They explore how our sense of detached observation can turn into intense discomfort.

Block practices a calculated deception in order to make this point: we learn in the final credits that the two social actors are, in fact, trained actors and that their interaction was not spontaneous but scripted. *No Lies* functions like a meta-commentary on the very act of documentary filmmaking itself by suggesting that we as an audience are put in a position similar to the young woman's. We are also subject to the manipulations and maneuvers of the filmmaker, and we, too, can be left unsettled and distressed by them. We are unsettled not only by the on-screen filmmaker's aggressive interrogation of the woman but also by the off-screen filmmaker's (Block's) deliberate misrepresentation of the film's actual status as a fiction. The actors play roles under contractual agreements rather than present themselves as social actors. The film becomes, potentially, a second rape, a new form of abuse, if we feel taken in or used by the deception, but the deception can also provide considerable relief. *No Lies* serves as an important comment on documentary film's potential for abuse by turning people into victims so that we can learn, voyeuristically, about their suffering and misery.

Issues often arise in relation to the question of how to relate to people ethically because of the degree to which the filmmaker stands apart from those he or she films. The filmmaker controls the camera and thus possesses a power others don't. Further, filmmakers, especially journalistic filmmakers, belong to organizations and institutions with their own standards and practices. Even independent filmmakers usually see themselves as professional artists, pursuing a career more than dedicating themselves to representing the interests of a particular group or constituency.

In their voice-over commentary on the DVD of *Jesus Camp*, Heidi Ewing and Rachel Grady, the co-directors, refer to their central figure, fundamentalist Becky Fischer, as "a great documentary subject" due to her charisma. Her appeal lies in her conviction and articulateness. That she professes a highly contentious set of fundamentalist beliefs is not something they indicate any desire to attack or defend. They want to make a good film and they clearly decided that a charismatic individual gives them considerable leverage: charisma virtually guarantees audience involvement, even if the exact nature of that involvement can range from reverence to revulsion.

The filmmakers let the audience decide how to respond to Ms. Fischer's efforts to convert young boys and girls into devout fundamentalists. They, in fact, go to some pains not to undercut what she says or to endorse it. This approach makes it possible for fundamentalists, including Ms. Fischer, to feel that the film represents them accurately and for those who question these religious views and practices to find ample evidence for concern. In this case the filmmakers adopt a professional detachment from the issues at hand. Ethics need not mean taking a stand for or against the values and beliefs of others so much as acting in ways that do not withhold respect from subjects or undermine trust from audiences. At the same time, some films like *Land without Bread* and *No Lies* will remind us that these values can also be put into question. Developing a sense of ethical regard becomes a vital part of the documentary filmmaker's professionalism.

FILMMAKERS, PEOPLE, AUDIENCES

"How should we treat the people we film?" is a question that reminds us of the various ways in which filmmakers can choose to represent others. How should we relate to one another and how much can the presence of a camera change the rules of the game? Very different forms of alliance can take shape between the three-fold interaction among (1) filmmakers, (2) subjects or social actors, and (3) audiences or viewers. One convenient way to think about this interaction involves a verbal formulation of this three-way relationship. A number of formulations recur frequently in documentary films. The most classic formulation is

I speak about them to you.

I. The filmmaker takes on a personal persona, either directly or through a surrogate. A typical surrogate is the voice-of-God commentator, whom we hear speaking in a voice over but do not see. This anonymous but surrogate voice arose in the 1930s as a convenient way to describe a situation or problem, present an argument, propose a solution, and sometimes to evoke a poetic tone or mood. Films like

Song of Ceylon (1934) and *Night Mail* (1936) rendered Ceylonese culture and the British postal service, respectively, in a poetic tone. The commentaries made the transmission of information secondary to the construction of a deferential, somewhat romanticized mood. The voice of God, and a corresponding voice of authority—someone we see as well as hear who speaks on behalf of the film, such as the field correspondents in *Harvest of Shame* (1960), who report on the conditions faced by migrant farm laborers, Roger Mudd in *The Selling of the Pentagon*, as he investigates the workings of the Pentagon's public relations machine, or Wynton Marsalis in *Jazz* (2000), as he offers his personal insights into the history of jazz in America—remains a prevalent feature of documentary film (as well as of television news programming).

Another possibility is for the filmmaker him- or herself to speak, either on-camera, as in *Sherman's March* and *Roger and Me*, or off-camera, heard but not seen, as in *The Thin Blue Line*, and *Nobody's Business* (1996), Alan Berliner's film about his cantankerous but loving father. In these cases the filmmaker becomes a persona or character within his or her own film as well as the maker of the film. The character may be thinly developed, as in the case of *The Thin Blue Line*, where we learn very little about Errol Morris himself, or quite richly developed, as in the case of *Roger and Me*, where filmmaker Michael Moore portrays a socially conscious nebbish who will do whatever is necessary to get to the bottom of pressing social concerns, a persona that he has adopted in his subsequent work as well (*TV Nation* [1994], *Bowling for Columbine* [2002], *Fahrenheit 9/11* [2004], *Sicko* [2007], and *Capitalism: A Love Story* [2009]).

Speaking in the first person edges the documentary form toward the diary, essay, and aspects of avant-garde or experimental film and video. The emphasis may shift from convincing the audience of a particular point of view or approach to a problem to the representation of a personal, clearly subjective view of things. The emphasis shifts from persuasion to expression. What gets expressed is the filmmaker's own personal perspective and unique view of things. What makes it a documentary is that this expressiveness remains coupled to representations about the social, historical world, including the world of the filmmaker as a social actor, going about his or her life among others. Much of the "new journalism" (Hunter Thompson's *Slouching toward Las Vegas*, for example) that stressed a personal point of view and documentary filmmaking influenced by it, such as Michael Rubbo's and Michael Moore's work, stressed just this combination of an idiosyncratic or personal voice coupled to reporting on a topical issue.

Speak about. The filmmaker represents others. The sense of speaking about a topic or issue, a people or individual lends an air of civic importance to the effort. Speaking about something may involve telling a story, creating a poetic mood, or constructing a narrative, such as the story of how the mail gets to its destination or how Nanook manages to find food for his family, but it also implies a content-oriented desire to convey information, rely on facts, and make points about the world we share. Compared to "What story shall I tell?" the question "What shall I speak about?" turns our minds to the public sphere and to the social act of speaking to others on a topic of common interest. Not all documentaries adopt this posture, but it is among the most common ways of structuring a documentary film.

Them. The third person pronoun implies a separation between speaker and subject. The I who speaks is not identical with those of whom it speaks. We as an audience receive a sense that the subjects in the film are placed there for our examination and edification. They may be rendered as rich, full-rounded individuals with complex psychologies of their own, a tendency particularly noticeable in observational documentaries (discussed in chapter 7), but just as often they seem to come before us as examples or illustrations, evidence of a condition or event that has happened in the world. This can seem reductive and diminishing, but it can also be highly compelling and effective. Early documentary, prior to the rise of the observational and participatory modes in the early 1960s, relied almost entirely on using individuals as examples or illustrations. The lack of ability to record speech synchronously encouraged treating shots of specific people as instances of larger concerns. Sometimes such individuals take on highly symbolic significance, as in the example of Rodney King, whose beating by Los Angeles policemen after a traffic stop was caught on video. Mr. King does not emerge as a full-blown character in the raw footage that circulated widely on the news and beyond. Instead he serves as a symbol of police brutality and institutional racism. The power and shock effect of the footage depends more on its graphic nature and apparent authenticity than on its portrayal of a personality. For some the use of individuals as examples diminishes the pleasure of documentary when compared to fiction; at the least, it suggests that the pleasure and satisfaction of documentary representation derives from more sources than character development alone.

You. Like "them," "you" suggests a separation. One person speaks and another listens. A filmmaker speaks and an audience attends. Documentary, in this sense, belongs to an *institutional* discourse or framework. People with a particular form of expertise, documentary filmmakers, address us. They bring us together, momentarily, as a "you." As an audience we are typically separated from both the act of representation and the subject of representation. We occupy a different social time and space from either; we have a role and identity of our own as audience members that is itself a distinct aspect of our own social persona: we attend the film as viewers and bring specific assumptions and expectations to this role. "They," the film's subjects, may be husbands and wives, lawyers and accountants, students and athletes, professionals and travelers, like us, and their actions may prove instructive in more direct ways than we expect from fiction. We need not ask if real army recruits are like Demi Moore's character in *G.I. Jane* (Ridley Scott, 1997); we can see real recruits in Joan Churchill and Nick Broomfield's documentary *Soldier Girls* (1980) or Fred Wiseman's *Basic Training* (1971). We may draw analogies about human conduct from the dramatic events in *G.I. Jane,* but we can draw conclusions about human conduct from the actual events represented in *Soldier Girls* and *Basic Training.*

"You" becomes consolidated as an audience when the filmmaker indicates that he or she is indeed addressing us, that the film reaches us in some way. Without this sense of active address we may be present *at* but not attend *to* the film. Filmmakers must find a way to activate our sense of ourselves both as the one to whom the filmmaker speaks (about someone or something else) and as members of a group or collectivity, an audience for whom this topic bears importance. The usual means of doing this is by recourse to techniques of rhetoric (discussed in chapter 4).

Rhetoric is the form of speech used to persuade or convince others about an issue for which no clear-cut, unequivocal answer or solution exists. Guilt and innocence in the judicial process often hinges not simply on evidence but on the convincingness of the arguments made regarding the interpretation of the evidence. The O. J. Simpson trial was a prime example, given that there was a considerable amount of incriminating evidence. Even so, the defense lawyers made a successful argument that this evidence might have been fabricated and was circumstantial; its value was suspect. A judgment about the truth, the verdict, lay outside the realms of science, poetry, or story telling. It came to pass within the arena of rhetorical engagement, the arena in which most documentary operates as well.

Georges Franju's *Blood of the Beasts* (1949), for example, uses irony and surreal imagery to persuade us of the strangeness of slaughtering cattle, in 1940s France, so that we may enjoy their flesh, whereas Frederick Wiseman's *Meat* (1976) observes the activities in a midwestern slaughterhouse with considerable detachment, in 1970s America, to show us the routine nature of the human interactions among workers and supervisors, men and animals. Wiseman focuses on issues of labor, Franju on myth and ritual. Wiseman regards the workers as typical or representative wage earners in a labor-management context, Franju regards the workers as mythical figures who perform astounding feats. Specific stylistic and rhetorical choices operate in both cases to activate our sense of being addressed and engaged in specific ways.

I speak about them to you may be the most common formulation of the three-way relationship among filmmaker, subject, and audience, but it is certainly not the only one. A chart could be made that would include all of the variations in pronouns that this sentence allows for. Each variation would carry a different set of implications for the relationships among filmmakers, subjects, and viewers. A few of the more pertinent ones are sketched out here:

It speaks about them (or it) to us.

This formulation betrays a sense of separation, if not alienation, between the speaker and the audience. The film or video appears to arrive, addressed to us, from a source that lacks individuality. It addresses a subject likewise separated from us, even if it lies within some proximity. This formulation characterizes what we might call an institutional discourse, in which the film, often by means of a voice-over commentary, perhaps even a voice-of-God commentator, informs us about some aspect of the world in an impersonal but authoritative manner. The subjects or social actors represented are usually represented as examples of a general situation or condition. *The City* (1939), for example, addresses the problem of urban poverty, decay, and alienation as "it": abstract topics of general interest. The people shown serve to illustrate the film's point: new cities must take on characteristics of the small town rather than the urban slum. We get to know none of them individually. The effect is compelling, not necessarily detached and cold at all, but it retains an aura of institutional address.

The City and films like it also appear to speak to "us" but address themselves to a largely undifferentiated mass. We should attend to the film because we need to know about its topic. Informational films and advertising messages, including trailers for forthcoming films, often adopt this framework. *The River* (1937), for example, not only uses a stentorian male commentator, it constantly refers to what "we" have done to the land and what "we" can do to change things, even though the actual culprit is quite removed from you or me today and from large segments of its original audience in 1938. The film wants all of us to take responsibility for soil erosion and flood control.

Films of this sort seem to arrive from nowhere in particular. They are not the work of a specific individual whom we could call the filmmaker; they are often not even the work of an institution as identifiable as CNN news with its on-camera representatives (anchor men and women, reporters, interviewees). They arrive as the utterances of an "it" that remains impersonal and unidentifiable. (The "it" may be the scientific community, the medical establishment, the government, or the advertising industry, for example.) This "it" speaks to an "us" that may be a function more of demographics than of collectivity. Such works convey information, assign values, or urge actions that invite us to find a sense of commonality within a framework that may be dryly factual or emotionally charged, but it is seldom organized to move beyond a statistical, generic, or abstract conception of who "we" are.

I (or we) speak about us to you.

This formulation moves the filmmaker from a position of separation from those he or she represents to a position of commonality with them. Filmmaker and subject are of the same stock. In anthropological filmmaking the turn to this formulation goes by the name of auto-ethnography: this refers to the efforts of indigenous people to make films and videos about their own culture so that they may represent it to "us," those who remain outside. The Kayapo Indians of the Amazon River basin have been exceptionally active in this practice, using their videos to lobby Brazilian politicians for policies that will protect their homeland from development and exploitation.

Often the sense of commonality hinges around the representing of family. Alan Berliner, for example, has made two exceptional films about his grandfather and father, *Intimate Stranger* (1992) and *Nobody's Business*, respectively. Jonathan Caouette's *Tarnation* (2003) is an intensely personal family portrait. It borders on art therapy to the degree that telling the story of his mother's descent into madness at the hands of misguided parents and relatives also serves as his opportunity to reunite with her. Marlene Booth has made an intriguing film about her family's experience as predominantly assimilated Jews living in Iowa, *Yidl in the Middle* (1998). After discovering in her adulthood that her father was Jewish, Lisa Lewenz travels to Europe to understand what her family's life was like in 1930s Germany in *Letter without Words* (1998). In a film that mixes staged enactments with documentary representations, Camille Billops describes what happens when she and the now grown daughter whom she gave up for adoption as a child reunite in *Finding Christa* (1991).

By speaking about an "us" that includes the filmmaker these films achieve a degree of intimacy that can be quite compelling.

One of the most striking examples of the first-person voice in a documentary is Marlon Riggs's extraordinary video *Tongues Untied* (1989). In it Riggs speaks about what it means to be a black, gay male in a subtle fusion of both *"I speak about us to you"* and *"I speak about myself to you"* formulations that stresses the linkages between personal and collective experience. He and other social actors speak on- and off-camera about their lives as black, gay men. Some recite poetry, some recount stories, some participate in sketches and reenactments. These are not the standard voices of authority. They are not stripped of ethnic identity or colloquial idiosyncrasy to approximate the dominant norm of standard, white, nonregional English. Inflection and rhythm, cadence and style attest to the power of individual perception and the strength of personal expression that makes *Tongues Untied* one of the milestones in documentary filmmaking.

These various formulations of the relation of speaker/subject/audience convey some sense of how the filmmaker adopts a specific position in relation to those represented in the film and those to whom the film is addressed. This position requires negotiation and consent. The outcome provides some measure of the respect accorded others, even in the face of disagreement, and of the trust established with the audience. Signs of trust and respect provide evidence of the ethical considerations that went into the film's conception, acknowledging that some films will deliberately challenge or subvert these values. These formulations suggest what kind of relationship the viewer may have with the film by suggesting what kind of relationship we may have with the filmmaker and his or her subjects. To ask what we do with people when we make a documentary film involves asking what we do with filmmakers and viewers as well as with subjects. Assumptions about the relationships that should exist among all three go a long way toward determining what kind of documentary film or video results, the quality of the relationship it has to its subjects, and the effect it has on an audience. Assumptions vary considerably, as we shall see, but the underlying question of what we do with people persists as a fundamental issue for the ethics of documentary filmmaking.

3   What Gives Documentary Films a Voice of Their Own?

If documentaries represent issues and aspects, qualities and problems found in the historical world, they can be said to speak about this world through both sounds and images. The question of speech raises the question of "voice," but finding and having a voice involves more than using the spoken word. When a documentary "speaks about" something, when "We speak about it to you," for example, it speaks through its composition of shots, its editing together of images, and its use of music, among other things. Everything we see and hear represents not only the historical world but also how the film's maker wants to speak about that world.

Just like the orator or public speaker who uses his entire body to give voice to a particular perspective, documentaries speak with all the means at their disposal. Questions of speech and voice are therefore not meant entirely literally. The spoken word, of course, does play a vital role in most documentary film and video: some films, like *Portrait of Jason* (1967), *Word Is Out* (1977), or *Shoah* (1985), seem, at first glance, to be nothing but speech. But when Jason tells us about his life in *Portrait of Jason*, a key avenue to understanding his words involves what we see of his inflections, gestures, and behavior, including his interaction with Shirley Clarke, the filmmaker, as she orchestrates their dialogue. And when the gay and lesbian subjects in *Word Is Out* or the various interviewees in *Shoah* speak to us about their past, a key aspect of understanding the force and severity of that past lies in registering its effect on their way of speaking and acting in the present. Even the most speech oriented of documentaries—often referred to as "talking head" films—convey meanings, hint at symptoms, and express values on a multitude of levels apart from what is literally said. What does it mean, then, to raise the question of "voice" in documentary?

In chapter 1 we said that documentaries represent the historical world by giving audible, visible shape "to a way of seeing the historical world directly rather than [shaping] a fictional allegory." As such documentaries become one voice among many that give shape to our world, from written histories to political parties and from religious leaders to urban planners. Collectively, these voices come together in an arena of social debate and contestation, an arena sometimes called the public sphere. The fact that documentaries are not a *reproduction* of reality gives them a voice of their own. They are, instead, a *representation* of the world. The voice of documentary makes us aware that someone is speaking to us from his or her own perspective about the world we hold in common with that person.

The voice of documentary can make claims, propose perspectives, and evoke feelings. Documentaries seek to persuade or convince us by the strength of their point of view and the power of their voice. The voice of documentary is each film's specific way of expressing its way of seeing the world. The same topic and perspective on it can be expressed in different ways. For example, "Freedom of choice is vital for women who must decide whether to have an abortion" is an argument, or point of view. One documentary might work performatively to convey what women in such a position feel or experience, as *Speak Body* (1987) does, with its evocative array of women's voices heard off-screen as we see fragments of female bodies on-screen. Another work might rely on interviews with women in different countries to underscore the social impact that access or barriers to abortion procedures create, as *Abortion Stories: North and South* (1984) does, with its variety of women who testify on-camera to their experience in different North and South American countries. *Speak Body* and *Abortion Stories* make basically the same argument, but they do so from distinctly different perspectives and hence with distinctly different voices.

The idea of voice is also tied to the idea of an informing logic overseeing the organization of a documentary compared to the idea of a compelling story organizing a fiction. Not mutually exclusive, there is nonetheless the sense that an informing logic, conveyed by a distinct voice, has dominance in documentary compared to the compelling story, conveyed by a distinct style, which has dominance in narrative fiction. Voice, then, is a question of *how* the logic, and perspective, of a documentary gets conveyed to us.

Documentary voice is clearly akin to film style: both rely on the same cinematic techniques (editing, speech, music, composition, lighting, etc.), but they function a bit differently in documentary than in fiction. Style operates differently in documentary than in fiction. The idea of a documentary voice indicates how we gain a sense that the film addresses us as socially situated viewers and speaks about our common world. Style in fiction gives us a sense of how a director constructs a distinct world that we enter into without being addressed directly. Instead of feeling addressed by a voice, a fiction typically unfolds on its own: as viewers we overlook and overhear what happens. As we do so, we develop various forms of emotional attachment to this fictive world. Documentary voice, on the other hand, derives from the director's attempt to translate his or her perspective on the actual historical world into audio-visual terms; it also stems from his or her direct involvement with the film's subject. Voice, that is, attests to how the filmmaker engages with the historical world in the course of making a film. It has an ethical component in ways we have already discussed in chapter 2. Voice is a measure of how a filmmaker responds to and speaks about the world he or she shares with us. If fictional style portrays a distinct, imaginary world of the director's making, documentary voice represents how the filmmaker engages with the historical world itself.

When Robert Flaherty films Nanook biting into a phonograph record to see what kind of thing this strange disc that makes sounds is, the inclusion, duration, and specific placement of the shot—elementary questions of style—reveal a willingness on Flaherty's part to let Nanook be the butt of a joke: Nanook "erroneously" uses his mouth where he should use his ear. The trust and collaboration between filmmaker and subject may appear in jeopardy, especially when viewed across the chasm of postcolonial studies that take some pains to examine the ways in which patterns of hierarchy persist in the everyday encounters between peoples of different cultures. The voice of the film betrays its maker's form of engagement with the world in a way that even he or she might not have fully recognized. It speaks from and reveals a distinct perspective on the world.

In another example, Jon Silver uses a long take at the opening of *Watsonville on Strike* (1989) (about a farmworker strike in the California coastal town of Watsonville), while we hear him arguing with the union director about whether he can continue to film inside the union hall. This stylistic choice (long take over editing) also bears witness to an existential necessity: Silver must negotiate his own right to be there, his own right to film, and he must do so right now, as he keeps filming. Everything is at risk at a precise instant of historical time that anything other than a long take could not authenticate in so direct a manner. The long take is a record of that moment seen from Silver's literal, and political, point of view as it gradually but dramatically reveals itself to us.

When the director threatens to have Silver thrown out of the hall, he responds by panning his camera to the onlooking Chicano/Chicana workers and asks them, in Spanish rather than in the English he uses with the Anglo director, "What do you say? Is it all right for me to film?" The record of his question and their enthusiastic response, all within the same shot as the director's intransigent refusal to grant permission, gives voice to Silver's desire to represent himself as a straightforward, above-board activist whose spontaneous loyalty lies with the workers rather than union representatives. We *see* him display this spontaneous loyalty when he pans the camera away from the director and toward the workers rather than cut to, possibly, another discussion at another time or place. He does not cut until the director has wagged his finger at him and warned, "If you put my picture on television, I'll sue you."

The voice of the film reveals Silver's willingness to acknowledge the reality of the moment rather than slip into the illusion that people act as if the camera, and filmmaker, were not there. His voice, represented in the long take and camera movement, as much as in what he actually says, reveals *how* he makes his argument on behalf of the worker's cause. Like style, but with an added sense of ethical and po-

Watsonville on Strike (Jon Silver, 1989). In this opening scene, the union director points and stares directly at the camera held by filmmaker Jon Silver. Such moments cause embarrassment within an observational framework or self-consciousness within a fictional framework. Here the director's direct confrontation with the filmmaker testifies to Silver's active, participatory role in the shaping of events. What we see would not have occurred had the camera, and the filmmaker, not been there to record it.

litical accountability, voice serves to give concrete embodiment to a filmmaker's engagement with the world.

The voice of documentary testifies to the character of the film-maker, like Robert Flaherty or Jon Silver, to *how* he acquits himself in the face of social reality, as much as to his creative vision. Style takes on an ethical dimension. The voice of documentary conveys a sense of what the filmmaker's social point of view is and of how this point of view becomes manifest in the act of making the film. This voice says, in so many words, "This is how I choose to act and film in relation to the world we hold in common; what do you make of it?"

The voice of documentary is not limited to the voices of unseen "gods" and visible "authorities" who represent the filmmaker's point of view—who speak *for* the film, or to social actors who represent their own points of view—who speak *in* the film. The voice of documentary speaks with all the means available to its maker. These means can be summarized as the selection and arrangement of sound and image; that is, the working out of an organizing logic. This entails, at least, the following decisions:

1. When to cut, or edit, and what to juxtapose
2. How to frame or compose a shot (close-up or long shot, low or high angle, artificial or natural lighting, color or black and white, whether to pan, zoom in or out, track or remain stationary, and so on)
3. Whether to record synchronous sound at the time of shooting, and whether to add additional sound, such as voice-over translations, dubbed dialogue, music, sound effects, or commentary, at a later point
4. Whether to adhere to an accurate chronology or rearrange events to support a point or mood
5. Whether to use archival or other people's footage and photographs or only those images shot by the filmmaker on the spot
6. Which mode of documentary representation to rely on to organize the film (expository, poetic, observational, participatory, reflexive, or performative).

CATEGORIES OF VOICE

When we represent the world from a particular point of view we do so with a voice that shares qualities with other voices. Genre conventions are one way to cluster such qualities. Some conventions are not specific to film but are shared with the essay, diary, autobiography, notebook, editorial, evocation, eulogy, exhortation, description, or report. (These kinds of categories or forms constitute the chapter headings for Erik Barnouw's informative history of documentary film, *Documentary: A History of the Non-fiction Film*, where he uses terms like "reporter," "advocate," "prosecutor," and "guerilla" to organize chapters on dif-

Bontoc Eulogy (Marlon Fuentes, 1995). Finding a voice. On first viewing we do not know that the person sitting in front of the old phonograph player is the filmmaker; nor do we know that the scratchy sounds dominating the sound track will eventually become the voice of the filmmaker's grandfather. In the course of the film, Fuentes embarks on his own voyage of discovery to learn more about his grandfather and his turn-of-the-century encounters with colonial anthropology. He combines archival footage, staged events (such as this one), and his own voice-over commentary to give to his film a voice that seeks to recover both family and Filipino history. *Photo courtesy of Marlon Fuentes.*

ferent trends in documentary.) Other conventions, such as the ones that characterize the various modes of documentary—expository and observational documentary, for example—are specific to the medium. This point is developed further in chapters 6 and 7.

Together, generic forms and modes establish some of the constraints that identify a given voice, but they do not wholly determine that voice. Each voice is unique. This uniqueness stems from the concrete utilization of forms and modes, techniques and styles, and from the specific pattern of encounter that takes place between filmmaker and subject. The voice of a documentary serves as evidence of both a perspective and an encounter. Our recognition that such a voice addresses us in a distinct way is a key part of our recognition of a given film as a documentary.

The fact that the voice of a documentary relies on all the means available to it, not just spoken words, means that the argument or point of view carried by a documentary can be more or less explicit. The most explicit form of voice is no doubt the one conveyed by spoken, or written, words. These are words that stand for the point of view of the film and are typically referred to as "voice-of-God" or "voice-of-authority" commentary. (We see and hear authorities who appear on behalf of a film but only hear "gods," who may be professional voice-over experts or others chosen for how their voice fits the needs of the film.)

Commentary, or direct address, is a voice that addresses us directly; it lays out its point of view explicitly. The comments can be passionately partisan, as they are in the bold graphic inter-titles of *Salt for Svanetia*, made in the Soviet Union in 1930 as Stalin was implementing a Five-Year Plan to accelerate industrialization and agricultural production. These titles proclaim the arrival of the road that will bring much-needed salt to this remote region as a massive triumph of the highest order. In other cases, comments can be seemingly impartial, as in the reportorial style of most television journalists. In both cases, the voice of direct address proposes a position that says, in effect, "See it this way." It can be a galvanizing voice or a reassuring one, but its tone provides us with a ready-made point of view to which we will, it is hoped, subscribe.

Some documentaries eschew this type of explicitness. Poetic documentaries, for example, may drop both voices of authority and God or use them to evoke, hint, or suggest rather than declare or explain. *Song of Ceylon* (1934) and *Night Mail* (1936) use a voice of God to evoke as well as explain. The voice of the film does not address us quite so directly. Evidence accrues, but evidence of what? A mood or tone, in part, as well as a proposal or argument.

A film's point of view may also become entirely implicit. In this case, the voice of the film lies embedded in all the means of representation available to the filmmaker *apart from* explicit commentary. In contrast to the voice of commentary, we might call this the voice of perspective. *Koyaanisqatsi* (1983) is a prime example of this tack but so is *Lessons of Darkness* (1992). These two films evoke feelings of loss and ruin in relation to environmental degradation and to the burning of the Kuwaiti oil fields during the first Iraq war, respectively. Neither relies on spoken commentary; the films speak through the images they select and arrange and the music that accompanies them.

A "voice of perspective" speaks through the filmmaker's specific decisions about the selection and arrangement of sounds and images. This voice advances an argument or makes proposals about the world by implication. The argument operates on a tacit level. We have to infer what the filmmaker's point of view, in fact, is. The effect is less "See it this way" than "See for yourself." Documentaries from the era of the silent cinema often spoke in this way, from *Berlin: Symphony of a Great City* (1927), a poetic portrait in images of Berlin, to *Rain* (1929), the story of the effect of a summer shower on street life in Amsterdam.

Although invited to see for ourselves, and to infer what is left tacit or unspoken, what we see is not a reproduction of the world but a specific form of representation with a specific perspective. The sense of a perspective—an informing logic and overall organization to the film—separates a documentary from mere footage or photographic records, where this sense of perspective is minimal. ("Mere footage" is the term used to refer to isolated shots, outtakes, raw footage, and other forms of unassembled, unedited material.) Mere footage may still possess some hint of a perspective but it is minimal: surveillance footage from a store that focuses on transactions at a cash register implicitly says something about which elements of customer/personnel interaction hold the highest priority.

Once we infer a perspective we know that we are not confronted by a mere reproduction of the historical world. Even if the voice of the film adopts the guise of a nonjudgmental, impartial, disinterested, or objective witness, it nonetheless offers a perspective. At the least, such a strategy of self-effacement testifies to the significance of the world itself and to a particular filmmaker's sense of solemn responsibility to report on it fairly and accurately.

The Thin Blue Line (1988), for example, uses no voice-over commentary at all, and yet through the perspective it offers it makes a clear argument for the innocence of a man convicted of murder. The voice of the film speaks to us through the juxtaposition of interviews with

TABLE 3.1. Forms of Documentary Voice

Direct Address

Embodied (see a person, social actor)	Disembodied (do not see the speaker)
Voice of Authority (news anchor, reporter)	Voice of God (voice-over commentary)
Interview (see interviewee, maybe see or hear the interviewer)	Titles/Inter-Titles (printed matterial addressed to us)

Indirect Address

Embodied (conveyed by social actors)	Disembodied (conveyed by film technique)
Observation (watch social actors go about their lives)	Film Form (the filmmaker tells us things by means of editing, composition, camera angle, music, effects, etc. It is up to us to interpret how these choices address us)

images that affirm or undercut what is said, in a spirit of critical irony similar to *The Life and Times of Rosie the Riveter*'s (1980) critical irony toward the official propaganda films that celebrated women's work during World War II. A key witness against the accused in *The Thin Blue Line* has her validity undercut by Errol Morris's decision to cut to scenes from a 1940s series of films about Boston Blackie, a former thief turned crime stopper who operates independently from the police. A scene of Blackie capturing a crook with the aide of his loyal female companion adds a comic note to the witness's solemn claims: through the juxtaposition of a lighthearted entertainment film with what was presumably decisive legal testimony, Morris gives voice to a point of view that, although tacit and indirect, remains hard to miss.

The different manifestations of the voice of documentary are summarized in Table 3.1. Some of the nuances of these distinctions are taken up further in chapters 6 and 7.

Direct address: address *to* the camera or audience. This creates the sense that the film is making a proposal to us about the nature of the historical world: "Things are like this, aren't they?" or even about how they might be altered: "Things could be like this, couldn't they?"

Indirect address: address *not* aimed at the audience directly, as in fiction. In documentary, this creates the sense that the film is offering a perspective on aspects or qualities of the historical world. It offers less overt guidance than a proposal or argument would but nonetheless enlists our consent and involvement: "This is one way to view the world; what do you make of it?"

DOCUMENTARY AND THE VOICE OF THE ORATOR

The voice of documentary is often that of an orator, or filmmaker, setting out to take a position or offer a proposal regarding an aspect of the historical world and to convince us of its merits. The position or proposal commonly addresses those aspects of the world that do not lend themselves to scientific proof. Issues subject to debate and interpretation, value and judgment, such as the role of government, the justifications for a war, our responsibility to the environment or for economic growth, require a way of speaking that is fundamentally different from logic (crucial to science) or story telling (central to fiction). The rhetorical tradition provides a foundation for this way of speaking. It can embrace reason and narrative, evocation and poetry, but does so for persuasive purposes. It seeks to inspire belief or instill conviction about the merit of a particular viewpoint on a contentious issue.

An Inconvenient Truth (2006), for example, about the perils of global warming, comes close to a scientific treatise but it actually addresses issues about which considerable debate exists, less about whether global warming is happening than about its primary causes and possible solutions. Former Vice President Al Gore, the film's voice of authority, relies on science, and logic, to make much of his case, but he also relies on narrative story telling and poetic evocation to give it compelling shape. He functions as an orator, making a case that will dispose us to see the world differently, more than as a logician or philosopher following a careful line of reasoning.

How do we proceed when we proceed rhetorically? In what forms, with what conventions do we speak? Classic rhetorical thinking identified three divisions (discussed in chapter 4) and five "departments," each of which carries over to documentary film: invention, arrangement, style, memory, and delivery. Cicero described their connection this way:

> [S]ince all the activity and ability of an orator falls into five divisions, . . .
> he must first hit upon what to say; then manage and marshal his discoveries, not merely in orderly fashion, but with a discriminating eye for
> the exact weight as it were of each argument; next go on to array them
> in the adornments of style; after that keep them guarded in his memory;
> and in the end deliver them with effect and charm. (*De oratore*, I.xxxi)

We can review the usefulness of these five divisions in turn.

Invention

Invention refers to the discovery of evidence or "proofs" in support
of a position or argument. (The word "proof" occurs in classic texts,
but we should remember that rhetoric and documentary film address
aspects of human experience where the certainty of *scientific* or strictly
logical proof is unavailable. What counts as proof is subject to social
conventions rather than to something as conclusive as the scientific
method.) Aristotle proposed two types of evidence. They correspond
to the division between reference to the facts of the matter—inartistic
or nonartificial proofs—and appeal to the feelings of the audience—artistic or artificial proofs. They amount to ideas or beliefs an audience
might already hold and to the ways an orator finds to activate them by
means of his or her voice.

Inartistic proof includes not just ideas and beliefs but also facts or
evidence that can be brought to bear and that lie beyond dispute. But
bear in mind that the *interpretation* of this factual evidence may be
very much in dispute. Examples of inartistic proof include witnesses,
documents (including photographs or archival footage), confessions,
physical evidence such as fingerprints, hair or blood samples, DNA,
and so forth. This type of evidence lies outside the right of the orator
or filmmaker to invent or create, although very much within his or her
power to evaluate or interpret

Yet more pertinent to our discussion of how documentaries speak
or acquire a voice of their own is artistic or artificial evidence or proof.
These proofs rely on the techniques used to generate the *impression*
of conclusiveness or proof. These techniques often interpret evidence
or put it in an interpretative frame. They are a product of the orator
or filmmaker's inventiveness rather than something found elsewhere

and introduced intact. In his *Rhetoric*, Aristotle divided artistic proofs into three types (ethos, pathos, logos). Each strives to convince us of an argument's or perspective's validity. All three have relevance to documentary film and video. They can be described as

- Credible or ethical (ethos): generating an impression of good moral character or credibility for the filmmaker, witnesses, authorities, and others
- Compelling or emotional (pathos): appealing to the audience's emotions to produce the desired disposition; putting the audience in the right mood or establishing a frame of mind favorable to a particular view, this "proof" has its basis in feelings rather than logic
- Convincing or demonstrative (logos): using real or apparent reasoning or demonstration; proving, or giving the impression of proving, the case.

If real reasoning or logic were totally satisfactory, the issue would be scientific or mathematical in nature rather than rhetorical. The mixture of hunks of real reasoning with veiled pieces of apparent, faulty, or misleading reasoning characterizes rhetorical address. This can be seen as a flaw from the point of view of pure logic, but it can also be seen as a necessary consequence of taking up issues for which there is no one interpretation or single solution. In this case, decisions will hinge on values and beliefs, assumptions and traditions rather than the weight of reason alone. The reasoning may be flawless but the initial premise deeply flawed; this is, in fact, a common problem and the viewer's challenge is to determine what the underlying premise is. For example, deciding whether to restrict land development because it will harm the environment or to promote land development because it will stimulate the economy admits, partially, of scientific or factual evidence, but the final decision will hinge heavily on values and beliefs and the basic assumptions that support them. Rhetoric facilitates giving expression to these quite real and very fundamental factors. Government policies in general are almost always subject to debate. Facts and evidence are involved, but whether a given course of action is wise or dangerous is also a matter of interpretation. Evidence will serve to support values and beliefs and rhetoric will make that support compelling. Debate is inevitable; the public sphere, to which documentary films contribute, facilitates incorporating that debate into the life of a society.

These three strategies call on the orator or filmmaker to honor the three Cs of rhetorical discourse: to be credible, convincing, and compelling. An important tendency within documentary film since the 1970s has been to shift the focus of these strategies from using experts and authorities to more personal, individual perspectives. A work like Rea Tajiri's *History and Memory* (1991), for example, does not try to provide an overarching history of the internment of Japanese Americans during World War II. Instead it is a more personal account of her family's experience. Similarly, Agnès Varda's *The Gleaners and I* (2000) does not examine the social implications of scavenging from an authoritative or global position. Instead it conveys Varda's personal response to those she meets, in fields and cities, who glean or scavenge as a way of life. Such works can be credible, convincing, and compelling without being definitive or conclusive.

The best of these personal works all successfully couple their accounts of personal experience to larger social, historical ramifications but retain a local focus. Examples include Tajiri's and Varda's films; Alan Berliner's two films, *Intimate Stranger* (1992) and *Nobody's Business* (1996), on his own hard-to-know and often absent grandfather and father; Deborah Hoffmann's *Complaints of a Dutiful Daughter* (1994), on the filmmaker's relation to her mother after she succumbs to Alzheimer's disease; Emiko Omori's *Rabbit in the Moon* (1999), on her family's internment during World War II and its consequences; Su Friedrich's *The Ties That Bind* (1984), on her relation to her German-born mother and to German history mediated through her mother; Marilu Mallet's *Unfinished Diary* (1983), on her life in Canada as a Chilean exile married to the Canadian documentary filmmaker Michael Rubbo; Ngozi Onwurah's *The Body Beautiful* (1991), on her relation to her white British mother and her black African father; Marlon Fuentes's *Bontoc Eulogy* (1995), on his relation to his grandfather and the legacy of colonialism in the Philippines; Ari Folman's personal memory of the Israeli-Lebanon war of 1982, *Waltz with Bashir* (2008); and Jonathan Caouette's haunting tale of his relation to his tormented mother and her family, *Tarnation* (2003).

History and Memory (Rea Tajiri, 1991). This image of a woman's hands holding a canteen beneath a stream of tap water recurs throughout Tajiri's film. It is, in one sense, an impossible image (for a documentary), since it is an image, Tajiri tells us, that appears in her dreams as if it were a memory of what living in the Japanese American internment camps during World War II was like for her mother. In her voice-over commentary Tajiri refers to this image as one of the inspirations for her effort to return to this suppressed history, a history that no one in her family wished to reexamine as much as she did. How could she build on this small scrap of a larger experience with its references to the desert, the primacy of water, the hands of her mother, and the sense of isolation or fragmentation that haunted the interred citizens? *History and Memory* is an eloquent answer to this question.

This coupling of the personal and the social often serves to establish credibility and conviction because the filmmaker starts from what she or he knows best—personal experience—and extends outward from there. Subjectivity itself compels belief: instead of an aura of detached truthfulness we have the honest admission of a partial but important, situated but impassioned perspective. These works also gain a compelling quality thanks to the intensity with which the filmmaker approaches aspects of his or her own life. The frankness and intimacy of the approach contrasts quite dramatically with the aura of detached objectivity that marked more traditional documentaries.

An example of a more traditional approach to oratorical address is television news broadcasting. The anchorperson, at the other end of the spectrum from the sensationalist talk show host, establishes a basic ethical proof: here is an honest, credible person, free of personal biases and hidden agendas; you can trust this person to relay the news to you without distortion.

On broadcast news shows, emotional proof operates in reverse fashion from usual: the show works to quiet, not arouse, emotion. What happened in the world need not perturb even if it does interest us. We need not take action other than attend to the news. The packaging and management of world affairs, the reassurance that almost any event, no matter how extraordinary, can be encapsulated within the daily format of a news item assures us that things may change but the news can consistently report such change. If there is an effort to compel belief, it lies in the news broadcast's effort to convince us of its own powers of reportage. We can feel safe and secure because the news carries on. Events happen, people die, leaders change, nations fall, but the news provides a constant reference point. We can trust it to give us a window onto the world indefinitely.

News broadcasts also must convince us. They must resort to demonstrative proofs, with their mix of real and apparent proof. The real proofs come from the factual evidence brought before us: statistical information on inflation or unemployment, eyewitness accounts of specific events, documentary evidence of a certain occurrence, and so on. One kind of apparent proof lies in the way such evidence may be interpreted to support a particular case. News coverage in the United States of the Gulf War against Iraq, for example, might provide authentic images of a speech by Saddam Hussein on Iraqi television but edit it and position it to support representations of his anti-American attitude and defiant belligerence, whether that was the main point of his speech or not.

An extensive source of apparent proof lies in how news program frame the news generally. The convention of situating the anchor in a TV studio that usually lacks a specific geographic location works to give the sense that "the news" emanates from somewhere apart from the events it reports, that it is above or beyond such events and is, therefore, free from partisan involvement in the events. At the same time, a second convention calls on the anchorperson to sketch out the

Rabbit in the Moon (Emiko Omori, 1999). A very personal film, *Rabbit in the Moon* involves the reflections of filmmaker Emiko Omori and her sister on their experience as young girls in the detention camps built during World War II to house citizens of Japanese ancestry on the West Coast of the United States and Canada. The film couples family interviews and the filmmaker's voice-over commentary with historical footage to place the personal story in a larger framework of lingering racism and government policies of "national security." *Photos courtesy of Emiko Omori.*

broad outline of a story or news item and then to call on a reporter for substantiation.

Unlike the anchor, who sets the tone of impartiality, hovering in an abstract space without geographic coordinates, the reporter is always "on the scene." This convention operates as if to say, I, the news anchor, have told you about this event but lest you doubt, I will prove what I said by having a reporter provide further detail from the very place where the story is unfolding. When we cut to reporters, they invariably occupy the foreground of the shot while the background serves to document, or prove, their location on the spot: the "Green Zone" in Baghdad, the White House in Washington, the Vatican in Rome, and so on.

In this case physical presence serves a rhetorical function. It functions as a metonymy. Whereas metaphors link together physically disconnected phenomena to suggest an underlying similarity (love is a battlefield, or marriage is a piece of cake, for example), metonymy makes associations between physically linked phenomena. They typically use one aspect of something to represent the whole thing: seafood restaurants set along the shore signify fresh fish metonymically because the ocean is only yards away, for example. (The fish may actually come from a wholesaler located miles away.) Similarly, reporters standing on the scene of a news event will get the true story because they are there, in physical proximity to the event itself.

Metaphor and metonymy are rhetorical or figurative devices rather than logical forms of proof. They are usually not literally true. Not all love is necessarily a battlefield, just as not all fish prepared in seaside restaurants is fresh. Similarly, not all commentary heard from reporters on the scene is true. This may do little to detract from its convincingness. The value of figures of speech like metaphor and metonymy is precisely that they offer a more vivid and compelling image of something, whether this image corresponds to any larger truth or not.

Television news is a sober business. It adopts the solemn airs of those other discourses of sobriety that address the world as it is, such as economics, business, medicine, or foreign policy. This sobriety, and the three Cs of rhetorical engagement, however, can be treated ironically as well. Films like *Land without Bread* (1932), *Blood of the Beasts* (1949), *Cane Toads* (1987), about the rampant growth of a toad population in Australia, and *Isle of Flowers* (1989), about the relation of garbage to the overall social system in Brazil, exemplify an ironic use of the three artistic proofs. The credibility of the commentators in all three films, for example, seems assured by their solemn intonation and objective style. They are also male voices, tapping into a culturally constructed assumption that it is men who speak about the actual world and that they can do so in an authoritative manner. But credibility unravels as *what* they say begins to undercut *how* they say it. Why is the commentator pointing out "another idiot," or praising a slaughterhouse worker as if he were a god, describing cane toads as if they were an invading army, or comparing people and pigs?

Conviction also erodes as we begin to sense that the ostensibly objective tone is itself a mock-scientific one. Is the commentator serious about his claims of a toad menace when we see the Australian landscape pass by from the literal point of view of a solitary toad inside a wooden crate set inside a railroad freight car? Is the heroism of the abattoir worker genuine when we see the still-twitching heads of slaughtered cows piled in a corner? Can we be getting a full picture of the life of the Hurdanos when the commentator likens their customs to those of "barbaric" people elsewhere? And can the apparent harmony and balance of everyone getting a slice of the pie make sense when scavenging pigs have priority over desperate people?

Finally, the films consciously refuse to compel belief in the truthfulness of their representations. The hints of partiality and exaggeration build to a conviction that what we see is *not* what careful scrutiny of the facts would reveal. The quirky point of view captures our attention; its idiosyncrasy urges us to believe in it as a representation that deliberately undercuts believability. These four films question our usual willingness to believe other films that adopt the very conventions these films subvert.

Irony involves *not* saying what is meant or saying the opposite of what is meant. Just as the ironic use of television's journalistic conventions provides an important clue that *This Is Spinal Tap* (1984) is a mock documentary, the ironic use of authoritative commentary in these four films is a vital clue that they want to provoke suspicion of documentary conventions themselves more than they want to persuade us of the validity of their actual representations about the world.

Land without Bread, Blood of the Beasts, Cane Toads, and *Isle of Flowers* all serve to remind us that beliefs stem from shared values and that shared values take on the form of conventions. These include conventional ways of representing the world in documentary (soberminded commentators, visual evidence, observational camera styles, location shooting, and so on) as well as conventional ways of seeing and thinking about the world itself. Subvert the conventions and you subvert the values that compel belief.

Arrangement

Arrangement involves organizing the parts of a rhetorical speech or, in this case, film, to maximum effect. One typical arrangement already discussed is the problem/solution structure. A more comprehensive treatment of arrangement, as recommended by classic orators, parallels the five-act structure of classic plays but advances a proposal, perspective, or argument instead of a story:

- An opening that catches the audience's attention
- A clarification of what is already agreed as factual and what remains in dispute, or an elaboration of the issue itself
- A concrete argument in support of one's case from a particular viewpoint
- A refutation that rebuts anticipated objections or opposing arguments
- A summation of the case that stirs the audience and predisposes it to a particular course of action.

Arrangement can be organized in various ways. Aristotle, for example, stressed two parts—stating an issue and making an argument about it—whereas Quintilian favored five parts that elaborated on Aristotle's scheme. However organized, classic oration retains two characteristics.

First, the inclusion of pro and con arguments inclines traditional rhetoric to place issues within a black or white, either-or frame such as right or wrong, true or false, guilty or innocent. It is particularly conducive to a problem/solution approach, judicial deliberation involving a plaintiff and defendant, or the balanced, "both sides of the question" convention of journalism that still allows for right and wrong, good and bad views. This makes rhetoric of particular value in polarized or action-oriented situations such as advertising—dedicated to guiding consumers to specific products—and propaganda—designed to advocate one and only one solution to a problem or issue.

Since the 1990s an appreciable number of documentaries have stressed the complexity and ambiguity of various situations or issues. Open-ended, nonjudgmental perspectives, such as the sense of perplexity and wonder conveyed by Errol Morris's *Fast, Cheap and Out of Control* (1997) or the complex interactions between the art and life of R. Crumb in Terry Zwigoff's film *Crumb* (1994), depart especially from the persuasive aspects of traditional rhetorical form. *Capturing the Friedmans* (2003) is another vivid example. It examines the complex, ambiguous issues that surround the arrest of Arnold Friedman and his son Jesse for pedophilia. They both wind up pleading guilty but for reasons that may or may not be connected to their actual guilt. They both deny the charges, despite their guilty pleas, and a number of the individuals (male high school students who took computer classes at the Friedman home) state that nothing happened. Other students have lurid, graphic stories about molestation and abuse. Were these stories the result of suggestions made by the police investigators? Were the Friedmans victims of a wave of hysteria about the sexual abuse of children in schools? Were they scapegoats or perpetrators?

The film does not set out to condemn or exonerate them—it does not save an innocent man as *The Thin Blue Line* successfully did—but it does convey a vivid sense of what it feels like to be immersed in a situation of fundamental uncertainty. It has more in common with a European art film by Michelangelo Antonioni like *L'Avventura* (1960), which explores relationships more than actions, than it does with a genre film like Billy Wilder's *Double Indemnity* (1944). The police found no physical evidence of sexual abuse by either Friedman. The charges hinge on the (to some degree coached and rehearsed) testimony of the Friedmans' students. The impenetrable cloud of doubt that neither Arnold nor Jesse can dispel simply by stating, "I am innocent," most deeply affects Elaine, wife and mother to the suspects. Another son, David, adamantly insists his father was framed, while Elaine's painful realization that Arnold has hidden his pedophilic past (events prior to the ones at issue) causes her considerable grief. The repercussions of this agonizingly complex situation are what the film explores. (Interestingly, a supplementary disk in the DVD release of the film contains additional information that strengthens the case for Arnold and Jesse's innocence, but it also deepens our understanding of Arnold's admitted pedophilia and how his past may have left room for uncertainty.)

Other films such as *Darwin's Nightmare* (2004), on the complex interdependencies of governments, businesses, workers, and their dependents that have led to a disastrous market in Nile perch from Lake Victoria (the perch, once artificially introduced, have consumed almost all the other fish species in the lake even as they provide a lucrative foreign exchange market for Tanzania) cast no moral judgment and offer no solution. *Darwin's Nightmare* does convey, powerfully, the full impact of a series of actions in which no one takes responsibility for the long-term consequences of day-to-day decisions. Similarly, films as different as *The War Room* (1993), on the behind-the-scenes strategizing that paved the way for President Clinton's election in 1992, and *Control Room* (2004), on the workings of the controversial Arab language news outlet Al Jazeera, watch and listen rather than frame and assert.

These films, along with others like *Hell House* (2001), about one church's effort to create an amusement park–like recreation of what hell is like for sinners, and *Jesus Camp* (2006), which follows the work of Becky Fischer as she strives to make converts to Christ from pre-pubescent boys and girls, all leave it to the viewer to come to his or her own conclusions. The filmmaker's own voice remains evident in the more subtle form of editing and mise-en-scène. Ambiguity exists; black-and-white alternatives ignore much gray and these films call our attention to the gray zone of uncertainty and complexity rather than to specific opinions or alternatives. Rhetoric continues to guide efforts to establish credibility for the filmmaker and convince of the complexity of what they show and the compellingness of its real or potential impact, but it does so detached from any urge to arrive at a conclusion, judgment, or solution.

Second, regardless of the balance between certainty and ambiguity, documentaries continue to exhibit a classic alternation between appeals to evidence and appeals to audience, factual appeals and emotional appeals. Given that the types of issues addressed by rhetoric always involve questions of value and belief as well as evidence and fact, this alternation makes good sense. It allows the documentary to add flesh to fact, to locate its arguments not in the abstract domain of impersonal logic but in the concrete domain of embodied experience and historical occurrence. Oration was originally a concrete, physical skill: it was how one person addressed others persuasively and eloquently face to face, using his or her entire body. The documentary preserves the sense of embodied, impassioned speech through a voice that speaks movingly as well as factually.

Much of the power of documentary, and much of its appeal to governments and other institutional sponsors, lies in its ability to couple evidence *and* emotion. How powerful it is to see Rodney King being beaten by the police as the videotape made of this event makes pos-

Solovky Power (Marina Goldovskaya, 1988). A monastery in the Middle Ages, the buildings became one of the first prisons in the Soviet Gulag. It is approximately 3,500 kilometers north of Moscow. The spirituality of the former monastery became appropriated by government propaganda made about the virtues of the prison. *Photos courtesy of Marina Goldovskaya.*

sible or to show images of abused detainees at Abu Ghraib prison in Iraq rather than only read accounts of alleged torture as Errol Morris's *Standard Operating Procedure* (2008) does. Such images not only provide visible evidence, they pack an emotional punch, boosted by the indexical whammy of our own belief in their authenticity. They locate a film all the more forcefully in relation to the historical world and our own engagement with this world.

Style

Style facilitates the documentary voice. Elements of style such as choice of camera angle, composition, and editing give the filmmaker the tools with which to speak to his or her audience, not in a purely factual, didactic way, but in an expressive, rhetorically, or poetically powerful way.

Familiarity with film style is an important part of the filmmaker's repertoire. Style involves all the uses of figures of speech and codes of grammar to achieve a specific tone. Introductory film textbooks usually cover elements of film style under the broad chapter headings such as camera, lighting, editing, acting, sound, and so on. These same elements clearly come into play in documentary work, tempered by the

Solovky Power (Marina Goldovskaya, 1988). Director Marina Goldovskaya discovered a 1927–1928 Soviet propaganda film that presented Solovky prison as a model of clean living, wholesome food, and redemptive hard work. The authorities had to withdraw the film from circulation: their enthusiasm to deceive led them to fabricate an environment better than that of most of the viewers. Citizens began to wonder why prisoners had nicer rooms and better food than they did! *Photo courtesy of Marina Goldovskaya.*

forms (diary, essay, etc.) and modes (expository, reflexive, etc.) most characteristic of documentary. Since all introductory film textbooks cover these elements quite thoroughly, they will be referred to in particular contexts here rather than reviewed in their entirety.

Memory

Memory holds crucial importance for speech delivered on the spot, such as in the heat of a debate. One could memorize a speech, or set of "talking points," or one could develop a "memory theater" as a

Solovky Power (Marina Goldovskaya, 1988). Marina Goldovskaya excavates the story of the prison through interviews with survivors, prisoner diaries, and official records that attest to the living conditions of extreme hardship. We see here some of the family photographs and letters of a Solovky prisoner. *Photo courtesy of Marina Goldovskaya.*

way to remember what needed to be said. This involves imaginatively placing the components of the speech in different parts of a familiar space such as one's house or a public place. This mental image then facilitates retrieval of the speech's components as the speaker "moves" through the imagined space to retrieve the arguments deposited there.

Because films are not delivered as spontaneous speech, the role of memory enters in more fully in two ways: first, film itself provides a tangible "memory theater" of its own. It is an external, visible representation of what was said and done. Like writing, film eases the burden to commit sequence and detail to memory. Films often become a source of "popular memory," giving us a vivid sense of how something happened in a particular time and place.

Second, memory enters into the various ways by which viewers draw on what they have already seen to interpret what they presently see. The act of retrospection, of remembering what has already been shown and making a connection with what is now being shown, can prove crucial, just as memory can prove crucial to the construction of a coherent argument. Although not part of rhetorical *speech* as such, it is part of the overall rhetorical *act*. When Errol Morris begins *The Thin Blue Line* with exterior, evening shots of abstract, impersonal Dallas skyscrapers coupled to the accused man's comment that Dallas seemed like "hell on earth," these images serve a metaphorical function that hovers over the remainder of the film, if we activate our memory of them in an appropriate manner. Similarly, our recall of the opening image of a man sitting on the floor playing a phonograph record becomes crucial to an overall understanding of Marlon Fuentes's *Bontoc Eulogy*. As the film unfolds we learn the identity of the man and the significance of his act. We gradually come to understand why the film begins as it does. We can only arrive at this understanding by remembering, by retroactively thinking back to the beginning after we acquire additional knowledge. This form of re-view is often crucial to a full grasp of a film's meaning.

Delivery

Because oration was originally a matter of direct, face-to-face encounter rather than communication by means of a medium like writing or film, delivery involved what was said, how it was said, and the expressions and gestures that accompanied it. This is somewhat analogous to the distinction between direct and indirect address and between embodied and disembodied forms of documentary expression, discussed above. All of these options remain capable of emotional impact, just like the multiple facets of classic delivery. Expression and gesture involve nonverbal communication. They are ways of "saying things" without reliance on words. They comprise a key aspect of what is meant by the presentation of self, for individuals.

This level of communication is vividly on display during interviews. Much of the fascination of interviews—and a major reason why "talking heads" are not necessarily boring—is that a great deal of emotional power resides in how a person uses his or her face and body in concert with what he or she says. Abraham Bomba, the Holocaust survivor who haltingly recounts his experience cutting the hair of those about to die; Lila Lipscomb, the mother who mourns the son she lost in Iraq in *Fahrenheit 9/11* (2004); Jonathan Caouette, the maker of *Tarnation*, as he interacts with his damaged mother; and Timothy Treadwell, as he naively befriends wild grizzly bears in the remote reaches of Alaska in *Grizzly Man* (2005) reveal as much through the use of their faces and bodies as through their words. Charisma correlates strongly with delivery in this expanded sense, and these characters all possess it.

Other vital aspects of delivery are the ideas of eloquence and decorum. Although these words now have a feel of the drawing room about them, this is a piece of cultural baggage that degrades their original importance. In classic rhetoric there was nothing overly refined about either concept. We can consider eloquence, for example, as an index of the clarity of an argument or the potency of an emotional appeal. We can consider decorum as the effectiveness of a particular argumentative strategy, or voice, in a specific context. Eloquence and decorum measure "what works," regardless of how refined or crude it might be. They stress the pragmatic, result-oriented nature of rhetoric in general. Not restricted to polite (or overly polite) speech, they apply to any form of speech or voice that seeks to move an audience in a given context.

The five departments of classic rhetoric provide a useful guide to the rhetorical strategies available to the contemporary documentarian. Like the orator of old, the documentarian speaks to the issues of the day, proposing new directions, judging old ones, measuring the quality of lives and cultures. These actions characterize rhetorical speech not as "rhetorical" in the sense of argument for the sake of argument, but in the sense of engaging with those pressing matters of value and belief for which facts and logic provide an inconclusive guide to proper conduct, wise decisions, or insightful perspectives. The voice of documentary testifies to engagement with the social order and to a perspective on the values that underlie it. It is this specific orientation to the historical world that gives documentary a voice of its own.

4

What Makes Documentaries Engaging and Persuasive?

THE TRIANGLE OF COMMUNICATION

For every documentary there are at least three stories that intertwine: the filmmaker's, the film's, and the audience's. These stories are all, in different ways, part of what we attend to when we ask what a given film is about. That is to say, when we watch a film we become aware that the film comes from somewhere and someone. There is a story about how and why it got made. These stories are often more personal and idiosyncratic for documentary and avant-garde film than they are for feature films. Leni Riefenstahl's production of *Triumph of the Will* (1935), for example, remains a controversial story of Riefenstahl's artistic ambitions to make great films of emotional power but free of propagandistic intent—according to her own accounts—together with the story of Nazi Party pressure for a film that would generate a positive image at a moment when its power was not fully consolidated and its leadership not fully concentrated in Hitler—from the point of view of most film historians. Interpretations of the film often pick up the thread of one or the other of these stories, praising the film as a great piece of film art or condemning the film as a blatant piece of Nazi propaganda. And audiences, of course, have responded differently as well. When released, well before World War II, it won awards and received praise from figures like John Grierson. After the war, with greater awareness of the Nazi Party's genocidal efforts, the film's naïve endorsement of Hitler and his henchmen shocked far more than it excited.

Triumph of the Will (Leni Riefenstahl, 1935). This dramatically choreographed entrance by the three Nazi leaders stresses the utter centrality of the all-powerful leader in relation to the attendant masses of troops. George Lucas replicated this choreography at the end of *Star Wars* as if the hero worship could be extracted from its fascist context and applied to Han Solo, Chewbacca, and Luke Skywalker as "good old boys."

We often want to consider a filmmaker's previous work and con-tinuing preoccupations, how the filmmaker might understand and explain his or her intentions or motives, and how these considerations relate to the general social context in which the work was made. This reference back to the filmmaker and the context of production is one of the ways in which we can discuss what a film is about. Such back-ground stories do not exhaust our curiosity, however, and we need to take statements of intention with a grain of salt since the effect of a work on others, and its interpretation, may be quite different from the intentions of its maker.

There is also the story of the film itself and our understanding and interpretation of its story. This is the standard task of critical analysis

Triumph of the Will (Leni Riefenstahl, 1935). By shifting to a different angle, Riefenstahl draws the leaders into closer proximity to the masses while still maintaining a vivid sense of physical distance and hierarchical distinction.

and the usual focus of film history and criticism. In this case we concentrate on what the film reveals about the relation between filmmaker and subject and what, for documentary, the film reveals about the world we occupy. This is where knowledge of the various forms, modes, and techniques of documentary filmmaker proves useful. We ask how the film represents a specific form of engagement with the world and a distinct type of encounter between filmmaker and subject.

Finally, there is the story of the viewer. Every viewer comes to a film with perspective and motives based on previous experience. Jean-Luc Godard's great fiction film *Contempt* (1963) refers to this phenomenon directly. A screenwriter, Paul, is given the task of revising an adaptation of Homer's *The Odyssey* for the screen. Meanwhile, his wife feels that he has betrayed their relationship by allowing the producer to make advances toward her. The writer slowly becomes defensive and jealous. In the midst of his own marital conflict he claims that the central theme of *The Odyssey* is infidelity. Why? Because, according to Paul, Penelope has cheated on Odysseus for some time. Odysseus deliberately delays his return to postpone the moment when he must face the full consequences of this betrayal!

Paul has reversed the usual interpretation of this classic text, where Penelope faithfully awaits her husband's return, as a result of projecting his own experiences onto the story itself. Although aberrant as an interpretation, this projection of personal experience onto Homer's story achieves a certain level of credibility. It is a perfect example of how the expectations and mindset of the viewer can change the story's meaning.

As audience members we often find what we want, or need, to find in films, sometimes at the expense of what the film has to offer others. Different audiences will see different things. Introducing or promoting a film in a particular way can coach viewers to regard it one way rather than others. This practice can help filter out interpretations that project stories of personal experience onto the story of the film. For example, the practices of members of other cultures can seem bizarre and "unnatural" to viewers from a different culture. Watching, without any preparation, *Les Maîtres Fous* (1955), in which Hauka tribesmen enter into a trance and become Hauka spirits, during which they froth at the mouth, drool, sacrifice a live chicken, and eat the flesh of a dog, or *The Nuer* (1970), in which a Nuer boy has several parallel incisions made across the width of his forehead as a rite of passage into male adulthood, can produce feelings of revulsion or nausea in Western audiences. These feelings say more about the audience's understanding of appropriate conduct, control of the body, and the sight of blood than they do about another culture's practices. Placing these films within an ethnographic frame that draws attention to the larger issues of cross-cultural interpretation and of cultural bias encourages a focus on the story told by the film over the story an audience may project onto it.

Our own predispositions and experiences cannot be screened out entirely, nor should they be. Documentaries often seek to tap into the assumptions and expectations we bring to them as a way of establishing rapport rather than revulsion or projection. This is the basis of the core rhetorical principle of making a film compelling. If a film can activate our predispositions and tap into emotions we already have toward certain values and beliefs, it can enhance their affective power. Documentaries may appeal to our sense of curiosity or our desire for an explanation of American policy toward the war against Vietnam, or Grenada, or Haiti, or Serbia, or Afghanistan and Iraq, for example. Our desire to hear a story that strengthens our preexisting assumptions and predispositions often draws us to particular documentaries. Liberals and progressives often find Michael Moore's films appealing for that reason. *Jesus Camp* (2006) can appeal to fundamentalists who want to see "one of their own" striving to make young boys and girls into devout, socially active Christians. Skill in the use of the rhetorical techniques for creating credible, convincing, compelling accounts depends on knowing how to enlist an audience's preexisting values and beliefs for specific ends.

For example, *Operation Abolition* (1960) describes protests against a set of hearings by the House Un-American Activities Committee (HUAC) into Communist agitation in the San Francisco Bay Area in May 1960 as the work of dangerous extremists. It deliberately taps into the stories some audience members already believe, sometimes fervently, about a looming, sinister Communist menace to American society.

By contrast, *Operation Correction* (1961) recounts the same events and uses much of the same footage, but it argues that the violence surrounding the protests was instigated by the police, not the demonstrators. By detailing the exact chronology of events, it demonstrates that *Operation Abolition* deliberately reverses chronology and falsely juxtaposes events to blame the protestors for what the police provoked. *Operation Correction* appeals most readily to audience members who are already suspicious that the Red Scare in postwar America was an exaggerated, if not paranoid, view of Soviet intentions.

The same technique crops up in *The Revolution Will Not Be Televised* (a.k.a. *Chavez: Inside the Coup*) (2002), a brilliant chronicle of the early days of Hugo Chavez's presidency in Venezuela. The filmmakers happened to be present during the 2002 military coup that overthrew Chavez, until his own palace guard played a crucial role in restoring him to power. In the days before the coup numerous street protests by supporters of Chavez against the established power structure that

Chavez opposed turned violent. Local television reports showed footage indicating that the police had to fire on crowds that had attacked them. This documentary turns the tables: it traces the exact chronology of the confrontations and shows that the police fired first, provoking the violence they blamed on the protesters. *The Revolution Will Not Be Televised* will appeal more strongly to audiences that come predisposed to think that right wing elements and paramilitary units are likely to incite violence than to those who assume that left wing protesters are willing to use any means necessary, including violence, to achieve their goals.

CONCRETE EVENTS AND ABSTRACT CONCEPTS

The concepts and issues we say documentaries are about are almost always abstract and invisible. We cannot see affluence or poverty as general concepts, for example. We can name them verbally, but we can only film specific signs and symptoms of an affluent lifestyle or a debased existence, to which we then assign the concepts "affluence" or "poverty." (Some viewers, following other dispositions, might assign other concepts to the same images, such as "the good life," "self-indulgence," "white trash," or "ghetto life.") Similarly, we cannot film "fear," "obedience," or "pain" directly, but we can film specific situations that give visible embodiment to these concepts. Rithy Panh's wrenching documentary *S 21: The Khmer Rouge Killing Machine* (2003), for example, reexamines what happened at S 21, a notorious prison in which thousands of Cambodians perished. Pain and suffering, and dignity as well, flash across the faces of the handful of survivors who revisit the prison and confront some of the very men who were their guards and tormentors. The situations that Panh films give haunting evidence of what pain, suffering, and dignity look and feel like at the level of personal experience.

That is to say, the documentary value of nonfiction films lies in how they give visual, and audible, representation to topics for which our written or spoken language gives us concepts. Photographic images do not present concepts; they embody them. (This is why so many documentaries rely on a spoken commentary to guide the viewer to the "correct" interpretation of the images that embody what's said.

The commentary, as spoken language, can name poverty or torture directly.) Documentaries offer the sensuous experience of sounds and images organized to move us: they activate feelings and emotions; they tap into values and beliefs, and, in doing so, possess an expressive power that equals or exceeds the printed word.

Frederick Wiseman's *Hospital* (1970), for example, observes a series of encounters between patients and staff in a generic urban hospital (New York City's Metropolitan Hospital) but amounts to more than an informational or instructional account of how the hospital works. The film becomes a perspective on how *hospitals* work. It possesses its own distinct voice or point of view. Wiseman's organization of these specific encounters embodies a perspective on basic concepts such as "medical ethics," "bureaucracy," "class difference," and "quality of life." We derive these concepts, intangible and invisible themselves, from the scenes Wiseman puts before us, just as we infer from his editing and organization of the film what Wiseman's views are on how well this particular hospital fulfills its duties and obligations.

Similarly, John Huston could say, in written English, "War is hell" or "The ordinary soldier pays with his life for what generals decide," but his film *The Battle of San Pietro* (1945) shows us what war is like so that we may arrive at such thematic abstractions from our experience of the specific incidents Huston chooses to show us. Huston's act of showing becomes more than a mere record or display because it is organized through the careful selection and arrangement of sound and image. For example, Huston accompanies his voice-over comment, as the narrator, to "Note the interesting treatment of the chancel" of the San Pietro town church with an image of its bombed-out ruins. The "incidental" reference to carnage couched in the tone and vocabulary of architectural design creates a vivid sense of irony: it is as if Huston were saying, "War is hell—and even more so when we do not even see it as such." In a more recent, equally critical film, *Why We Fight* (2005), Eugene Jarecki argues that the United States goes to war in large measure to feed the huge military-industrial complex. This idea was first stated by President Eisenhower at the end of the 1950s, but Jarecki gives it emotional punch by his choice of concrete sounds and images, matched with clarifying interviews. The result is a compelling (but not necessarily conclusive) argument for alternative policies.

Put differently, documentary films usually contain a tension between the specific and the general, between historically unique moments and generalizations. Without generalizing, documentaries would be little more than records of specific events and experiences. Were they nothing but generalizations, documentaries would be little more than abstract treatises. It is the combination of the two, the individual shots and scenes that locate us in a particular time and place and the organization of these elements into a larger whole, that gives the documentary tradition its power and fascination.

Most of the topics that we identify as common topics in documentary filmmaking, such as war, violence, biography, sexuality, ethnicity, and so on, are abstractions derived from specific experiences. They are ways of bundling experience into larger categories, frames, or gestalts. The whole is greater than the sum of the parts. Documentary films bundle shots and scenes into larger categories or gestalts. They invoke or allude to concepts. This is what allows us to treat them as something other than mere footage or factual documents. Documentaries are *organized* sequences of shots that are about something conceptual or abstract because of this organization (such as a problem/solution structure, a story with a beginning and end, a focus on a crisis, an emphasis on a tone or mood, a way of seeing things, and so on).

COMMON ISSUES, RECURRING TOPICS

If a concept is not in doubt, such as the condensation of liquids as temperatures fall or the evaporation of liquids as temperatures rise, there is little call for a documentary film to address it. An informational or instructional film may still be of use to explain and exemplify the concept, but its organization is strictly devoted to conveying factual information and consolidating our grasp of an undisputed concept rather than coloring or inflecting our very understanding of the concept itself. Its interest as documentary is close to nil. It is *debated concepts* and *contested issues* that documentaries routinely address.

What specific kind of concepts or issues do documentaries address then? In general, they address those concepts and issues over which there is appreciable social concern or debate or experiences to which the filmmaker can contribute a distinct perspective. This can range

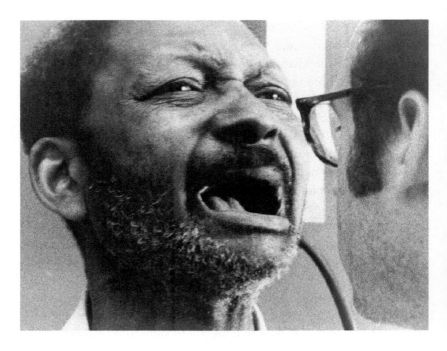

Hospital (Frederick Wiseman, 1970). Frederick Wiseman exhibits a relentless empiricism that carries hints of surrealism and the theater of the absurd for some viewers. His focus on institutions and social practices from high schools to department stores provides a remarkable study of contemporary American life. His mosaic-like pattern of numerous events that do not follow a single character or issue and that are not united by a voice-over commentary demands that the viewer respond to the often intense charge of the immediate moment and discern the larger patterns of power and control, need and response within the specific social framework that the film addresses. *Photo courtesy of Zipporah Films, Inc., Cambridge, Massachusetts.*

from aspects of the filmmaker's own life such as we find in *The Gleaners and I* (2000), as Agnès Varda journeys around France discovering a wide variety of gleaning styles that have clear bearing on her own life, to the powerful *Trouble the Water* (2008), an incisive look at what it took for Kim and Scott Roberts to survive Hurricane Katrina in New Orleans before any external assistance arrived. Be it questions of scavenging as a lifestyle or our government's response to disasters, documentaries explore questions and adopt perspectives that present their subjects in distinct, compelling ways.

Debates and contestation surround the basic social institutions and practices of our society. Social practices are precisely that: the conventional way of doing things. They could be otherwise. For example, many serious issues of law are resolved by juries in the United States and by judges in Europe. A different judge or jury may very well come to a different conclusion about the same issue. Children may feel they owe a debt to their parents after they become adults themselves, or not, depending on the conventions of a culture and an individual's own relation to those conventions and to his or her actual parents. A woman may feel she deserves, and may be prepared to demand, opportunity and treatment equal to that given men, or not, depending on the prevailing social practices and her personal attitude toward them.

With most social practices, where more than one way of doing things is possible and where more than one set of values or beliefs exist, different approaches must contend with each other. Dominant values must struggle to remain dominant. Alternative values must struggle to gain legitimacy. We enter contested terrain where different ideals and values compete for our allegiance. This competition gets played out in an ideological arena rather than by coercive means. Dominant and alternative practices seek to persuade us of their value rather than physically force us to comply. (Force remains a last resort.) Persuasion, though, requires a means of representing an acceptable way of doing things, a desirable course of action, a preferable solution that makes these options ones we will feel disposed to make our own. Persuasion requires communication, and communication depends on a means of representation, from written languages to body language, from television to film, from video to the web. These sign systems are the fundamental means of persuasive representation.

THE CHALLENGE OF PERSUASION

In the Western tradition, the different uses to which spoken and written language can be put has led to a classification scheme that sketches out three broad categories:

- Narrative and poetics (for telling stories and evoking moods)
- Logic (for rational, scientific, or philosophic inquiry)

- Rhetoric (for creating consensus or winning agreement on issues open to debate).

Although each of these three great divisions of language has a particular sphere to which it is most appropriate, they are not mutually exclusive. Elements of narrative (suspense and point of view) and poetic figures of speech (metaphor and simile) color both scientific and rhetorical discourse; persuasive tactics sometimes play a central role in both story telling and scientific reasoning. (Galileo, for example, had to couch much of his scientific argument against considering the earth as the center of the universe in terms that would persuade the Church hierarchy and not seem blasphemous; this challenge called for rhetorical skill as much as for logical proof.)

In general, then, documentary bears witness to the distinct, sometimes unusual perspective from which filmmakers see aspects of the world we share. Documentary films mount an effort to convince, persuade, or predispose us to a particular view of the world we have in common. Documentary work does not appeal exclusively to our aesthetic sensibility: it may entertain or please, but does so in relation to a rhetorical or persuasive effort aimed at the existing social world. Documentary not only activates our aesthetic awareness (unlike a strictly informational or training film), it also activates our social consciousness. This is a disappointment to some, who yearn for the pleasure of escaping into the imaginary worlds of fiction, but it is a source of stimulation for others, who hunger for imaginative, passionate engagement with pressing social issues and individual concerns.

In ancient times rhetoric, or oratory, garnered less respect than logic, or philosophy, because it seemed to be a concession to those aspects of human affairs not yet subject to the rule of reason. Our experience of the course of some 2,000 years of additional history, our acquaintance with Sigmund Freud and the idea of the unconscious, and our awareness of the links between power and knowledge, belief and ideology give us reason to suspect that rhetoric is not the bastard child of logic but more likely its master. At the very least we can say that rhetoric is an indispensable ally in those situations where we must speak about unresolved social issues. Put differently, if an issue has not yet been definitively decided, or if agreement cannot be definitively achieved, documentary film is one important means for disposing us to see that issue from a specific perspective. Most social practices—from family life to social welfare, from military policy to urban planning— occupy contested territory. Documentary film and video engages us on just such territory.

Rhetoric, or oratory, then, is the use of language of particular interest to the study of documentary film and video. The topics that documentary is about often belong to the three kinds of issues that were considered the proper domain of rhetoric. These issues fall into the three classic divisions of rhetoric. These three divisions identify most, but not all, of the issues documentaries address.

Deliberative: What to Do?

This is the domain of encouraging or discouraging, exhorting or dissuading others on a course of public action. Political issues of social policy such as war, welfare, conservation, abortion, artificial reproduction, national identity, and international relations belong to this domain. Deliberations face toward the future and pose questions of what is to be done. A problem/solution structure fits deliberation comfortably; it allows the expediency or harmfulness of different choices to receive careful scrutiny. Films from *Smoke Menace* (1937), favoring gas heat over smog-producing coal, to *The City* (1939), with its proposal of "green" suburban centers as alternatives to the mayhem of the inner city, to *An Inconvenient Truth* (2006), with its call for a halt to global warming, exemplify the deliberative use of rhetoric in documentary.

Judicial or Historical: What Really Happened?

This is the domain of accusing or defending, justifying or criticizing previous actions. The filmmaker looks toward the past and poses questions like, "What really happened?" These are questions of fact and interpretation, where guilt or innocence is at stake in relation to the law and truth or falsehood is at stake in relation to history.

In judicial and historical rhetoric, questions of framing and interpretation are put to the test. Trials exist to put doubt to rest, to arrive at a conclusion, just as historical accounts seek to "set the record straight" but do so on the basis of evidence that is, in its totality, open to more

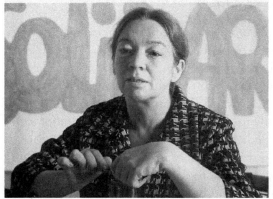

Far from Poland (Jill Godmilow, 1984). Jill Godmilow explores the dilemma facing the documentarian who cannot be there, on the spot where events occur. The Solidarity movement transformed Polish society, but Godmilow could not secure a visa to enter Poland as a filmmaker. How could she represent the movement and her own dilemma? She opted for a technique older than Flaherty's *Nanook of the North:* reenactment.

Instead of treating reenactments as if they were fully authentic, however, Godmilow makes it clear to us that what we see represents situations and events we cannot see directly. Godmilow recruits individuals to play the roles of Solidarity participants for her film. She herself plays the role of a filmmaker trying to make a film about the Solidarity movement. *Photos by Mark Magill, courtesy of Jill Godmilow.*

than one interpretation. That we turn to more than one account of events to form our own view hints at the fundamental undecidability of the past. *Shoah* (1985), on questions of guilt and responsibility for the Holocaust, *The Thin Blue Line* (1988), on an individual case of guilt or innocence, *The Fall of the Romanov Dynasty* (1927), on the history of Russia leading up to the revolution of 1917, and *Eyes on the Prize* (1987, 1990), about the history of the civil rights movement in the United States, exemplify the range of documentary filmmaking in the judicial and historical domain.

Commemorative or Critical: What Is He or She Really Like?

This branch of rhetoric assigns praise or blame to others, or, quite possibly, a mix of both. It evokes qualities and established attitudes toward individuals and their accomplishments. The genre of biography is dedicated to this pursuit. Autobiography, diary, and essay films can give this question a reflexive turn as filmmakers explore their own lives and sensibilities. Individual character can be represented, or misrepresented, by a variety of means; fairness and impartiality are not always honored. Just as demonstrative proofs rely as much on the appearance of logic as genuine logic, so commemorative or critical rhetoric relies on the impression of fairness and accuracy rather than scrupulous adherence to fact.

A striking example is a film by Jay Rosenblatt, *Human Remains* (1998), in which five dictators (Mao, Hitler, Stalin, Franco, and Mussolini) tell us, in their own words, about their daily habits and idiosyncrasies. None make reference to their political acts or their murderous ways. The voice-over commentary is entirely in the first person, as if we are listening to a reading of their diaries. It turns out that Rosenblatt did extensive research and selected authentic details from a variety of sources, which he then rewrote as if it were a first-person account. The impression of authenticity is only partly valid because, as with the editing of images, the editing of words generates new meanings that, in this case, are far more Rosenblatt's than the dictators'. The film, for instance, creates a deliberate dissonance between our preexisting knowledge of these men as infamous public figures and their quaint, amusing, sometimes quite bizarre habits and tastes.

Commemorative or critical rhetoric selects a person or situation and supplies an affective, moral coloration. It seeks to render people, places, and things in pleasing or off-putting tonalities so that we may deem them worthy of emulation and respect or demonization and rejection. As with questions of what to do and what really happened, the true nature of individuals remains open to considerable debate. We are once again in the realm of what is very often disputed or undecidable. It is the task of rhetoric to move us toward decision and judgment, although at times it may also serve to prolong a sense of wonder at the complex contradictions of individuals. Many of Errol Morris's films, from his early portrait films like *Vernon, FL* (1981), about a few of the eccentric inhabitants of this small Florida town, to *Standard Operating Procedure* (2008), a far more elaborate study of the military police who participated in and took the infamous photographs of abuse at Abu Ghraib, stress the ambiguous motives and uncertain impulses that surround human action.

Nanook of the North (1922), with its portrait of Nanook as a worthy hunter and father; *N!ai: Story of a !Kung Woman* (1980), as the portrait of a hard-pressed but strong-willed !Kung woman over a period of some 20 years; *Lonely Boy* (1962), on Paul Anka, as a dubious example of the making of a young male singing sensation; and *Paris Is Burning* (1990), as a sympathetic and respectful description of the lives of individuals within a black and Latino urban gay subculture of masquerade and performance, give some idea of the range of films that take up topics to which commemorative rhetoric applies.

THE POWER OF METAPHOR

One final generalization about recurring topics in documentaries is that they involve those concepts and issues we need metaphors to de-scribe. That is to say, some topics lend themselves to straightforward description; few issues are involved, and a prosaic, linear account is all we want or need. The manufacture of silicon chips might be such a topic, and the use of various grips and strokes in tennis another. Love, war, and family, on the other hand, are topics that a straightforward, dictionary-style definition does not exhaust. We may know what these subjects mean in a dictionary sense ("strong affection for or attraction to another," "armed, hostile conflict between states," "the basic unit in society, having as its nucleus at least one parent and one child") but still debate whether they are a blessing or a curse, heaven or hell. We may debate such questions about love, war, family, and other topics in gen-eral, or we may focus on specific instances: Perhaps war is a necessary evil, but was America justified in bombing North Vietnam, or Kosovo? Maybe families are a sacred form of union, but is the Loud family exemplary of such union? (The Louds are the family at the center of the multiple-part television documentary *An American Family* [1972].) Documentary films contribute their distinct persuasive powers to the debate. They furnish a way of saying, "Families are snake pits" or "a haven in a heartless world" in their own unique, engaging way. These metaphors enrich and enliven our grasp of the world.

Social practices, basic domains of human experience from working to medical care, lend themselves to metaphor. We can know how to define "family" and still want to know what family is *like* in a more metaphorical sense. Metaphors give us ways of likening war or love or family to something else that has similar qualities or values. Depending on whether we say that a family is a haven in a heartless world, as *Black Is, Black Ain't* (1995) suggests when Marlon Riggs explores his New Orleans roots and extended family, or a family is a battlefield, as *A Married Couple* (1970) suggests when Allan King films a couple in the process of breaking apart acrimoniously, our view of family life will differ considerably. Similarly, if war is a kind of hell and if hell is a painful, undesirable state, then war must be something to avoid, as *The Battle of San Pietro* suggests. If war is a rite of passage or test of manhood, and if such rites and tests provide a sense of identity and even glory, then war must be something to embrace, as *The Spanish Earth* (1937) suggests. It all depends on the values we assign to war in general or to a specific war or a given side in a war. Values we favor or reject are often intensified by metaphor.

Metaphors help us understand things in terms of how they look or feel; they establish a likeness that involves our own physical or experiential encounter with a situation rather than our knowledge of a standard dictionary definition. Metaphors draw on basic forms of personal experience like physical orientation (up, down, above, below) to assign values to social concepts. Success, for example, may be represented as *rising* to a *higher* station in life, not literally moving to a place of greater altitude but metaphorically moving to a social position of greater esteem. It activates what can be called muscle memory of rising or standing up and the feelings of achievement and power that act can generate. Many metaphors have a root in direct, tangible experience but link such experience to more abstract or intangible qualities.

Tangible representations are at the heart of cinema. The documentary image is always of something concrete and specific. We can show someone ascending an actual slope as a metaphor for success or show images of fallen bodies as a metaphor for war as hell. The selection and arrangement of sounds and images are sensuous and real; they provide an immediate form of audible and visual experience, but they also become, through their organization into a larger whole, a metaphorical representation of what something in the historical world is like.

What is it like to negotiate the marriage of a young woman in Turkana society? It is *like this* when, in *Wedding Camels* (1980), we see the particular negotiations surrounding a particular wedding but understand them to stand for a representation of wedding negotiations in the culture as a whole. Love is *like this* in *A Married Couple, Sherman's March* (1985), or *Silverlake Life* (1993); war is *like this* in *The Anderson Platoon* (1966), *Victory at Sea* (1952–1953), or *Gunner Palace* (2004); family is *like this* in *Finding Christa* (1991), *Complaints of a Dutiful Daughter* (1994), or *Nobody's Business* (1996).

We hunger for metaphorical representations to help us understand what values to attach to social practices. Documentaries help us understand how others experience situations and events that fall into familiar categories (family life, health care, sexual orientation, social justice, war, death, and so on). Documentaries offer an orientation to the experience of others and, by extension, to the social practices we share with them.

Whether we accept the perspectives and proposals made by documentary films as our own or not will depend heavily on the film's stylistic and rhetorical power, as well as our prior orientation. The oscillation between the specific and the general in documentary, though, comes from allowing a particular representation to (metaphorically) stand for a general orientation or assessment of a given issue or topic. Metaphorical understanding is often the most meaningful and persuasive way of convincing us of the merit of one perspective over others. A definition of genocide may sound appalling ("the deliberate and systematic destruction of a racial, political, or cultural group"), but the sound and image of a specific bulldozer pushing a large mass of individual naked bodies into an open trench at a given, historical moment *is* appalling in a more vivid, indelible way. If genocide is *like this*, as the representation of it in *Night and Fog* (1955) suggests, the metaphor presents us with a concrete yet metaphorical image of formidable power.

It is here that animated documentaries have made considerable impact. Animated images tap the full resources of the creative imagination and, in documentaries, become yoked to specific situations and events and, often, to the voices of actual people. *Waltz with Bashir* (2008) is a striking example as it gives a rich, embodied feel for what it was like for Ari Folman, the filmmaker, to be complicit with a horrendous massacre during Israel's invasion of Lebanon in 1982. The event haunts him for years afterward and the animated images give graphic representation to the agony, isolation, and despair that he, and others, subsequently felt. Similarly, Dennis Tupicoff's *His Mother's Voice* (1997) registers the panic and fear that engulf a mother after she learns her son has been shot. The sound track consists of an authentic audio recording of her account of what happened, while the image track provides an animated representation of what it felt like to drive to the scene of the shooting without knowing if her son was dead or alive. With this alone, Tupicoff would have achieved a touching, compassionate work of commemorative respect, but in the middle of the film he repeats the sound track from the beginning. This time the animation style changes and we remain at her home instead of travelling to the scene of the shooting. The camera lingers on her son's room and the objects that bear metaphorical significance such as posters, clothing, and a guitar. The animation encourages us to imagine what these objects and this room conjure for the bereaved mother. It is an extraordinarily powerful piece of filmmaking.

Personal identity, sexual intimacy, and social belonging are another way of defining the subjects of documentary film. What we speak about in documentary then are those subjects that engage us most passionately, and divisively, in life. These subjects follow the pathways of personal desire as we come to terms with what it means to take up an identity, to establish intimate relationships, and to achieve a sense of social belonging. Along the paths marked out by our relationship to ourselves, to loved ones, and to society more broadly, we find such basic subjects as biography and autobiography, gender and sexuality, family and kinship, labor and class, power and hierarchy, violence and war, economics, nationality, ethnicity, race, social justice, history, and culture. Documentaries provide us with representations of what encounters with these different forms of social practice have been like for people from a perspective designed to predispose us toward adopting a perspective of our own.

Waltz with Bashir (Ari Folman, 2008). Stark, often phantasmagoric images assail us in this film as the filmmaker rejects the usual device of historical footage and opts for highly subjective, emotionally powerful animation to convey what it feels like to experience a traumatic event. *Courtesy of Sony Picture Classics/Photofest.*

The Fall of the Romanov Dynasty, for example, recounts the story of the final years of Romanov rule in Russia and the early days of the Soviet revolution. It sets up a series of striking parallels and contrasts between life for the czar and his family and court and life for the majority of the Russian people. Life under the Romanovs becomes a world of vivid oppositions: leisure or labor, wealth or poverty, elegance or necessity. Esther Shub provides this perspective by way of archival film material that she reassembles into an indictment. She accentuates the contrasts with inter-titles, juxtapositions, and individual shots that sometimes ironically and sometimes caustically declare the moral bankruptcy of a regime indifferent to the condition of its subjects.

In one shot, for example, a count and his wife take tea at an outdoor table. After they rise to leave, a servant appears to remove the tea service. The class relation is clearly revealed through these actions alone, but Shub's archival clip goes one step further: when we look closely we see that the servant is standing in the deep background of the shot all along, waiting for his cue to move forward and reclaim the tea service.

His Mother's Voice (Dennis Tupicoff, 1997). By using the mother's account of her son's shooting twice, Dennis Tupicoff can offer two subjective visions of the event: what it felt like to travel to the scene of the shooting and learn what happened and what it felt like to recount this story while images of her son and his room flood her mind. *Courtesy of the filmmaker.*

Shub has found an early home movie that this count staged to document his estate life in the way that landscape paintings documented the wealth of the landed gentry, only now the document's moral value is reversed: it stands as a condemnation of what it once celebrated. The very act of staging the rituals of domination and servitude, which was perhaps meant to pass unnoticed originally, becomes, itself, evidence of the willingness to use others to maintain privilege that Shub argues brought the Romanovs down.

In another documentary of social change, Jill Godmilow provides an account of the rise of the Solidarity movement in Poland and the collapse of Communist rule. In contrast to Shub, Godmilow does not have access to a bounty of archival footage, nor does she even have access to events as they unfold. Various obstacles keep her in New York as Solidarity makes its advances toward power. How can Godmilow represent what she cannot witness? *Far from Poland* (1984) adopts a reflexive rather than an expository strategy. Godmilow makes the film into a work that is, all at once, *about* the difficulties of representation, about the convention of "being there" as testament to the truth of what is said, about the motivations filmmakers have for representing others when this act distorts as readily as it reveals, and about this specific historical moment of social transformation. The perspective is one that warns us about the powers of documentary representation at the same time as it expresses a clear solidarity with the social movement it can only partially and incompletely represent.

The Fall of the Romanov Dynasty (Esther Shub, 1927). This documentary image of a count and his wife clearly required not simply its subjects' consent but their active orchestration: as a home movie, it demonstrates their everyday ritual, in prerevolutionary Russia, of taking tea in the garden. The couple leaves the frame, and we may assume the shot has fulfilled its usefulness. But no; the shot continues, and a pair of servants enters to remove the used tea service. Shub converts the home movie into a social document of class structure and hierarchy. In a good print it is even possible to see the male servant waiting in the background, behind the shrubs, for his cue to enter the foreground, or, no doubt in Shub's mind, the historical stage.

Similarly, Robert Gardner's *Dead Birds* (1963) is an ethnographic account of life among the Dani of the New Guinea Highlands, a tribe still living in a nearly precontact state at the time of this expedition in 1961. The film has as a central preoccupation ritual violence among the Dani. Adopting a poetic, meditative tone, Gardner suggests that

Far from Poland (Jill Godmilow, 1984). Shooting "on location" for the film, but with Shamokin, Pennsylvania, standing in for the coal mines of Poland. Through her self-conscious style, Godmilow adds a reflexive note that makes us aware of the substitutions. This may prompt us to question the limitations and values of the trade-off between a sense of authenticity and the forms of truth it supports. Her tactics, at the very least, contrast strikingly with those of the television newscasts of the same events. *Photo by David Dekok, courtesy of Jill Godmilow.*

the rigors and hazards of ritual warfare, in which large contingents of men from neighboring groups hurl spears and shoot arrows at each other until they wound or kill someone, plays a vital role in defining individual and cultural identity. Life is *like this*, Gardner suggests, when we engage in regulated forms of social aggression, the better to maintain a sense of social coherence.

By contrast, Mitchell Block's *No Lies* (1973), like Godmilow's *Far from Poland*, takes a more reflexive view of ritual violence. Block uses the psychic violence of an intrusive, tactless filmmaker who persists in drawing out, and judging, the story of how his friend was raped as a commentary not only on the problem of rape and our social attitudes toward it, as men and women, but also on the problem of the ritual violence of representing the victims of rape as targets for a medium that perpetuates the victimization of the original act. The filmmaker psychically abuses his subject just as her assailant physically abused her. By representing this process of abuse as a function of documentary representation, Block calls into question the ethical underpinnings of the relation between filmmaker and subject in a direct and pointed way. He asks whether the act of filming an interview with a woman who has been raped in *this* way is *like* the actual rape she has already experienced.

As a final example, consider two representations of family relations. In *Four Families* (1959), Margaret Mead adopts the expository mode (a voice-over commentary) to compare and contrast family life among four families from four different cultures: France, India, Japan, and Canada. She applies conceptual categories such as child raising, discipline, male and female roles, and so on to make points about the many similarities and some of the differences among cultures. The specific families we see serve as examples, as shots of individuals typically did in the documentaries of the 1930s. We do not get to know individual family members in any complex sense. The film presents examples of their behavior to illustrate broad cultural qualities rather than individual differences. Margaret Mead informs us that family life in each of the four cultures is *like this.*

This representation of the family as a culturally homogenous entity, best understood when compared to families from other cultures, contrasts sharply with Ngozi Onwurah's *The Body Beautiful* (1991). Onwurah adopts a performative approach to the subject of her relationship to her own mother. The filmmaker is the product of a mixed-race marriage between her African father and her British mother. This already throws into question Mead's assumption that every national culture is distinctly different: the subject herself embodies two different cultures. Via a poetic voice over and reenacted childhood scenes that feature her actual mother, the filmmaker describes the ambivalence she felt as a child toward her working-class and, from her youthful perspective, unattractive mother. Only in retrospect does she come to recognize the hardship her mother experienced and the sacrifices she made, beginning with the choice to see her pregnancy with Ngozi to term, even when it meant that she would have to undergo a radical mastectomy for a cancer that might have been treated without removing her breast, had she done so during the pregnancy when treatment would have posed a risk to her growing fetus.

Onwurah enacts a drama of reconciliation and love that is highly performative. It emphasizes the filmmaker's own subjective investment in the subject, her mother, and conveys that investment forcefully to the audience. (At one point, Onwurah stages an imaginary seduction and love scene between her mother and a younger black man that carries a powerful emotional charge.) We learn no statistical facts about mixed-race marriages or the complexities of identifying differences in family structure at the level of national cultures. Instead, *The Body Beautiful* immerses us in a representation that suggests, "An ambivalent relationship to one's own mother is *like this*." The metaphor is all the more potent when based on her complex relationship to her own mother.

The affective power of these two films is radically different, as are the claims to general social knowledge that each makes. Mead's film suggests that families can be understood in terms of a cross-cultural, comparative examination of categories exemplified by four families chosen to stand for the four cultures, whereas Onwurah's film suggests that families can be understood in terms of a highly localized, embodied sense of what the conflicts and dilemmas in one particular family, her own, were like. Just as Mead's film allows for particularization through the four families selected but downplays it, Onwurah's film allows for generalization to issues of race, class, and nationality but downplays it in favor of specificity. Both films adopt a "Family life is *like this*" form of metaphorical assertion, but they do so in very different ways.

Focusing on particulars rather than generalizations has become the preferred choice for many contemporary filmmakers. The large categories into which specific situations and events fall (family, love, war, culture, and so on) remain in play but it also remains more up to the viewer to draw inferences and make connections rather than to receive assertions and arguments about these categories directly. *Tongues Untied* (1989) and *Silverlake Life* adopt this tack in relation to different aspects of gay life; *Tarnation* (2003) and *Capturing the Friedmans* (2003) dwell on complex forms of ambivalence in family relationships;

The Body Beautiful (Ngozi Onwurah, 1991). Sian Martin poses during a fashion shoot in Onwurah's film about her relation to her own mother. The world of fashion photography represents an escape from the drab existence associated with her mother. An imaginary seduction scene that Onwurah stages with her own mother as one of the participant/actors suggests an attempt to transport her mother out of her ordinary existence into a world of fantasy. The larger theme of the film, however, is the process by which Onwurah comes to accept both her mother and all of the blunt realities of her mother's own life. *Photo courtesy of Women Make Movies.*

and *Bus 174* (2002) and *Grizzly Man* (2005) explore the life of a specific disenfranchised or marginalized individual, respectively. The larger categories and metaphorical associations can still be made, but their stress is attenuated compared to the emotional intensities that swirl around specific situations and individuals.

In sum, documentary films and videos speak about the historical world in ways designed to move or persuade us. They address aspects of experience that fall into the general categories of social practices and institutionally mediated relations: family life, sexual orientation, social conflict, war, nationality, ethnicity, history, and so on. They draw on evidence but are not themselves documents. They possess a voice and a perspective of their own with which they communicate to us. As such they become one voice among many in the arena of social debate and contestation. This is the arena in which we vie for the support and belief of others in the name of a particular cause or system of values. It is, ultimately, an ideological arena that establishes our commitment to or detachment from the dominant practices and values of our culture. Rhetorical techniques are crucial in this arena since neither logic nor force can readily prevail. The arena may be the small but compelling one in *The Body Beautiful* or the large and galvanizing one in *The Fall of the Romanov Dynasty*. In either case, documentary film and video moves us to understand and engage the historical world in ways that matter.

5

How Did Documentary Filmmaking Get Started?

Our discussion of documentary would not be complete without some consideration of how this form of filmmaking found its voice. The voice of documentary relates to the ways in which documentary film and video speaks about the world around us, but from a particular perspective. When a documentary makes a proposal or offers a perspective, "voice" refers to how it does so. When did some films begin to speak in this distinctive form of voice? How is it related to other forms of cinema? How did documentary gain a voice of its own?

We should note that no one set out to invent this voice or build a documentary tradition. The effort to construct the history for documentary film, a story with a beginning, way back then, and an end, now or in the future, comes after the fact. It comes with the desire of filmmakers and writers, like myself, to understand how things got to be the way they are. But to those who came before us, back then, how things are now was a matter of idle speculation. Their goals were more immediate: make a film that answers to their own needs and intuitions about how to represent the subject of their choosing.

Early filmmakers did not set out to blaze a trail for a tradition that did not yet exist. Their great passion was in exploring the limits of cinema, in discovering new possibilities and untried forms. Some of these efforts would jell into what we now call documentary film. Looking backward, though, the existence of a documentary tradition obscures the blurred boundaries between fiction and nonfiction, narrative and rhetoric, poetry and spectacle, documenting reality and formal experimentation that fueled these early efforts. This tradition of experimentation continues to this day but in relation to new forms and new techniques from animation to reenactments: it is what allows documentary itself to remain a lively, vital genre.

A standard way of explaining the rise of documentary involves the story of the cinema's love for the surface of things, its uncanny ability to capture life as it is, an ability that served as a hallmark for early cinema and its immense catalog of people, places, and things culled from around the world. Like photography before it, the cinema was a revelation. People had never seen images that possessed such extraordinary fidelity to their subject, and they had never witnessed apparent motion that had imparted such a convincing sense of motion itself. As film theorist Christian Metz noted in the 1960s, to duplicate the impression of movement is to duplicate its reality. Cinema achieved this goal at a level no other medium had ever attained.

The capacity of photographic images to render such a vivid impression of reality, including movement as a vital aspect of life that painting and sculpture had been able to allude to but unable to duplicate, prompts two complementary myths to unfold—one about the image and one about the filmmaker. Both stand in need of correction.

REALISM AND THE DESIRE TO EMBODY IT: INSUFFICIENT GROUNDS FOR DOCUMENTARY

The remarkable fidelity of the photographic image to what it records gives such an image the appearance, and often the status, of a document. It offers visible evidence of what the camera saw. The underlying sense of authenticity in the films of August and Louis Lumière made at the end of the nineteenth century, such as *Workers Leaving the Lumière Factory, Arrival of a Train, Watering the Gardener,* and *Feeding the Baby* (all 1895), seem but a small step away from documentary film proper. Although they are but a single shot and last but a few minutes, they seem to provide a window onto the historical world. Fiction films often give the impression that we look in on a private or unusual world from outside, from our vantage point in the historical world, whereas documentary images often give the impression that we look out from our corner of the world onto some other part of the same world. The departing workers in *Workers Leaving the Lumière Factory*, for example, walk out of the factory and past the camera for us to see as if we were there, watching this specific moment from the past take place all over again.

Many point to these early works as the "origin" of documentary. Many claim them as the "origin" of realism for the fiction film. In either case, by maintaining a "faith in the image" of the sort the influential French critic André Bazin admired, the Lumières' films seem to record everyday life as it happened. Shot without adornment or editorial rearrangement, they reveal the shimmering mystery of events. They appear to reproduce the event and preserve the mystery. A note of humility was in the air. The cinema was an instrument of extraordinary power; it required no exaggeration or spectacle to win our admiration for what it could do.

The second myth involves the filmmaker. The remarkable accuracy of the image as an indexical representation of what the camera saw fascinated those who took the pictures. A compelling need to explore this source of fascination drove early cinematographers to record diverse aspects of the world around them. Even if they staged aspects of the action or decorated the scene, as Georges Méliès did in works such as his *A Trip to the Moon* (1902), a fascination with the power of the photographic image to record whatever came before it and to present the result to an audience by means of the film strip, capable of projection over and over, took precedence over the niceties of story telling and character development.

We have, then, two origin myths: (1) the filmmaker was a hero who travelled far and wide to reveal hidden corners and remarkable occurrences that were part of our reality, and (2) film images possessed the power to reproduce the world by dint of a photomechanical process in which light energy passed through a lens onto a photographic emulsion. These two qualities form, for some, the mythic foundation for the rise of documentary film. The combination of a passion for recording the real and an instrument capable of great fidelity attained a purity of expression in the act of documentary filming.

Workers Leaving the Lumière Factory (Louis Lumière, 1895). The early films of the Lumière brothers clearly document qualities of everyday life without pretense and yet they are not entirely unstaged either. The workers, all well dressed for the occasion, stream out of the entrance in a carefully defined plane perpendicular to the camera so that the focus remains sharp and the overall composition pleasing. None look at the camera. The impression of reality, though, remains quite strong since all the action unfolds in a single take. *Courtesy of Photofest.*

As we will see, however, a considerable leap has yet to be made from the cinematic document to the documentary film. The conventional story of the origins of the documentary film, though, culminates in the dual attainments of the narrative polish with which Robert Flaherty brought Inuit life to the screen in *Nanook of the North* (1922) and the marketing skills with which John Grierson established an institutional base for documentary film. Grierson spearheaded the government sponsorship of documentary production in 1930s Britain as Dziga Vertov had done throughout the 1920s in the Soviet Union and as Pare Lorentz would do in the mid-1930s in the United States. In point of fact, Vertov promoted documentary quite a bit earlier than Grierson but remained more of a maverick within the fledgling Soviet film industry; he did not attract a corps of like-minded filmmakers nor gain anything like the solid institutional footing that Grierson achieved. John Grierson became the prime mover of the British and, later, the Canadian documentary film movements. Despite the valuable example of Dziga Vertov and the Soviet cinema generally, it was Grierson who secured a relatively stable niche for documentary film production.

Coupling the uncanny power of film to document preexisting phenomena with the rise of an institutional base corresponds to the emergence of the four constituents of documentary film discussed in chapter 1. These developments generated a group of practitioners, an institutional frame, a body of films, and an audience attracted to these distinguishing qualities. That the image's incredibly accurate rendering of reality, including movement, and Grierson's pivotal role in creating an institutional base are over 30 years apart suggests, however, the beginnings of a problem. Why was there no Grierson in 1895? How were these extremely realistic representations received from 1895 to the late 1920s? What we have so far amounts to necessary but insufficient conditions. This origin story amounts to a myth.

DOCUMENTARY AS THE CONVERGENCE
OF MULTIPLE FACTORS

One of the problems with this mythic origin is that the capacity of film to provide rigorous documentation of what comes before the camera leads in at least two other directions besides documentary: science and spectacle. Their presence indicates that the indexical quality of the image did not lead directly to documentary film. Both directions begin with early cinema (roughly from 1895 to 1906, after which narrative cinema gains dominance). Both science and spectacle contribute to documentary film development but are hardly synonymous with it. The differences can be noted briefly.

First, the capacity of the photographic image (and later of the recorded sound track) to generate a precise replica of aspects of its source material forms the basis for scientific modes of representation. These modes rely heavily on the indexical quality of the photographic image. An indexical sign bears a physical relation to what it refers to: a fingerprint replicates exactly the pattern of whorls on the fleshy tips of our fingers; the asymmetrical shape of a windswept tree reveals the strength and direction of the prevailing wind.

The value of this indexical quality to scientific imaging depends heavily on minimizing the degree to which the image, be it a fingerprint or X-ray, exhibits any sense of a perspective or point of view distinctive to its individual maker. A strict code of objectivity, or institutional perspective, applies. The indexical image serves as empirical or factual evidence. It offers no perspective and has no voice, or a very faint one. It is the trained analyst or interpreter whose voice brings meaning to the image.

Documentary flourishes when it gains a voice of its own. Producing accurate documents or visual evidence does not, on its own, grant it such a voice. In fact, it can detract from it. The early cinema of Lumière and others, like that of science, still lacked the voice that would come to characterize documentary. Documentary does not depend on the indexical quality of the image for its identity. It is not science. In fact, early documentary embraced reenactments that could not possibly be authentic records of actual events, just as recent documentaries have embraced animation. Documentary commonly makes use of indexical images as evidence or to create the impression of evidence for the proposals or perspectives it offers. Robert Flaherty, for example, created the impression that some scenes took place inside Nanook's igloo when, in fact, they were shot in the open air with half an oversized igloo as a backdrop. This gave Flaherty enough light to shoot but required his subjects to act as if they were inside an actual igloo when they were not. *Night Mail* (1936) created a sense of what it felt like to hurdle across England on the overnight express mail train, bearing mail to Scotland, but the interior scenes of sorting mail were shot on a sound stage, not on the train. For *The Thin Blue Line* (1988), Errol Morris shot a series of reconstructions that represent the murder of a Dallas police officer as various figures in the film describe it. Not only are the reconstructions discrepant from each other, raising the question of "What really happened?" but every one of them was shot in New Jersey, not Dallas. These choices all represent tactics by the filmmaker to generate the effect he or she desires on an audience. These tactics may amount to bad science, but they are part and parcel of documentary representation.

When we believe in something without conclusive proof in the validity of our belief, this becomes an act of faith, or fetishism. Documentary film often invites us to take on faith that "what you see is what there was." This act of faith may derive from the indexical capacity of the photographic image without being fully justified by this quality, as reenactments suggest. For the filmmaker, creating trust, getting us to suspend doubt or disbelief, by rendering an *impression* of reality, and hence truthfulness, corresponds to the priorities of rhetoric more than to the requirements of science. A documentary not only documents events but conveys a distinct perspective on or proposal about them. Its perspective or proposal will be one among many. We accept the evidentiary value of images as proof of any one perspective's validity with some peril.

Second, spectacle also differs from documentary. Early cinema not only supported the scientific use of images, it also led to what film historian Tom Gunning has termed a "cinema of attractions." The cinema of attractions relied on the image as document to present viewers with sensational sketches of the exotic and unusual depictions of the everyday. The term refers to the idea of circus attractions and their open delight in showing us a wide variety of unusual phenomena. Such attractions could both whet the curiosity and satisfy the passion of early cinematographers and audiences alike for images that represented the odder aspects of the world around them. A tone of exhibitionism prevailed that differed radically both from the sense of looking in on a private, fictional world and from generating scientific evidence. Like scientific images, attractions hold a different form of appeal from documentary perspectives or proposals.

The "cinema of attractions" pitched its appeal directly to the viewer and took delight in the sensationalism of the weird, exotic, and bizarre. It sought to amuse, surprise, titillate, and shock rather than deliberate, evaluate, or commemorate. (Part of its legacy is the vast array of reality TV shows that have proliferated since the 1990s.) The distinctive point of view of the filmmaker took second place to the spectacle reported.

Mondo Cane (Gualtiero Jacopetti and Franco E. Prosperi, 1962). A slew of "mondo" films has followed in the wake of *Mondo Cane*. The sense of spectacle and sensationalism goes back to early cinema and clearly carries over to contemporary "reality TV" shows from *Cops* to *Survivor*, which function to present a succession of fantastic images and scenes, as if to say little more than, "Isn't that amazing!"

Louis Lumière sent scores of camera operators around the world armed with his newly patented *cinématographe* (an invention that not only shot film like a modern motion picture camera but also served to develop and project it!). We remember the names of only a handful of them. What they shot mattered more than how they shot it.

Aspects of this tradition of a "cinema of attractions" linger on just as scientific uses of the photographic image remain strong. It is vividly on display in a variety of films that peek into the underbelly of everyday life. We find it, for example, in "mondo" movies, beginning with the classic tour of outrageous customs and bizarre practices, *Mondo Cane* (1962), with its catalogue of bare-breasted women, the mass slaughter of pigs, and august pet cemeteries in different corners of the world. We find a similar display of "attractions" in programs like *Australia's Funni-*

est Home Movie Show and *Monster Kid Home Movies* (2005), as well as the adult movies, where an exhibitionist tone seems to know no limits. Safari films and travelogues on everything from surfing to architecture also rely heavily on this exhibitionist impulse to appeal to us directly with the wonders of what the camera discovered. Clearly an element of documentary film, this "cabinet of curious attractions" is often treated as an embarrassing fellow traveler rather than as a central component.

THE 1920S: DOCUMENTARY FINDS ITS LEGS

Neither an emphasis on showing off (a "cinema of attractions") nor on gathering evidence (scientific documentation), even though both rely on the indexical image, provides an adequate basis for documentary film. A direct line does not exist from Louis Lumière's train arriving in a station to Hitler arriving at Nuremberg (in *Triumph of the Will* [1935]) nor from the fascination with movement itself to fascination with moving audiences to see the world one way rather than another. We continue to lack a sense of the filmmaker's oratorical voice in these early tendencies. If there were a linear path from these qualities of early cinema to documentary, we would expect documentary to develop in parallel with narrative fiction through the 1900s and 1910s rather than only gain widespread recognition in the late 1920s and early 1930s.

We can, instead, identify four key elements that form the basis for documentary film. It is only when all four converge that a documentary tradition comes into being:

- Indexical documentation (shared with scientific images and the cinema of attractions)
- Poetic experimentation
- Narrative story telling
- Rhetorical oratory

The recognition of documentary as a distinct film form becomes less a question of the origin or evolution of these different elements than of their remarkable convergence at a given historical moment. That moment came in the 1920s and early 1930s and is discussed further in chapter 8. We can review the nature of these additional three elements here briefly.

Poetic Experimentation

Poetic experimentation in cinema arises largely from the cross-fertilization between cinema and the various modernist avant-gardes that flourished in the early part of the twentieth century. This poetic dimension plays a vital part in the emergence of a documentary voice. The poetic potential of cinema, though, remains largely absent in the "cinema of attractions," where "showing off" took higher priority than "being poetic." It is clearly absent from scientific imaging practices as well. Classic examples of poetic filmmaking include the work of 1920s French impressionist artists and critics such as Jean Epstein (*L'Affiche* [*The Poster*], 1924), Abel Gance (*La Roue* [*The Wheel*], 1923), Louis Delluc (*Fièvre* [*Fever*], 1921), Germaine Dulac (*The Smiling Madame Beudet*, 1922), and René Clair (*Paris Qui Dort*, a.k.a. *The Crazy Ray*, 1924) and the experimental work of Dutch filmmaker Joris Ivens (*The Bridge*, 1928; *Rain*, 1929), the German artist Hans Richter (*Rhythmus 23*, 1923; *Inflation*, 1928), the Swedish artist Viking Eggeling (*Diagonal Symphony*, 1924), the French artist Marcel Duchamp (*Anemic Cinema*, 1926), the Ukranian filmmaker Alexander Dovzhenko (*Zvenigora*, 1928), the expatriate American Man Ray (*Le Retour à la Raison*, 1923), and the surrealist collaborators Salvador Dali and Luis Buñuel (*Un Chien Andalou*, a.k.a. *An Andalusian Dog*, 1929).

It was within the avant-garde that the sense of a distinct point of view or voice took shape. This voice refused to subordinate personal perspective to spectacle or fact. Avant-garde work often began with photographic images of everyday reality, although some, such as Man Ray's "rayograms," were made without a lens by exposing undeveloped film to various objects. These indexical images of a recognizable world quickly veered in directions other than fidelity to the object and realism as a style. The filmmaker's way of seeing things took higher priority than demonstrating the camera's ability to record what it saw faithfully and accurately. Visible evidence served as a vehicle for poetic expression.

Voice clearly came to the fore in modernist works such as Dimitri Kirsanoff's *Ménilmontant* (1926), a tale of love betrayed, murder, and contemplated suicide told from a woman's point of view; Alberto Cavalcanti's *Rien que les Heures* (1926), a day in the life of Paris that flips whimsically between images of reality and the reality of images (images of a woman descending a staircase become a strip of film that is torn up and tossed into the street, for example); Joris Ivens's *The Bridge*, with its "story" of the rise and fall of a bridge told primarily through beautifully composed but fragmented shots of the bridge's structure; and Man Ray's *L'Etoile de Mer* (1928), a surreal series of events in the life of a Parisian woman.

The empirical ability of film to produce a photographic record of what it recorded struck many of these artists as a handicap. If a perfect copy was all that was desired, what room was left for the artist's desire to see the world anew? A film technician would do. French impressionist theory in the 1920s celebrated what Jean Epstein termed *photogénie*, whereas Soviet film theory championed the concept of montage. Both were ways of overcoming the mechanical reproduction of reality in favor of the construction of something new in ways only cinema could accomplish. Such an impulse proved vital to the development of a documentary film tradition.

Photogénie referred to what the film image offered that supplemented or differed from what it represented. A machine-governed, automatic reproduction of what came before the camera became secondary to the magic worked by the cinematic apparatus. Details of reality could become wondrous when projected onto a screen. The image offered a captivating rhythm and a seductive magic all its own. The experience of watching film differed from looking at reality in ways that words could only imperfectly explain.

Abel Gance's *La Roue*, for example, used single-frame flashbacks and numerous motifs of wheels, rotation, and movement to capture the delirium of a train engineer caught up in an impossible love. Robert Flaherty, in a spirit different from the French impressionists, also suggests what this sense of wonder can be like when he begins *Louisiana Story* (1948) with a slow, enchanting journey through the Louisiana bayou as seen from the pirogue of a young boy.

The idea of *photogénie* and editing, or montage, allowed the filmmaker's voice to take center stage. Ruttmann's *Berlin: Symphony of a Great City* (1927), for example, has a poetic but nonanalytic voice; it celebrates the diversity of daily life in Berlin unrelated to any clear social or political analysis of urban life. Dziga Vertov's *The Man with a Movie Camera* (1929), by contrast, adopts a poetic but also reflexive

Berlin: Symphony of a Great City (Walter Ruttmann, 1927). This publicity still for the film uses photomontage to celebrate the dynamism and energy of the modern city but does so without the sharp, political edge that photo and film montage achieved elsewhere in 1920s Germany and in 1920s Soviet cinema and Constructivist art. Montage can stress formal relationships or political associations. The editing of *Berlin*, like the photomontage in this still, opts for the poetic over the political.

voice to examine the transformative power of the masses as they, like the machinery of cinema, go about the business of producing a new, postrevolutionary Soviet society.

The avant-garde flourished in Europe and Russia in the 1920s. Its emphasis on seeing things anew, through the eyes of the artist or filmmaker, had tremendous liberating potential. It freed cinema from replicating what came before the camera to celebrate how this "stuff" could become the raw material not only of narrative filmmaking but of a poetic cinema as well. This space beyond mainstream cinema became the proving ground for voices that spoke to viewers in languages distinct from feature fiction.

Narrative Story Telling

The period after 1906 not only saw the emergence of a poetic avant-garde but also heralded the development of an even more dominant narrative cinema. This element also plays a vital role in the rise of documentary film. History and biography, for example, usually take the form of narratives but in a nonfiction mode from *The River* (1937) to *Born into Brothels* (2004). In narrative story telling, style (from the style of individual filmmakers to group styles such as expressionism, neo-realism, and surrealism) couples with plot (the sequence in which events unfold on the screen) to tell a story, be it factual or fabricated. The shape of the story, composed as it is of plot and style, simultaneously reveals the voice of the filmmaker on the world he or she represents directly in nonfiction or creates allegorically in fiction.

What mattered most for the development of documentary was the refinement of specifically cinematic story-telling techniques, from the parallel editing of D. W. Griffith to the use of different camera lenses and distances to frame characters and events. Story telling also elaborated the many ways in which an action or event could be told from different perspectives (from the perspective of an omniscient narrator, the perspective of a third-person observer, or the points of view of different characters, for example). These perspectival options promoted the search for a voice with which to represent the historical world in ways that were not necessarily spoken but, instead, embedded in film form (editing, framing, music, lighting, and so forth).

Narrative perfects the sense of an ending by returning to problems or dilemmas posed at the beginning and resolving them. Narratives resolve conflict and achieve order. The problem/solution structure of many documentaries makes use of narrative techniques as well as rhetoric to achieve resolution. Narrative welcomes suspense, or delay, where complications can mount and anticipation grow. It provides ways of elaborating a sense of character, not only through the performance of actors trained to act for the camera but through the techniques of lighting, composition, editing, reenactment, and interviews, among others, that can be readily applied to nonactors. Narrative refined the techniques of continuity editing to give a seamless sense of coherent time and space to the locations characters inhabited. Even when documentaries turned to evidentiary editing and the assembly of material from various times and places to support a line of thought, the techniques learned from narrative continuity facilitated the smooth flow of one image to another by matching movement, action, eyeline, or scale from one shot to another. All of these developments found uses in documentary, most vividly, perhaps, in strictly observational films (such as *Primary* [1960] or *Salesman* [1969]) that looked in on the lives of people and invited the audience to interpret what it saw as if it were a fiction.

Writing in the postwar years in France, André Bazin celebrated the achievements of Italian neo-realism for reasons similar to those later used to celebrate participatory and observational documentary. The Italian films demonstrated what Bazin considered a profound respect for reality by finding a narrative "voice" that was humble and modest but hardly silent.

The neo-realists eschewed attempts to evoke the quality of *photogénie* through extremes of stylization favored by the French impressionists. They avoided the expressionist techniques favored by German directors such as Robert Wiene (*The Cabinet of Dr. Caligari,* 1920), F. W. Murnau (*Nosferatu,* 1922), and Fritz Lang (*Metropolis,* 1927) that also modified the look of the image to suggest a distorted, unbalanced world of menacing forces and unstable personalities. The neo-realists shunned the montage techniques favored by Soviet directors such as Sergei Eisenstein (*October,* 1927), Vsevolod Pudovkin (*The End of St. Petersburg,* 1927), and Dziga Vertov (*The Man with a Movie Camera*) that juxtaposed shots to jar the spectator and produce new insights from the way different shots are brought together. They coupled narrative to the documentary purity of Lumière to achieve a style of enduring significance.

Neo-realists such as Roberto Rossellini (*Rome, Open City,* 1945), Vittorio De Sica (*Bicycle Thieves,* 1948), and Luchino Visconti (*La Terra Trema,* 1948) stressed narrative qualities in tune with film's potential for indexical documentation: a casual, unadorned view of everyday life; a meandering, coincidence-laden series of actions and events; natural lighting and location shooting; a reliance on untrained actors; a rejection of close-ups doting on the faces of stars; and a stress on the problems confronting ordinary people in the present moment rather than the historical past or an imagined future. Here was an important strand of narrative filmmaking that contributed directly to the development of documentary.

This sense of an indexical or photographic realism, of revealing what life has to offer when it is filmed simply and truly, is not, in fact, a truth but a style. It is an effect achieved by using specific but unassuming, definite but self-effacing means. It corresponds to what amounts to one of three important ways in which the term "realism" applies to documentary film.

- *Physical* or *empirical realism. Photographic realism* authenticates or appears to authenticate what actually happened in front of a camera. The indexical quality of the image can generate a realism of time and place through location photography, straightforward filming, and continuity editing that minimize the distorting and subjective uses of editing favored by the avant-garde.
- *Psychological realism* conveys the inner states of characters or social actors in plausible and convincing ways. A person's feelings of anxiety, happiness, anger, ecstasy, and so on appear accessible to the viewer. We feel that we have access to the inner life of a character. This calls for inventiveness on the part of the director, such as eliciting revealing expressions and gestures, holding a shot longer than usual, using close-ups expressively, adding suggestive music, or juxtaposing one image or sequence with another. A documentary filmmaker with a strong feel for the dramatic qualities of a situation or event can achieve compelling examples of psychological realism.
- *Emotional realism* results from creating an appropriate emotional state in the viewer. A stirring musical number can generate a feeling of exuberance in the audience even though there is little psychological depth provided to the characters and the physical setting is clearly a fabrication. We recognize a realistic dimension to the experience of exuberance or other emotions: the emotion itself is familiar and genuinely felt. Marching music, for example, often produces a sense of emotional realism in both fiction and documentary films dealing with war.

Documentary relies heavily on an empirical realism of time and place. It generates psychological realism by seeking out people, or social actors, who reveal themselves in front of a camera with an

Bicycle Thieves (Vittorio De Sica, 1948). The genius of Vittorio De Sica lay in
drawing out stories that felt as if they were intimately tied to a concrete sense
of time and place. This type of story-telling skill reverberated throughout
the Italian neo-realist film movement, with its use of location photography,
nonactors, and stories of everyday life and basic survival. (The original Italian
title correctly translates as *Bicycle Thieves*, but in keeping with a Hollywood
emphasis on the individual, it was initially translated as *The Bicycle Thief.*)

openness and lack of self-consciousness similar to what trained professionals achieve. Finally, documentaries exude emotional realism
by the use of cinematic techniques and a documentary voice to tap
the preexisting emotional reservoir of their audience. Neo-realism
and other forms of narrative story telling, along with the tradition of
the avant-garde, enhanced the expressive possibilities of documentary
filmmaking.

Rhetorical Oratory

Indexical documentation, narrative story telling, and poetic experimentation provide three of the four foundation stones for documentary
film. The fourth, the rhetorical tradition of oratory, is also shared with
other forms of filmmaking but flourishes most vividly in documentary
film itself.

ANGORA OCT /923

Grass: A Nation's Battle for Life (Merian C. Cooper and Ernest B. Schoedsack, 1925). The two men who made this film later produced *King Kong* and other films. The woman, Marguerite Harrison, shown sitting between the two men, was a pioneering journalist who had spied for the United States in Europe after World War I and published several books. She plays a reporter in the film as the trio sets out to depict the life of the nomadic Bakhtyari, mainly in modern day Iran. *Courtesy of Milestone Film and Video.*

The classic voice of oratory sought to speak about the historical world—addressing questions of what to do, what really happened, or what someone or something was really like—in ways that convey a particular perspective. It sought to persuade us of the merits of a perspective as well as to predispose us to action or to the adoption of sensibilities and values favored by the speaker. Such a voice was clearly heard in Robert Flaherty's *Nanook of the North* as it had been by a smaller audience for the great photographer Edward S. Curtis's 1914 film *In the Land of the Head Hunters* (a film restored and reissued in 1972 as *In the Land of the War Canoes*). Curtis's film, like Flaherty's, combined elements of a "cinema of attractions" with a narrative story, the poetic orchestration of scenes, and an oratorical voice to affirm his distinct perspective on the vanishing world of Native American culture.

Grass: A Nation's Battle for Life (Merian C. Cooper and Ernest B. Schoedsack, 1925). This original poster for the film demonstrates how graphic design can evoke a spirit of adventure in an exotic, distant land, perhaps better than a photographic image from the film itself. *Courtesy of Milestone Film and Video.*

Along with Flaherty's *Moana* (1926), about Polynesian culture, other early works such as Merian C. Cooper and Ernest B. Schoedsack's *Grass: A Nation's Battle for Life* (1925), about the nomadic peoples of Turkey and Persia, Victor A. Turin's *Turksib* (1929), on the construction of an important new rail link between far-flung parts of the Soviet Union, and Jean Vigo's *À Propos de Nice* (1930), a savage look at class differences at the beach resort, affirmed the vitality of the documentary voice. This voice adapted the "cinema of attractions," or spectacle, indexical documentation, story telling, and poetic expressiveness to speak about the historical world in ways that engaged the thoughts and feelings of its audience.

In the 1920s, such developments took distinctive shape in the Soviet Union, where an earlier, prerevolutionary period of experimentation in the arts known as Constructivism continued to flourish in the early years of the new Soviet state. Soviet cinema drew heavily from Constructivism and its determination to remake the world anew. (The gradual imposition of an "official" state style of art and film, Socialist Realism, eliminated almost all experimentation by the mid-1930s.)

In an influential essay, the Constructivist painter, designer, and photomontage artist Aleksandr Rodchenko argued against the "synthetic portrait," which would capture a whole personality in a single painting. Instead, he championed a series of documentary photographs, each revealing a different facet of a complex figure. Soviet theories of film montage echoed this idea. In another essay, "Constructivism in the Cinema" (1928), the Russian artist Alexei Gan called for a new type of cinema, both poetic and demonstrative:

> It is not enough to link, by means of montage, individual moments of episodic phenomena of life, united under a more or less successful title [*Berlin: Symphony of a Great City* may have been the type of work Gan had in mind]. The most unexpected accidents, occurrences and events are always linked organically with the fundamental root of social reality. While apprehending them with the shell of their outer manifestations, one should be able to expose their inner essence by a series of other scenes. Only on such a basis can one build a vivid film of concrete, active reality—gradually departing from the newsreel, from whose material this new ciné form is developing. ("Constructivism in the Cinema," in Stephen Bann, ed., *The Tradition of Constructivism*, p. 130)

Dziga Vertov also championed an attitude of bold, poetic reconstruction. Editing and the interval (the effect of the transitions between shots) formed the core of his style of nonfiction cinema called *kino-eye*:

- Editing during observation—orienting the unaided eye at any place, any time.
- Editing after observation—mentally organizing what has been seen, according to characteristic features [akin to the functions of invention and memory in classic rhetoric].
- Editing during filming—orienting the aided eye of the movie camera in the place inspected in step 1.
- Editing after filming—roughly organizing the footage according to characteristic features. Looking for the montage fragments that are lacking.
- Gauging by sight (hunting for montage fragments)—instantaneous orienting in any visual environment so as to capture the essential link

The Prince Is Back (Marina Goldovskaya, 1999). The family: this group portrait of the Meschersky family from 1912, in prerevolutionary Russia, affirms both their kinship and their good standing within the Russian aristocracy.

The prince: in the 1990s, Prince Meschersky decides to reclaim his family estate from the government and restore it. *Photos courtesy of Marina Goldovskaya.*

    shots. Exceptional attentiveness. A military rule: gauging by sight, speed, attack.

- The final editing—reveal minor, concealed themes together with the major ones. Reorganizing all the footage into the best sequence. Bringing out the core of the film-object. Coordinating similar elements, and finally, numerically calculating the montage groupings. ("Kino-Eye," 1926, in Annette Michelson, ed., *Kino-Eye: The Writings of Dziga-Vertov*, p. 72)

These writings address issues of film form, specifically the assembly of shots into a pattern that both discloses less visible aspects of the world and affirms the voice of the filmmaker. This call for montage or assembly often relies on indexical documentation but moves beyond finding "attractions" or making scientific observations. Soviet theories of constructivist art and cinematic montage harnessed the power of formal expression to a collective desire to remake the world in the image of a radically new society.

Montage stressed shaping events from fragments, or shots. By juxtaposing shots that did not "naturally" go together, the filmmaker constructed new impressions and insights. Eisenstein likened traditional realism to an imposed ideology:

    Absolute realism is by no means the correct form of perception. It is simply the function of a certain form of social structure. Following a

The Prince Is Back (Marina Goldovskaya, 1999). The estate: this model suggests how the prince's palace looked prior to the 1917 Revolution. The problem: 80-plus years after the Revolution. Can one man and his family restore what's left of the family home? Can a country move forward if its citizens want to go backward? Marina Goldovskaya raises larger issues only implicitly in her intimate portrait of the prince's pursuit of a dream. *Photos courtesy of Marina Goldovskaya.*

> state monarchy, a state uniformity of thought is implanted. ("The Cinematographic Principle and the Ideogram," in *Film Form and the Film Sense,* Jay Leyda, ed., p. 35)

What did Eisenstein see as an alternative? Molding and reshaping reality through montage to create a radically new vision of it.

> Is this not exactly what we of the cinema do . . . when we cause a monstrous disproportion of the parts of a normally flowing event, and suddenly dismember the event into "close-up of clutching hands," "medium shot of the struggle," and "extreme close-up of bulging eyes," in making a montage disintegration of the event in various planes? In making an eye twice as large as a man's full figure! By combining these monstrous incongruities we newly collect the disintegrated event into one whole, but in *our* aspect. According to the treatment of our relation to the event. ("The Cinematographic Principle," p. 34; italics in original)

The Soviet cinema was a vividly rhetorical cinema. In the work of many of its practitioners, from the famous films of Sergei Eisenstein himself (*Strike,* 1925; *Battleship Potemkin.* 1925; *October; The Old and the New,* 1929; etc.) to the less-well-known but pioneering compilation documentaries of Esther Shub (*The Great Road,* 1927; *The Fall of the Romanov Dynasty,* 1927; and *The Russia of Nicholas II and Leo Tolstoy,*

1928), techniques of montage laid the groundwork for the celebrity that John Grierson brought to documentary in the Great Britain of the 1930s.

Rhetoric in all its forms and all its purposes provides the final, distinguishing element of documentary. The recorder of facts, exhibitor of attractions, teller of stories, and poet of *photogénie* coalesce into the figure of the documentary filmmaker as orator, speaking in his or her own voice about a world we all share.

These elements first came together in the Soviet Union of the 1920s as the challenge of constructing a new society took precedence in all the arts. This particular melding of elements took root in other countries in the late 1920s and early 1930s as other governments, thanks to advocates like John Grierson, saw the value of using film to promote a sense of participatory citizenship and to support the role in government in confronting the most difficult issues of the day, such as inflation, poverty, and the Great Depression. Answers to these problems varied widely from democratic Britain to fascist Germany and from a New Deal United States to a communist Russia, but in each case, the voice of the documentarian contributed significantly to framing a national agenda and a common course of action.

6

How Can We Differentiate among Documentaries? Categories, Models, and the Expository and Poetic Modes of Documentary Film

In chapter 1 we defined documentary as a form of cinema that speaks to us about actual situations and events. It involves real people (social actors) who present themselves to us in stories that convey a plausible proposal about or perspective on the lives, situations, and events portrayed. The distinct point of view of the filmmaker shapes this story into a proposal or perspective on the historical world directly, adhering to known facts, rather than creating a fictional allegory.

Helpful though this definition is for documentaries in general, it scarcely begins to distinguish different types of documentary. Many documentaries violate any specific definition and mockumentaries deliberately blur the border zone between fiction and documentary in any case. There are no laws and few genuine rules when it comes to creative expression. What actually counts as a documentary remains fluid, open to debate across institutions, filmmakers, audiences, and the films themselves. Institutions, from television channels to foundations that support specific types of documentary film; filmmakers, from the extraverted Michael Moore to the self-effacing D. A. Pennebaker; films, from the searing *Night and Fog* (1955) to the hilarious *Super Size Me* (2004); and audience expectations that range from "show me the truth" to "entertain me" all co-exist. Favored styles come and go. Institutional opportunities and constraints, technological innovations, creative inspiration, and evolving audience expectations constantly change the landscape of what counts as a documentary and what constitutes its horizon of possibility.

Rather than regret the failure of documentary films to comply with any one, single definition, and rather than lament the ability of any one definition to identify all the possible types of documentary, we can accept this fluidity as cause for celebration. It makes for a dynamic, evolving form. Fluid, fuzzy boundaries are testimony to growth and vitality. The amazing vigor and popularity of documentary films over the last 25 years is firm evidence that fluid boundaries and a creative spirit yield an exciting, adaptable art form.

This said, distinctions can still be made. New documentaries continue to bear strong resemblances to previous documentaries. In fact, it is possible to note a number of tendencies, or modes, such as the poetic and expository modes, at work in documentary. The modes were sketched out in chapter 1 and receive fuller consideration here and in the next chapter. These modes identify the different ways in which the voice of documentary manifests itself in cinematic terms. They differentiate documentaries in terms of formal, cinematic qualities. These qualities have existed as potential resources for decades, but in different proportions and with different emphases. Most films incorporate more than one mode, even though some modes are more prominent at one time or place than another. These modes serve as a skeletal framework that individual filmmakers flesh out according to their own creative disposition. But before we break down documentary representation into a number of modes, it is useful to take a brief, more distant view of documentary film as one component of cinema in general.

How we categorize and divide up a domain of experience is seldom a purely objective act in which we follow the natural fault lines given to us by a preexisting world. Science, which deals with the natural world, can classify in this way, but when what we want to classify is the product of our own human activity, natural fault lines quickly disappear. In relation to documentary film these categories belong to a continuing dialogue among institutions, filmmakers, films, and audiences rather than to the natural world. They evolve, change, consolidate, and scatter in unpredictable ways. The needs they meet at one moment may no longer be met in another. Filmmakers are usually among the first to notice this as they seek new ways to tell stories and convey their point of view. Categories and concepts often play catch-up, trying to give coherence to the extraordinary array of works created by human activity.

DOCUMENTARY FILM AND ITS RELATIONSHIP TO OTHER KINDS OF FILM

From an adequate distance, we might see film clustered into fiction and nonfiction films that can be represented by two overlapping circles or spheres (Table 6.1).

Exclusively in the left-hand circle is fiction per se. Here we find the majority of fiction films that are readily identifiable as works that conjure up an imaginary world populated by actors who play assigned roles (characters). These characters appear to go about their business as if the camera that beholds them were in no way part of their world. What they say and, even more, what they do may be incredible, fantastic, seemingly impossible, and hence amazing, but it all unfolds as if such occurrences were a plausible part of the world the characters inhabit.

Exclusively in the right-hand circle is nonfiction, which includes documentary film, informational or "how to" films, scientific films, surveillance footage, and more. Here we find the majority of documentary films that are identifiable by (1) their representations in sound and image of a preexisting, historical world, (2) their reliance on social actors who present themselves rather than take on assigned roles, and (3) the intricate relationship that may arise between the interaction of the filmmaker and the film's social actors who clearly co-exist in the same historical world. It is from this interaction that the film's story, proposal, or perspective frequently arises.

In both circles, nestled in the zone of overlap, are forms that borrow from both traditions and get classified as one or the other according to the goals and purposes of the analyst. Most critics consider neo-realism fiction because the performers, even if not trained actors, play assigned roles; the films possess a clear narrative shape, and the restrained, understated style gives little sense of a documentary voice. These qualities, however, are also present in observational documentaries, as we shall see, but these films are routinely counted as documen-

TABLE 6.1. The Relation of Fiction to Nonfiction

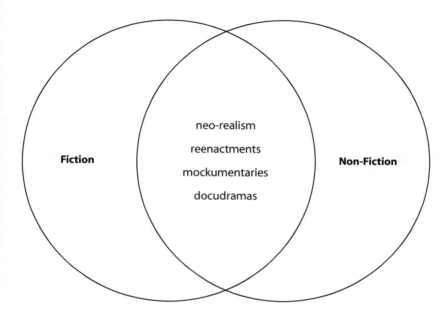

taries because the stories they tell seem to be primarily of the social actor's own making.

In contrast to neo-realism, reenactments, mockumentaries, and docudramas, although they adopt many fictional techniques and are generally considered fundamentally fictions, get roped into discussions of documentary. This is because reenactments typically occur as one part of a documentary or informational film and take much of their meaning and value from that larger context. Mockumentaries clearly engage in a teasing dialogue with documentary conventions and audiences' expectations, and docudramas draw much of their plot structure and character depiction from actual events.

Once we shift our attention to the nonfiction side of the diagram in Table 6.1, we find that it, too, breaks down into two overlapping categories: documentary and nondocumentary films, which Table 6.2 illustrates.

In the zone of overlap are those forms that can be treated in either documentary or not documentary, depending on the critic's goals and

TABLE 6.2. The Relation of Documentary to Nondocumentary Films

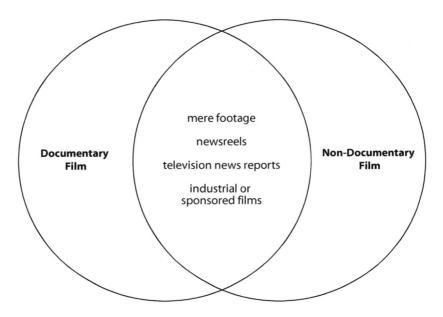

purpose. Mere footage is raw footage, often a single shot or take such as surveillance footage or Abraham Zapruder's famous Super 8 footage of President John F. Kennedy's assassination. By itself mere footage lacks any pronounced voice or perspective but it can easily be drawn into either a documentary or nondocumentary work. Oliver Stone's *JFK* (1991), a narrative fiction, strives to present Zapruder's footage as scientific evidence of a conspiracy (and multiple assassins). Going in the opposite direction, Jean Painlevé made scientific recordings of aquatic life, mere footage, into captivating documentary poems such as *The Sea Horse* (1934). His films are often considered scientific documents, but numerous museums also include them in their collections of documentaries.

Industrial or sponsored films usually address a very limited clientele or openly promote a specific business or product. Advertisements, which may have some documentary elements, are highly promotional. Their partisanship urges the purchase of a product, a more limited goal than most documentaries, although they share many of the same rhetorical techniques. Sponsored films such as Robert Flaherty's *Loui-*

siana Story (1948), sponsored by Shell Oil, carry less pointed messages (the film is about a young Cajun boy; that his traditional world and the world of oil extraction can co-exist was sufficient message for Shell). Here sponsorship is akin to that of governments when they underwrite documentaries: the film promotes a perspective or way of seeing the world more than a specific act of consumption.

Documentaries are not documents. They may use documents and facts, but they always interpret them. They usually do so in an expressive, engaging way. This lends documentaries the strong sense of voice that nondocumentaries lack. This voice distinguishes documentary films. We sense a voice addressing us from a particular perspective about some aspect of the historical world. This perspective is more personal and sometimes more impassioned than that of standard news reports. Television news adheres to journalistic standards that have a strongly informational bias although they are far from free of qualities of voice. Bias, framing the context within which to present information, assumptions about who counts as an expert or authority, and choices of words and tone can all push news reporting toward the documentary camp while journalistic standards of objectivity and accuracy pull in the direction of the informational film.

Nondocumentary films such as scientific films, surveillance footage, and informational or "how to" films exhibit a minimal sense of voice: they function more like documents than documentaries, conveying information in a straightforward, often didactic manner. They speak about aspects of the world with a high degree of transparency or indexicality. This is what lends evidentiary value to what they show: the footage retains a highly indexical relation to preexisting situations and events such as footage of animal behavior or a spaceship launch. Clarity and simplicity are often at a premium in scientific films, whereas expressivity, style, and sometimes ambiguity are prized qualities in documentary films.

MODELS FOR AND MODES OF DOCUMENTARY FILM

If we accept these general categorizations as a useful starting point, remembering that they could be redrawn, for other purposes, in other ways, we can then ask, Once a documentary tradition came into being, what categories help us characterize different types of documentary films?

This book proposes two major ways of dividing up documentaries:

- Preexisting nonfiction models. Documentaries adopt models such as the diary, biography, or essay. Documentary film belongs to a long, multi-faceted tradition of nonfiction discourse that continues to evolve (essays, reports, manifestos, blogs, etc.). Erik Barnouw used some of these models to categorize documentaries in his international history, *Documentary: A History of the Non-fiction Film.* (Barnouw treats "documentary" and "nonfiction" as synonyms.)
- Distinct, cinematic modes. Documentaries adopt modes such as the expository or observational mode. Documentaries select and arrange sounds and images in distinct ways, using specifically cinematic techniques and conventions. These forms did not preexist the cinema. Many have since carried over to television, digital production, and the internet. Like the cinematic techniques developed in the early cinema, which helped define the contours of the narrative feature film, the modes help define the shape and feel of the documentary film. They identify the qualities that distinguish an expository documentary from an observational one, for example, regardless of whether the film uses the diary, report, or biography as its model.

The emphasis here will be on the modes of documentary, but one additional point needs clarification: we can classify any one documentary in either of two ways:

- What model it adopts from other media
- What mode it contributes to as cinema.

The classifications are not mutually exclusive. In fact, they are complementary: together, they give us a better sense of the structure of any one documentary film.

Table 6.3 provides a list of some of the primary nonfiction models from which documentary draws and of the six cinematic modes that characterize the bulk of documentaries. (The film examples listed under the heading "Nonfiction Models" also appear in the right-hand column, "Documentary Modes," according to the documentary mode to which they belong most strongly and vice versa.)

TABLE 6.3. Some Major Models and Modes for Documentary Film

NONFICTION MODELS	DOCUMENTARY MODES
Investigation/Report (assemble evidence, make a case or offer a perspective)	**Expository** (speak directly to viewer with voice over)
Bus 174	Afrique, je te plumerai
Control Room	Chile, Obstinate Memory
Enron: The Smartest Guys in the Room	The Civil War
Gunner Palace	The Corporation
Harvest of Shame	Dead Birds
Real Sex (HBO series)	Grass
	Grizzly Man
	Harvest of Shame
	An Inconvenient Truth
	Les Maîtres Fous
	The March of the Penguins
	Nanook of the North
	Night and Fog
	Night Mail
	The Plow That Broke the Plains
	The Power of Nightmares
	The River
	Roger and Me
	Seven Days in September
	Sicko
	Stranger with a Camera
	Super Size Me
	Unfinished Diary
	Victory at Sea

TABLE 6.3. (continued)

NONFICTION MODELS	DOCUMENTARY MODES
	Why We Fight series *Wild Safari 3D: A South African Adventure* (an IMAX film)
Advocacy/Promotion of a Cause (stress convincing, compelling evidence and examples; urge adoption of a specific point of view)	**Poetic** (stress visual and acoustic rhythms, patterns, and the overall form of the film)
The Corporation	*The Bridge*
An Inconvenient Truth	*Koyaanisqatsi*
Night Mail	*The Maelstrom*
The Plow That Broke the Plains	*Rain*
The Power of Nightmares	
Sicko	
History (recount what really happened, offer an interpretation or perspective on it)	**Observational** (look on as social actors go about their lives as if the camera were not present)
The Civil War	*Control Room*
An Injury to One	*Gunner Palace*
Night and Fog	*High School*
Seven Days in September	*Jesus Camp*
Victory at Sea	*The Last Waltz*
	Metallica: Some Kind of Monster
	N!ai: Story of a !Kung Woman
	Primary
	Salesman
	Up the Yangtze
	Wedding Camels

NONFICTION MODELS	DOCUMENTARY MODES
Testimonial (assemble oral history or witnesses who recount their personal experience)	**Participatory** (filmmaker interacts with his or her social actors, participates in shaping what happens before the camera: interviews are a prime example)
The Fog of War *Las Madres de la Plaza de Mayo* *The Life and Times of Rosie the Riveter* *Shoah* *The Women's Film* *Word Is Out*	*Bus 174* *Enron: The Smartest Guys in the Room* *The Fog of War* *Las Madres de la Plaza de Mayo* *The Life and Times of Rosie the Riveter* *Nobody's Business* *Real Sex* (HBO series) *Sherman's March* *Shoah* *Wild Parrots of Telegraph Hill* *The Women's Film* *Word Is Out*
Exploration/Travel Writing (conveys the distinctiveness and often the allure of distant places, may stress exotic or unusual qualities)	**Reflexive** (calls attention to the conventions of documentary filmmaking and sometimes of methodologies such as fieldwork or the interview)
Grass *The March of the Penguins* *Nanook of the North* *Up the Yangtze* *Wild Safari 3D: A South African Adventure* (an IMAX film)	*Man with a Movie Camera* (not in the models column; see text below for discussion) *Reassemblage* *Stranger with a Camera*

TABLE 6.3. (continued)

NONFICTION MODELS	DOCUMENTARY MODES
Sociology (the study of subcultures: normally involves fieldwork, participant-observation with subjects, and both description and interpretation)	**Performative** (emphasizes the expressive quality of the filmmaker's engagement with the film's subject; addresses the audience in a vivid way)
High School	*Chile, Obstinate Memory*
Jesus Camp	*Complaints of a Dutiful Daughter*
Primary	*Finding Christa*
Salesman	*The Gleaners and I*
Stranger with a Camera	*An Injury to One*
	Tarnation
	Tongues Untied
	Waltz with Bashir
Visual Anthropology/Ethnography (the study of other cultures; similar to sociological fieldwork with language acquisition usually added; reliance on informants to provide access to the culture studied)	
Dead Birds	
Les Maîtres Fous	
N!ai: Story of a !Kung Woman	
Reassemblage	
Wedding Camels	
First-Person Essay (a personal account of some aspect of the author/filmmaker's experience or point of view; autobiography is similar but stresses individual development)	
Chile, Obstinate Memory	
Nobody's Business	
Roger and Me	
Super Size Me	

NONFICTION MODELS	DOCUMENTARY MODES
The Bridge	
Koyaanisqatsi	
The Maelstrom	
Rain	
Diary/Journal (daily impressions that may begin and end somewhat arbitrarily)	
Afrique, je te plumerai	
The Gleaners and I	
Sherman's March	
Unfinished Diary	
Individual or Group Profile/Biography (recounts the story of a person or group's maturation and distinctiveness)	
7 Up (and successors: *7 Plus Seven* to *49 Up*)	
Grizzly Man	
The Last Waltz	
Metallica: Some Kind of Monster	
The Wild Parrots of Telegraph Hill	
Autobiography (a personal account of someone's experience, maturation, or outlook on life)	
Complaints of a Dutiful Daughter	
Finding Christa	
Tarnation	
Tongues Untied	
Waltz with Bashir	

A few points about this table call for elaboration.

- First, the categorizations reflect individual judgment rather than precise measurement. Many films can be classified in relation to multiple models and modes. To emphasize this, *Stranger with a Camera* (1999) appears under the expository and the reflexive modes and *Chile, Obstinate Memory* (1997) appears under the expository and the performative modes. Similarly, *Night Mail* (1936) has a strongly poetic quality to its voice-over commentary (written by W. H. Auden) and might be discussed as a film beholden to poetry and the poetic mode rather than advocacy and the expository mode. *Nanook of the North* (1922) corresponds to anthropology as well as exploration since it has served as a touchstone for many discussions and debates within visual anthropology and ethnographic film. Its emphasis on the character Nanook also argues for biography as a model. These are valid choices. They stress specific qualities, just as placing *Nanook* within the observational mode stresses Flaherty's remarkable patience and willingness to let events unfold in their own time, even if it took Flaherty's active hand to set up events like the seal hunt or igloo building. Different viewers respond more or less strongly to different aspects of the same film and classify it accordingly.
- The expository mode contains the most examples by far. This is partly a result of the specific films chosen as examples, but it also suggests the prevalence of this mode. Expository documentaries arose at the start of the documentary tradition and remain prominent today, even if some of the films listed here could be associated with other modes as well. This mode gives priority to the spoken word to convey the film's perspective from a single, unifying source. This, in turn, facilitates comprehension.
- Films like *Enron: The Smartest Guys in the Room* (2005) and *Sicko* (2007) demonstrate how one mode can combine with other modes especially in the use of interviews. We can stress the guiding role of the direct address commentary in *Sicko*

(expository mode) or the interviews and what they reveal in *Enron* (participatory mode). In each film interviews are quite central. In *Enron* they provide some of the most crucial information and demonstrate how public interviews and comments by company officers hid rather than revealed the truth, which interviews with others make clear. In *Sicko*, the interviews generate considerable insight, and humor, thanks to Michael Moore's use of mock naïveté and guerilla tactics to catch interviewees off guard in ways other techniques never would. Stressing Michael Moore's own role as commentator argues for a primarily expository emphasis as his voice guides us through the complexities of health care and how to provide it. Such commentary has become a trademark signature in his films. Both expository and participatory modes are clearly present in each film. Which prevails depends, in large part, on what aspects of the film we want to explore further. Neither is right or wrong in any fundamental sense.

This practice of mixing modes holds true for many films. It does not mean that the categories are inadequate so much as that filmmakers frequently adopt a fluid, pragmatic approach to their material, blending different models and modes to achieve a distinct result. This is quite different from an "anything goes" approach in which the filmmaker invents structures and patterns on the spot, without recourse to precedent. As is true of other arts, those filmmakers who are familiar with previous work and aware of the basic characteristics of different models and modes typically exhibit a fluidity and grace in their ability to use a wide range of conventions and techniques to create a style, and voice, uniquely their own.

- The reflexive mode is clearly under-represented. This, however, is not too surprising if we consider that many reflexive documentaries call attention to the formal conventions of the documentary film itself. In other words, they question the principles that underlie the other five modes rather than the various models drawn from other media like the printed word. There is no reason why they might not also be reflexive in relation to the nonfiction models, though, drawing attention to the conventions of the diary, biography, or visual anthropology, for example.

Stranger with a Camera, however, does prompt a reflexive awareness of anthropological and sociological assumptions involving fieldwork. The film dwells at length on two individuals: Canadian filmmaker Hugh O'Connor, who went to film Appalachian residents in the late 1960s, and Hobart Ison, the local resident who shot and killed Mr. O'Connor. The filmmaker, Elizabeth Barret, reflexively questions how massive cross-cultural misunderstandings and stereotypes led to this tragic end. In doing so she peels away many of the assumptions viewers might have about impoverished citizens and entitled filmmakers to prompt deeper consideration of the underlying issues of social representation.

Similarly, *Reassemblage* (1982) looks at aspects of West African culture but does so primarily to question the traditional assumptions of anthropological methodology. Other reflexive films such as *Man with a Movie Camera* (1929; not listed in the models column) draw attention to the filmmaking process itself and how filmmakers construct a distinct perspective on the historical world cinematically. Its maker, Dziga Vertov, was adamant about not adopting preexisting models. He sought to forge new ones unique to the cinema. His film, therefore, does not fall under any of the models listed in the left-hand column even though there are traces of sociology, poetry, and the first-person essay in it.

• The expository and poetic modes often harvest, glean, or compile images from the world with relative indifference to the specific individuals or situations captured in order to shape proposals or perspectives on a general topic. The sense of any extended engagement between the filmmaker and the subject is frequently modest, at best. *The River* (1937), for example, contains numerous shots of specific people and places as it tells the story of how the Tennessee Valley Authority tamed the Mississippi and brought electrical power to a vast region. Some of these people and places may be named, in passing, but their personal history and individual relation to the film's goals remain scantly addressed. The classic poetic film *Rain* (1929), adopts a similar attitude: we see scores of people caught in a summer shower in Amsterdam but none of them emerge as characters with names and personalities. The poetic power of the film lies elsewhere.

Images culled from other films yield a compilation film that joins these fragments together in a distinct way. The actual interaction between the filmmaker and the social actors is usually of nominal concern since the images contribute to the big picture proposed by the film. Images are harvested and assembled into a whole greater than the individual parts. This is true of the great majority of the shots in the *Why We Fight* series (1942–1945) because the films advocate U.S. involvement in World War II rather than tell the story of specific individuals. The filmmaker's relation to those who appear before the camera generally holds less importance than the overall proposal or perspective shaped from the resulting images.

- The observational, participatory, and performative modes work differently. The relationship between the filmmaker and the person filmed becomes more direct, personal, and complex. The viewer senses that the image is not just an indexical representation of some part of the historical world but also an indexical record of the actual encounter between filmmaker and subject. The sense of extended engagement between filmmaker and subject is often acute. The individuality of specific social actors, people, matters greatly. The filmmaker enters into the social actor's world through interviews, conversation, provocation, or other forms of encounter and has the power to alter that world. Something is at risk in the encounters. We realize that the filmmaker exists on the same plane of human existence as his or her social actors rather than on the more detached plane of commentator or poet. Discussions of ethical conduct in documentary often revolve around the nature of these interactions. (Ethical discussions also involve questions of distortion, misrepresentation, and deception that span all the modes.)

DOCUMENTARY MODES AND THE FILMMAKER'S VOICE

Like every speaking voice, every cinematic voice has a style or "grain" all its own that acts like a signature or fingerprint. It attests to the individuality of the filmmaker or director or, sometimes, to the determining power of a sponsor or controlling organization. Television news has a voice of its own just as Fred Wiseman or Chris Marker, Esther Shub or Barbara Kopple do.

Individual voices lend themselves to an auteur theory of cinema, while shared voices lend themselves to a genre theory of cinema. We routinely group fiction films into subcategories known as genres such as melodrama and horror, westerns and science fiction. Genre study considers the qualities that characterize these various groupings of films. In many instances, documentary can be treated as a genre similar to the western or gangster film, with conventions and expectations that routinely inform it. Chapter 1 addressed documentary at this level to a considerable degree. But to fine-tune our discussion, we need to differentiate among different types of documentary films. It is to this end that the notion of models and modes comes into play. The models are not specific to the cinema, whereas the modes are. These modes, in fact, deserve extended discussion because they form the conceptual backbone of most documentary film production.

These six modes establish a loose framework of affiliation within which individuals may work. They set up conventions that a given film may adopt, and they provide specific expectations viewers anticipate having fulfilled. Each mode possesses examples that we can identify as prototypes or models: these prototypes seem to give exemplary expression to the most distinctive qualities of that mode. A prototype cannot be duplicated verbatim, but it can be emulated as other filmmakers, in other voices, set out to represent aspects of the historical world by using a prototype that they inflect with their own distinct perspectives.

The order of presentation for these six modes appears to correspond roughly to the chronology of their introduction. This is not literally true since performative and reflexive tendencies were evident from the outset. The greatest temporal divide is before and after 1960, roughly. This is when portable synchronous sound recording became a reality and the observational and participatory modes gained prominence. They differ quite vividly from the expository and poetic modes because the filmmaker's actual physical presence in a given historical moment takes on new and profound importance.

The different documentary modes may seem to provide a history of documentary film, but they do so imperfectly. Not only were most of them present from the outset, a film identified with a given mode need not be so entirely. A reflexive documentary can contain sizable portions of observational or participatory footage; an expository documentary can include poetic or performative segments. The characteristics of a given mode give structure to a film, but they do not dictate or determine every aspect of its organization. Considerable latitude remains possible. The modes do not constitute a genealogy of documentary film so much as a pool of resources available to all.

A performative documentary can exhibit many qualities common to poetic documentaries, for example. The modes do not represent an evolutionary chain in which later modes demonstrate aesthetic superiority over earlier ones and vanquish them, although a temptation to make such claims often arises. Once well established through a set of conventions and prototypical films, a given mode remains available to all. Each mode expands the sense of the possible in documentary representation. Expository documentary, for example, goes back to the 1920s but remains highly influential today. Most television news and reality TV shows depend heavily on its quite dated conventions, as do almost all science and nature documentaries, biographies such as the A&E *Biography* series, and the majority of large-scale historical documentaries such as *The Civil War* (1990), *Eyes on the Prize* (1987, 1990), *The People's Century* (1998), or *The War* (2007).

To some extent, each mode of documentary representation arises in part through a growing sense of dissatisfaction among filmmakers with other modes. New technological possibilities often play a significant role. The observational and participatory modes of representation became highly attractive once lightweight 16mm cameras and portable but high-quality sync tape recorders came onto the scene in the 1960s. Similarly, the advent of digital cameras and recording devices, computer-based editing programs, and the internet have spawned a wave of documentary work that promises to alter many basic assumptions about the form. From cell phone video recorded in the heat of a highly volatile moment to spoofs of popular culture icons and almost nonstop video diaries, these new technologies are expanding the sense of the possible in dramatic ways.

As an example, an official White House "photostream" exists on Flickr.com, a website devoted to the display of images. The photos are captioned and often tell stories about the president's activities. In 1963, Robert Drew organized an observational study of the White House during the peak of the struggle to desegregate schools in the South: *Crisis: Behind a Presidential Commitment* (1963). It provided a behind-the-scenes view of the confrontation between President Kennedy and Governor George Wallace of Alabama. Critics praised its access to the corridors of power and its insider-like ability to get behind the scenes. Now these activities become a daily update on Flickr by the White House itself, the story content and image of the president a carefully crafted result of those who once rarely allowed outsiders to view the inner workings of the White House in any detail at all. It is a small indication of how new technology and creative minds constantly alter the documentary landscape.

The desire to come up with different ways of representing the world contributes to the formation of each mode, as does a changing set of circumstances. New modes arise partly in response to perceived deficiencies in previous ones, but the perception of deficiency comes about partly from a sense of what it takes to represent the historical world from a particular perspective at a given moment in time. The seeming neutrality and "make of it what you will" quality of observational cinema arose at the end of the quiet fifties and during the heyday of descriptive, observation-based forms of sociology. It flourished as the embodiment of a presumed "end of ideology" and as a fascination with the everyday world. It had less obvious affinity with the social plight or political anger of those who occupy the margins of society.

Similarly, the emotional intensity and subjective expressiveness of performative documentary took fullest shape in the 1980s and 1990s. Its deepest roots are among those groups whose sense of commonality had grown during this period as a result of identity politics. This form of political, often militant organizing on a basis other than class affirmed the relative autonomy and social distinctiveness of marginalized groups. These films rejected techniques such as the voice-of-God com-

The Day after Trinity (Jon Else, 1980). Post-1960s reconsiderations of cold war rhetoric invited a revision of the postwar record. Film-makers such as Connie Field in *The Life and Times of Rosie the Riveter* and Jon Else in *The Day after Trinity* recirculate historical footage in a new context and give it new meaning. In this case, Else reexamines Robert J. Oppenheimer's hesitancies and doubts about the development of the atomic bomb as a lost, or suppressed, voice of reason during a period of near hysteria. Oppenheimer himself was accused of treason. *Photo courtesy of Jon Else.*

mentary not because these techniques lacked humility but because they belonged to an entire epistemology, or way of seeing and knowing the world, no longer deemed acceptable. Tired of hearing others speak about them, members of these groups set out to speak for themselves.

We do well to take with a grain of salt any claims that a new mode advances the art of cinema and captures aspects of the world never before possible. What changes is the *mode* of representation, not the quality or ultimate status of the representation. A new mode is not so much better as it is different, even though the idea of "improvement" is frequently touted, especially among champions and practitioners of a new mode or new technology. Every change brings a different set of emphases and implications. But every new mode or new way of making and distributing work will eventually prove vulnerable, in turn, to criticism for limitations that some type of alternative promises to overcome.

New modes signal less a better way to represent the historical world than a new way to organize a film, a new perspective on our relation to reality, and a new set of issues and desires to preoccupy an audience. We can now say a bit more about each of the modes in turn.

THE POETIC MODE

As we saw in chapter 5, poetic documentary shares a common terrain with the modernist avant-garde. The poetic mode sacrifices the conventions of continuity editing and the sense of a specific location in time and place that follows from such editing. The filmmaker's engagement is with film form as much as or more than with social actors. This mode explores associations and patterns that involve temporal rhythms and spatial juxtapositions. Social actors seldom take on the full-blooded form of characters with psychological complexity and a specific view of the world. People more typically function on a par with other objects as raw material that filmmakers select and arrange into associations and patterns of their choosing. We get to know none of the social actors in Joris Ivens's *Rain*, for example, but we do come to appreciate the lyric impression Ivens creates of a summer shower passing over Amsterdam.

The poetic mode is particularly adept at opening up the possibility of alternative forms of knowledge to the straightforward transfer of information, the prosecution of a particular argument or point of view, or the presentation of reasoned propositions about problems in need of solution. This mode stresses mood, tone, and affect much more than displays of factual knowledge or acts of rhetorical persuasion. The rhetorical element remains underdeveloped but the expressive quality is vivid. We learn in this case by affect or feeling, by gaining a sense of what it feels like to see and experience the world in a particular, poetic way.

Laszlo Moholy-Nagy's *Play of Light: Black, White, Grey* (1930), for example, presents various views of one of his own kinetic sculptures to emphasize the gradations of light passing across the film frame rather than to document the material shape of the sculpture itself. The effect of this play of light on the viewer takes on more importance than the object it refers to in the historical world. Similarly, Jean Mitry's *Pacific*

Pacific 231 (Jean Mitry, 1949). The locomotive begins its journey in a roundhouse and is soon hurtling down the rails. Mitry's film is one of the cinema's great tributes to the railroad, a vehicle, like film, that swiftly transports us to distant places. *Courtesy of Photofest.*

231 (1949) is in part a homage to Abel Gance's *La Roue* (1923) and in part a poetic evocation of the power and speed of a steam locomotive as it gradually builds up speed and hurtles toward its (unspecified) destination. The editing stresses rhythm and form more than it details the actual workings of a locomotive. The film's poetic power is all the more apparent when we compare it to the Lumière brothers' *Arrival of a Train* (1895). *Pacific 231* builds a vivid sense of the dynamic rhythms of an extended journey that is completely lacking from the long take of a gradual but dramatic arrival in the earlier film.

The documentary dimension to the poetic mode of representation stems largely from the degree to which modernist films relied on the historical world for their source material. Some avant-garde films such as Oskar Fischinger's *Composition in Blue* (1935) use abstract patterns of form or color or animated figures and have minimal relation to a documentary tradition of representing *the* historical world rather than *a* world of the artist's imagining. Poetic documentaries, though, draw on the historical world for their raw material but transform this material in distinctive ways. Francis Thompson's *N.Y., N.Y.* (1957), for example, uses shots of New York City that provide evidence of how New York looked in the mid-1950s but gives greater priority to how specific shots can be selected and arranged to produce a poetic impression of the city as a mass of volume, color, and movement. Thompson's film continues the tradition of the city symphony film and affirms the poetic potential of documentary to see the historical world anew.

This sense of the affective tone of lived reality takes considerable prominence in animated documentaries, many of which have strong poetic qualities even if they also address a specific event or type of experience. Sylvie Bringas and Orly Yadim's moving account of Tana Ross's experience of the Holocaust as a little girl, *Silence* (1998), is told largely through animation. The haunting, ghostly quality of the animation stresses the unspoken and unspeakable history that her family carried forward but did not acknowledge. It takes on a half-life of its own, felt and experienced obliquely rather than directly, just as the animation evokes the world of the death camps and the surreal illusions of Theresienstadt, which the Nazis used as a "show camp" to create the impression that prisoners were well treated, with memorable power.

In a similar spirit, Jonathan Hodgson's *Feeling My Way* (1997) uses animation to evoke the highly subjective world imagined by the film's narrator as he travels to work. Nothing is quite real but everything bears an uncanny resemblance to reality. The narrator, "John," applies categories and labels to what he sees, but these seem to do little to reduce the affective power of a world that teems with mystery and, sometimes, threat. When he finally arrives at work it is to pass through a door labeled "Parallel Universe." The question becomes: is the parallel universe what we would understand as reality or is it yet a wilder variation on the subjective world we have just experienced? These films and many others like them use animation to achieve poetic goals mixed with autobiographical, diaristic, and performative models and modes.

The poetic mode began in tandem with modernism as a way of representing reality in terms of a series of fragments, subjective impressions, incoherent acts, and loose associations. These qualities were often attributed to the changes wrought by industrialization generally

Rain (Joris Ivens, 1929). Images such as this convey a feeling or impression of what a rain shower is like rather than convey information or an argument. This is a distinct and distinctly poetic perspective on the historical world. Pursuing such a perspective was a common goal of many who would later identify themselves more specifically as documentary or experimental filmmakers. *Photo courtesy of the European Foundation Joris Ivens.*

and the effects of World War I in particular. The modernist world no longer seemed to make sense in traditional narrative, realist terms. Breaking up time and space into multiple perspectives, denying coherence to personalities vulnerable to eruptions from the unconscious, and refusing to provide solutions to insurmountable problems had the sense of honesty about it even as it created works of art that were puzzling or ambiguous in their effect. Although some films explored more classical conceptions of the poetic as a source of order, wholeness, and unity, this stress on fragmentation and ambiguity remains a prominent feature of many poetic documentaries.

Un Chien Andalou (Luis Buñuel and Salvador Dali, 1929) and L'Age d'or (Luis Buñuel, 1930), for example, give the impression of a documentary reality but then populate that reality with characters caught up in uncontrollable urges, abrupt shifts of time and place, and more puzzles than answers. Filmmakers like Kenneth Anger continued aspects of this poetic mode in *Scorpio Rising* (1964), a representation of ritual acts performed by members of a motorcycle gang, as did Chris Marker in *Sans Soleil* (1982), a complex meditation on filmmaking, memory, and postcolonialism. (At the time of their release, works like Anger's seemed firmly rooted in an experimental film tradition, but in retrospect we can see how they combine experimental and documentary elements. How we place them depends heavily on the assumptions we adopt about categories and genres, models and modes.)

By contrast, works like Basil Wright's *Song of Ceylon* (1934), on the untouched beauty of Ceylon (Sri Lanka) despite the inroads of commerce and colonialism, Bert Haanstra's *Glass* (1958), a tribute to the skill of traditional glass blowers and the beauty of their work, or Les Blank's *Always for Pleasure* (1978), a celebration of Mardi Gras festivities in New Orleans, return to a more classic sense of unity and beauty and discover traces of them in the historical world. The poetic mode has many facets, but they all emphasize the ways in which the filmmaker's voice gives fragments of the historical world a formal, aesthetic integrity peculiar to the film itself.

Péter Forgács's remarkable reworking of amateur movies into historical documents stresses poetic, associative qualities over transferring information or winning us over to a particular point of view. *Free Fall* (1997), for example, chronicles the fate of European Jews in the 1930s and 1940s through the home movies of a successful Jewish businessman, Gyorgy Peto, and *Danube Exodus* (1998) follows the journeys of a Danube cruise ship as it takes Jews from Hungary to the Black Sea on their flight to Palestine and then takes Germans from Bessarabia (the northern part of Romania at the time) as they are driven out by the Russians and evacuated to Germany, only to be relocated in Poland. The historical footage, freeze frames, slow motion, tinted images, selective moments of color, occasional titles to identify time and place, voices that recite diary entries, and haunting music build a tone and mood far more than they explain the war or describe its course of action. The poetic quality Forgács adds to the original home movies imbues these films with an affective dimension that stems from the blind spots and pleasures of everyday experience rather than from the drama and intensity of world-shaking events.

THE EXPOSITORY MODE

This mode assembles fragments of the historical world into a more rhetorical frame than an aesthetic or poetic one. It is the mode that first combined the four basic elements of documentary film described in chapter 5 (indexical images of reality; poetic, affective associations; story-telling qualities; and rhetorical persuasiveness). The expository mode addresses the viewer directly, with titles or voices that propose a perspective or advance an argument. Some expository films adopt a voice-of-God commentary (the speaker is heard but never seen) such as we find in the *Why We Fight* series, *Victory at Sea* (1952–1953), *The City* (1939), *Blood of the Beasts* (1949), and *Dead Birds* (1963). Others utilize a voice-of-authority commentary (the speaker is heard and also seen) such as we find in *America's Most Wanted, The Selling of the Pentagon* (1971), *16 in Webster Groves* (1966), John Berger's *Ways of Seeing* (1974), Michael Moore's *Fahrenheit 9/11* (2004), and Zana Briski and Ross Kaufman's *Born into Brothels: Calcutta's Red Light Kids* (2004).

The voice-of-God tradition fostered the cultivation of the professionally trained, richly toned male voice of commentary that proved a hallmark of the expository mode even though some of the most impressive films chose less-polished voices precisely for the credibility gained by avoiding too much polish.

Joris Ivens's great film urging support for the Republican defenders of Spanish democracy, *The Spanish Earth* (1937), for example, exists in at least three versions. None has a professional commentator. All three have identical image tracks, but the French version uses an ad-libbed commentary by the famous French film director Jean Renoir, while the English versions rely on Orson Welles and Ernest Hemingway. Ivens chose Welles first, but his delivery proved a bit too elegant; it bestowed a humanistic compassion on the events, where Ivens hoped for a tougher sense of visceral engagement. Hemingway, who had written the commentary, proved the more effective voice. He brought a matter-of-fact but clearly committed tone to a film that wanted to galvanize support more than compassion. (Some prints still credit the voice over to Welles even when the actual voice is Hemingway's.)

Expository documentaries rely heavily on an informing logic carried by the spoken word. In a reversal of the traditional emphasis

Yosemite: The Fate of Heaven (Jon Else, 1988). The tension between public access and conservation is the focus of this film. Robert Redford's commentary falls into the category of voice-of-God address inasmuch as we never see Mr. Redford. To the extent that Mr. Redford's long-time advocacy for environmental issues makes him a more informed speaker than an anonymous commentator would be and that we already have an image of what Mr. Redford looks like with us from his many film roles, he also fulfills the function of a voice of authority. *Photo courtesy of Jon Else.*

in film, images serve a supporting role. They illustrate, illuminate, evoke, or act in counterpoint to what is said. The commentary is typically presented as distinct from the images of the historical world that accompany it. It serves to organize these images and make sense of them similar to a written caption for a still image. The commentary is therefore presumed to come from some place that remains unspecified but associated with objectivity or omniscience. It shows signs of intelligence and represents the organizing logic of the film. The commentary, in fact, represents the film's perspective. We take our cue from the commentary and understand the images as evidence or illustration for what is said. Television news descriptions of famine in

Ethiopia as "biblical," for example, appear proven by wide-angle shots of great masses of starving people clustered together on an open plain.

Editing in the expository mode generally serves less to establish a rhythm or formal pattern, as it does in the poetic mode, than to maintain the continuity of the spoken argument or perspective. We call this evidentiary editing. Such editing may sacrifice spatial and temporal continuity to rope in images from far-flung places if they help advance the argument or support a proposal. The expository filmmaker often has greater freedom in the selection and arrangement of images than the fiction filmmaker. In *The Plow That Broke the Plains* (1936), shots of arid prairie landscapes came from all over the Midwest, for example, to support the claim of widespread erosion. Cutting shots from Kansas and Texas together enhanced rather than detracted from the claim that the Great Plains stood in severe danger of permanent damage.

The expository mode emphasizes the impression of objectivity and a well-supported perspective. The voice-over commentary seems literally "above" the fray; it has the capacity to judge actions in the historical world without being caught up in them. The professional commentator's official tone, like the authoritative manner of news anchors and reporters, strives to build a sense of credibility from qualities such as detachment, neutrality, disinterestedness, or omniscience. These qualities can be adapted to an ironic point of view such as Charles Kuralt's commentary for *16 in Webster Groves* or subverted even more thoroughly in a film such as *Land without Bread* (1932), with its implicit attack on the very notion of objectivity. More recently, filmmakers such as Michael Moore, Su Friedrich, Jill Godmilow, Travis Wilkerson, Alan Berliner, Trinh Minh Ha, and Patricio Guzmán speak in their own voice on the sound track. This change stresses the personal perspective of the maker and foregoes the claim to ultimate wisdom or impartial truth that is common to voice-of-God commentary. It is part of a larger change that has emphasized personal perspectives over institutional authority in documentary generally and in other forms of discourse as well.

The expository mode also affords an economy of analysis since points can be made succinctly and pointedly in words. Expository documentary is an ideal mode for conveying information or mobilizing support within a framework that preexists the film. In this case, a

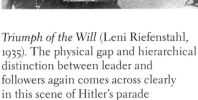

Triumph of the Will (Leni Riefenstahl, 1935). The physical gap and hierarchical distinction between leader and followers again comes across clearly in this scene of Hitler's parade through the streets of Nuremberg.

The Spanish Earth (Joris Ivens, 1937). Ivens's support for the Republican cause against the Nazi-backed rebellion of General Franco followed from his political commitment to democratic and socialist ideals. His de-emphasis on hierarchy in this shot of an officer and a soldier contrasts sharply with Riefenstahl's shooting style.

film will add to our stockpile of knowledge but not challenge or subvert the categories that organize and legitimate such knowledge in the first place. Common sense makes a perfect basis for this type of representation about the world because common sense, like rhetoric, is less subject to logic than to belief.

Frank Capra could organize much of his argument for why young American men should willingly join the battle during World War II in the *Why We Fight* series, for example, by appealing to a mix of native patriotism, the ideals of American democracy, the atrocities of the Axis war machine, and the malignant evil of Hitler, Mussolini, and Hirohito. In the black-and-white alternatives of a "free world" versus a "slave world," who would not defend a free world? Common sense made the answer simple—to the predominantly white audience thoroughly imbued with a "melting pot" belief in American values.

Some 50 years later, Capra's appeal seems remarkably naïve and overblown in its treatment of patriotic virtue and democratic ideals. For example, no minorities, no problems of social justice, poverty, or hunger intrude into the film. White Americans represent all Americans and all Americans oppose a fascist enemy. When Ken Burns

Triumph of the Will (Leni Riefenstahl, 1935). The soldier's salute, left, parallels this low-angle view of the German eagle and Nazi swastika. Like Hitler, the eagle serves as a symbol of German power. It presides over the stream of marching troops that pass below it, galvanizing their movement into a tribute to national unity.

The Spanish Earth (Joris Ivens, 1937). In contrast to the pageantry of Riefenstahl's endless parades and speeches, Ivens captures the modest quality of everyday rural life in 1930s Spain, right. This image of the town, Fuenteduena, situated near the shifting battlefront, suggests how ordinary lives are jeopardized, not galvanized, by the fascist rebellion.

retold the story of World War II in *The War,* a 7-part TV series, he learned firsthand that he could not invoke a Capraesque vision of melting pot unity so easily. An episode focusing on Sacramento, California, during the war made scant reference to the efforts of Mexican Americans and protests quickly arose. Burns, a fundamentally conservative historian and filmmaker, albeit a very talented one, beat a hasty retreat and added references to Mexican Americans but retained his overall melting pot perspective. Despite the afterthought quality, Burns's acknowledgement of a marginalized minority community that experienced discrimination and injustice makes clear that the expository mode need not serve to promote only the dominant point of view. World War II looked very different when seen from the perspective of Hispanics in Sacramento, of women confronting sexism in wartime factory work, or Japanese Americans enduring forced confinement to relocation camps. The proposals and perspectives of specific expository films may become dated far more than quickly than the mode itself. It persists and is quite probably the most prevalent mode in use today.

7

How Can We Describe the Observational, Participatory, Reflexive, and Performative Modes of Documentary Film?

THE OBSERVATIONAL MODE

Poetic and expository modes of documentary often sacrificed direct engagement with specific individuals to construct formal patterns or compelling perspectives. The filmmaker gathered the necessary raw materials and then fashioned a meditation, perspective, or proposal from them. What if the filmmaker were simply to observe what happens in front of the camera without overt intervention? Would this not be a new, compelling form of documentation?

Developments in Canada, Europe, and the United States in the years after World War II culminated around 1960 in various 16mm cameras such as the Arriflex and Auricon and tape recorders such as the Nagra that could be easily handled by one person. Speech could now be synchronized with images without the use of bulky equipment or cables that tethered recorders and camera together. The camera and tape recorder could move freely about a scene and record what happened as it happened.

Many filmmakers now chose to abandon all of the forms of control over the staging, arrangement, or composition of a scene made possible by the poetic and expository modes. Instead, they chose to observe lived experience spontaneously. Honoring this spirit of observation in postproduction editing as well as during shooting resulted in films with no voice-over commentary, no supplementary music or sound effects, no inter-titles, no historical reenactments, no behavior repeated for the

Victory at Sea (Henry Salomon and Isaac Kleinerman, 1952–1953). Like *Night and Fog, Victory at Sea* returns to the recent past to tell the story of World War II. Made as a television series for CBS, it adopts a commemorative stance. It recalls battles and strategies, setbacks and victories from the perspective of the survivor or veteran. It celebrates naval power and its contribution, giving scant attention to the ground war or the civilian consequences that are at the heart of *Night and Fog*. Both films, however, rely on compilation of footage shot contemporaneously with the events to which the films now return. Compilation films invariably alter the meaning of the footage they incorporate. Here, both films use footage for purposes that are possible only to those who reflect on the meaning of the past rather than report the occurrences of the moment.

camera, and not even any interviews. What we saw was what there was, or so it seemed in *Primary* (1960); *High School* (1968); *Les Racquetteurs* (Michel Brault and Gilles Groulx, 1958), about a group of Montrealers enjoying various games in the snow; portions of *Chronicle of a Summer* (1960), which profiles the lives of several individuals in the Paris of 1960; *The Chair* (1962), about the last days of a man condemned to death; *Gimme Shelter* (1970), about the Rolling Stones' infamous concert at Altamont, California, where a man's death at the hands of the Hell's Angels is partially caught on-camera; *Dont Look Back* (1967), about

Bob Dylan's tour of England in 1965; *Monterey Pop* (1968), about a music festival featuring Otis Redding, Janis Joplin, Jimi Hendrix, the Jefferson Airplane, and others; or *Jane* (1962), profiling Jane Fonda as she prepares for a role in a Broadway play.

The resulting footage often recalled the work of the Italian neorealists. We look in on life as it is lived. Social actors engage with one another, ignoring the filmmakers. Often the characters are caught up in pressing demands or a crisis of their own. This requires their attention and draws it away from the presence of filmmakers. The scenes tend, like fiction, to reveal aspects of character and individuality. We make inferences and come to conclusions on the basis of behavior we observe or overhear. The filmmaker's retirement to the position of observer calls on the viewer to take a more active role in determining the significance of what is said and done.

The observational mode poses a series of ethical considerations that involve the act of observing others go about their affairs. Is such an act in and of itself voyeuristic? Does it place the viewer in a necessarily less comfortable position than in a fiction film? In fiction, scenes are specifically contrived for us to oversee and overhear, whereas documentary scenes represent the lived experience of actual people that we happen to witness. This position, "at the keyhole," can feel uncomfortable if a pleasure in looking seems to take priority over the chance to acknowledge and interact with the one seen. This discomfort can be even more acute when the person is not an actor who has willingly agreed to be observed playing a part in a fiction.

For some, the Mayles brothers' portrait of Edith and Edie Bouvier Beale in *Grey Gardens* prompted just this sort of acute discomfort. The two women, scions of Jacqueline Kennedy Onassis's family, live in a huge but dilapidated mansion in the fashionable Hamptons outside New York City. They are at ease with the camera and spontaneous in their interactions but seem to have no idea that others will judge their eccentric, reclusive, highly co-dependent lifestyle bizarre if not unhealthy. How can the filmmakers simply observe and pass along what they see if what we now see becomes fodder for diagnoses of illness or judgments of dysfunction? Did they have no ethical obligation to confront these concerns more directly? Of course, these questions now enter into the arena of ethical debate regarding the documentary filmmaker's responsibilities, but the act of entering this arena is not as praiseworthy as acknowledging the issue and attempting to resolve it in the moment rather than observe it and possibly exploit it.

The impression that the filmmaker is not intruding on the behavior of others also raises the question of unacknowledged or indirect intrusion. Do people conduct themselves in ways that will color our perception of them, for better or worse, in order to satisfy a filmmaker who does not say what it is he wants? Does the filmmaker seek out others to represent because they possess qualities that may fascinate viewers for the wrong reasons? This question often comes up with ethnographic films that observe, in other cultures, behavior that may, without adequate contextualization, seem exotic or bizarre, more part of a "cinema of attractions" than science. Has the filmmaker sought the informed consent of participants and made it possible for such informed consent to be understood and given? To what extent can a filmmaker explain the possible consequences of allowing behavior to be observed and represented to others?

Fred Wiseman, for example, requests consent verbally when he shoots but assumes that when he shoots in tax-supported, public institutions he has a right to record what happens; he never grants participants any control over the final result. Even so, many participants in *High School* found the film fair and representative although most critics have considered it a harsh indictment of school regimentation and discipline. A radically different approach occurs in *Two Laws* (1981), about Aboriginal land rights, where the filmmakers did not film anything without both the consent and collaboration of the participants. Everything from content to camera lenses was open to discussion and mutual agreement.

Since the observational filmmaker adopts a peculiar mode of presence "on the scene" in which he or she appears to be invisible and nonparticipatory, the question also arises of when the filmmaker has a responsibility to intervene? What if something happens that may jeopardize or injure one of the social actors? Should a cameraman film the immolation of a Vietnamese monk who, knowing that there are cameras present to record the event, sets himself on fire to protest the Vietnam War, or should the cameraman refuse or try to dissuade the monk? Should a filmmaker accept a knife as a gift from a participant in the course of filming a murder trial and then turn that gift over to the police when blood is found on it (as Joe Berlinger and Bruce Sinofsky do in their film *Paradise Lost* [1996])? This last example moves us toward an unexpected or inadvertent form of participation rather than observation as it also raises broad issues about the filmmaker's relationship with his or her subjects.

Observational films exhibit particular strength in giving a sense of the duration of actual events. They break with the dramatic pace of mainstream fiction films and the sometimes hurried, montage assembly of images that support expository or poetic documentaries. When Fred Wiseman, for example, observes the making of a 30-second television commercial for some 25 minutes of screen time in *Model* (1980), he conveys the sense of having observed everything worth noting about the shooting. His 25 minutes of screen time, however, condenses what was hours and hours of actual shooting time for the commercial.

Similarly, when David MacDougall films extended discussions between his principal character, Lorang, and one of his peers about the bride price for Lorang's daughter in *Wedding Camels* (1980), he shifts our attention from what the final agreement is or what new narrative issue arises because of it to the feel and texture of the discussion itself: the body language and eye contact, the intonation and tone of the voices, the pauses and "empty" time that give the encounter the sense of concrete, lived reality.

MacDougall himself describes the fascination of lived experience as something that is most vividly experienced as a difference between rushes (the unedited footage as it was originally shot) and an edited sequence. The rushes seem to have a density and vitality that the edited film lacks. A loss occurs even as structure and perspective take shape:

> The sense of loss seems related to positive values perceived in the rushes and intended by the filmmaker at the time of filming but unrepresented in the completed film. It is as though the very reason for making films is somehow contradicted in the act of making them. The process of editing a film from the rushes involves both reducing the overall amount of screen time and cutting most shots to shorter lengths. Both these processes progressively highlight particular meanings. Sometimes filmmakers appear to recognize this when they try to preserve some of the qualities of the rushes in their films, or reintroduce those qualities through other means. ("When Less Is Less," *Transcultural Cinema*, p. 215)

The presence of the camera "on the scene" testifies to its presence in the historical world. This affirms a sense of commitment or engagement with the immediate, intimate, and personal as it occurs. This also affirms a sense of fidelity to what occurs that can pass on events to us as if they simply happened when they have, in fact, been constructed to have that very appearance. One modest example is the "masked interview." In this case the filmmaker works in a more participatory way with his subjects to establish the general subject of a scene and then films it in an observational manner. David MacDougall has done this quite effectively in several films. An example is the scene in *Kenya Boran* (1974) where, without paying heed to the camera but in accord with the general guidelines established before shooting began, two Kenyan tribesmen discuss their views of the government's introduction of birth control measures. Almost all contemporary filmmakers who rely on interviews meet and talk to their subjects first, often prerehearsing what will be said on-camera to ensure, at the very least, that it is terse and coherent. Of practical advantage, it also provides an opportunity to shade a perspective or emphasize a tone in accord with the filmmaker's needs rather than the subject's experience.

A more complex example is the event staged to become part of the historical record. Press conferences, for example, may be filmed in a purely observational style, but such events would not exist at all if it were not for the presence of the camera. This is the reverse of the basic premise behind observational films, that what we see is what would have occurred were the camera not there to observe it.

This reversal took on monumental proportions in one of the first "observational" documentaries, Leni Riefenstahl's *Triumph of the Will* (1935). After an introductory set of titles that set the stage for the German National Socialist (Nazi) Party's 1934 Nuremberg rally, Riefenstahl observes events with no further commentary. Events—predominantly parades, reviews of troops, mass assemblies, images of Hitler, and speeches—occur as if the camera simply recorded what would have happened anyway. At 2 hours running time, the film can give the impression of having recorded historical events all too faithfully and unthinkingly.

And yet, very little would have happened as it did were it not for the express intent of the Nazi Party to make a film of this rally. Riefenstahl

Roy Cohn/Jack Smith (Jill Godmilow, 1994). Godmilow's film, like many documentaries of music concerts, observes a public performance; in this case she records two one-man plays by Ron Vawter. Given that such events are understood to be performances in the first place, they allow the filmmaker to avoid some of the accusations that the presence of the camera altered what would have happened had the camera not been there. *Photo courtesy of Jill Godmilow.*

had enormous resources placed at her disposal, and events were carefully planned to facilitate their filming, including the repeat filming of portions of some speeches at another time and place when the original footage proved unusable. (The repeated portions are reenacted so that they blend in with the original speeches, hiding the collaboration that went into their making.)

Triumph of the Will demonstrates the power of the image to represent the historical world at the same moment as it participates in the construction of the historical world itself. Such participation, especially in the context of Nazi Germany, carries an aura of duplicity. This was the last thing observational filmmakers like Robert Drew, D.A. Pennebaker, Richard Leacock, and Fred Wiseman wanted in their own work. The integrity of their observational stance successfully avoided it, for the most part, and yet the underlying act of being present at an event but filming it as if absent, as if the filmmaker were simply a "fly

Roy Cohn/Jack Smith (Jill Godmilow, 1994). Godmilow makes use of editing to create a distinct perspective on Ron Vawter's performance as gay underground filmmaker Jack Smith and right-wing, anti-Communist (and closeted gay) lawyer Roy Cohn. By intercutting the two separate performances she draws increased attention to the contrasting ways in which the two men dealt with their sexuality during the 1950s. *Photo courtesy of Jill Godmilow.*

on the wall," invites debate as to how much of what we see would be the same if the camera were not there or how much would differ if the filmmaker's presence were more readily acknowledged. That such debate is by its very nature undecidable continues to fuel a certain sense of mystery, or disquiet, about observational cinema.

THE PARTICIPATORY MODE

Also appearing around 1960 with the advent of new technologies that allowed for sync sound recording on location is the participatory mode. Here the filmmaker does interact with his or her subjects rather than unobtrusively observe them. Questions grow into interviews or conversations; involvement grows into a pattern of collaboration or confrontation. What happens in front of the camera becomes an index of the nature of the interaction between filmmaker and subject. This mode inflects the "I speak about them to you" formulation into something that is often closer to "I speak with them for us (me and you)" as the filmmaker's interactions give us a distinctive window onto a particular portion of our world.

The participatory mode has come to embrace the spectator as participant as well. Interactive websites and installations allow the viewer to chart a path through the spectrum of possibilities made possible by the filmmaker. A vivid example of this shift is the difference between Péter Forgács's film, *Danube Exodus* (1998), about the passage of Jews during World War II from central Europe to the Black Sea aboard a cruise ship and the return passage of Germans from Bessarabia to Germany. Forgács builds his film from the home movie footage of the ship's captain and the result is an extremely powerful, poetic, but also provocative study of the displacement and exodus of two populations. Later, Forgács, in collaboration with the Labyrinth Project, which has created a number of interactive "database documentaries" on DVD, turned the footage into an installation. A computer controls the projection of footage from the film onto a large screen, but now audience members can interact with the computer to make choices about how the footage is displayed, opting to follow different strands or themes in the original footage. In addition, other computers house outtakes, interviews, and other primary source documents that can be accessed in patterns of the viewer's choosing. Individual lives can be examined in greater detail and more learned than the original film made possible.

Such innovations suggest that the participatory mode is particularly ripe for exploitation in digitally based, computer-driven forms that grant far more control to the viewer than the standard fixed and unalterable structure of the film-based documentary. Because the filmmaker or database artist retains ultimate control over what gets into the database and how it can be accessed, the overall experience will possess aesthetic and rhetorical qualities that exceed those of a general archival depository, but the participatory emphasis shifts from the interaction between filmmaker and subject to the one between viewer and assembled material. Such database documentaries occupy very fertile ground between the very open structure of the ordinary archive and the much more linear structure of the average documentary.

The participatory mode has antecedents in other media and disciplines. Radio has long featured direct interactions between talk show hosts and guests, a form that migrated readily to television before taking root in cinema as well. In addition, the social sciences have long promoted the study of social groups by means of direct interaction and investigation. Anthropology, for example, remains heavily defined by the practice of field work, where an anthropologist lives among a people for an extended period of time, learns the language and customs, and then writes up what he or she has learned. Such research usually calls for some form of participant-observation. The researcher goes into the field, participates in the lives of others, gains a corporeal or visceral feel for what life in a given context is like, and then reflects on this experience, using the methods of anthropology or sociology to do so. "Being there" calls for participation; "being here" allows for observation. That is to say, the field worker does not allow him- or herself to "go native," under normal circumstances, but retains a degree of detachment that differentiates him or her from those about whom he or she writes. Anthropology has, in fact, consistently depended on this complex act of engagement and separation between two cultures to define itself.

Documentary filmmakers also go into the field; they, too, live among others and speak about or represent what they experience. The practice of participant-observation, however, has not become a paradigm. The methods of social science research have remained subordinate to the more prevalent rhetorical practice of moving and persuading an audience. Observational documentary de-emphasizes persuasion to give us a sense of what it is like to *be* in a given situation but without a sense of what it is like for the filmmaker to be there, too. Participatory documentary gives us a sense of what it is like for the filmmaker to be in a given situation and how that situation alters as a result. We experience the representation of an encounter that can be quite acute in films such as *Nobody's Business* (1996), about the filmmaker's blunt but evasive father, or *Tarnation* (2003), about the filmmaker's efforts to understand why his mother became mentally ill and his own childhood a nightmare, that draw on the diary, confession, or essayistic traditions for their model. In fact, biography, autobiography, history, essays, confessions, and diaries are among the most popular models for participatory documentaries. Like the performative mode, discussed below, the filmmaker's presence, and perspective, often contributes significantly to the film's overall impact.

When we view participatory documentaries we expect to witness the historical world as represented by someone who actively engages with others, rather than unobtrusively observing, poetically reconfiguring, or argumentatively assembling what others say and do. The filmmaker steps out from behind the cloak of voice-over commentary, steps away from poetic meditation, steps down from a fly-on-the-wall perch, and becomes a social actor (almost) like any other. (Almost like any other because the filmmaker retains the camera, and with it, a certain degree of potential power and control over events.)

Participatory documentaries like *Chronicle of a Summer; Portrait of Jason* (1967); or *Word Is Out* (1977) involve the ethics and politics of encounter. This is the encounter between one who wields a movie camera and one who does not. How do filmmaker and social actor respond to each other? Does a sense of respect, despite disagreement, emerge, or is there a feeling of deception, manipulation, distortion at work? How do they negotiate control and share responsibility? How much can the filmmaker insist on testimony when it is painful to provide it? What responsibility does the filmmaker have for the emotional aftermath of putting others on-camera? What goals join filmmaker and subject and what needs divide them?

Many find the ambush interview practiced on CBS's *60 Minutes* and refined into a major ploy by Michael Moore in all of his films an example of where an ethical borderline exists. To catch someone who is unprepared and perhaps ill equipped to engage in an interview can signal disrespect as well as irreverence. In many cases, the targets of Moore's ambushes seem to deserve what they get: Dick Clark, who owns the restaurant where a welfare mother barely earns enough to cover the costs of her daily commute and day care for her children, hastily beats a retreat rather than try to explain himself to Moore in *Bowling for Columbine* (2002), but Charlton Heston cannot flee his own home after he lets Mr. Moore inside. A rising sense of discomfort comes over many viewers as they realize Mr. Heston's faltering responses are at least partly due to a case of Alzheimer's disease, making

Grizzly Man (Werner Herzog, 2005). Werner Herzog uses footage of grizzly bears shot by Timothy Treadwell to reflect on man's relation to nature and Treadwell's relation to sanity. Treadwell records his own thoughts in footage he shoots of himself without assistance as he camps out in the wilderness. Herzog then adds his own voice-over commentary to Treadwell's footage as well as introducing interviews with others. Treadwell's extraordinary footage, shown here, frequently places him in the same frame as wild bears, miles from civilization. The indexical power of deep focus long takes lends an overwhelming authenticity to his footage. It's beyond dispute: he and the bear co-exist in the same frame just as they co-existed in the remote Alaskan wilderness. *Courtesy of Lions Gate Films/Photofest.*

Moore seem insensitive and disrespectful rather than tough minded. Moore does a similar thing in *Roger and Me* (1989) when he snares Miss Michigan to quiz her about economic conditions in Flint. Clearly unfamiliar with the specifics and not someone who pretends to any authoritative knowledge of plant closings and the global economy, Moore makes her look foolish, but for some the insensitivity to her individuality as a person makes the filmmaker appear callous in his pursuit of irreverence.

The sense of bodily presence, rather than absence, that arises from sync sound exchanges between filmmaker and subject locates the filmmaker "on the scene." We expect that what we learn will hinge on the nature and quality of the encounter between filmmaker and subject. We may see as well as hear the filmmaker act and respond on the spot, in the same historical arena as the film's subjects. The possibilities of serving as mentor, critic, interrogator, collaborator, or provocateur arise.

Participatory documentary can stress the actual, lived encounter between filmmaker and subject in the spirit of Dziga Vertov's *The Man with a Movie Camera* (1929), Jean Rouch and Edgar Morin's *Chronicle of a Summer*, Jon Alpert's *Hard Metals Disease* (1987), Claude Lanzmann's *Shoah* (1985), or Ross McElwee's *Sherman's March* (1985). The filmmaker's presence takes on heightened importance, from the physical act of "getting the shot" that figures so prominently in *The Man with a Movie Camera* to the political act of joining forces with one's subjects, as Jon Silver does at the start of *Watsonville on Strike* (1989) when he asks the farmworkers if he can film in the union hall in defiance of the union boss. In other cases, the filmmaker's presence takes on a highly personal and sometimes poignant quality, as in *Complaints of a Dutiful Daughter* (1994), as Deborah Hoffmann, the filmmaker, struggles to cope with her mother's descent into dementia, or *Finding Christa* (1991), as filmmaker Camille Billops wrestles with her decision to locate the daughter she gave up for adoption some 20 years earlier.

This style of filmmaking is what Rouch and Morin termed "cinéma vérité," translating into French Dziga Vertov's title for his newsreels of Soviet society, *kinopravda*. As "film truth," the idea emphasizes that this is the truth of an encounter rather than absolute or untampered truth. We see how the filmmaker and subject negotiate a relationship, how they act toward one another, what forms of power and control come into play, and what levels of revelation or rapport stem from this specific form of encounter. Cinéma vérité reveals the reality of what happens when people interact in the presence of a camera.

If there is a truth here it is the truth of a form of interaction that would not exist were it not for the camera. In this sense it is the opposite of the observational premise that what we see is what we would have seen had we been there. In participatory documentary, what we see is what we can see only when a camera, or filmmaker, is there

Takeover (David and Judith MacDougall, 1981). The MacDougalls have evolved a collaborative style of filmmaking with the subjects of their ethnographic films. In a series of films made on Aboriginal issues, of which *Takeover* is a prime example, they have often served as witnesses to the testimonial statements of traditions and beliefs that Aboriginal people offer in their disputes with the government over land rights and other matters. The interaction is highly participatory, although the result can seem, at first, unobtrusive or observational since much of the collaboration occurs prior to the act of filming. *Photo courtesy of David MacDougall.*

instead of ourselves. Jean-Luc Godard once claimed that cinema is truth twenty-four times a second: participatory documentary makes good on Godard's claim.

Chronicle of a Summer, for example, involves scenes that result from the collaborative interactions of filmmakers and their subjects, an eclectic group of individuals living in Paris in the summer of 1960. In one instance Marcelline Loridan, a young woman who later married the Dutch filmmaker Joris Ivens, speaks about her experience as a Jewish deportee who is sent to a German concentration camp from France during World War II. The camera follows her as she walks through the Place de la Concorde and then through the former Parisian market,

Sherman's March (Ross McElwee, 1985). In this still, director Ross McElwee adopts the pose of a Confederate officer, but for the bulk of the film he simply records his journey through the American south, looking, ostensibly, for love. The film is a classic example of an essay film in which the filmmaker's personal perspective shapes not only what we see but how we see it. The most memorable scenes involve interactions between McElwee and various women as they discuss his search for love. *Courtesy of First Run Features/www.firstrunfeatures.com.*

Les Halles. She offers a quite moving monologue on her experiences, but only because Rouch and Morin planned the scene with her and gave her a tape recorder to carry. If they had waited for the event to occur on its own so they could observe it, it never would have occurred. They pursued this notion of collaboration still further by screening parts of the film to the participants and filming the ensuing discussion. Rouch and Morin also appear on-camera, discussing their aim to study "this strange tribe living in Paris" and assessing, at the end of the film, what they have learned.

Filmmakers who seek to represent their own direct encounter with their surrounding world and those who seek to represent broad social issues and historical perspectives through interviews and compilation footage constitute two large components of the participatory mode. They differentiate, loosely speaking, into essayists and historians. As viewers we have the sense that we are witness to a form of dialogue between the filmmaker and his or her subject—be it an issue like a labor strike or a person like the filmmaker's mother—that stresses situated engagement, negotiated interaction, and emotion-laden encounter. These qualities give the participatory mode of documentary filmmaking considerable appeal as it roams a wide variety of subjects from the most personal to the most historical. Often, in fact, this mode demonstrates how the personal and political intertwine to yield representations of the historical world from specific perspectives that are both contingent and committed.

In *Not a Love Story* (1981), for example, Bonnie Klein, the filmmaker, and Linda Lee Tracy, an ex-stripper, discuss their reactions to various forms of pornography as they interview participants in the sex industry. In one scene, Linda Lee poses for a nude photograph and then discusses how the experience made her feel. The two women embark on an exploratory journey in a spirit similar to Rouch and Morin's and partly confessional/redemptive in an entirely different sense. The act of making the film plays a cathartic, redemptive role in their lives; it is less the world of their subjects that changes than their own.

In some cases, such as Marcel Ophuls's *The Sorrow and the Pity* (1970), on French collaboration with Germany during World War II, the filmmaker serves as a researcher or investigative reporter. In such cases, the filmmaker's voice emerges from direct, personal involvement in the events that unfold. The investigative reporter commonly makes

his or her own personal involvement in the story central to its unfolding. Another example is the work of Canadian filmmaker Michael
Rubbo, such as his *Sad Song of Yellow Skin* (1970), where he explores
the ramifications of the Vietnam War among the civilian population
of Vietnam. Another is the work of Nick Broomfield, who adopts a
brasher, more confrontational—if not arrogant—style in films like *Kurt
and Courtney* (1998). Exasperation with Courtney Love's evasiveness
about her possible complicity in Kurt Cobain's death compels Broomfield to film his own apparently spontaneous denunciation of her at a
ceremonial dinner sponsored by the American Civil Liberties Union.

In other cases, we move away from the investigative stance to
take up a more responsive and reflective relationship to unfolding
events that involve the filmmaker. This latter choice moves us toward
the diary and personal testimonial. The first-person voice becomes
prominent in the overall structure of the film. It is the filmmaker's
participatory engagement with unfolding events that holds our attention. It is Emiko Omori's effort to retrace the suppressed history of her
own family's experience in the Japanese American relocation camps
of World War II, for example, that gives form to *Rabbit in the Moon*
(1999). Marilu Mallet offers an even more explicitly diary-like structure
to her portrait of life as a Chilean exile living in Montreal married to
Canadian filmmaker Michael Rubbo in *Unfinished Diary* (1983), as
does Kazuo Hara to his chronicle of the complex, emotionally volatile
relationship he revives with his former wife as he and his current partner follow her over a period of time in *Extremely Personal Eros: Love
Song 1974* (1974). The film includes a mind-boggling scene in which
Hara films his former wife giving birth on the floor of her apartment.
These films make the filmmaker as vivid a persona as any other in his
or her films. As testimonial and confession, they often exude a self-
revelatory power.

As noted above, not all participatory documentaries stress the ongoing, open-ended experience of the filmmaker or the interaction between filmmaker and subjects. The filmmaker may wish to introduce
a broader perspective, often one that is historical in nature. How? The
most common answer involves the interview and the archive. The
result often takes the form of a compilation film and recounts history
from above (about major figures and events), or from below (about the

Crumb (Terry Zwigoff, 1994). Terry Zwigoff adopts a highly participatory relationship to the cartoon strip artist R. Crumb. Many of the conversations and interactions clearly would not have occurred as they do had Zwigoff not been there with his camera. Crumb takes a more reflective attitude toward himself and a more probing attitude toward his brothers as he collaborates with Zwigoff's desire to examine the complexities and contradictions of his life.

experience of ordinary people in relation to a historical event). The vast archive of previously shot footage that now exists provides historical footage to accompany the voices of those who were there or who know about what happened.

The interview stands as one of the most common forms of encounter between filmmaker and subject in participatory documentary. Interviews are a distinct form of social encounter. They differ from ordinary conversation and the more coercive process of interrogation by dint of the institutional framework in which they occur and the specific protocols or guidelines that structure them. Interviews occur in anthropological or sociological field work; they go by the name of the "case history" in medicine and social welfare; in psychoanalysis, they take the form of the therapeutic session; in law the interview becomes the pretrial deposition and, during trials, testimony; on television, it forms the backbone of talk shows; in journalism, it takes the form of both the interview and the press conference; and in education, it ap-

Las Madres de la Plaza de Mayo (Susana Muñoz and Lourdes Portillo, 1985). These two women filmmakers (Susana Muñoz and Lourdes Portillo) adopt a highly participatory relationship with the mothers who risked their lives to stage public demonstrations during Argentina's "dirty war." The sons and daughters of these women were among the "disappeared" whom the government abducted, and often killed, without any notice or legal proceedings. Muñoz and Portillo could not shape the public events, but they could draw out the personal stories of the mothers whose courage led them to defy a brutally repressive regime. *Photo courtesy of Lourdes Portillo.*

pears as Socratic dialogue. Michel Foucault argues that these forms all involve regulated forms of exchange, with an uneven distribution of power between client and institutional practitioner, and that they have a root in the religious tradition of the confessional.

Filmmakers make use of the interview to bring different accounts together in a single story. The filmmaker's voice emerges as it weaves together in a distinctive way, contributing voices and the material brought in to support what they say. This compilation of interviews and supporting material has given us numerous film histories, from *In the Year of the Pig* (1969), on the war in Vietnam, to *Eyes on the Prize* (1987, 1990), on the history of the civil rights movement, and from

The Devil Never Sleeps (El Diablo Nunca Duerme) (Lourdes Portillo, 1994). Director Lourdes Portillo as a hard-boiled private eye. The film recounts her journey to Mexico to investigate the suspicious death of her uncle. Reflexive and ironic at times, Portillo nonetheless leaves the question of whether her uncle met with foul play, possibly at the hands of a relative, open. *Photos courtesy of Lourdes Portillo.*

Shoah, on the aftermath of the Holocaust for those who experienced it, to *Jazz* (2000), on the history of jazz in America.

Compilation films such as Esther Shub's *The Fall of the Romanov Dynasty* (1927), which relies entirely on archival footage found by Shub and reedited to tell a social history, date back to the beginnings of documentary film. Shub draws out insights and themes by how she edits shots together, just as later directors like Emile de Antonio draw out a broad historical perspective by how they edit interviews together. Some, such as Barbara Kopple's *Harlan County, U.S.A.* (1977), on a coal miner's strike in Kentucky, or Michael Moore's *Fahrenheit 9/11* (2004), dwell on events in the present moment as the film is made and in which the filmmmaker participates. Others, such as Errol Morris's *The Thin Blue Line* (1988), Leon Gast's *When We Were Kings* (1996), on the 1974 fight between Muhammad Ali and George Foreman, or Ray Müller's *The Wonderful, Horrible Life of Leni Riefenstahl* (1993),

The Devil Never Sleeps (El Diablo Nunca Duerme) (Lourdes Portillo, 1994).
The filmmaker, in the course of an interview, in search of clues, and, ideally,
the confession that will solve the mystery. Although she never obtains a
confession, the sense that she *might* do so lends an air of narrative, film
noir–like suspense to the film. *Photos courtesy of Lourdes Portillo.*

on Riefenstahl's controversial career, center on the past and how those
with knowledge of it now recount it.

The experience of gays and lesbians in the days before Stonewall
could be recounted as a general social history, with a voice-over commentary and images that illustrate the spoken points. (In 1969, gay
patrons of the Stonewall bar in New York city battled police who tried
to raid the bar; it sparked the rise of the gay rights movement.) It could
also be recounted in the words of those who lived through those times
by means of interviews. The Mariposa collective's *Word Is Out* (1977)
opts for the second choice. The filmmakers, like Connie Field for *The
Life and Times of Rosie the Riveter* (1980), screened scores of possible
subjects before settling on the dozen or so who appear in the film.
Unlike Field or Emile de Antonio, the Mariposa collective opts to
keep supporting material to a bare minimum; they compile the history
primarily from the "talking heads" of those who can put this chapter

Cadillac Desert (Jon Else, 1997). *Cadillac Desert* is another excellent example of a film that couples archival footage and the tradition of the compilation film with contemporary interviews that add a fresh perspective to historical events without resorting to a voice-over commentary. *Cadillac Desert* retraces the history of water use in California and its devastating impact on the inland valleys of the state. *Photos courtesy of Jon Else.*

of American social history into their own words. The articulateness and emotional directness of those who speak gives films of testimony such as this a highly compelling quality. The form is similar to but different from the oral history, an extended recounting of past events by participants. Oral histories serve as primary source material and generally lack the careful selection and arrangement of the interview material into a greater whole or a broader perspective.

THE REFLEXIVE MODE

If the historical world provides the meeting place for the processes of negotiation between filmmaker and subject in the participatory mode, the processes of negotiation between filmmaker and viewer become the focus of attention for the reflexive mode. Rather than following the filmmaker in his or her engagement with other social actors, we now attend to the filmmaker's engagement with us, speaking not only about the historical world but about the problems and issues of representing it as well. This intensified level of reflection on what representing the world involves distinguishes the reflexive mode from the other modes.

Trinh Minh-ha's declaration that she will "speak nearby" rather than "speak about" or "speak with" the native people of West Africa, in *Reassemblage* (1982), symbolizes the shift that reflexivity produces: we now attend to *how* we represent the historical world as well as to *what* gets represented. Instead of *seeing through* documentaries to the world beyond them, reflexive documentaries ask us to *see documentary* for what it is: a construct or representation. Jean-Luc Godard and Jean-Pierre Gorin carry this to an extreme in *Letter to Jane* (1972), a 45-minute "letter" in which they scrutinize in great detail a journalistic photograph of Jane Fonda during her visit to North Vietnam. No aspect of this apparently factual photo goes unexamined.

Just as the observational mode of documentary depends on the filmmaker's apparent absence from or nonintervention in the events recorded, the documentary in general depends on the viewer's neglect of his or her actual situation, in front of a movie screen, interpreting a film, in favor of imaginary access to the events shown on the screen as if it is only these events that require interpretation, not the film. The motto that a documentary film is only as good as its content is compelling is what the reflexive mode of documentary calls into question.

One of the issues brought to the fore in reflexive documentaries is the one taken up in chapter 2: What to do with people? Some films, like *Reassemblage; Daughter Rite* (1978); *Bontoc Eulogy* (1995); or *Far from Poland* (1984), address this question directly by calling the usual means of representation into question: *Reassemblage* breaks with the realist conventions of ethnography to question the power of the camera's gaze to represent, and misrepresent, others; *Daughter Rite* subverts reliance on social actors by using two actresses to play sisters who reflect on their relationship to their mother, using insights gathered from interviews with a wide range of women but withholding the voices of the interviewees themselves; *Bontoc Eulogy* recounts the family history of the filmmaker's own grandfather, who was taken from the Philippines to appear as part of an exhibit of Filipino life at the St. Louis World's Fair in 1904 through staged reenactments and imagined memories that call conventional rules of evidence into question; *Far from Poland's* director, Jill Godmilow, addresses us directly to ponder the problems of representing the Solidarity movement in Poland when she has only partial access to the actual events. These films set out to heighten our awareness of the problems of representing others as much as they set out to convince us of the authenticity or truthfulness of representation itself.

Reflexive documentaries also tackle issues posed by realism as a style. Realism seems to provide unproblematic access to the world; it takes form as physical, psychological, and emotional realism (see chapter 5) through techniques of evidentiary or continuity editing, character development, and narrative structure. Reflexive documentaries challenge these techniques and conventions. *Surname Viet Given Name Nam* (1989), for example, relies on interviews with women in Vietnam who describe the oppressive conditions they have faced since the end of the war, but then halfway through the film we discover (if various stylistic hints haven't tipped us off) that the interviews were staged in more ways than one: the women who play Vietnamese women in Vietnam are actually immigrants to the United States reciting, on a stage set, accounts transcribed and edited by Trinh Minh-ha from interviews conducted in Vietnam by someone else with other women!

Similarly, in *The Man with a Movie Camera*, Dziga Vertov demonstrates how the impression of reality comes to be constructed by beginning a scene with the cameraman, Mikhail Kaufman, filming

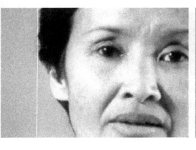

Surname Viet Given Name Nam (Trinh T. Minh-ha, 1989). These three
successive shots, each an extreme close-up that omits portions of the interviewee's
face, correspond to the preproduction storyboard designed by the filmmaker.
Their violation of the normal conventions for filming interviews both calls
our attention to the formality and conventionality of interviews and signals
that this is not a (normal) interview. *Photos courtesy of Trinh T. Minh-ha.*

people riding in a horse-drawn carriage from a car that runs alongside
the carriage. Vertov then cuts to his editing room, where the editor,
Elizaveta Svilova, Vertov's wife, assembles strips of film that represent
this event into the sequence we have, presumably, just seen. The overall result deconstructs the impression of unimpeded access to reality
and invites us to reflect on the process by which this impression is itself
constructed through editing.

Other films, such as *David Holzman's Diary* (1968); *No Lies* (1973);
Daughter Rite; and *The Blair Witch Project* (1999), represent themselves, ultimately, as disguised fictions. They rely on trained actors to
deliver the performances we initially believe to be the self-presentation
of people engaged in everyday life. Our realization of this deception,
sometimes through hints and clues during the film, or at the end, when
the credits reveal the fabricated nature of the performances we have
witnessed, prompts us to question the authenticity of documentary in
general: What "truth" do documentaries reveal about the self; how is
it different from a staged or scripted performance; what conventions
prompt us to believe in the authenticity of documentary performance;
and how can this belief be productively subverted?

The reflexive mode is the most self-conscious and self-question-
ing mode of representation. Realist access to the world; the ability to
provide persuasive evidence; the possibility of indisputable proof; the

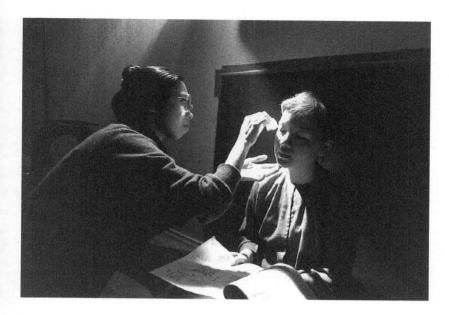

Surname Viet Given Name Nam (Trinh T. Minh-ha, 1989). Makeup and costume are a more frequent consideration for documentary filmmakers than we might assume. Here filmmaker Trinh T. Minh-ha prepares actress Tran Thi Bich Yen for a scene where she will play an interviewee describing her life in Vietnam. The interview appears to be set in Vietnam but was actually shot in California. Like *Far from Poland*, this film explores the question of how to represent situations not directly available to the filmmaker. *Photos courtesy of Trinh T. Minh-ha.*

solemn, indexical bond between an indexical image and what it represents—all these notions come under suspicion. That such notions can compel fetishistic belief prompts the reflexive documentary to examine the nature of such belief rather than attest to the validity of what is believed.

At its best, reflexive documentary prods the viewer to a heightened form of consciousness about his ore her relation to a documentary and what it represents. Vertov does this in *The Man with a Movie Camera* to demonstrate how we construct our knowledge of the world; Buñuel does this in *Land without Bread* (1932) to satirize the presumptions that accompany such knowledge; Trinh does this in *Reassemblage* to question the assumptions that underlie a given body of knowledge or mode of inquiry (ethnography); and Chris Marker, in *Sans Soleil* (1982), questions the assumptions that underlie the act of making films of the lives of others in a world divided by racial and political boundaries.

Achieving a heightened form of consciousness involves a shift in levels of awareness. Reflexive documentary sets out to readjust the assumptions and expectations of its audience, more than to add new knowledge to existing categories. "Let's reflect on *how* what you see and hear gets you to believe in a particular view of the world," these films seem to say.

In pursuit of this invitation to reflection and a heightened form of consciousness, documentaries can be reflexive from both formal and political perspectives.

From a formal perspective, reflexivity draws our attention to our assumptions and expectations about documentary form itself. Trinh does this vividly in *Sur Name Viet Given Name Nam* as she undercuts our assumptions about the interview as a privileged form of access to what people wish to recount. It is only as the film unfolds that we realize that apparent interviews of women who suffered from Communist rule in Vietnam are in fact entirely staged and that the women deliver stories told not by themselves but by others. It is a way, perhaps, to highlight the prescripted, if not stereotyped, nature of tales of hardship, suffering, and victimization. At the very least the revelation that the interviews are not what they appear to be prompts the viewer to rethink his or her assumptions about the truth value and credibility of what is said. In a similar spirit the numerous "confessions" of sex addiction made by the filmmaker Caveh Zahedi in *I Am a Sex Addict* (2005) involve so many obviously exaggerated or stylized reenactments that their ultimate validity comes into question. Although less insistently reflexive than Trinh's film, Zahedi encourages the viewer to bring a heightened skepticism to the credibility of his own confessions.

From a political perspective, reflexivity points toward our assumptions and expectations about the historical world more than about film form. The rise of feminist documentaries in the 1970s provides a vivid example of works that call social conventions into question. Films such as *The Woman's Film* (1971), *Joyce at 34* (1972), and *Growing Up Female* (1971) followed most of the conventions of participatory documentary, but they also sought to produce a heightened consciousness about discrimination against women in the contemporary world. They counter the prevailing (stereotypical) images of women with radically different representations and displace the hopes and desires fueled by advertising and melodramas with the experiences and demands of women who have rejected these notions in favor of radically different ones. Such films challenge entrenched notions of the feminine and also serve to give name to what had lain invisible: the oppression, devalorization, and hierarchy that can now be called sexism. Individual experiences join up to support a new way of seeing, a distinct perspective on the social order.

Both perspectives rely on techniques that jar us, that achieve something akin to what Bertolt Brecht described as "alienation effects," or what the Russian formalists termed *ostranenie*, or "making strange." This is similar to the surrealist effort to see the everyday world in unexpected ways. As a formal strategy, making the familiar strange reminds us how documentary works as a film genre whose claims about the world we can receive too unthinkingly. As a political strategy, it reminds us how society works in accord with conventions and codes we may too readily take for granted.

Brecht's term, "alienation" (a conscious mode of detachment or distantiation), separates us from prevailing assumptions. Formal reflexivity makes us aware of formal assumptions; political reflexivity provokes awareness of the assumptions that support a given social structure. They both tend, therefore, to induce an "aha!" effect, where we grasp a principle or structure at work that helps account for how we understand and represent the world. We take a deeper look. Our heightened consciousness opens up a gap between knowledge and desire, between what is and what might be. Politically reflexive documentaries point to *us* as viewers and social actors, not to films, as the agents who can bridge this gap between what exists and the new forms we can make from it.

THE PERFORMATIVE MODE

Like the poetic mode of documentary representation, the performative mode raises questions about what knowledge actually amounts to. What counts as understanding or comprehension? What besides factual information goes into our understanding of the world? Is knowl-

Wedding Camels (David and Judith MacDougall, 1980). In this trilogy of films on the Turkana of northern Kenya, David and Judith MacDougall adopt several reflexive strategies to make us aware of the filmmakers' active involvement in shaping the scenes we see. Sometimes it is a question put by the filmmakers that prompts discussion, sometimes it is written titles that remind us of the complex process of representing members of another culture in a form members of an English-speaking culture can understand. Such reflexive acts were rare at the time in ethnographic film. Many such films want to give the impression *Nanook of the North* gave: we witness customs and behavior as they "naturally" occur, not as a result of interaction between filmmaker and subject. *Photo courtesy of David MacDougall.*

edge best described as abstract and disembodied, based on generalizations and the typical, in the tradition of Western philosophy? From this perspective, knowledge can be transferred or exchanged freely and those who perform the transfer or exchange are but conduits for knowledge that remains unaltered by their personal involvement with it. But is knowledge better described as concrete and embodied, based on personal experience, in the tradition of poetry, literature, and rhetoric? From this perspective, knowledge can be demonstrated or evoked but

Corpus: A Home Movie for Selena (Lourdes Portillo, 1999). Director Lourdes Portillo investigates the repercussions that followed from the murder of the popular Tex-Mex singer Selena. Was she a positive role model for young women who learn to channel their energies into becoming popular singers, or was she herself a young woman encouraged to recycle stereotypical images of female sexuality? Portillo does not answer such questions so much as pose them in an engaging way. She does so partly by shooting in video to create a family portrait of Selena and her legacy. *Photo courtesy of Lourdes Portillo.*

those who perform the demonstration or evocation imbue what they do with a distinctiveness that cannot be easily replicated. Performative documentary endorses the latter perspective. It sets out to demonstrate how embodied knowledge provides entry into an understanding of the more general processes at work in society.

Meaning is clearly a subjective, affect-laden phenomenon. A car or gun, hospital or love affair will bear different meanings for different people. Experience and memory, emotional involvement, the precise context, questions of value and belief, commitment and principle all enter into our understanding of those aspects of the world most often addressed by documentary: the institutional framework (governments and churches, families and marriages) and specific social practices (love and war, competition and cooperation) that make up a society (as discussed in chapter 4). Performative documentary underscores the complexity of our knowledge of the world by emphasizing its subjective and affective dimensions.

Works like Marlon Riggs's *Tongues Untied* (1989), Ngozi Onwurah's *The Body Beautiful* (1991), Marlon Fuentes's *Bontoc Eulogy*, Agnès Varda's *The Gleaners and I* (2000), Jonathan Caouette's *Tarnation*, and Ari Folman's *Waltz with Bashir* (2008) stress the emotional complexity of experience from the perspective of the filmmaker him- or herself. An autobiographical note enters into these films that bears similarity to an essayistic or diaristic model for participatory filmmaking. Performative films give added emphasis to the subjective qualities of experience and memory. Marlon Riggs, for example, makes use of recited poems and enacted scenes that address the intense personal stakes involved in black, gay identity; Onwurah's film builds up to a staged sexual encounter between her own mother and a handsome young man; Fuentes enacts a fantasy about his grandfather's escape from captivity as an object of display at the 1904 St. Louis World's Fair; Varda speculates on time and mortality as she interviews a host of urban and rural gleaners; Caouette invokes powerful, disturbing memories of his chaotic, trauma-laden youth as he tries to understand why his mother became mentally unstable; and Folman recounts a horrific wartime incident by means of animation. Actual occurrences become amplified by imagined ones. The free combination of the actual and the imagined is a common feature of the performative documentary.

What these films and others such as Isaac Julien's *Looking for Langston* (1988), about the life of Langston Hughes, or Julien's *Frantz Fanon: Black Skin, White Mask* (1996), about the life of Frantz Fanon; Robert Gardner's *Forest of Bliss* (1985), about funeral practices in Benares, India; Chris Choy and Renee Tajima-Peña's *Who Killed Vincent Chin?* (1988), about the murder of a Chinese American by two out-of-work auto workers who reportedly mistook him for Japanese; and Rea Tajiri's *History and Memory* (1991), about her efforts to learn the story of her family's internment in detention camps during World War II share is a deflection of documentary emphasis away from a realist representation of the historical world and toward poetic liberties, more unconventional narrative structures, and more subjective forms of representation. The referential quality of documentary that attests to its function as a window onto the world yields to an expressive quality that affirms the highly situated, embodied, and vividly personal perspective of specific subjects, including the filmmaker on that world.

This use of the word "performative" differs from the well-known use given it by the philosopher J. L. Austin in his book *How to Do Things with Words*. For Austin, speech normally refers to things external to it and does not alter this reality. Performative speech was an exception. In this case saying something becomes a form of doing: commands and pronouncements by those with the authority to utter them and promises meant to be kept are examples. The officer who says, "Fire!" to a firing squad, the minister who says, "I pronounce you man and wife," and the person who says, "I will pay you back" do something by means of speech. The nature of reality changes.

Performative documentaries do not do something in this sense. Performance here draws more heavily on the tradition of acting as a way to bring heightened emotional involvement to a situation or role. Performative documentaries bring the emotional intensities of embodied experience and knowledge to the fore rather than attempt to do something tangible. It they set out to do something, it is to help us sense what a certain situation or experience feels like. They want us to feel on a visceral level more than understand on a conceptual level. Performative documentaries intensify the rhetorical desire to be compelling and tie it less to a persuasive goal than an affective one—to have us feel or experience the world in a particular way as vividly as possible.

Ever since at least *Turksib* (1929), *Salt for Svanetia* (1930), and, in a satiric vein, *Land without Bread*, documentary has exhibited many performative qualities, but they seldom have served to organize entire films. They were present but not dominant. Some participatory documentaries of the 1980s, such as *Las Madres de la Plaza de Mayo* (1985) and *Roses in December* (1982), include performative moments that draw us into subjective, "as if" renderings of traumatic past events (the "disappearance" of the son of one of the mothers who protested government repression in Argentina and the rape of Jean Donovan and three other women by El Salvadoran military men, respectively), but the organizing dominant to the films revolves around a linear history that includes these events. Performative documentaries primarily address us emotionally and expressively rather than factually.

Tongues Untied, for example, begins with a voice-over call that ricochets from left and right, in stereo, "Brother to brother," "Brother to brother . . . ," and ends with a declaration, "Black men loving black men is the revolutionary act." The course of the film over a series of declarations, reenactments, poetic recitations, and staged performances that all attest to the complexities of racial and sexual relations within gay subculture urges us to adopt the position of "brother" for ourselves, at least for the duration of the film. We are invited to experience what it feels like to occupy the subjective, social position of a black, gay male, such as Marlon Riggs himself.

Just as a feminist aesthetic may strive to move audience members, regardless of their actual gender and sexual orientation, into the subjective position of a feminist character's perspective on the world, performative documentary seeks to move its audience into subjective alignment or affinity with its specific perspective on the world. Like earlier works such as Listen to Britain (1941), on resistance to German bombing by the British people during World War II, or Three Songs of Lenin (1934), on the mourning of Lenin's death by the Soviet people, recent performative documentaries try to give representation to a social subjectivity that joins the particular to the general, the individual to the collective, and the personal to the political.

Here, too, animation has proven a powerful tool. His Mother's Voice (1997), discussed in chapter 4, helps us grasp what it feels like to learn your son has been shot by using two different animated treatments of what might go through the mother's mind as she recounts this horrifying experience. Folman's Waltz with Bashir draws us strongly into the experience of war as a disorienting, surreal nightmare in which individual autonomy and responsibility dissolve into chaos and confusion. Chris Landreth's Ryan (2004) gives powerful visual form and emotional expressiveness to how a prominent animation artist at the National Film Board of Canada, Ryan Larkin, might see the world from his wildly schizophrenic perspective. The film is both an homage to Ryan's artistry and a lament for a life shattered by mental illness.

Paris Is Burning (Jennie Livingston, 1990). *Paris Is Burning* enters into a distinct, black, gay subculture in which young men cluster into "houses," which compete against each other in various categories of mimicry and drag at "balls." Organized partly to explain this subculture to nonparticipants, *Paris Is Burning* also immerses us performatively in the quality and texture of this world to a degree that *16 in Webster Groves* or *Dead Birds* does not.

The emotional intensities and social subjectivity stressed in performative documentary is often that of the underrepresented or misrepresented, of women and ethnic minorities, gays and lesbians. Performative documentary can act as a corrective to those films in which "We speak about them to us." They proclaim, instead, "We speak about ourselves to you," or "I speak about myself to you." Performative documentary shares a rebalancing and corrective tendency with auto-ethnography (ethnographically informed work made by members of the communities who are the traditional subjects of Western ethnography, such as the numerous tapes made by the Kayapo people of the Amazon River basin and by the Aboriginal people of Australia). It does not, however, counter error with fact, misinformation with information. Instead, performative documentaries adopt a distinct mode of representation in which gaining knowledge and understanding require an entirely different form of engagement.

Like early poetic and expository documentaries—before the observational mode placed priority on the direct filming of social encounter—performative documentary freely mixes expressive techniques that give texture and density to fiction (point-of-view shots, musical scores, renderings of subjective states of mind, flashbacks, and freeze frames, etc.) with oratorical techniques for addressing social issues that neither science nor reason can resolve.

Performative documentary approaches the poetic domain of experimental or avant-garde cinema but gives, finally, less emphasis to the self-contained formal rhythms and tones of the film or video. Its expressive dimension refers us back to the historical world for its ultimate meaning. We continue to recognize the historical world by means of familiar people and places (Langston Hughes, Detroit cityscapes, the San Francisco Bay Bridge, and so on) and the testimony of others (participants in *Tongues Untied* who describe the experiences of black, gay men; the personal voice-over confidences of Ngozi Onwurah about her relationship to her mother in *The Body Beautiful*; and Jonathan Caouette's harrowing home movie footage of his mother and himself as they struggled to maintain their dignity and sanity in a hostile universe).

The world as represented by performative documentaries becomes, however, suffused by evocative tones and expressive shadings that constantly remind us that the world is more than the sum of the visible evidence we derive from it. An early, partial example of the performative mode, Alain Resnais's *Night and Fog* (1955), about the Holocaust, makes this point vividly. The film's voice-over commentary and images of illustration nominate *Night and Fog* for the expository mode, but the haunting, personal quality of the commentary moves it toward the performative. The film is less about history than memory, less about history from above—what happened when and why—and more about history from below—what one person might experience and what it might feel like to undergo that experience. Through the elliptic, evocative tone of the commentary by Jean Cayrol, a survivor of Auschwitz, *Night and Fog* sets out to represent the unrepresentable:

Night and Fog (Nuit et brouillard) (Alain Resnais, 1955). Much of the footage presented in Night and Fog was shot by concentration camp officers, then discovered after the war by the Allies. Alain Resnais compiles this footage into a searing testimony to the horrors of inhumanity. His film offers far more than visual evidence of Nazi atrocities. It urges us to remember, and never forget, what happened long ago in these camps. It links the past to the present and gives to memory the burden of sustaining a moral conscience.

the sheer inconceivability of acts that defy all reason and all narrative order. Visible evidence abounds—of belongings and bodies, of victims and survivors—but the voice of Night and Fog extends beyond what evidence confirms: it calls for an emotional responsiveness from us that acknowledges how understanding this event within any preestablished frame of reference is an utter impossibility (even as we may arrive at a judgment of the heinous monstrosity of such genocide).

In a similar spirit, Hungarian filmmaker Péter Forgács has described his goal as not to polemicize, not to explain, not to argue or judge, so much as to evoke a sense of what past experiences were like for those who lived them. His extraordinary documentaries are made from home movies reorganized into performative representations of

Free Fall (Péter Forgács, 1996). Péter Forgács relies entirely on found footage, in this case, home movies from the 1930s and 1940s. Such footage reveals life as it was seen and experienced at a given time. Forgács reworks the footage, cropping images, slowing down motion, adding titles and music, to combine a sense of historical perspective with a form of emotional engagement. The result is quite poetic, radically different in tone from the classic World War II documentaries in an expository mode such as the *Why We Fight* series. *Photos courtesy of Péter Forgács.*

the social turmoil caused by World War II: *Free Fall* (1997), recounts the life of a successful Jewish businessman in the 1930s, Gyorgy Peto, who is eventually caught up in Germany's decision, late in the war, to apply their "final solution" to Hungarian Jews.

By focusing on specific events, seen from the viewpoint of a participant rather than a historian, Forgács suggests something about the overall tone of the war: he suggests how, for some participants, the war hovered on the horizon, seemingly at a remove from everyday pleasures and distractions. We, with benefit of hindsight, know better. Forgács maintains a strong level of suspense by means of this disparity in knowledge. Gyorgy Peto's life is destined to fall apart. We know and he doesn't. This alone is a potent way of invoking the power of history performatively: we experience what it feels like to have historical knowledge and yet also realize we cannot alter what has already come to pass.

Forgács leaves evaluation and judgment to us but postpones this kind of reflection while we experience a more directly subjective encounter with these historical events. He invokes affect over effect, emotion over reason, not to reject analysis and judgment but to place them on a different basis. Like Resnais, Vertov, and Kalatozov before him, and like so many of his contemporaries, Forgács sidesteps readymade positions and prefabricated categories. He invites us, as all great documentarians do, to see the world afresh and to rethink our relation to it. Performative documentary restores a sense of magnitude to the local, specific, and embodied. It animates the personal so that it may become our port of entry to the political.

We can summarize this general sketch of the six modes of documentary representation in the Table 7.1. As already discussed, the modes are not a genealogy and the table is not a family tree. It only suggests how each mode possesses distinct qualities, qualities that are sometimes a matter of emphasis more than hard and fast distinctions. The qualities of each mode, along with the models that filmmakers also adopt, provide a rich toolbox of resources from which to fashion distinctive new documentaries.

TABLE 7.1. Some Specific Qualities of Documentary Modes

Quality	Expository	Poetic	Observational	Participatory	Reflexive	Performative
An Alternative To	Fiction/avant-garde	Fiction/exposition	Classic oration and poetic expression	Passive observation and classic oration	Realist representation that ignores the formal process of representing the world or social assumptions about the nature of the world	Empirical, factual, or abstract forms of knowledge
Limited By	Didacticism	Formal abstractions that lose touch with historical reality	What occurs in front of the camera (hard to represent historical events)	May cede control and point of view to others, lose independence of judgment	Increased sense of formal abstraction, detachment, loss of direct engagement with social issues	Personal pov or vision may become private or dissociated from more broadly social perceptions
Treats Knowledge As	Disembodied or abstract ideas, concepts, or perspectives	Affective, a new way to see and comprehend the world; see the familiar in fresh way	Tacit sense of what we learn by watching, listening, observing, and making inferences about the conduct of others	What we learn from personal interactions; what people say and do when confronted or engaged by others; what can be conveyed by interviews and other forms of encounter	Contextual. Always framed by institutional constraints and personal assumptions that can be exposed and changed; asks what we learn when we ask how we learn	Embodied. Affective and situated. What we learn from direct, experiential encounter rather than second-hand from experts or books

Sound	Expressive, used for pattern and rhythm but with filmmaker holding a high degree of control as in the expository mode	Expressive and cognitive, fully under the control of the filmmaker; no indexical link to the image it supports; often in a voice-over form	Tied to the image by the indexical link of synchronous recording. Filmmaker gives up full control of sound to record what is said and heard in a given situation; refrains from voice over	Stress the speech between filmmaker and subject, especially in interviews. Heavy reliance on sync sound but may also utilize voice over; filmmaker retains only partial creative control of sound	May meta-communicate about how communication takes place. Talk about talking about something as well as sync or nonsync sound	Often relies on filmmaker's own voice to organize the film; stress introspective, testimonial, essayistic forms of speech and dialogue. Mixes sync and nonsync; uses music and sound expressively
Time and Space	Discontinuous. Uses images that build mood or pattern without full regard for their original proximity	Discontinuous. Uses images from many different times and places to illustrate a perspective or argument	Continuous. Strong sense of continuity that links the words and actions of subjects from shot to shot	Continuous. May interconnect a present tense time and space with a past tense (historical time and space)	Contextualized. Draw attention to how time and space may be manipulated by systems of continuity or discontinuity	Varies according to the expressive goals. May stylize time and space to emphasize its affective dimension
Ethical Concerns	Use of actual people, places, and things without regard for their individual identity; may distort or exaggerate for aesthetic effect	Historical accuracy and verifiability; fair representation of others, avoid making people into helpless victims; develop the viewer's trust	Passive observation of dangerous, harmful, or illegal activity can lead to serious difficulties for subjects. Questions of responsibility toward subjects can become acute	Manipulate or goad others into confessions or actions they may regret; a strong responsibility to respect the rights and dignity of subjects. Questions of manipulation and distortion arise	Use or abuse subjects to pose questions that are those of the filmmaker and not the subjects	Degree of honesty and self-scrutiny vs. self-deception; misrepresentation or distortion of larger issues, lapses into wholly idiosyncratic
A Voice Characterized By	An expressive desire to give new forms and fresh perspectives to the world represented	Classic oration in pursuit of the truth and seeking to inform and move an audience	Patience, modesty, self-effacing. Willingness to let audience decide for itself about what it sees and hears	Engagement, strong investment in the encounter with others or in presenting a historical perspective	Self-questioning, a voice of doubt, even radical doubt about the certainty or fixity of knowledge	Strongly personal, engaged orator pursuing the truth of what it feels like to experience the world in a particular way

8   How Have Documentaries Addressed Social and Political Issues?

PEOPLE AS VICTIMS OR AGENTS

When we first asked "What to do with people?" in chapter 2, our discussion fell primarily within an ethical frame. What consequences follow from different forms of response to and engagement with others? How may we represent or speak about others without reducing them to stereotypes, pawns, or victims? Similar questions arose in the discussion of the observational and participatory modes. These questions allow few easy answers, but they also suggest that the issues are not ethical alone. To act unethically or to misrepresent others involves politics and ideology as well.

In a harsh critique of the documentary tradition, especially as represented by television journalism, Brian Winston argues that 1930s documentary filmmakers in Great Britain took a romantic view of their working-class subjects; they failed to see the worker as an active, self-determining agent of change. Instead, the worker suffered from a "plight" that others, namely government agencies, should do something about.

Housing Problems (1935), for example, gave slum dwellers the opportunity to speak for themselves, in a synchronous sound interview format set within their own homes. The words of actual workers appeared on British screens for the first time, a sensational achievement in the days long before television or reality TV. But they appeared as if they came with hat in hand, to explain their miserable living conditions politely in the hopes that someone else would agree to do something about it. (*Housing Problems* had the Gas Light and Coke Company as a sponsor since government slum clearance, the proposed "solution" to the workers' plight, served the company's own interests of ultimately increasing gas consumption.) There was less militancy than supplication. The stage was set for a politics of charitable benevolence.

As Winston notes, the urge to represent the worker romantically or poetically, within an ethics of social concern and charitable empathy, denied the worker a sense of equal status with the filmmaker. The filmmaker kept control of the act of representation; collaboration was not in the air. A professional corps of filmmakers would go about representing others in accord with their own ethics and their own institutional mandate as government-sponsored propagandists, in the case of John Grierson and his colleagues, and as film and television journalists in the "tradition of the victim" that Winston argues followed from this example. A few years of such films and "The worker would stand revealed as the central subject of the documentary, anonymous and pathetic, and the director of victim documentaries would be as much of an 'artist' as any other filmmaker" ("The Tradition of the Victim in Griersonian Documentary," in Alan Rosenthal, ed., *New Challenges for Documentary*, p. 274).

Parenthetically, we should note that this "tradition," if that is the right word for a form of class prejudice, did not prevail everywhere or with everyone. As we shall see later in the chapter, the 1920s and 1930s Film and Photo Leagues of various nations chose displays of worker resistance such as strikes and protests for their subject matter, and Joris Ivens and Henri Storck made their own clearly partisan and highly activist account of a Belgian coal mine strike, *Misère au Borinage* (1934), as an act of solidarity with the defiant workers. It is a precursor to Barbara Kopple's Oscar-winning documentary, *Harlan County, U.S.A.* (1977). Stephanie Black's *Life and Debt* (2001) continues the practice of granting agency to presumed victims: it is those Jamaicans whose livelihood is crippled by IMF (International Monetary Fund) and World Bank lending practices who explain how stringent rules leave locally raised or grown food unable to compete with inferior food products from abroad, devastating the economy and building a negative balance of trade. They are just as articulate as and much more honest than the well-heeled IMF spokesman who sees the fund's intervention only as a long-term good, with no need to ameliorate its at least short-term devastation. It is a far cry from the supplicating innocence embedded in *Housing Problems*. The target of Winston's ire is less independent documentaries and more those government- or network-television-sponsored reports that prefer to present workers as docile and helpless but needy.

For Winston one question constitutes a litmus test for the politics of documentary representation: "But if it is the case that housing problems are unaffected by fifty years of documentary effort, what justification can there be for continuing to make such films and tapes?" Winston notes that a failure to achieve social change was not inevitable; it stemmed from the politics of representation put into practice:

> There was nothing, though, in this ambition to be the propagandists for a better and more just society (shared by the entire documentary movement) that would inevitably lead to the constant, repetitive, and ultimately pointless exposure of the same set of social problems on the televisions of the West night after night. . . . Benchmarks were thereby established for all subsequent work both in film and in television for the entire English-speaking world and beyond. ("Victim," p. 270)

We may take exception to the blanket condemnation of documentary and to the assumption that more radical documentaries alone would solve issues such as housing problems, or, conversely, that the failure to solve pressing issues necessarily demonstrates the impotence of those documentaries that attempt to represent them, without regard to other social and political forces at work in a given historical moment. The degree of activism among workers, the political balance of power in government, the policies and actions of industries implicated in the question of housing, for example, would all have significant bearing— as much as, if not more than, the rhetorical persuasiveness and political efficacy of documentaries on this issue. We can agree, however, that the politics of representation locates documentaries within a larger arena of social debate and contestation. A regard for ethics entails a regard for political, and ideological, consequences as well.

All documentaries have a voice of their own, but not all documentary voices address social and political issues directly. (Poetic documentaries may seem far removed from social issues; this may be a political choice on one level, but it shifts our primary attention to other considerations.) We will look here at some of those documentaries that do address the political directly. These are films such as *Housing Problems; Coal Face* (1935); and *Smoke Menace* (1937), among the British documentaries of the 1930s, for example, and *Sicko* (2007); *Enron: The Smartest Guys in the Room* (2005); and *Trouble the Water* (2008) that enter into the ongoing debates of the day about social values and beliefs more than about accepted facts or poetic visions.

CONSTRUCTING NATIONAL IDENTITY

Among the many specific debates that documentaries have addressed over their history, we will focus on the construction of nationality and nationalism, and on the relation of documentary filmmaking to the interests of governments in power and to the interests of the dispossessed. Karl Marx once said, "They [the working class] cannot represent themselves; they must be represented." This is a statement to which much documentary film and video production by those who have been the presumed "victims" of the documentary tradition—women, ethnic minorities, gays and lesbians, Third World peoples—gives the lie.

The construction of national identities involves the construction of a sense of community. "Community" invokes feelings of common purpose and mutual respect, of reciprocal relationships closer to family ties than contractual obligations. Shared values and beliefs are vital to a sense of community, whereas contractual relationships can be carried out despite differences of value and belief. A sense of community often seems like an "organic" quality that binds people together when they share a tradition, culture, or common goal. As such it may seem far removed from issues of ideology, where competing beliefs struggle to win our hearts and minds.

On the other hand, the most insidious forms of ideology may be precisely the ones that make community seem natural, or organic. We seldom pause to give careful consideration to such questions as: Who do we choose to emulate or identify with, and why? Who do we choose as objects of sexual desire, or love, and why? Who do we choose to join with as members of a community, and why? The need for role models, loved ones, and social belonging seems profoundly human. These forms of interdependence "just happen," or so it seems.

And yet, within different societies, at different points in time, individuals enter into very different forms of relationships with one another. Whatever basic drives or needs are involved, they take a variety of concrete forms, and these forms seem, at least in modern times, susceptible to social construction. Be it a bill of rights or a five-year plan, a benign despotism or a competitive spirit, ideologies come into play to provide stories, images, and myths that promote one set of values over others. The sense of community always comes at the price of alternative values and beliefs deemed deviant, subversive, or illegal. The politics of documentary film production address the ways in which this work helps give tangible expression to the values and beliefs that build, or contest, specific forms of social belonging, or community, at a given time and place.

Take the Soviet cinema of the 1920s, for example. All filmmaking depended on state support after the Russian Revolution of 1917. Like the Soviet art movement known as Constructivism, Soviet cinema explored how film could serve the revolutionary aspirations of the moment: How could it represent the "new man" of communist society; how could it construct a distinct culture freed from bourgeois tradition; how could it transcend old class divisions in the cities, near-feudal relations in the country, and parochial loyalties in the various republics to foster a sense of community revolving around the *union* of Soviet socialist republics and the leadership of the Communist Party?

Answers varied but, on the whole, Soviet cinema adopted a strongly rhetorical means of expression. Persuasive styles and forms predominated, and few were more persuasive in their advocacy of specific strategies than Sergei Eisenstein and Dziga Vertov. Eisenstein's theory of montage and Vertov's ideas about editing insisted on the necessity for the filmmaker to juxtapose images, or shots, in ways that jarred the viewer into achieving new insights. Fragments of what could be put before the camera, combined into a vision of the new, of what the filmmaker, like other members of a new society, could fashion in the moment. Eisenstein more than Vertov relied on narrative structure to tell stories of social transformation. He reenacted historical events and invented composite or typical ones. His work inspired many but his achievement has been assigned, oddly enough, primarily to the development of narrative fiction film. This comes at the expense of his formative contribution to the expressive and poetic qualities of documentary, a contribution as great as Vertov's. Eisenstein may well have been surprised to find himself considered mainly a fiction film-maker by later generations: like early documentarians in other countries, Eisenstein's films, such as *Strike* (1925), *Battleship Potemkin* (1925), *October* (1927), and *The Old and the New* (1929), set out to give tangible expression to a sense of community in the process of construction. He celebrates masses of people joining together to achieve goals unattainable by any other means. There was little in basic intent to separate him from more avowedly pure documentarists like Dziga Vertov.

Vertov, like the observational filmmakers of the 1960s, eschewed all forms of scripting, staging, acting, or reenacting. He exaggerated his differences with Eisenstein since Eisenstein relied on narrative principles to a greater degree. Vertov wanted to catch life raw-handed and then to assemble from it a vision of the new society in the process of emergence. His own term for the cinema, *kinopravda* (film truth), insisted on a radical break with all forms of theatrical, literary structure for film: these forms depended on narrative structures that crippled the potential of cinema to help construct a new visual reality and, with it, a new social reality. His forty-three weekly newsreels made in 1918–1919 on current events, his *kinopravda* series of reports on life in the postrevolutionary Soviet Union (1923–1925), his first feature-length film, *Kino Glaz* (a.k.a. *Kino-Eye*; 1924), and his best-known film, *The Man with a Movie Camera* (1929) all attest to his belief that the cinema could *see* a world invisible to the human eye and help bring such a world into existence.

Cinema and revolution go hand in hand. As Vertov himself put it,

> I am kino-eye, I create a man more perfect than Adam, I create thousands of different people in accordance with preliminary blue-prints and diagrams of different kinds.
> I am kino-eye.
> From one person I take the hands, the strongest and most dexterous, from another I take the legs, the swiftest and most shapely; from a third, the most beautiful and expressive head—and through montage I create a new, perfect man. ("Kinoks: A Revolution" [1923], in Annette Michelson, ed., *Kino-Eye: The Writings of Dziga Vertov*, p. 17)

Kino-eye is understood as "that which the eye doesn't see,"
as the microscope and telescope of time . . .
[as] "life caught unawares," etc. etc.

All these different formulations were mutually complementary,
since implied in kino-eye were:

- all cinematic means,
- all cinematic inventions,
- all methods and means that might serve to reveal and show the truth.
- Not kino-eye for its own sake, but truth through the means and possibilities of film-eye, i.e., kinopravda ["film truth"].
- Not "filming life unawares," for the sake of the "unaware," but in
  order to show people without masks, without makeup, to catch them
  through the eye of the camera in a moment when they are not acting,
  to read their thoughts, laid bare by the camera.
- Kino-eye as the possibility of making the invisible visible, the unclear
  clear, the hidden manifest, the disguised overt, the acted nonacted,
  making falsehood into truth.
- Kino-eye as the union of science with newsreel to further the battle
  for the communist decoding of the world, as an attempt to show the
  truth on the screen—Film-truth. ("The Birth of Kino-Eye" [1923], in
  Michelson, pp. 41–42)

Vertov did not need to coin a word like "documentary," since he
believed that his films embodied the essence of cinema, not the traits
of a genre. For Vertov *all true cinema* fell under the banner of kino-eye
and *kinopravda*. Ironically, the term *kinopravda* returned to common
use through the homage paid to Vertov by Jean Rouch and Edgar
Morin when they named their new form of documentary filmmaking
cinéma vérité (French for *kinopravda*), as a *type* (or mode) of documentary, rather than as an all-inclusive category. A term that had begun
with Vertov as the definition of all true cinema became associated not
only with the more delimited area of one genre, documentary, but also
with the further delimited mode of participatory documentary!

Kino-eye contributed to the construction of a new society by demonstrating how the raw materials of everyday life as caught by the
camera could be synthetically reconstructed into a new order. Vertov
did not return to the historical past since that demanded reenactment
with costumes, scripts, and performances. He favored the compilation films of Esther Shub to the reconstructions of historical events

by Eisenstein, Dovzhenko, Pudovkin, and others, but even more he favored discovering situations and events in the present that could be refashioned to reveal the shape of the future.

Vertov, like many artists of the early twentieth century, held great reverence for technologies of the machine and for radical experimentation with traditional forms. In his hands, a reverence for the perfection of the kino-eye facilitated the construction of a Soviet community that gave priority to collectivity over individuality, change over stasis, and unity as one nationality, with one central leader (Lenin, then Stalin). His dedication to formal innovation, though, would cause him, and most of the other leading figures of Soviet cinema and Constructivist art, increasing difficulty in the late 1920s and early 1930s as the state began to impose a more accessible, and formulaic, style of representation that came to be known as "Socialist Realism" (a return to linear narratives, recognizable characters with familiar psychological profiles, and themes of heightened consciousness that prompt heroes to dedicate themselves to "the people" and the state). By 1939, Vertov lacked the state sponsorship that was necessary to make a film. As he recorded in his diary of that year,

> I feel as if I'm way at the bottom. Facing the first step of a long, steep staircase. My violin lies at the very top, on the landing. I move the bow . . . on air. I ask to be allowed to get my violin. I climb onto the first step. But the person in charge of the step pushes me aside and asks: "Where are you going?"
>
> I point to my bow and explain that my violin's up there. "But what do you plan to play on the violin? Tell us, describe it to us. We'll discuss it; we'll correct it; we'll add to it; we'll coordinate it with the other steps; we'll reject or confirm it."
>
> I say that I'm a composer. And I write not with words, but with sounds.
>
> Then they ask me not to worry.
>
> And take away my bow.

Perhaps they handed the bow to John Grierson. Grierson, along with Flaherty, is often called the father of documentary, a term he is credited with coining in a review of Flaherty's *Moana* [1926]; Vertov had little need for such a word since his theory encompassed all of cinema. He persuaded the British government to do with film in 1930 what the Soviet government had done: make use of an art form to fos-

The River (Pare Lorentz, 1937). The power of the river is matched by the power of the voice over. Soon, we are told, the turbulent violence of floods will yield to the harnessing power of dams, thanks to federal sponsorship of the Tennessee Valley Authority. *Photo courtesy of the National Archives.*

ter a sense of national identity and shared community commensurate with its own political agenda. By establishing a film unit at the Empire Marketing Board from 1930 to 1933 and then at the Government Post Office (G.P.O.) from 1933, Grierson gave the documentary film an institutional base, cultivated a community of practitioners, championed selected forms of documentary convention, and encouraged a specific set of audience expectations.

Grierson extended his example first to Canada, where he became the first film commissioner of the National Film Board of Canada in 1939, and then to the United Nations, where he served as coordinator of mass media for UNESCO in 1947. The model of government sponsorship for documentary film spread to numerous other countries, including the United States, initially through the single-minded de-

The River (Pare Lorentz, 1937). "A year's income" hangs in the balance. The soft, dry, hard-to-gather cotton contrasts with the wild fury of the river. *The River* personalizes the issue of conservation by profiling the "little guy" rather than the larger business interests that also seek the benefits of flood control. And, as in *The City*, the "little guy" cannot do for himself what the government must do for him. *Why We Fight*, seeking to motivate men to go to war, will restore a sense of populist initiative that these films in support of the New Deal opted to de-emphasize. *Photo courtesy of the National Archive.*

termination of Pare Lorentz, who produced *The Plow That Broke the Plains* (1936) and *The River* (1937) for different government agencies, and later, thanks to World War II, through the efforts of converted Hollywood filmmakers like Frank Capra (the *Why We Fight* series, 1942–1945), John Ford (*The Battle of Midway*, 1942), Alfred Hitchcock (*Bon Voyage* and *Aventure Malgache*, both 1944), and John Huston (*Report from the Aleutians*, 1943, and *The Battle of San Pietro*, 1945).

John Grierson, like Pare Lorentz, shied away from the formal or poetic innovation of Dziga Vertov or the European avant-garde generally to stress the role of the documentary filmmaker as orator. These were films designed to enter into the arena of social policy and to orient or predispose public opinion to preferred solutions. From slum clearance in *Housing Problems* to combat in *Prelude to War* (1941), the first of the seven-part *Why We Fight* series, these films strove to orient the viewer toward a particular perspective on the world that called for national consensus on the values and beliefs advanced by the film. The government of the nation-state served the common good, and the common man should therefore serve the government with diligence and good faith. Such efforts affirmed a sense of national identity and inclusive community. Individuals joined in common cause to uphold treasured ideals, as specific films attest, such as *Coal Face*, made by Alberto Cavalcanti in 1935 for the G.P.O. film unit under Grierson as a respectful homage to the working-class men who mine the coal that underpins Britain's industrial power, and *The River*, made by Pare Lorentz in 1937 for the Farm Security Administration with its promotion of the Tennessee Valley Administration as the solution to the problem of destructive flooding and a desperate need for rural electrical power.

John Grierson often defined his position in contrast to the romantic idealism of Robert Flaherty. He addressed the issues of the contemporary world and promoted a commonsensical approach to nationalism and community rather than a reverence for the qualities of a bygone world and a mythical vision of kinship and affinity. Grierson's contribution to documentary represented not only a more practical, hard-headed approach to social issues but also a more conservative version of Soviet film aesthetics. Rather than fostering the revolutionary potential of the dispossessed of the world, Grierson promoted the ameliorative potential of parliamentary democracy and government intervention to ease the most pressing issues and most serious abuses of a social system that remained fundamentally unquestioned. This ameliorative impulse no doubt contributes to the "tradition of the victim" described by Brian Winston.

John Grierson also disparaged but left unchallenged the economic dominance of feature fiction filmmaking. He saw documentary as a morally superior alternative to fiction: not quite as entertaining, but better for us. Made-up stories and poetic experimentation had their place, but on a lower rung of a culture's totem pole. Grierson aligned his concept of documentary with social purpose and public policy, eliminating Vertov's more inclusive claim for kino-eye as *the* essential element to *all* true cinema, not just documentary.

The expansiveness and power of Soviet film theory narrowed into a set of issues surrounding a more limited sense of what documentary as a nonfiction genre could mean or do. The construction of a sense of community and national identity revolved around the coordination of individual aspiration with government policies and priorities by means of a documentary form stripped of its boldest ambitions. John Grierson gave us our prototypical image of the documentary film that, handled with the invention and sensitivity of an Alberto Cavalcanti, Basil Wright, or Humphrey Jennings, could be a thing of beauty but more often became, in the hands of government and corporate-sponsored hacks, a thing of tedious didacticism.

CONTESTING THE NATION-STATE

John Grierson gave his vision of documentary film form a level of prominence and respectability but at a cost not all filmmakers were willing to pay. Other filmmakers proposed a sense of community based on actions, and changes, that governments seemed unprepared to accept, or make. Their films took up positions that opposed the policies of governments and industries. These filmmakers constituted the political avant-garde of documentary filmmaking.

In the United States, such activity traces back to the efforts of the Workers' Film and Photo Leagues of the 1920s and 1930s, which produced information about strikes and other topical issues from the perspective of the working class. Aligned with the Communist Party, similar leagues arose in Britain, Japan, the Netherlands, and France. They adopted a participatory mode of filmmaking, consistently identifying and collaborating with their worker-subjects, thus avoiding the risk of portraying them as powerless victims. This was a cinema of empowerment that sought to contribute to the radical social movements of the 1930s and to build community from a grass-roots, oppositional level rather than from a top-down, governmentally orchestrated one.

Individuals who had their beginnings in the Film and Photo League broke away in the mid-1930s to form other organizations dedicated to producing films of greater ambition than the sometimes perfunctory newsreels of the league. Figures from writers like Lillian Hellman and Clifford Odets to filmmakers like Leo Hurwitz and Joris Ivens lent their support to this effort. Frontier Films, for example, produced *Heart of Spain* (1937), to garner support for the Republican cause in the Spanish Civil War as the government struggled but failed to prevent a right-wing military coup. Contemporary Historians, a more ad hoc group of supporters from John Dos Passos to Ernest Hemingway, sponsored the production of Joris Ivens's powerful documentary *The Spanish Earth* (1937) for the same cause.

Joris Ivens can, in fact, be regarded as another one of the many possible "fathers" of documentary, alongside Louis Lumière, Esther Shub, Dziga Vertov, John Grierson, and Robert Flaherty, but his career, which began illustriously with the poetic, experimental films *The Bridge* (1928) and *Rain* (1929), almost disappeared from sight after World War II, when his political beliefs took him to the other side of the Iron Curtain. Ivens made numerous films in Russia (*Komosol*, 1932), East Germany (*Song of the Rivers*, 1954), North Vietnam (*The Seventeenth Parallel*, 1968), and the People's Republic of China (*Before Spring*, 1958; *How Yukong Moved the Mountains*, 1976; *Tale of the Wind*, 1988). They form little or no part of standard documentary histories in the West, although most of them possess the same degree of artistic merit as his earlier works. To this day Ivens is a revered figure in China, for example, for his epic and still powerful series about the now discredited Cultural Revolution, *How Yukong Moved the Mountains*. Revealingly, the Internet Movie Database (IMDB) website, which is usually very comprehensive in its coverage of filmmakers, has no information about this series of films at all. Like other work by Ivens it remains a victim of cold war politics.

For Ivens, collaboration proved an essential ingredient to his filmmaking practice. Those forms of rehearsal, reenactment, or staging that might disconcert Vertov were of real value to Ivens if they enhanced the sense of collective effort and common cause forged in the heat of social conflict. (It was not until *after* the advent of observational filmmaking in the 1960s that these practices became subject to intense criticism; reflexive and performative documentaries have restored them to the filmmaker's repertoire.) In making *Misère au Borinage*, in collaboration with Belgian filmmaker Henri Storck, for example, about a massive coal-mine strike in the Borinage region of Belgium, Ivens came to realize that capturing "life unawares" was not enough: one also had to guard against the artistic norms that might color a filmmaker's perspective and diminish his political voice. As Ivens notes in his book, *The Camera and I,*

> When the clean-cut shadow of the barracks window fell on the dirty rags and dishes of a table the pleasant effect of the shadow actually destroyed the effect of dirtiness we wanted, so we broke the edges of the shadow. Our aim was to prevent agreeable photographic effects distracting the audience from the unpleasant truths we were showing. . . . There have also been cases in the history of documentary when photographers became so fascinated by dirt that the result was the dirt looked interesting and strange, not something repellent to the cinema audience. The filmmaker must be indignant and angry about the waste of people before he can find the right camera angle on the dirt and on the truth. (p. 87)

This gritty realism culminates in the final scene of the film, when the workers reenact a protest march that had taken place before Ivens and Storck arrived. Not only did the workers collaborate by determining the exact nature of the march, they found themselves reexperiencing the sense of community or solidarity they had experienced in the original march! The participatory *act* of filming helped bring about the very sense of community Ivens wanted to represent. It is this sense of collective solidarity that Jon Silver also ignited when he enlisted the workers in his effort to film inside their union hall in *Watsonville on Strike* (1989), discussed in chapter 3.

Ivens and Storck collaborated not with the government, or the police, but with the very people whose misery no government had yet addressed, let alone eliminated. Their participatory involvement helped generate the very qualities they sought to document, not as spectacle to fascinate aesthetically and subdue politically, like *Triumph of the Will* (1935), but as activism to engage aesthetically and transform politically. A cinema of oratory made in collaboration with the "wretched of the earth" claimed a solid foundation that would go on to support numerous other examples of politically engaged filmmaking from the other side of the barricades.

Constructing consensus along the lines of national identity, be it in affirmation of or in opposition to established governments, played a defining role in the first few decades of documentary. Many early ethnographic filmmaking efforts partook of a similar perspective in relation to other cultures. All these efforts tended to categorize individuals in ways that minimized individuality and maximized typicality: shots of specific people stood for larger qualities, a trend partly encouraged by the difficulty of recording sync sound and partly by a preference for political generalization and poetic expressiveness. In ethnography, voice-over commentary or poetic editing techniques identified individual behavior as representative or typical and thereby turned our attention to the characteristics of the culture as a whole. *Trance and Dance in Bali* (1952), *Les Maîtres Fous* (1955), *Dead Birds* (1963), and *The Hunters* (1957), for example, follow the example of *Nanook of the North* (1922) in treating the individual as gateway to a unified, homogenized sense of community and culture. Along with "national identity" comes "national character" as a reductive, melting-pot idea; ethnography suffered from it as much as state-sponsored documentaries did.

But an alternative conception of individuals and the community to which they belong stands in opposition to this reductionism and the stereotyping to which it is susceptible. Communities do not align themselves perfectly with nation-states; differences remain and distinguish the one from the many, subcultures from the dominant culture, minorities from the majority. The melting pot remains only partially blended. Communities of descent—ethnic identities inherited from generation to generation despite diaspora and exile, and communities of consent—collective identities formed by an active choice to adopt and defend the practices and values of a given group, also gain representation. They serve as evidence of the mythic dimension to claims of full equality and the assumptions of a nationalism that knows no differences of race, class, or color.

The work of some filmmakers questioned the ideology of a singular national character and a transcendental national purpose. They sought radical change more than social amelioration. From the Film and Photo League's reports on hunger marches in the 1930s to Luis Buñuel's *Land without Bread* (1932), these filmmakers rejected Grierson's willingness to work for governments rather than challenge them. *Land without Bread*, for example, drew attention to a region of misery outside the norms acceptable to the Spanish government (they banned the film for many years); Leo Hurwitz's *Strange Victory* (1948) questioned the

Borinage (a.k.a. *Misère au Borinage,* Joris Ivens and Henri Storck, 1934). In contrast to Jill Godmilow in *Far from Poland,* Joris Ivens was able to be there, on location, during a coal mine strike. But he, too, opts for reenactment, in this case to shoot a strikers' march that had already occurred. Ivens has no desire to be reflexive and draw attention to the problems of representation. On the contrary, that the workers regained their sense of militant spirit during the reenactment added a level of authenticity to the filming that Ivens fully endorsed. The intensity of emotion during the reenactment itself blurs the distinction between history and re-creation, document and representation, in ways that point to the formative power of the documentary filmmaker. *Photo courtesy of the European Foundation Joris Ivens.*

victorious postwar mood of triumph over fascism when class conflict and racial discrimination remained an entrenched fact of American life, and Joris Ivens's *Indonesia Calling* (1946) supported the Indonesian independence movement against the colonial rule of the Netherlands (the film made him unwelcome in his native land for years afterward).

The 1960s and 1970s brought this tendency to represent "history from below"—from the point of view of those who remained marginalized and dispossessed—to even sharper focus. The most notable example of collective filmmaking, for example, is the American filmmaking group called Newsreel. With highly active filmmaking centers in New York and San Francisco and distribution support in several other cities, Newsreel made or distributed dozens of films from 1967 onward that reported on the war in Vietnam, draft resistance, college strikes (at Columbia University and San Francisco State), national liberation movements around the world, and the women's movement.

Newsreel films identified themselves with a logo composed of a flickering machine gun with the word "Newsreel" emblazoned on its side. There was no doubt that these were agit-prop films, like the early newsreels of Dziga Vertov in 1918–1919. The films strove to foster political resistance to government actions and policies. They bore no individual credits. The effort was a collective one, and the idea of an individual artistic vision came second to the commitment of the group to a radical political position. San Francisco Newsreel went so far as to set up a rotating work plan, where members would take jobs for a period of time and pool their earnings to support the group and its film-making initiatives. Distributing their own films and showing them on campuses, in community centers, and on the walls of buildings, prior to the availability of videocassettes, DVDs, and the internet, Newsreel contributed to the grass-roots political activism of the 1960s and early 1970s. It is an important precursor to websites like MoveOn.org that mobilize political activism today.

San Francisco Newsreel's film *The Woman's Film* (1971), for example, represented the perspective of a range of working-class women on how their everyday experience gave rise to an awareness of oppression. *The Woman's Film,* made primarily by women members of the group, stands out as one of the first feminist documentaries of the postwar era. Its series of interviews coupled with scenes of each participant's everyday life confirmed women as *filmmakers* and as political activists rather than as the "victims" identified by Brian Winston as a troubling legacy of the 1930s British documentary.

BEYOND NATIONALISM: NEW FORMS OF IDENTITY

"We speak about us to you" took on a new inflection that rippled into a wide range of neglected corners of social life, from the experience of women to that of African Americans, Asian Americans, and Native Americans, Latinos and Latinas, gays and lesbians. Associated with the rise of a "politics of identity" that celebrated the pride and integrity of marginalized or ostracized groups, the voice of documentary gave memorable form to cultures and histories that had remained ignored or suppressed beneath the dominant values and beliefs of society. Standing in support of or in opposition to government policies became secondary to the more localized (and sometimes insular) task of retrieving histories and proclaiming identities that myths, or ideologies, of national unity denied. *Imagining Indians* (1993) and *Color Adjustment* (1991), for example, cast a critical eye on the misrepresentation and stereotyping of Native Americans in films and of African Americans on television, respectively. They challenged the taken-for-granted assumptions that perpetuated distorted and demeaning representations of not just these specific minorities but any minority.

This process of giving form, name, and visibility to an identity that had never known one was most vividly displayed in relation to issues of sexuality and gender, although work by African Americans and a wide variety of Fourth World people (individuals with roots in the Third World but living in the industrialized world) demonstrates a comparable vividness. *The Woman's Film* began the process, but other films arrived to buttress the women's movement with work that explored experiences of oppression, recovered lost histories, and profiled currents of change. Geri Ashur and Peter Barton's *Janie's Janie* (1971), like *The Woman's Film*, linked oppression with exploitation, sexism with economic deprivation. Like *Housing Problems* long before, these two films gave voice to working-class experience but in a sustained, participatory mode that refused to turn the disadvantaged into victims awaiting charitable assistance. Women commanded the camera's attention rather than having their voices subsumed within an argument or perspective belonging solely to the filmmaker.

By contrast, Julia Reichert and Jim Klein's *Growing Up Female* (1971) and Joyce Chopra and Claudia Weill's *Joyce at 34* (1972) deemphasized economics to present middle-class views of sexism as a primarily psychological experience that is nonetheless shared by large numbers of women. Yvonne Rainer's *A Film about a Woman Who . . .* (1974) and Chantal Ackerman's *Jeanne Dielmann, 23 Quai du Commerce, 1080 Bruxelles* (1975) pushed this aspect of feminism yet further. Their works came close to fiction in the invention of characters and situations but brought autobiographical and essayistic qualities to bear,

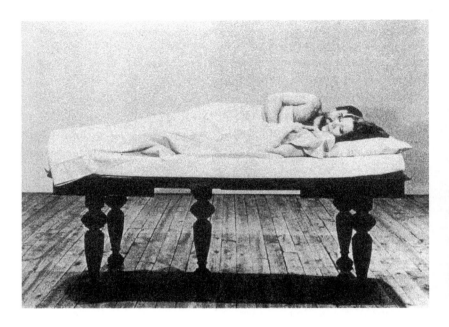

A Film about a Woman Who . . . (Yvonne Rainer, 1974). This film illustrates the subtle boundary between documentary and avant-garde films as Yvonne Rainer uses vivid stylistic techniques, carefully composed scenes, and a pointed political agenda to explore women's experience of the world. *Courtesy of Zeitgeist Films.*

including a highly performative, Brechtian style in Rainer's case and an intensely ethnographic, hyper-realist style in Ackerman's. The result in each instance was to open a window on feminist perspectives on romance and housework, objectification and self-determination that had never been seen before.

Julia Reichert, Jim Klein, and Miles Mogulescu's *Union Maids* (1976) and Lorraine Gray, Lynn Goldfarb, and Anne Bohlen's *With Babies and Banners* (1979) adopted a participatory, compilation film approach through the use of interviews and archival footage to tell the stories of labor organizing and mass strikes during the 1930s from a women's point of view. They pick up the thread of an earlier suffragette movement and carry it forward, providing valuable historical context to the story of wartime work opportunities and their postwar disappearance told in Connie Field's *The Life and Times of Rosie the Riveter* (1980).

Maquilapolis (Vicki Funari and Sergio de la Torre, 2006). This image illustrates
the participatory collaboration of filmmakers and subjects as some of the
women workers display the products of their labor. Staged and dramatic, the
image sheds light on what goes on inside the maquiladoras themselves, such
as the one in the background of the shot. *Courtesy of California Newsreel.*

These works portray the subjects and perspectives that documentaries from the 1930s had not addressed in their emphasis on the unifying
rhetoric of nation building or male-dominated forms of working-class
resistance. The dispossessed, whom Edward R. Murrow featured in
his ground-breaking television expose, *Harvest of Shame* (1960), about
migrant farmworkers in 1960, gained not only coverage but a voice in
works like Lorraine Gray's *The Global Assembly Line* (1986) and Vicki
Funari and Sergio de la Torre's *Maquilapolis* (2006). Funari and de
la Torre make a special effort not only to represent the plight of the

predominantly female workers in the maquiladoras (factories owned by multi-national corporations along the border that legally sidestep many of the basic civil rights and labor laws of both the United States and Mexico), they include two women workers in the shaping of the film. Carman Durran and Lourdes Lujan become labor activists, spurred by paltry wages, minimal benefits, rampant pollution, and indifferent management. *Maquilapolis* celebrates the conversion of potential victims into active combatants in the modern arena of global capital.

Documentaries of the early women's movement have their parallel in documentaries of the early gay and lesbian movement. Here, too, we find work that explores the experience of oppression, recovers lost histories, and profiles currents of change. The collectively made *Word Is Out* (Mariposa collective, 1977) used a series of interviews with gays and lesbians who recount their discovery of their sexuality and social resistance to it in the days before the gay rights movement took shape. A more fundamentally historical perspective on homosexual experience dominates Greta Schiller and Robert Rosenberg's *Before Stonewall: The Making of a Gay and Lesbian Community* (1984). (Stonewall was a gay bar in New York City; a "routine" police raid turned into a battle with enraged gay customers. This confrontation is used to mark the beginning of a militant gay and lesbian movement.) Here interviewees not only refer to personal experience but also adopt the voice of witnesses and experts to make perceptible the highly invisible experience of closeted gay life. The subjects are themselves members of the community they describe. They provide an insider's perspective. *Before Stonewall*, like most other films engaged with identity politics, eschews the commentary of outside experts and authorities in the classic model of sociology and journalism to turn to the self-perceptions and self-descriptions by members *of* the community that forms the film's subject.

In a similar spirit, Rob Epstein and Richard Schmiechen's Oscar-winning portrait of the first openly gay politician in San Francisco, *The Times of Harvey Milk* (1984), relies heavily on interviews and television news coverage of Milk's career as a city council member. It tells a tale of defiant resistance to stereotypes and of remarkable political skill. The indelible portrait it offers of Harvey Milk clearly played a significant role in informing how Sean Penn constructed his own representation

Nitrate Kisses (Barbara Hammer, 1992). *Nitrate Kisses* uses experimental film technique to explore the history of the representation of gay and lesbian culture in cinema. Hammer also explores dimensions of sexuality routinely suppressed, such as sexual intimacy between those who have passed beyond the "body beautiful" phase of the human life cycle. The advertising and entertainment industries would have us believe that sexual relations rarely occur before the age of 15 or after the age of 50.

Anthem (Marlon Riggs, 1991). Marlon Riggs's *Anthem* continues,
in a post-Stonewall context, what *Word Is Out* began. A stirring
celebration of gay pride, *Anthem* exemplifies the affective, emotion-
laden quality of performative documentary. As in *Tongues Untied*, Riggs
incorporates the direct, powerful poetry of Essex Hemphill, above.

of Mr. Milk for Gus Van Sant's *Milk* (2008), a fictional account of this
exceptional man.

Other works took up related themes. For example, Barbara Hammer's *Nitrate Kisses* (1992) recovers the history of doubly suppressed
homosexual experiences such as that of older lesbians and of interracial
couples. It also departs from the standardized interview format. Hammer adopts experimental film techniques along with some graphic
sexual enactments to represent the texture and subjectivity of such
experience as well as its historical outlines. *Nitrate Kisses* sketches out,
in evocative, performative terms, the qualities and texture of what the
community its subjects constructed is like. The result is closer to Péter
Forgács's *Free Fall* (1997) than to the Mariposa collective's *Word Is Out*
in its emphasis on a poetic, evocative tone of remembrance.

Tongues Untied (Marlon Riggs, 1989). Neither Marlon Riggs's previous work on stereotypical images of African Americans in popular culture (*Ethnic Notions*, 1986) nor his follow-up documentary on the representation of race on television (*Color Adjustment*, 1991) prepared viewers for *Tongues Untied*. Highly personal, poetic, and polemical, Riggs's video fractured the myth of a gay identity blind to race. With a frank acknowledgment of the impact of AIDS, on gays in general and on himself in particular, Riggs, pictured here with poet Essex Hemphill, established a visual form of testimonial statement comparable in impact to Rigoberta Menchú's written testimonial of her experience as a Guatemalan Indian, *I, Rigoberta*.

As gay film critic Tom Waugh has pointed out, it is within a performative mode of representation that gay and lesbian documentary has primarily flourished. Performance itself has been central to an understanding of gendered identity. Most thoroughly, and radically, articulated in Judith Butler's book *Gender Trouble*, the performative dimension of sexuality does not simply imply a choice of drag or camp as a parody of sexual norms but also insists on the construction of any sexual identity, straight or gay, as a performative act in which sexual identity can only be established by what one *does* rather than what one presumably *is* or *says*. This question of the flexible presentation of self in a social context where discrimination has warped the field of play makes the performative mode particularly appealing. It is a way for members of an oppressed minority to express the emotional tones that color personal experience and fuel political activism.

Jean Genet's *Un Chant d'amour* (1950), a film of lust and longing among male prisoners and their guards, shocked some audiences and outraged most censors in 1950. Along with Kenneth Anger's *Fireworks* (1947), a depiction of a young man's highly charged erotic dream, it paved the way for later, highly expressive work. Usually treated as short fictions or avant-garde works, these two films gave vivid embodiment to the performative impulse. They celebrate homoerotic desire graphically but with flourishes of imagination and defiance that proved inspirational to later filmmakers. Jan Oxenberg's pioneering lesbian film, *A Comedy in Six Unnatural Acts* (1975), for example, relies primarily on a performative mode of representation to shatter stereotypes and myths about lesbians, much to the consternation of some early viewers. Later films such as Marlon Riggs's *Tongues Untied* (1989) and *Anthem* (1991) utilize staged performance, reenactment, poetry, and confessional commentary as well as, in *Anthem*, a music video editing style to affirm the active construction of homoerotic desire and black gay identity. *Tarnation* (2003), with its almost florid use of montage and split-screen assemblies of shots to embody what it feels like to experience mental anguish and sexual confusion, is virtually unimaginable without the precedent of Genet and Anger.

In a somewhat different spirit, Jennie Livingston's *Paris Is Burning* (1990) uses a mix of the observational and participatory modes to describe the rich subculture of black and Latino "houses" of gay men who share a life that revolves around the mimicry and, often, elaborate parody of fashion, dress, and everyday "straight" behavior. Livingston enters into a subculture that has the potential for exotic representation, with its staged balls and vogueing contests. Whether she successfully avoids this potential hazard has stimulated considerable debate. The sense of participatory collaboration between filmmaker and subjects that characterizes *Tongues Untied* or *The Times of Harvey Milk* seems more muted here since Livingston's own sexual orientation remains unacknowledged and performance functions more to draw attention *to* the subject than to the relation *between* camera and subject.

Hoop Dreams (Steve James, Frederick Marx, Peter Gilbert, 1994). A publicity still for the "stars" of *Hoop Dreams.* Although pitched as a familiar, suspenseful narrative of "Will they or won't they succeed?" *Hoop Dreams* is also an extraordinary example of the filmmakers' commitment to the gradual unfolding of individual lives. Many films are shot during a few months of production, but *Hoop Dreams* was shot over a period of 6 years. *Photo courtesy of Fine Line Features.*

These performative films on gender and sexuality step away from a specific political agenda, issues of social policy, or the construction of a national identity. Instead, they enlarge our sense of the subjective dimension to "forbidden" lives and loves. Like many other works, they contribute to the social construction of a common identity among members of a given community. They give social visibility to experiences once treated as exclusively or primarily personal; they attest to a commonality of experience and to the forms of struggle necessary to overcome stereotyping, discrimination, and bigotry. The political voice of these documentaries embodies the perspectives and visions of communities that share a history of exclusion and a goal of social transformation.

At their best these documentaries generate a feeling of tension between the film and the world that stands beyond it. They convey a sense of incommensurate magnitudes: a film represents the world in ways that always leave more unsaid than said, that confesses to a failure to exhaust a topic through the mere act of representing it. The world is of a greater order of magnitude than any representation, but representations can make our awareness of this discrepancy more vivid. Experience does not boil down to explanations. It always exceeds them. We understand this intuitively. Documentaries that remain open to a difference in orders of magnitude between themselves and what they represent allow us to remain open to the real, historical process of forging a society and culture, with values and beliefs, that are never reducible to a single mold or a fixed system.

REDEFINING THE POLITICS OF IDENTITY

Documentaries that address a politics of identity also address the question of alliances and affinities among various subcultures, groups, and movements. This represents another shift from the earlier construction of national identities to the recognition of partial or hybrid identities that seldom settle into a single, permanent category. Such categories, with their elusive, variable nature, even call into question the adequacy of any notion of community that can be permanently labeled and fixed. This process of labeling aids in the creation of group identity, and pride, but it also risks producing a false sense of security or permanence. As a result, an emphasis on hybridity and diaspora, exile and displacement exists in tension with the more sharply defined contours of an identity politics.

Gay men and lesbian women, for example, also live their lives in relation to class and ethnic identities; Jews live their ethnic identity in relation to superimposed national, class, and gender identities. The model of any one fundamental identity is also put into question by the upheavals and transformations of modern history that suggest that all identities are provisional in their construction and political in their implications. To take on the primary identity of a Jew or a Bosnian, a black male or an Asian female has a contingent, political dimension to it, pegged to a specific historical context, that runs counter to any notion of a fixed or essentialized group identity. This sense of fluid, liminal boundaries that defy categories and blur identities has itself become the subject of documentary representation.

Two films about the travails of some of the young men from the war-torn Sudan who eventually find their way to the United States exemplifies this complexity: *Lost Boys of Sudan* (2003) and *God Grew Tired of Us: The Lost Boys of Sudan* (2005). The boys' national, tribal, linguistic, and religious identities are stripped away as they take up their new lives as "African" Americans, not fully accepted by the African American community and not easily embraced by all white Americans either. The earlier *Lost Boys of Sudan* pulls fewer punches in its depiction of disorientation, loneliness, and discrimination that the boys meet with a resolute sense of good will and patience. *God Grew Tired of Us* adopts a softer, more uplifting tone, exemplified, perhaps, by the choice of Nicole Kidman to provide a thoughtful commentary that reassures more than it criticizes.

In a far more reflexive vein, Chris Marker examines the experience of dislocation and displacement in his stunningly complex film *Sans Soleil* (1982). A female voice reads letters written by an itinerant film-maker, Sandor Krasna, whose experience seems an uncanny parallel for Marker's own. Images flow between Africa, Greenland, and Japan as "Krasna" tries to make some sense of the global interrelationships among nations and people and of his own fragmented encounters over many years and many films. The film refuses to identify a concrete thesis, let alone "add up" to a conclusion. Instead it works to convey the subjective experiences of cruelty and innocence, place and displace-ment, memory and time that characterize our passage through the landscape of modern events.

Trinh Minh-ha's *Surname Viet Given Name Nam* (1989) adopts a similar thesis about the instability of categories. Its complex mix of fact and fiction, of staged and unstaged scenes, of scripted and spontaneous interviews, prompts us to rethink the usefulness of any notion of docu-mentary as a form that conveys information unproblematically. The film also prompts us to rethink what it means to understand another person's life, in this case the lives of Vietnamese women in Vietnam and in the United States.

Trinh, like Marker, wants us to remember that any claim to knowl-edge that we take away comes thoroughly filtered through the *form* in which that knowledge reaches us. The style of the acted interviews with women in Vietnam gives a sense of a controlled or stage-managed performance through the careful lighting and composition, the super-imposition of printed versions of what the women say over their images, and the slow, deliberate way in which they appear to speak, or recite, their comments. The style of the interviews with the same women in their "real" roles as women living in San Jose, California, exhibits the spontaneity of interaction found in classic participatory documentaries like *Chronicle of a Summer* (1960) or *Roger and Me* (1989) through the dependence on available light, less formal, more catch-as-catch-can framing, the lack of superimposed versions of what is said, and the more rapid, unguarded manner in which the women speak.

The result, though, is less to confirm the San Jose scenes as "true" and the staged Vietnam scenes as "false" than to put on display two different forms of representation as our means of access to the historical world. Categories and concepts are our own social creation—some-times useful, sometimes a bane. People, social actors, migrate through these abstractions, including concepts of personal and collective iden-tity, in ways that attempt to pin categories down to dictionary defini-tions. That the women in *Surname Viet Given Name Nam* are from Vietnam but now belong to an immigrant community that is itself part of a war-induced displacement, or diaspora, is no coincidence: hybrid identities, provisional alliances, and a tension between past and present realities render most categories less a reassuring source of knowledge than a disturbing form of incompleteness. Trinh tries to lead us to *understand* this without falling into the trap of providing yet another category to *explain* it. It is, however, an understanding that looks at immigrant life in America far less critically than indigenous life in Vietnam: in Vietnam social oppression looms large but racism is absent; one might argue that the converse might apply in San Jose—op-portunities abound but racism persists— but there is no exploration of this in the film. Even reflexive films can have blind spots about what they take for granted.

In a similar but more familiarly personal vein, Marilu Mallet's *Unfinished Diary* (1983) stresses the experience of exile from her native Chile, which she fled after the defeat of the Allende government and the installation of a dictatorship under General Pinochet. She must learn French and adapt to Quebec customs. She must also learn Eng-

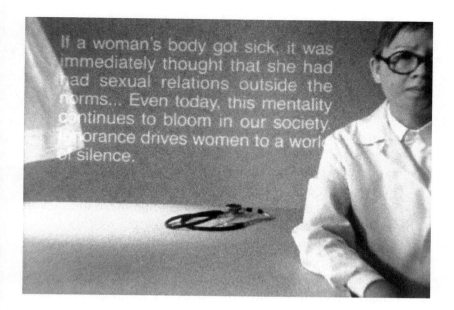

Surname Viet Given Name Nam (Trinh T. Minh-ha, 1989). Another use of "subtitles." Trinh superimposes a version of the words spoken by the interviewee simultaneously with her speech. This produces a split in our attention. This split may also heighten our awareness of the staged quality to interviews: scenes seem less "natural" when filmmakers alter the conventions to which we have grown accustomed. *Photo courtesy of Trinh T. Minh-ha.*

lish and use it in her relationship with her Australian-born husband, Canadian filmmaker Michael Rubbo. Mallet experiences daily issues of loss and exile that separate her from a feminism that assumes the stability of national identity in order to address the issues of gender hierarchy. A gap separates Mallet from those who locate themselves within other social categories. Identity, it seems, must be negotiated *across* categories as much as, if not more than, within them.

In a more direct confrontation with exile and the past, another Chilean filmmaker, Patricio Guzmán, returns to Chile from exile after the fall of the repressive Pinochet government. Guzmán had made the powerful documentary *The Battle of Chile* (1975, 1977, 1979), on the rise of President Salvador Allende, the first democratically elected socialist in Latin America. But on September 11, 1973, Allende was deposed and killed and Guzmán went into exile. *Chile, Obstinate Memory* (1997) is the story of his return. His goal is to examine the effect of some 30 years of military dictatorship on the country, especially on how the nation's history has become remembered, distorted, or forgotten. The film is a compelling exploration of this issue, utilizing interviews with participants in Allende's rise to power and with a much younger generation of Chileans who have no direct knowledge or memory of those events. Guzmán reminds us that memory itself is an arena of political struggle as different political forces strive to write the official history of what has happened and how it shapes the present.

This sketch of some of the ways in which documentary reveals a political voice has focused on the issue of community. It touched on (1) the construction of national identity in terms of a melting-pot homogeneity up through the 1950s and early 1960s, (2) the challenges to this construct associated with political confrontation (worker militancy, antiwar protests, civil rights protests) in the 1960s and 1970s, (3) the emergence of an identity politics that gave voice to suppressed minorities in the 1970s and 1980s, and, finally, (4) the acknowledgment of the hazards of categories and identities themselves in a time of catastrophic events, trauma, exile, and diaspora in the 1990s and since.

This is more a sketch than a comprehensive history of political representation in documentary. It suggests how the choices of modes of representation and topics for representation change not only from internal technological and aesthetic opportunities but also in relation to a larger historical context. Nationalism and transnational issues like global warming, identity politics, diaspora, hybridity, and exile do not originate with documentary but in society at large. Documentary filmmakers strive to find the means to represent these issues in ways that retain a sense of their magnitude in the lives of the people who confront them.

SOCIAL ISSUES AND PERSONAL PORTRAITURE

Two different emphases characterize the political voice of many of the films discussed in this chapter. These emphases present a spectrum of possibilities more than an either/or choice, and they can be found at work in all six modes of documentary representation. We can call them an emphasis on social issues and an emphasis on personal portraiture.

Social issue documentary might seem to go with the expository mode and an earlier moment in documentary, whereas personal portraiture might seem to go with observational or participatory modes and contemporary debates about the politics of identity. Even though there is a grain of truth to this generalization, both these emphases proliferate across the full range of documentary representation.

Social issue documentaries take up public issues from a social perspective. Individuals recruited to the film illustrate or provide perspective on the issue. *Why We Fight*, for example, relies on the unseen voice of Walter Huston to guide us through the complexities of World War II. No individuals presented in the films rise to the level of well-developed characters. In a radically different tone, Adam Curtis's *The Power of Nightmares: The Rise of the Politics of Fear* (2004) is a stunning reexamination of the nation-state and those who have used either the lure of fanaticism, particularly in the Middle East, or the fear of terror, mainly in the West, to advance antidemocratic agendas. Curtis relies on a style of montage editing akin to that of *Why We Fight* but with even bolder, attention-grabbing claims and juxtapositions. Individuals who have played a major role in promoting a politics of hate or fear get considerable attention but only for the political role they have played, not as rounded individuals.

Sometimes one or two individuals become the gateway to larger social issues. In this case, there may be some character development but it is often minimal since the individual's primary importance is what they can tell us about the larger issue. Errol Morris's *The Fog of War*, Oscar winner in 2003, for example, recounts a great deal of the history of the Vietnam War but exclusively from the perspective of Robert McNamara as he looks back on his role as secretary of defense. We learn only basic facts about Mr. McNamara as an individual and a great deal about his current views on his previous actions. Similarly, Alex Gibney's *Taxi to the Dark Side*, Oscar winner in 2007, explores how decisions at the highest levels of government about the use of torture as defined by the Geneva Conventions end up claiming the life of one detainee, Dilawar, a taxi driver who had no involvement in terrorism. We learn only the broad outlines of Dilawar's life but we learn a great deal about the various actions, taken by individuals from the White House to Abu Ghraib, that contributed to his death. In both cases, the larger issues take precedence over the complexities of the personal lives of the central characters.

Personal portrait films place their focus on the individual rather than the social issue. At their best they reveal the one by means of the other. It is another way to move from the specific to the general. (Some personal portraits, or biographies, will repress the political in favor of a concept of the subject as a self-contained, self-determining entity.) The films described here demonstrate an intimate connection between the personal and the political, whereas most social issue documentaries tend to assume that public issues command our attention on their own merits: the personal domain remains private or out of bounds as long as we turn our public self to the issue at hand. Works such as Péter Forgács's *Free Fall*, Marlon Riggs's *Tongues Untied*, or Carl Deal and Tia Lessin's *Trouble the Water* occupy a border zone between the extremes of either emphasis: they clearly build outward from central characters to larger issues but also flesh out their characters with considerable care.

In personal portrait documentaries if broader social issues are implicitly evoked by the film, they remain in the background. Individuals featured in the film attest to or implicitly live out the underlying issue without even necessarily identifying it. *Nanook of the North*, for example, relies on the portrait Flaherty constructs of Nanook and his family to give us a sense of what it takes to survive given the harsh realities of Eskimo culture. Jumping ahead some 80-plus years, Kimberly and Scott Roberts lived in the 9th Ward in New Orleans and Kimberly had just bought a video camera when Hurricane Katrina hit. *Trouble the Water* incorporates a great deal of her footage into its tale of how this couple and their friends survived the hurricane. There is less direct criticism of the Bush administration's actions than in Spike Lee's *When the Levees Broke* (2006), but what they must do for themselves and what government agencies fail to provide makes for a devastating critique. Foremost, though, is the portrait of two individuals and how they survived. In a similar spirit *Nobody's Business* (1996) and *Intimate Stranger* (1992) tell the complex and fascinating stories of the filmmaker's, Alan Berliner's, father and grandfather, respectively. Berliner's family members were Jewish immigrants to the United States, but these two stories do not address this larger phenomenon directly even though his father's

Trouble the Water (Carl Deal and Tia Lessin, 2008). Scott Roberts, one of the two people profiled in the film, is in desperate need of shelter as a result of Hurricane Katrina. Here he confronts a National Guard unit that denies him, and others, access to an unused school. The irony that President Kennedy had ordered out the National Guard to ensure that African American children gained access to previously all-white public schools in Alabama, in the early days of the civil rights movement, is not lost on many viewers. *Courtesy of Zeitgeist Films.*

and grandfather's values and actions remain suggestive of experiences shared by many others with similar backgrounds.

Shirley Clarke's *Portrait of Jason* (1967) allows us to unravel layers of performance and negotiation between Ms. Clarke and her subject, Jason, a black gay hustler filmed over the course of a single, protracted encounter. Her interactions with Jason and Jason's frank disclosures introduce issues of race, gender, and the filmmaker's complicity in what takes place before the camera in ways that many observational films ignore. Ms. Clarke confirmed what Jean Rouch and Edgar Morin had shown in *Chronicle of a Summer*: the relation between filmmaker and subject is a vital part of the act of representation. The film stands as a portrait of its subject and its maker and, through them, of questions of racial relations and gender politics in the 1960s.

Twenty-five years later, *Silverlake Life: The View from Here* (1993) offers a touching self-portrait of Mark Massi and Tom Joslin in what began as Tom Joslin's home movie. Simultaneously, it provides a sense of the devastation wrought upon millions of people by HIV. When the filmmaker, Mr. Joslin, dies from AIDS, the project is brought to completion by Mark Massi and a friend, Peter Friedman. Joslin's subject, Mark Massi, becomes the filmmaker, and the filmmaker, Tom Joslin, becomes the subject. This reversal reveals dimensions to both individuals that the usual separation of responsibilities masks. Through the complex portrayal of one loving relationship brought to an untimely end by the AIDS epidemic, the film raises much larger questions but only indirectly.

Not all documentaries fall neatly into one camp or the other. A considerable number of films explore larger social issues as their primary emphasis but do so through the distinct perspective of one or more individuals. Performative documentaries like *History and Memory* (1991), *Tongues Untied,* and *Who Killed Vincent Chin?* (1988) address the Japanese American internment camp experience and its repercussions, the intersection of sexual and racial identities, and the mixture of racism, sexism, and zenophobia that contribute to one man's death, respectively. They do so through strongly personal perspectives just as *The Fog of War* revisits the Vietnam War but only as remembered and explained by Robert McNamara, the film's sole subject.

Two Spirits: Sexuality, Gender and the Murder of Fred Martinez (2009) tackles the unrecognized phenomenon of two-spirited individuals (those who see themselves as both male and female) in the context of Native American culture. The film revolves around a portrait of Fred Martinez, a Navajo boy who also saw himself as a girl. He was murdered during an assault motivated by homophobia while he was still

Two Spirits: Sexuality, Gender and the Murder of Fred Martinez (Lydia Nibley, 2009). This historical photograph is one of the pieces of evidence used in the film to describe how individuals who identified as both male and female were an esteemed part of traditional Navajo culture. Their respected status places them in a category quite different from that of most gays, lesbians, bisexuals, and transsexuals in contemporary culture. *Courtesy of Lydia Nibley.*

a teenager. Around the story of Fred's own life director Lydia Nibley weaves commentaries that both link Fred's life to that of bisexuals and cross-dressers in the larger American culture and also explain how individuals who possessed "two spirits" were revered as shamans and seers in traditional Navajo culture. Their elevated status as individuals who were sought out for specific needs in earlier times is incomparable to that of individuals who possess a similar gender orientation in contemporary culture, whether Native American or not. The film's intimate portrait of Fred ripples out into an examination of the oppression that often meets those who fail to conform to social norms.

Other films adopt a similar strategy. *Born into Brothels* (2004) profiles a handful of children whose mothers are prostitutes in India, along with the filmmaker's personal efforts to help them. We learn a great deal about the children and Zana Briski, the filmmaker, but almost everything we learn relates to the broader question of how to provide a decent chance for a successful life to disadvantaged children. *Trouble the Water* puts considerable focus on the failure of all levels of government to respond effectively to the havoc caused by Hurricane Katrina but does so primarily as these failures come to bear on the lives of the two individuals it profiles: Kimberly and Scott Roberts. The selection of individuals who display psychological complexity but whose experience also vividly points to larger social issues combines the social issue and personal portrait tendencies into an effective hybrid that many documentary filmmakers have utilized.

The differences between these two main emphases is represented in Table 8.1. The task of documentaries is to move us toward a predisposition or perspective regarding some aspect of the world. This goal calls for close attention to the three Cs of credible, convincing, and compelling rhetoric. Drawing our attention to the social issues that unite and divide us as a people and profiling the complex and revealing lives of specific individuals are two of the most recurring choices filmmakers make. Films that combine these two tendencies demonstrate that we are dealing with a spectrum of possibilities rather than a black-and-white choice. Across this spectrum films adopt a rhetorical voice aimed at the questions of what happened or what we should do, on the one hand, and to questions of the strengths and weaknesses of individuals,

Strange Fruit (Joel Katz, 2002). Billie Holliday was unparalleled as a performer, and "Strange Fruit" was her best known, and most powerful, song. It has come to stand as a compelling lament for the lives lost to the horrific practice of lynching. Katz brilliantly fuses a personal portrait of Billie Holliday and Abel Meeropol, the song's writer, with the larger social history to which the song refers in this memorable film. *Photo by Charles Peterson, courtesy of Don Peterson.*

on the other. Each poses different ethical issues for the filmmaker regarding the basic question, "What to do with people?" and each approaches the realm of political engagement from a distinct angle. Collectively, they remind us that whether we approach a question from the perspective of the individual or from that of society as a whole, or from somewhere in between, it is in the interrelationship between the individual and society that questions of power and hierarchy, ideology and politics stand most forcefully revealed.

TABLE 8.1. Two Emphases in Documentary

Social Issue Documentary	Personal Portrait Documentary
Voice of filmmaker or agency as authority, plus voice of witnesses and experts to corroborate what's said. Filmmaker interacts with subjects in relation to the social issue. May rely heavily on rhetoric to engage or persuade the viewer	Voice of social actors (people) who speak for themselves rather than as representatives of a cause or issue. Filmmaker interacts with subjects more personally, which may include discussion of the interaction itself. May rely heavily on style to engage or involve the viewer
Discourse of sobriety. Style is secondary to content; content is what counts—the real world as it exists or existed	Poetic or subjective discourse. Style counts as much as content; form is what matters—what the world feels like from a particular perspective
Stresses disembodied, conceptual knowledge, enduring importance of social issues and historical events	Stresses embodied, situated knowledge, enduring importance of specific moments and individual experiences
Public issues	Private moments
The right to know or serving the greater good guides the quest for knowledge	The right to privacy and the boundary between the personal and the political is a conscious consideration
Characters gain minimal psychological depth relative to the exploration of broad concepts or issues	Characters convey considerable psychological complexity; larger issues emerge implicitly or indirectly
Individuals are often represented as: Typical (representative of a larger category) Victim Expert or witness	Individuals are often represented as: Unique or distinctive (idiosyncratic) Mythic Charismatic
Directs maximum attention to an issue, problem, or concept that is expressly named: sexism, global warming, AIDS, etc.	Direct maximum attention to the qualities and challenges of an individual, usually with indirect or implicit reference to larger issues
Stresses filmmaker's social mission or political purpose over his or her stylistic aplomb or personal expressiveness	Stresses filmmaker's style or personal expressiveness over his or her focus on a social issue

Social Issue Documentary	Personal Portrait Documentary
Filmmaker, or his voice-over surrogate, functions in an omniscient, transcendent realm that is distinct from the world of the film's subjects or social actors. Interviews, if present, serve the needs of this omniscient perspective	Filmmaker functions in the same social, historical realm as the subjects or social actors he or she interacts with. These interactions (especially interviews) may be a key element of the film
Commonly possesses a problem/ solution structure; often offers explanations for specific issues (poverty, welfare, war, social injustice, environmental harm)	Commonly presents a problem, situation, or individual without providing a solution or strong sense of closure; often invites understanding and empathy (of crises, intense experiences, maturation, personal growth or change, effect of experiences)
Stresses drama of finding a viable solution to a common problem	Stresses drama of experiencing the world from an individual's distinct perspective
Examples: *Before Stonewall; Berlin: Symphony of a Great City; The City; Enron: The Smartest Guys in the Room; Eyes on the Prize; Harvest of Shame; In the Year of the Pig; An Inconvenient Truth; An Injury to One; Isle of Flowers; Land without Bread; The Life and Times of Rosie the Riveter; The Man with a Movie Camera; Midnight Movies; Night and Fog; The Power of Nightmares; Taxi to the Dark Side; This Film Is Not Yet Rated; Tribulation 99; Ways of Seeing (I–IV); Why We Fight*	Examples: *Antonia: Portrait of a Woman; Bontoc Eulogy; Capturing the Friedmans; Derrida; Dont Look Back; Fast, Cheap and Out of Control; Hotel Terminus: The Life and Times of Klaus Barbie; Man on Wire; Metallica: Some Kind of Monster; Murderball; My Architect; Nanook of the North; Portrait of Jason; Primary; Ryan; S 21; Salesman; Sherman's March; Silverlake Life; Standard Operating Procedure; Tarnation; The Wild Parrots of Telegraph Hill*

CODA

Some documentaries set out to *explain* aspects of the world to us. They analyze problems and propose solutions. They seek to mobilize our support for one position instead of another. Other documentaries invite us to *understand* aspects of the world more fully. They observe, describe, or poetically evoke situations and interactions. They try to enrich our understanding of aspects of the historical world by means of their representations. They complicate our adherence to positions by undercutting certainty with complexity or doubt.

We need explanations to get things done. If we know what causes poverty or sexual abuse, pollution or war we can then take measures to address the issue. We need understanding, with its qualities of empathy and insight, to grasp the implications and consequences of what we do. Actions rely on values, and values are subject to question. Lives are at stake. Understanding, like critical perspective, leavens explanations, policies, solutions. Social actors are not pawns but people.

Documentary film and video constitutes a tradition that has addressed exactly this point, sometimes imperfectly, sometimes eloquently. It moves forward in relation to all the work that has gone before, addressing issues, exploring situations, engaging viewers in ways that will continue to instruct and please, move and compel. Its history belongs to the future and to those efforts yet to come. It is these future works that will enlarge an existing tradition and contribute to shaping a world we have yet to create.

How Can We Write Effectively about Documentary?

This chapter assumes some general familiarity with essay writing for film. All introductory film texts cover the topic and other helpful guides to essay writing also exist. This chapter gives sharper focus to writing about documentary film, but the basic principles pertain to almost any research topic in the humanities. Some suggestions for further reading, including more introductory guides to writing about film, can be found in the "Notes on Source Material" section of this book.

Crucial to successful writing is having a purpose. It may be, on one level, to get a grade or pass a course, but, on a more concrete level, the specific topic calls for an investment of curiosity, enthusiasm, and effort. A specific purpose, such as defending a position, advancing a point of view, or exploring an issue, endows an essay with interest. Simply summarizing a film, repeating what others have said about it, or describing parts of it without evaluating them—in essence, withholding a personal perspective—detract from an essay's interest. Finding a theme or idea that holds genuine personal interest typically yields a better essay than simply going through the motions of completing an assignment.

We will explore effective writing by using a concrete example: an essay assignment on *Nanook of the North* (1922). The hypothetical essay question below invites the student to assess the film and respond to it.

> Documentary addresses the historical world by shaping its representa-
> tion of this world from a distinct perspective or point of view. Identify
> the point of view adopted by Robert Flaherty in *Nanook of the North*

and consider some of its implications for you, based on what you have learned about documentary film. Demonstrate research on this topic by including at least three research citations in your essay. Length: 850–1,000 words.

The first step for writing any essay is preparation. Seeing *Nanook* is the most obvious preparation, but seeing it more than once is also important. On first viewing we become immersed in the viewing experience. We may ask ourselves some questions about what we are seeing, but on second viewing this process of asking and thinking about what we see becomes more central. We might ask, for example, Why does Flaherty begin the way he does? What does this set up for the rest of the film? Why does he end as he does? How does this relate to the beginning? What kind of relationship is there between Flaherty, or the camera, and Nanook? How are scenes edited? What scenes stand out and why? How is one scene joined to another? What does the narrative structure of the film revolve around? How does Flaherty represent people from another culture? How does he characterize them or convey a sense of their individuality?

Questions like these might be guided by a specific idea we already have for a paper or they may guide note taking prior to developing a specific idea. In either case, they increase our awareness of Flaherty's distinct approach.

Some viewers like to make notes on the first viewing of a film; others find it distracting. But on repeat viewing notes provide the raw material that will later support critical writing about the film. In general, notes can track such things as

- The chronology of scenes (what comes first, second, and so on).
- The types of camera shots (wide angle, telephoto, tracking shots, zooms, composition within the frame, etc.).
- Editing techniques (continuity editing, point-of-view shots, unusual juxtapositions or jumps in time and space).
- The role of speech (dialogue, commentary), written words (titles, subtitles, inter-titles), music, or sound effects in a scene.
- Character development: how the film makes choices to enhance our sense of individual characters or personalities (camera angle, editing, organization of scenes, selection of

Nanook of the North (Robert Flaherty, 1922). Nanook bites a record. Is this an act of playful hamming for the camera, or is this Flaherty's way of demonstrating the backwardness of his subject? The two sample essays that follow take different paths in interpreting this classic documentary film.

what is said, and, possibly, hints as to what is left unsaid or omitted).

- Rhetorical technique (how the film makes itself seem credible, convincing, and compelling, or not).
- Modes and models (what modes and models the film relies on to organize itself and how it inflects them in a distinct way).
- Other unusual qualities such as the degree of acknowledged presence of the filmmaker in scenes and the political perspective, if any, that the film conveys.
- Aesthetic or emotional responses to specific qualities of the film and what seems to prompt them in terms of technique or subject matter. Taking notes is a selective business. We can attend to only so many aspects of a film. We may choose to focus on the camera style or poetic editing, on the filmmaker's own presence or the development of social actors as complex

characters, but we cannot concentrate on everything at once. Notes provide a record of some of preoccupations and interests. When done in relation to an essay, they provide source material for the points we plan to make in our commentary.

Let's assume that two hypothetical students, Robert and Roberta, have seen *Nanook* once and have formed an initial opinion. Let's talk through the process of moving forward toward a finished essay.

Robert   What did you think of *Nanook*?
Roberta I hated it.
Robert   Oh, I loved it.

As a comprehensive response to the film this type of comment barely registers as a half-hearted attempt. It does provide a valuable starting place for thinking about the film, however. Each viewer has a strong response, and that response can motivate writing an essay. It furnishes a purpose: to defend a basic feeling about the film. To do so, however, this initial judgment has to be shaped into a critical analysis that relies on substantive support to make its points.

At this point our path branches in two directions. One leads to film reviews and one to film criticism. A useful distinction is that a reviewer writes for those who have not seen the film, as a kind of consumer guide. A critic writes for those who have, as part of a critical dialogue. Although some professional reviewers also pose issues that contribute to a critical dialogue among those who have seen the film, classroom essays seldom serve as reviews: the professor has already seen the film. The assigned essay topic on *Nanook* clearly expects the essay to be part of a critical dialogue among those who have already seen the film.

One important consequence: there is no need to summarize the plot. In film criticism, unlike film reviewing, once an essay begins to summarize a film or describe a scene the essay's analytic momentum may come to a halt. Summaries are largely redundant since the reader has already seen the film and, once begun, they often compel the writer to go on, summarizing more and more until the entire plot is clearly stated. This reverses priorities. For criticism, it is more vital to make a point and then provide supporting evidence through references to the film than to give a summary and then connect it to an over-all opinion. Developing arguments that convey your own considered thoughts about the film has the highest priority. Describe scenes or techniques that support your argument but avoid summaries that do not advance your own point of view.

Robert and Roberta's initial statements of love and hate are un-substantiated opinions (they have not offered any supporting evidence yet) and do not yet qualify as criticism. Let's take them a bit further.

> Robert I loved the way Flaherty showed me things about Eskimo cul-ture I hadn't seen before.
> Roberta I hated the way Flaherty made Nanook act like a typical primitive who knew all about nature but couldn't figure out a phono-graph record.

This gets the ball rolling. Each student has given us some sense of *why* he or she loves or hates the film. Robert has begun to put his finger on the quality he admires about Flaherty. From here he could begin to think about what Flaherty shows him and how Flaherty shows him these things: what about the representation seems to deserve admira-tion? Roberta has begun to link Flaherty with a set of misrepresenta-tions in which traditional cultures appear like earlier, or more infantile, versions of our own. From here she could begin to think about what Flaherty does to give her this feeling and how Flaherty's style contrib-utes to it. Film viewing notes will help this process.

Robert and Roberta may now make a preliminary thesis statement or an outline for their papers and review the film again, looking for scenes and moments that will support their theses. They may conduct additional research as well, but let's first see how they can elaborate their initial argument a bit more with a thesis statement and then see how research can help support their evolving argument in written form. The goal of the statement or outline is to indicate concisely what the main argument or point of the final paper will be.

> Robert I loved the way Flaherty adopts the perspective of a single fam-ily as a way to understand Eskimo culture. This gives us a convenient handle since we are already familiar with family roles but not familiar with the specific problems and tasks facing this family. Flaherty in-volves us mainly with Nanook but also shows how the kids begin to

learn Eskimo ways and how Nyla, Nanook's wife, contributes to the success of the group. Flaherty has a way of letting scenes linger; they don't rush to a conclusion. This is a really harsh environment, and men must be very determined and skilled to survive.

Roberta I hated Flaherty's hackneyed attempt to make us love Eskimos by making us love Nanook. This is a trite way of saying that we should admire other cultures because the people are cute and colorful, the sort of thing I see in travel brochures for exotic locales all the time. Nanook acts like a ham when Flaherty gives him a chance to respond to the camera, especially at the trading post. He's more in his element when hunting seals, but that's where we expect him to be most at ease. Is this Flaherty's way of keeping him in his place? Nanook seems like Eskimo brawn to the white man's brain.

This is better. These statements are clearly not final papers but they succeed in sketching out the authors' viewpoints and indicating what some of the supporting evidence might be. They jump around a bit and do not yet reflect any research. Roberta uses an anachronistic judgment: she finds Flaherty wanting because he reminds her of travel brochures she's seen. These brochures, though, would most likely have come 80 or more years after the film. A much more telling point would be to see if this type of travel brochure existed in the 1910s or 1920s so that Roberta could then argue they may have actually influenced Flaherty's approach or perhaps the marketing of the film. (The publicity still for *Grass* [1925] in chapter 5 suggests that travel brochures and ads may well have had an impact of film promotion in the 1920s.) Both essays still lack adequate substantiation, but the points that need support are also becoming clear. Robert will want to find articles or books that share his appreciation for Flaherty's method and Roberta will want to find material that takes a much more skeptical view.

Robert and Roberta can now conduct research on issues they want to clarify or substantiate, see the film, or parts of the film, again, and prepare a final draft. Ideally, this final draft will sit at least a day or two, then be revised one last time to address weak points, gaps in the argument, and grammatical errors. Flaws like these are often more apparent with the detachment a little time affords. The opening sentences of each student's statement, for example, begin with "I loved" and "I hated." These bald expressions of likes and dislikes can be dropped entirely as the emphasis shifts from the authors' opinion to what the film achieves or does not achieve. We could rewrite Robert's sentence as, "Flaherty adopts the perspective of a single family as a way to understand Eskimo culture." This becomes a more forceful assertion about the film itself and could even serve as a declaration of the essay's thesis. It marks the beginning of a critical perspective. What's lacking is further clarification of the thesis, substantiation, and a stronger overall organization. This is where research plays a role.

Conducting research normally involves utilizing two distinct sources of research material—the World Wide Web and the library. Each offers a wealth of information in three different forms:

- Primary source material is original source material rather than analyses or descriptions of it. The film itself is a primary source, as is any other material that provides direct access to the thoughts and actions of those involved in the film such as diaries, oral histories, and autobiographies. As documents, such material awaits analysis and interpretation.
- Secondary source material is the body of writing that has accumulated about the primary source material; it represents the results of analysis and interpretation. This material takes many different perspectives, just as Robert and Roberta do. Books, articles, reviews, websites, blogs, and other, similar material about *Nanook of the North* would all be secondary source material.
- Tertiary source material is information derived from secondary sources that synthesizes, summarizes, or popularizes this material, such as encyclopedia entries. It may provide helpful background but seldom plays a central role in the actual paper since it usually lacks a distinct perspective and recycles information from elsewhere. The entry on *Nanook* in *The International Encyclopedia of Documentary Film,* for example, would be tertiary source material.

A focused sense of curiosity guides engagement with all the source material: the writer reads with the idea of gaining additional information or insight for his or her specific essay. This is very similar to the process of reviewing the film. Robert, for example, will look for work, or portions of work, that demonstrate why *Nanook* deserves respect and appreciation. Roberta will look for material that questions the value of the film and helps indicate how Flaherty's bias and cultural limitations helped shape it.

Libraries are an invaluable source of information. Almost everything in a library has been selectively acquired over a considerable period of time. Secondary source material usually has considerable credibility as the work of established authors or as the publication of reputable presses. Libraries used to provide access to their holdings via card catalogues: thousands and thousands of cards, stored in tiers of drawers, through which a researcher could comb to find authors, titles, or subjects of interest. These no longer exist. Access is now via internet catalogues that contain the same information. Not only is this enormously more convenient, it also means that the most geographically nearby library is not the only resource: searches can be done in other, much larger libraries and any useful material found there requested by inter-library loan, purchased from a vendor, or, sometimes, located in an on-line form.

The vast holdings at the University of California, for example, can be searched by going to http://melvyl.cdlib.org. More selectively the holdings (both books and films) at the University of California at Berkeley (UCB) can be searched by going to http://lib.berkeley.edu/. The listings will include the films held at the Pacific Film Archive along with program notes and other information. Similarly, the rich resources of the University of California at Los Angeles (UCLA) Library, which includes oral histories and the personal papers of many film figures, can be searched by going to the UCLA website, http://www.ucla.edu/, and following the links to the university library.

The internet is also tremendously useful as a research tool. As with on-line library catalogues, vast amounts of material are just a click away. The main problem with the internet is that the ultimate source of the information and its permanence are always in doubt. Material may be present one day and gone the next or significantly altered. It may be copied from another site or a book; it may be the work of an amateur or a skilled professional. It may match something also published in hard copy or modify such material to a greater or lesser extent. For these reasons, it is advisable to double-check information found on the web and, when citing it, not only to provide the URL (the web address at which it was found) but also the date when the site was visited.

Robert and Roberta might well find the same material when they conduct their research, but they will use it differently. In general, they will be looking for material that gives them fresh ideas or adds support to ideas they already have. Research may, sometimes, indicate that the initial idea was ill conceived and perhaps unsupportable. It may encourage a change or modification in the topic.

Robert and Roberta may quote directly from their research in the final paper or simply absorb it as background information. Typically, they will choose to quote a passage when it provides a clear, concise idea that is memorably phrased or important because of its context. What someone said in a review of *Nanook* in 1922, for example, could be summarized, but a quote will give a concrete example of the film's initial reception. Source material is normally not quoted if it conveys common knowledge, generalizations, or could just as readily be rephrased in the author's own words. We can illustrate what their research might look like by surveying some results from both a web and library search.

If we begin with the web, we might also begin with a couple of heavily used sites: IMDB and Wikipedia. By themselves, they are inadequate. Both are tertiary sources, but they can be a good place to begin since they provide basic information and lead to other, more substantial primary and secondary source material. As a database, IMDB collects pertinent information about films, and as an encyclopedia, Wikipedia is one of the most-often-used tertiary sources on the web. Both sites cover *Nanook of the North*. IMDB provides basic information on the production and various options for buying a copy of the film. It also has a link to external reviews by accredited film reviewers and to reviews by users of the website. The external reviews include Roger Ebert's relatively recent and appreciative review of the film along with nineteen other reviews of quite varying quality.

The entries at Wikipedia do not bear their authors' names, nor do they indicate the level of each author's expertise. Corrections of errors or revision can occur at any time, or an error may linger and go undetected indefinitely since there is no in-house editorial staff at Wikipedia guaranteeing that all entries conform to specific standards.

As tertiary material for the most part, the entries are also not likely to advance a particular point of view or generate new knowledge as much as summarize existing knowledge. In this case the entry, as expected, covers familiar themes. It also lists several additional sources of information that can be accessed on the web. The entry also has a sidebar provided by Wikipedia that describes one way to give acknowledgment for information found on the site. If anything from the discussion of the film on Wikipedia is used, it says, the URL and date of access need to be noted like this:

> No author [or "Wikipedia contributors,"] *Nanook of the North*, Wikipedia, the Free Encyclopedia. http://en.wikipedia.org/wiki/Nanook_of_ the_North (accessed June 16, 2009).

The on-line Wikipedia entry, largely a distillation of other work, proves a useful starting point not so much for what the entry itself says but for what it leads to. Among the references in the Wikipedia article are the following:

> The story of the film and the people it was made among is told in *The Long Exile: A True Story of Deception and Survival Amongst the Inuit of the Canadian Arctic*, by Melanie McGrath.
> *Kabloonak* is a 1994 film about the making of *Nanook of the North*. Charles Dance plays Flaherty and Adamie Quasiak Inukpuk (a relative of Nanook) plays Nanook.
>
> **External Links**
> * *Nanook of the North* at the Internet Movie Database
> * *Nanook of the North* at Allmovie
> * Great Movies: *Nanook of the North* (1922) by Roger Ebert
> * How I Filmed *Nanook of the North* by Robert J. Flaherty
> * *Media Worlds*, essay by Faye D. Ginsburg
> * Swiss Jazz band Q3 composes a new *Nanook of the North* soundtrack
> * June 12, 1922 review of *Nanook of the North* in the *New York Times*

Each of these links can be pursued by clicking on it (on Wikipedia). (The first two items mentioned, a book, *The Long Exile*, and a film, *Kabloonak*, must be located elsewhere.) Following the links for the other items will lead to a wide range of material, from IMDB, as already discussed, to primary source material (a segment of Flaherty's own account of making the film) and scholarly secondary material

(Faye Ginsburg's essay is a chapter in a book she co-edited, *Media Worlds*, published by University of California Press). The researcher must use discretion in determining the relative value and credibility of these sources.

The general principle of internet research involves beginning with some likely websites or with googling for the title or filmmaker and then sifting through what turns up, making notes, copying selected passages, and recording where and when the research occurred. One website may not have particularly valuable content as such but it may still provide links to other sites that do. One thing leads to another and serendipity frequently opens up an entirely new perspective on the issue at hand. Whether to incorporate specific material into the essay arises later. For now the point is to find additional information about the film that supports an opinion or thesis about the film.

Research continues by going to an on-line library catalogue. "Investigator," the on-line catalogue for San Francisco State University, for example, yields several book titles when searches are done for *Nanook of the North* as keywords in a title search and for "Robert Flaherty" as author and as subject. Among these are

- *My Eskimo Friends, "Nanook of the North,"* by Robert Flaherty and Frances Flaherty
- William Rothman, *Documentary Film Classics*
- Daniel Bernardi, editor, *The Birth of Whiteness: Race and the Emergence of U.S. Cinema*
- Richard Griffith, *The World of Robert Flaherty*
- Alexander Calder-Marshall, *The Innocent Eye*
- Frances Flaherty, *The Odyssey of a Filmmmaker*
- Paul Rotha (edited by Jay Ruby), *Robert Flaherty: a Biography*

The information provided above is just a list, not a bibliography, since it is meant only to aid research on this topic. Not all of these items will be examined. Works consulted will have their bibliographic details noted and, if used, included in the essay. What is important to note down is the call number for each item so that it can be located in the library. For example, the call number for Rothman's *Documentary Film Classics* is PN 1995.9 D6 R69 1997.

In addition, this book, *Introduction to Documentary*, in the section at the back of the book entitled, "Notes on Source Material," lists Barry Grant and Jeannette Sloniowski's edited collection of essays that examine important documentary films, *Documenting the Documentary*. Their anthology includes a slightly modified version of the essay that also appears in Rothman's own book, *Documentary Film Classics*. It will not be obvious at this point, but it turns out that Daniel Bernardi's edited volume, *The Birth of Whiteness*, appeared in the search because it includes "Taxidermy and Romantic Ethnography: Robert Flaherty's *Nanook of the North.*" This is a chapter from Fatimah Tobing Rony's *The Third Eye: Race, Cinema and Ethnographic Spectacle* (Durham, N.C.: Duke University Press, 1996). This book offers access to the same material as Bernardi's book; it is a trenchant critique of Flaherty's approach and almost certain to be of strong interest to Roberta.

Libraries typically separate book searches from searches for magazine or journal articles. These are located by using databases that contain reference to, and sometimes, the entire text of, articles that appeared in the specific list of magazines and journals covered by that particular database. Some databases cover the sciences or social sciences; many cover the humanities, and a number of them include numerous sources of articles on films and filmmakers.

For example, a search of the Humanities Full Text database for "Nanook of the North" reveals, among other entries, the following article:

> *Title* "Exploration as construction: Robert Flaherty and *Nanook of the North*"
> *Personal Author* Grace, Sherrill
> *Journal Name* Essays on Canadian Writing
> *Source* Essays on Canadian Writing no. 59 (Fall 1996) p. 123–46
> *Publication Year* 1996
> *Abstract* Part of a special issue on representations of the North. The writer interrogates the making and marketing of Robert Flaherty's film *Nanook of the North*, focusing on his construction of Canada, the Arctic, and the Inuit. She challenges the use of the term "documentary" when discussing Flaherty's film, arguing that he created an "elegiac romance" in which he constructed an ethnographic other named "Nanook." She situates Flaherty's activities as an American explorer/filmmaker within the wider problematic of representing Canada and the North.

Subject(s) Motion pictures/Documentary films; Arctic regions/Discovery and exploration; Arctic regions in motion pictures; Inuit in motion pictures; *Nanook of the North* (Motion picture)

The abstract summarizes the basic argument of the essay and the entire essay can be read on-line. A useful passage from the essay could be cut and pasted into a research paper directly. (The citation would be credited to the essay in a footnote.) Its reassessment of Flaherty in light of a broader understanding of ethnographic research might have particular appeal for Roberta.

Another valuable database is FIAF, organized by the International Federation of Film Archives. A search of this database for "Nanook of the North" yields nineteen results. An example is an article by Richard Leacock, a filmmaker whose pioneering work in the observational mode of documentary has received mention elsewhere in this book. The entry for his essay is

Film Culture.
Leacock, Richard. Film Culture, nr 79 (Winter 1996), p. 1–6. *In defense of the Flaherty traditions.* Article; Illustration(s)
Accession Number: 48603919
Film Description: LOUISIANA STORY (US, Robert Flaherty, 1948), MAN OF ARAN (UK, Robert Flaherty, 1934), MOANA (US, Robert Flaherty, 1926), NANOOK OF THE NORTH

The title suggests that Leacock will defend Flaherty from those who found his method wanting; it may be of particular interest to Robert.

After selectively looking at some of this source material, making notes and selecting passages for possible quotation, Robert and Roberta return to their preliminary thoughts to complete a draft of their respective essays.

Robert: "Flaherty's Abiding Respect and Humane Consideration of Others"
Flaherty adopts the perspective of a single Eskimo family as our entry into the entirety of Eskimo culture. This strategy may be one reason for the film's enormous popularity. Another may be the way Flaherty succeeds in giving us the impression that he draws his insights from what Nanook and his family naturally do. Apart from his introduction of the family all piling out of a kayak and some hamming it up at the trading

post, Flaherty respectfully observes Nanook's family as they go about the difficult business of survival in the forbidding north.

Nanook's family has a strongly representative quality. His wife complements his own skills and clearly has skills of her own, such as tending the children and preparing their food. Nanook gradually earns our respect as a hunter. If he seems a bit of a buffoon in the early scenes, this may be Flaherty's way of letting us feel somewhat superior to this "savage," but it is not a feeling he lets us indulge for long.

Nanook may foolishly bite into a phonograph record as if this could help him find the sound, for example, but if biting and tasting things is an essential part of survival in the wilderness, who is more foolish, Nanook for doing it or us for laughing at him? Flaherty goes on to demonstrate how Nanook's ability to provide for his family through his hunting prowess deserves our full respect. Nanook's biting episode may not fit into the etiquette of a trading post, and of the civilized world the post stands for, but it is part and parcel of his own world. The later scene of Nanook and his family chewing their leather boots to soften them functions as proof of Nanook's ultimate wisdom. Biting into things generates important information. Flaherty's inclusion of this act remind us of our own folly in judging too quickly.

The point was not lost on early viewers, if the initial review in the *New York Times* is any indicator. The unidentified author notes,

> When Nanook, the master hunter and a real Eskimo, matches himself against the walrus, there is no pretense about the contest. Nanook's life depends upon his killing the walrus, and it is by no means certain that he will kill him. Some day he may not. And then Nanook will die. So the spectator watches Nanook as a man engaged in a real life-and-death struggle. And how much more thrilling the sight is than the "battle" between two well-paid actors firing blank cartridges at each other![1]

The reviewer clearly senses the radical break with fiction that filming real acts on real locations entails. However much Flaherty helped set up the scene, the risk was real and it is Nanook himself who confronts that risk. Not only does *Nanook* urge us not to judge too quickly, it also urges us to exercise patience in coming to an understanding of what we see. Several times Flaherty introduces us to a scene without fully explaining what is going on. This puts us in a state of suspense. The suspense is not the highly charged tension of a shoot-out but it does involve life and death in terms of whether Nanook can survive and how actions we don't immediately understand help him do so.

For example, when Nanook builds an igloo a title tells us that one more thing remains to be done. What, we ask ourselves? Instead of telling us, Flaherty just watches as Nanook finds a piece of clear ice and cuts it free. When he plunks it onto the side of the igloo we may figure out what is going on, or it may take us another minute or so, as Nanook cleans and buffs the ice, to realize that he has made a window for the igloo!

This quiet revelation is what brought wonder to the eyes of Richard Leacock, who worked with Flaherty on *Louisiana Story* and went on to make numerous films himself. In a 1996 article he writes, "Flaherty believed that film-making was a relatively simple process and that he could do it all himself with the help of local people. To this day I agree with his position."[2]

This shooting style is one of Flaherty's great contributions to documentary. He lets his camera follow actions so that they unfold at their own rhythm. We discover the meaning of events by observing them rather than having a meaning imposed by comments, titles, or editing. The scene when Nanook finds a hole in the ice, suspends a thread across it, and then waits, and waits, is another great example. We are not at all sure what he's doing, but when he finally hurls his spear into the hole because he's seen the thread quiver, we realize just how skillful a hunter Nanook really is, even if it takes a little longer to learn that there's a seal on the end of the line.

Professor Edmund Carpenter has written that Flaherty's method was highly appropriate to Eskimo culture. Carpenter says that an Eskimo carver doesn't set out to carve a seal from ivory. He examines the ivory, mulls it over, and begins to carve aimlessly, trying to find the form already inside it. "Then he brings it out; Seal, hidden, emerges. It was always there: he didn't create it; he released it; he helped it step forth."[3] When we realize what Nanook is doing in scenes like the window making or the seal hunting we suddenly discover what his world is like. It was always there; Flaherty just helps it step forth.

[929 words, excluding footnotes]

1. Cited on Wikipedia entry for *Nanook of the North*: http://query .nytimes.com/gst/abstract.html?res=9A00E2DB1E3EEE3ABC4A52DFB 0668389639EDE (accessed June 15, 2009).

2. Richard Leacock, "In Defense of the Flaherty Traditions," *Film Culture*, Winter 1996, p. 1.

3. Edmund Carpenter, "Notes on Eskimo Art Film," cited in Arthur Calder Marshall, *The Innocent Eye*. Based on research material by Paul Rotha and Basil Wright (Baltimore, Maryland: Penguin Books, 1970), p. 70.

Robert has developed a very solid essay. He has presented a clear thesis: Flaherty involves us in Eskimo culture through the familiar figure of the family but then urges us to discover what this culture is like by observing events and inferring meaning for ourselves, in a spirit similar to the way Eskimos approach their own art. He has also provided good substantiation through reference to specific scenes. The writing is clear and the paragraphs well organized. Opinion is present, but more as a motivation for critical argument than as an end in itself. Quotes substantiate Robert's position, showing that his view has a basis in what others have also appreciated in Flaherty's work. A clear theme developed in relation to specific cinematic qualities allows an interpretation of the film to emerge that acknowledges both the actual form of the film and Robert's experience of it.

Now let's see what Roberta's essay looks like.

Roberta   "Flaherty: Seeing Others the Way You Need to See Them"

Robert Flaherty can be considered the first filmmaker to make use of the participant-observation style of documentary and a pioneer in ethnographic filmmaking, but if this is so, it may demonstrate more about the problems with ethnography than the virtues of Flaherty.

For example, in an early scene Nanook comes to the trading post to trade his furs for commodities. This is the only reference to Western goods in the film. Why doesn't Nanook acquire supplies that will help him the most, like a rifle for hunting? Why doesn't the film identify the post with Revillon Frères, the film's sponsor? By making the trader a benevolent patriarch who doles out treats for the kids and amusements for Nanook, Flaherty makes this an implicit ad for how well Revillon treats the natives. Nanook is as easily distracted by gadgets as his kids are by biscuits and lard. The phonograph scene presents Nanook as a clown. Technology poses no threat; it's just a curiosity. Nanook and his family go away happy. Everyone benefits, or so it seems.

Flaherty observes more than he participates, at least on-camera. Behind the scenes, Flaherty participates more than he admits. Why, if the family gets treated to a feast at the trading post, are they soon in danger of starvation? Is Flaherty prepared to film Nanook starving to death? It is more likely that this is what is called a "hook" in fiction films: it's a way to involve us in a drama by inventing a dramatic angle. Will Nanook find food? Stay tuned and we'll see. This is Flaherty actively working, off-camera, to set the stage for the drama to come. The trick is that he then presents this drama as if he just happened to be there to record it.

For example, in the scene where Nanook and other men (where did they come from, Central Casting?) spear a walrus, Flaherty is nearby, filming. According to Flaherty's own account, the men begged him to use his rifle to kill the walrus, but Flaherty pretended not to hear them. This forced them to risk their lives unnecessarily, but it also allowed Flaherty to "observe" an "authentic" hunt as if he wasn't there. As Flaherty himself admits in his diary, "For a long time it was nip and tuck—repeatedly the crew called for me to use the gun—but the camera crank was my only interest then and I pretended not to understand."[1]

Flaherty's whole effort is a form of fraud. He wants to give us an infantalized image of a culture populated by innocents. He wants to act as if that culture had no contact with our own when Flaherty himself, and the trading post, is proof that it does. Flaherty doesn't want to explore the consequences of these relationships, at least in the film. He is willing to take money from Revillon to make the film, and he is willing to treat Nanook as a friend, at least as long as it takes to make the film. As Fatimah Tobing Rony bluntly puts it, "What has been called Flaherty's 'slight narrative' thus fits perfectly with a racializing representation of the Inuit, which situates indigenous peoples outside modern history."[2] Such a view may preserve them as images of a quaint past but it can also fuel considerable passion and for Flaherty this passion spilled over into a love affair with Maggie Nujarlutuk, who plays "Nyla" in the film: she bore him a child.[3] Since he was married to Frances Flaherty at the time and had her accompany him on the trip to make the film, this part of the Flaherty myth gets swept under the rug.

According to our class discussion, this kind of film apparently fits a model of "salvage ethnography," where ethnographers describe other cultures as they were before contact with the Western world in an attempt to salvage a record of what will soon be lost. This served a valuable purpose in giving us a record of cultures before they disappeared. But it also denied the reality of ethnographers, or filmmakers, interacting with the same cultures they described as having no contact with whites. Where did that leave the filmmaker? It's the filmmaker who disappears, along with all the bargaining and negotiation that happens so that he can get his information.

Fatimah Tobing Rony also describes a film made in 1988, *Nanook Revisited*, that clarifies how much Flaherty hid. An Inuit man tells how the polar bear skin clothing, the igloo set (half exposed to the weather), and the seal hunt were all distortions. Any documentary that wants to represent a previous historical period has to re-create or reenact it, but when the re-creation is passed off as the way it really was rather than a re-creation, deception is in the air. Rony also refers to how the man who "played" Nanook, Allakariallak, couldn't help laughing much of the time because what Flaherty asked him to do was so hopelessly funny. Flaherty clearly enlisted Allakariallak and other Inuits to help him make his film, but as the film hero's impish laughter suggests, it may be because, for them, this was a fictional comedy far more than an ethnographic document.

[867 words]

1. Robert J. Flaherty, "How I Filmed *Nanook of the North.*" This portion of the text cited online at http://www.cinemaweb.com/silentfilm/bookshelf/23_rf1_2.htm (accessed June 14, 2009). Erik Barnouw quotes this passage in his book, *Documentary,* but hesitates to pass judgment on Flaherty. Flaherty's refusal seems justifiable to Barnouw since it enables Flaherty to film the Eskimo's "traditional ways," despite the risk and despite intervening to set up the scene in the first place. Barnouw, *Documentary* (New York: Oxford University Press, 1993), p. 37.

2. Fatimah Tobing Rony, *The Third Eye: Race, Cinema and Ethnographic Spectacle* (Durham, N.C.: Duke University Press, 1996), p. 103.

3. Melanie McGrath, *The Long Exile* (New York: Alfred A. Knopf: 2007), pp. 21–22. The book is written in a novelistic style, like Jon Krakauer's fact-based stories (*Into the Wild, Into Thin Air, Under the Banner of Heaven*) and, like his books, is strongly based on facts; it includes a bibliography and reference to an extensive set of interviews with Inuit people and others.

Roberta has also developed a solid, coherent thesis with ample supporting material. Her research has given her valuable information that could not be derived from the film alone (precisely because Flaherty masked what she reveals). There is a strongly accusatory tone that may not do justice to the complexity of Flaherty's achievement, or to the reasons for its having been considered such a great film despite the failings she identifies. The reference to "Central Casting," for example, is somewhat gratuitous, "stay tuned" creates a somewhat frivolous tone, "fraud" is probably too strong a word for Flaherty's mixture of concealment and reenactment, and the reference to Flaherty's affair with one of his actors has only an indirect bearing on the film's status as a film. In other words the writing style has a sharp, indignant tone to it that may detract from the less judgmental and more reflective goal of the assignment.

A longer paper might examine why a revision to Flaherty's reputation and achievement has been so slow in coming rather than adopt a tone of indignation that Flaherty has gotten away with something. Clearly, another challenge would be to see if we can understand Flaherty's film in a way that would take account of both Robert and Roberta's arguments. Robert's thesis, in fact, parallels the view of Flaherty that prevailed until the early 1980s or so, while Roberta's has more in common with recent revisions of the "Flaherty myth." This does not invalidate either one but helps to locate them within a larger historical context.

Both papers, though, fulfill the assignment: they move away from opinion and toward analysis. They identify a distinct perspective belonging to Flaherty and examine some of its implications or consequences successfully. They also demonstrate how it is possible for the specific facts and events present in a film to lead to more than one interpretation. The apparent authenticity or indexicality of the image, the location shooting, and the long takes do not clinch the case for a single argument or conclusion any more than the forensic evidence put before a jury automatically clinches the case for guilt or innocence. An interpretative or explanatory frame must be introduced. The one proposed by the filmmaker will clearly be one of them, but it will just as clearly not be the only one.

As the essays demonstrate, Flaherty's film can be read in many ways. Part of the challenge of film history and criticism is to understand how analyses vary with time and place as different viewers, with different perspectives, bring their critical skills to bear on a given film. But both of these essays give us a better idea of how basic techniques of film analysis can be applied to the study of documentary films.

Notes on Source Material

Since the publication of Bill Nichols, *Representing Reality* (Bloomington: Indiana University Press, 1991), and, 2 years later, Michael Renov, ed., *Theorizing Documentary* (New York: Routledge, 1993), the field of documentary film study has blossomed remarkably as scholars and critics explore the many ways in which the field of documentary poses as rich and perplexing an array of questions as any other. An annual conference, held in cities around the world, Visible Evidence (http:// visibleevidence.org/), brings people together to share thoughts and pursue ideas about documentary film. Journals like *Documentary Box*, from Japan, and *Studies in Documentary Film*, from Australia, provide extensive coverage of documentary film. Many other journals, from *Jump Cut*, on-line, to *Cineaste*, a monthly publication, offer extensive coverage of documentary film and video.

These source notes highlight books since most books include bibliographies and footnotes that help point to the considerably larger periodical literature. The full bibliographic reference for books discussed here is only included on their first mention. Chapter 9 provides additional guidance on how to conduct a search for articles, as well as for books and on-line material.

Going further in an exploration of how to define or conceptualize documentary is best done through works that are devoted specifically to documentary film and video. Some caution is advisable when referring to standard introductory film textbooks and basic film history textbooks. These books invariably place their emphasis on narrative fiction and often overlook documentary, provide idiosyncratic or dated definitions, and may lack nuance in their discussion of documentary definitions, history, and form.

Defining documentary as a form, genre, or particular type of social practice is taken up by *Representing Reality* in some detail. The issues involved in a definition of documentary as a "fuzzy" concept are explored quite helpfully in Carl R. Plantinga, *Rhetoric and Representation in Nonfiction Film* (New York: Cambridge University Press, 1997). Invaluable for a full understanding of definitions that are less factual and concrete than conceptual and fuzzy is George Lakoff and Mark Johnson's classic book, *Metaphors We Live By* (Chicago: University of Chicago Press, 1980).

Among the books that offer a broad overview are three standard documentary histories. All are now dated but they nonetheless capture much of the excitement and experimentation that characterized the rise of documentary film. They are Eric Barnouw, *Documentary: A History of the Non-fiction Film*, 2nd ed. (New York: Oxford University Press, 1993); Richard Meran Barsam, *Nonfiction Film* (New York: Dutton, 1973); and John Ellis, *The Documentary Idea* (Englewood Cliffs, N.J.: Prentice-Hall, 1989). A revised version of Ellis's book, *A New History of Documentary Film*, with Betsy McLane as co-author (London: Continuum, 2005), is updated but remains strongest on developments in documentary film up to the 1980s. (It also takes on a more negative tone toward vigorous critical inquiry.) Covering criticism as well as history, Ian Aitkin, ed., *The International Encyclopedia of Documentary Film* (New York: Routledge, 2005), treats a host of historical topics as well as individual filmmakers, critics, and representative films. It is the best single tertiary source on documentary currently available.

Going further back, Paul Rotha's still pertinent history, *Documentary Film* (New York: Norton, 1939), set the model for a sensitive, chronological account of the form. Restricted to American filmmakers, but much more rigorous in its methodology, is Jonathan Kahana's *Intelligence Work: The Politics of American Documentary* (New York: Columbia University Press, 2008). Kahana gives a high degree of attention to the linkages between the documentary film form and larger currents in American society.

Other books that offer a valuable overview but that, like *Repre-senting Reality*, are more conceptual than historical, include Michael Renov, ed., *Theorizing Documentary*, and Renov's collected essay, *The Subject of Documentary* (Minneapolis: University of Minnesota Press, 2004). The latter book, a collection of essays, explores the complex ways in which documentary films embody a subjective point of view and how this has a bearing on topics from memory and historical representation to the confession and autobiography. Michael Renov, Faye Ginsburg, and Jane Gaines serve as editors of the Visible Evidence series at the University of Minnesota Press. Spanning a wide variety of topics from feminism and documentary to the fake documentary, the series consistently takes up important topics and addresses them from a variety of perspectives. An early volume, Micheal Renov and Jane Gaines, eds., *Collecting Visible Evidence* (Minneapolis: University of Minnesota Press, 1999), offers an excellent set of essays on topics that retain contemporary interest.

Brian Winston, *Claiming the Real* (London: British Film Institute, 1995), challenges much of the received wisdom about John Grierson to argue that his efforts in the 1930s turned documentary away from active social engagement. John Corner, *The Art of Record: Critical Introduction to the Documentary* (Manchester: University of Manchester Press, 1996), provides an intelligent, well-researched overview of issues in documentary, while John Izod, *An Introduction to Television Documentary* (New York: St. Martin's Press, 1997), gives an informative account of television documentary in Great Britain. A. William Bluem's *Documentary in American Television* (New York: Hastings House, 1965), although older, offers a broad perspective on the rise of documentary and its place in television history. More recently, Pat Aufderheide has written *Documentary Film: A Very Short Introduction* (New York: Oxford University Press, 2007), a work that also gives close attention to television documentary as well as providing the broad outlines of a documentary film history.

Of considerable value to the newcomer to documentary is Barry Grant and Jeannette Sloniowski, eds., *Documenting the Documentary* (Detroit: Wayne State University Press, 1998), a collection of essays each of which is devoted to a particular documentary film. (It is more selective than the *International Encyclopedia of Documentary Film* but both works contain very insightful essays on individual films.) William Rothman, *Documentary Film Classics* (New York: Cambridge University Press, 1997), covers similar ground from a more personal point of view. More recently, Stella Bruzzi has published *New Documentary*, 2nd ed. (New York and London: Routledge, 2006). It offers elements of a historical survey and discusses a few contemporary topics and individual filmmakers. Alan Rosenthal, ed., *New Challenges for Documentary* (Berkeley: University of California Press, 1988), collects a large number of very useful essays; Rosenthal's earlier *The New Documentary in Action* (Berkeley: University of California Press, 1971), also provides a revealing set of interviews with documentary filmmakers. Lewis Jacobs's *The Documentary Tradition*, 2nd ed. (New York: Norton, 1979), is a valuable collection of older essays that gives a good sense of the development of both documentary film and discussions about it.

Timothy Druckery, ed., *Electronic Culture: Technology and Visual Representation* (New York: Aperture, 1996), provides both a conceptual and a historical guide to the implications of digital technology for visual representation generally, while Winston's *Technologies of Seeing* (London: British Film Institute, 1996), offers a useful historical perspective on technology and representation. His *Claiming the Real* also takes this issue up in passing. Lev Manovich's *The Language of New Media* (Cambridge, Mass.: MIT Press, 2001) explores many of aspects of new media. Although not specifically focused on documentary film, it contains valuable implications for how documentary and new media may intersect.

Some useful books for those who want to know more about how to make a documentary film are Ilisa Barbash and Lucien Taylor, *Cross-Cultural Filmmaking* (Berkeley: University of California Press, 1997); Michael Rabiger, *Directing the Documentary* (Boston: Focal Press, 1987); Alan Rosenthal, *Writing, Directing, and Producing Documentary Films* (Carbondale: Southern Illinois University Press, 1990); and Dai Vaughn, *For Documentary* (Berkeley: University of California Press, 1999). Vaughn's book is a wonderful set of observations by one of the most respected editors of documentary film. Sheila Curran Bernard's comprehensive *Documentary Storytelling for Film and Videomakers* (Oxford, UK: Elsevier Press, 2004), stresses the use of narrative techniques in documentary production and includes interviews with a number of important filmmakers.

For questions of ethics in documentary film and video, *Honest Truths: Documentary Filmmakers on Ethical Challenges in Their Work* (Washington, D.C.: Center for Social Media, 2009), a short pamphlet that is also available on-line at http://www.centerforsocialmedia.org/, offers guidelines for filmmakers based on the actual experience of professional documentarians. It does not establish an ethical code as much as identify ethical issues and the principles used to address them by practicing filmmakers. Another extremely useful text is Larry Gross, John Stuart Katz, and Jay Ruby, eds., *Image Ethics* (New York: Oxford University Press, 1988). *Representing Reality* includes a chapter devoted to ethical considerations in relation to documentary film form and style. *New Challenges for Documentary* includes Brian Winston's essay "The Tradition of the Victim in Griersonian Documentary," which is a scathing attack on the tendency to treat people as victims, especially in television news and special reports. Books that gather together interviews with filmmakers, such as Alan Rosenthal's collection of interviews, *The Documentary Conscience* (Berkeley: University of California, 1970), or that include essays by filmmakers, such as Kevin MacDonald and Mark Cousins, eds., *Imagined Reality* (London: Faber and Faber, 1996), inevitably touch on ethical considerations.

Another useful reference are the codes of ethics developed by the American Sociological Association, the American Anthropological Association, and the Society of Professional Journalists. They can be found on-line at the websites for these organizations. These codes address many of the issues that arise when researchers enter into the lives of people markedly different from themselves. Many universities adopt somewhat similar codes for experiments and research and sometimes require student filmmakers to comply with their codes.

Issues of the relationship between speaker and recipient and the role of pronouns in such formulations as "*I speak about them to you*" is addressed by the linguist Emile Benveniste in his *Problems in General Linguistics* (Coral Gables, Fla.: University of Miami Press, 1971), while Christian Metz explores some of the implications for film study in his *The Imaginary Signifier: Psychoanalysis and the Cinema* (Bloomington: Indiana University Press, 1982). Judith Butler adds additional nuance to the discussion in her important book, *Excitable Speech* (New York: Routledge, 1997), about issues surrounding hate speech and other uses of language to produce a direct, immediate effect.

The general question of film genres is well addressed in Charles Altman, *Film/Genre* (London: British Film Institute, 1999). It is also taken up by Barry Grant, ed., *Film Genre: Theory and Criticism* (Metuchen, N.J.: Scarecrow Press, 1977), and by Stephen Neale, *Genre* (London: British Film Institute, 1980). The background to and original debates about observational documentaries are well addressed in Stephen Mamber, *Cinema Verite in America: Studies in Uncontrolled Documentary* (Cambridge, Mass.: MIT Press, 1974). Another valuable treatment of this mode is Dave Saunders, *Direct Cinema: Observational Documentary and the Politics of the Sixties* (London: Wallflower Press, 2007).

The overlap and interrelationship of the genres of ethnographic and experimental film is a central concern of Catherine Russell, *Experimental Ethnography* (Durham, N.C.: Duke University Press, 1999). The intriguing case of docudrama is taken up by Derek Paget, *No Other Way to Tell It* (Manchester: Manchester University Press, 1998). Mock documentaries, or films that appear to be but are not, by most standards, documentary, provide a great entry point for efforts to address what makes documentary film a distinct form or genre. Two books that explore this terrain effectively are Jane Roscoe and Craig Hight, *Faking It: Mock-Documentary and the Subversion of Factuality* (Manchester: University of Manchester Press, 2001), and Alexandra Juhasz and Jesse Lerner, eds., *F Is for Phony: Fake Documentary and Truth's Undoing* (Minneapolis: University of Minnesota Press, 2006).

Documentary practices occur in many media from historical accounts to news reporting. The characteristics of such practices in a given period are illuminatingly discussed in William Stott, *Documentary Expression in Thirties America* (New York: Oxford University Press, 1973), and in Paula Rabinowitz, *They Must Be Represented* (New York: Verso, 1994), a book that also focuses on the 1930s. William Alexander, *Films on the Left: American Documentary Film from 1931 to 1942* (Princeton, N.J.: Princeton University Press, 1981), also addresses this period but primarily in terms of the documentary film tradition.

Considerations of voice in documentary, in the sense discussed in chapter 3, occur in *Representing Reality*. Voice in the more literal sense of the use of spoken words in film is itself an important concept that has been well explored, particularly from a feminist perspective. Kaja Silverman, *The Acoustic Mirror* (Bloomington: Indiana University Press, 1988), and Sara Kozloff, *Invisible Storytellers: Voice-Over Narration in American Fiction Film* (Berkeley: University of California Press, 1988), are the most directly relevant books. On sound and voice more generally, Charles Altman has edited a special issue of *Yale French Studies* on "Cinema/Sound" (no. 60, 1980); John Belton and Elisabeth Weis have edited *Film Sound: Theory and Practice* (New York: Columbia University Press, 1985); and Michel Chion has written an influential book, *The Voice in Cinema* (trans. Claudia Gorbman, New York: Columbia University Press, 1999; originally *Le Son au cinema*, Paris: Editions de L'Etoile, 1992).

Discussions of rhetoric are abundant as it has remained a source of lively debate since ancient times. Of particular use for the treatment of rhetoric here are Cicero, *De Oratore* (English and Latin), 2 vols. (Cambridge, Mass.: Harvard University Press, 1967–1968); Quintillian, *Instituto Oratorio*, 4 vols. (Cambridge, Mass.: Harvard University Press, 1953); and Aristotle, *The "Art" of Rhetoric* (Cambridge, Mass.: Harvard University Press, 1975). A contemporary and very insightful rethinking of rhetorical terms and categories occurs in Richard Lanham, *A Handlist of Rhetorical Terms*, 2nd ed. (Berkeley: University of California Press, 1991).

The idea that a sense of voice can be collective as well as individual, as members of a community or subculture find common forms of expression, receives examination in Chris Holmlund and Cynthia Fuchs, eds., *Between the Sheets, in the Streets: Queer, Lesbian and Gay Documentary* (Minneapolis: University of Minnesota Press, 1997), and in Diane Waldman and Janet Walker, eds., *Feminism and Documentary* (Minneapolis: University of Minnesota Press, 1999). The idea of an individual "voice" as used here also slides toward the idea of personal "vision" or individual style (although the terms are not entirely identical). There are numerous studies of individual filmmakers in documentary. These can be found by searching a library database using the filmmaker's name as a subject heading. The bibliographic material on documentary filmmakers, contemporary and historical, found at www.lib.berkeley.edu/MRC/documentary.bib.html provides a useful starting point. It is a list of all the relevant documentary books and articles in the UC Berkeley library.

All of the standard histories of documentary as well as almost all basic film history books provide an account of the form's beginnings and subsequent development, although the argument advanced here differs from the emphasis in these other books. This book argues against the notion of early cinema (1895–1906) as the origin of the documentary genre. André Bazin, *What Is Cinema?* vol. 1 (Berkeley: University of California Press, 1967), traces the rise of cinema generally to a desire to preserve or embalm that has strong implications for documentary film. (His entire aesthetic is very sympathetic to documentary qualities in narrative cinema generally.)

The 1920s avant-garde film movement in Europe and the Constructive art and Soviet cinema initiatives in the USSR, the arenas from which documentary film takes shape in the account given here, are covered in a number of books. Among them are Richard Abel, *French Film Theory and Criticism, 1907–1939,* 2 vols. (Princeton, N.J.: Princeton University Press, 1988); Kees Bakker, ed., *Joris Ivens and the Documentary Context* (Amsterdam: Amsterdam University Press, 1999); Stephen Bann, ed., *The Tradition of Constructivism* (New York: Viking, 1974); Sergei Eisenstein, *Film Form and the Film Sense,* Jay Leyda, ed. (New York: Meridian Books, 1968); Stephen C. Foster, ed., *Hans Richter: Activism, Modernism and the Avant-Garde* (Cambridge, Mass.: MIT Press, 1998); Jay Leyda, *Kino: A History of the Russian and Soviet Film* (New York: Macmillan, 1960); Alan Lovell, *Anarchist Cinema* (on Jean Vigo, Georges Franju, and Luis Buñuel) (London: Peace Press, 1967); Amos Vogel, *Film as a Subversive Art* (New York: Random House, 1974); and Thomas Waugh, *Joris Ivens and the Evolution of the Radical Documentary, 1926–1946* (Ann Arbor, Mich.: University Microfilms, 1981). Siegfried Kracauer, *From Caligari to Hitler* (New York: Noonday Press, 1959), contains a relevant appendix, "Propaganda and the Nazi War Film." Joris Ivens's autobiographical account, *The Camera and I* (New York: International Publishers, 1969), gives a first-hand account of the social and aesthetic issues he faced during this period.

Italian neo-realism is one of the film movements that perches on the boundary of documentary and fiction. André Bazin discusses it informatively in *What Is Cinema?* and Robert Kolker, *The Altering Eye* (New York: Oxford University Press, 1983; also available on-line at http://otal.umd.edu/~rkolker/AlteringEye/preface.html), gives a more critical but still appreciative account of this movement. David Mac-Dougall, *Transcultural Cinema* (Princeton, N.J.: Princeton University Press, 1998), a collection of this distinguished filmmaker's most important essays, makes many valuable references to Italian neo-realism and its continuing influence.

The broader issue of realism itself is helpfully addressed in most introductory film textbooks as well as in John Hill and Pamela Church Gibson, eds., *The Oxford Guide to Film Studies* (New York: Oxford University Press, 1998); Linda Nochlin, *Realism* (Baltimore: Penguin, 1976); Jacques Aumont et al., *Aesthetics of Film* (Austin: University of Texas Press, 1992); and Ien Ang, *Watching Dallas* (New York: Methuen, 1985). The Ang book gives a valuable account of psychological and emotional realism. Bill Nichols, *Engaging Cinema* (New York: W. W. Norton, 2010), is a general introduction to film but with an emphasis on film's social significance. It has chapters on documentary film and on realism, modernism, and postmodernism as the three most important stylistic movements in film.

The role of narrative in film, both fiction and documentary, is taken up in a number of works. Among the most important for a broad perspective on the use of narrative in nonfiction is Hayden White, *The Content of the Form* (Baltimore, Md.: Johns Hopkins University Press, 1987). In terms of film study Tom Gunning, *D. W. Griffith and the Origins of American Narrative Film* (Urbana: University of Illinois Press, 1991), traces the rise of narrative technique. Gunning's important essay on the early "cinema of attractions" is in Thomas Elsaesser and Adam Barker, eds., *Early Cinema: Space, Frame, Narrative* (London: British Film Institute, 1990). David Bordwell, *Narration in the Fiction Film* (Madison: University of Wisconsin Press, 1985), and two of Christian Metz's books, *Film Language: A Semiotics of Cinema* (New York: Oxford University Press, 1974), and *The Imaginary Signifier: Psychoanalysis and the Cinema* (Bloomington: Indiana University Press, 1982), also contain much valuable information.

Various ways exist to divide up documentary film and video into different clusters, movements, or modes. Four of the modes discussed here (expository, observation, participatory [previously called interactive], and reflexive) are treated further in *Representing Reality*, while the performative mode receives a separate chapter in Bill Nichols, *Blurred Boundaries: Questions of Meaning in Contemporary Culture* (Bloomington: Indiana University Press, 1994). Carl Plantinga takes up the question of categories in *Rhetoric and Representation in Nonfiction Film*, and Michael Renov advances an alternative set of divisions in his edited volume, *Theorizing Documentary*.

The poetic mode can be placed in a broader context through reference to readings devoted to the avant-garde and experimental film mentioned above. Laszlo Moholy-Nagy, *Painting, Photography, Film* (Cambridge, Mass.: MIT Press, 1969), is a stimulating survey of the potential of each of these media. Richard Abel, *French Film Theory and Criticism*, contains many essays by filmmakers and early theorists on the poetic possibilities of cinema. P. Adams Sitney has contributed two useful books on experimental cinema that can also be read with documentary film in mind: *Visionary Film: The American Avant-Garde*, 2nd ed. (New York: Oxford University Press, 1979), and the edited volume *The Avant-Garde Film: A Reader of Theory and Criticism* (New York: New York University Press, 1978). Jeffrey Skoller's brilliant book, *Shadows, Specters, Shards: Making History in Avant-Garde Film* (Minneapolis: University of Minnesota Press, 2005), explores the powerful legacy of the modernist avant-garde and its poetic techniques for filmmakers who address questions of history and memory in innovative ways; all of the works he discusses can be considered documentary as well as avant-garde.

Expository documentary receives discussion in Thomas Waugh, ed., *"Show Us Life!": Toward a History and Aesthetic of the Committed Documentary* (Metuchen, N.J.: Scarecrow Press, 1984), and in Jay Leyda, *Film Begets Film* (New York: Hill and Wang, 1964). Although Leyda's book does not use that term for the structure of the compilation film, his treatment of such films is a crucial link in understanding the exposition, compilation, and historical representation. Additional discussion of this mode occurs in Bill Nichols, *Ideology and the Image* (Bloomington: Indiana University Press, 1988).

Observational cinema is well covered by Stephen Mamber, *Cinema Verite in America*, and by portions of David MacDougall, *Transcultural Cinema*. Gary Evans, *In the National Interest: A Chronicle of the NFB of Canada from 1949–1989* (Toronto: University of Toronto Press, 1991), offers insight into the Canadian contribution to this mode. Barry Grant, *Voyage of Discovery: The Films of Frederick Wiseman* (Urbana: University of Illinois Press, 1992), examines the films of one of this mode's purest practitioners. Paul Hockings, ed., *Principles of Visual Anthropology*, 2nd ed. (Berlin: Mouton, 1995), includes several essays that discuss the implications of observational modes of film for ethnography and visual anthropology.

Although sometimes mistakenly thought of as expository because of its propagandistic uses, *Triumph of the Will* is one of the early examples of observational documentary, one that raises rich questions about the line between observing and staging. Additional discussion of this film takes place in Brian Winston, *Claiming the Real*; Linda Deutschman, *Triumph of the Will: The Image of the Third Reich* (Wakefield, N.H.: Longwood Press, 1991); and David Hinton, *The Films of Leni Riefenstahl* (Metuchen, N.J.: Scarecrow Press, 1991). Richard M. Barsam has provided a useful bibliographic reference, *Filmguide to "Triumph of the Will"* (Bloomington: Indiana University Press, 1975).

Important references for the participatory mode of documentary include, at the general level of the interview and confession, Michel Foucault, *The History of Sexuality*, vol. 1 (New York: Vintage, 1980); Jack Douglas, *Creative Interviewing* (Beverly Hills: Sage, 1985); and Philip Bell and Theo Van Leeuven, *The Media Interview: Confession, Contest, Conversation* (Kensington: University of New South Wales Press, 1994). Paul Hockings, ed., *Principles of Visual Anthropology*, addresses some of the issues involved with field work, a process that has appreciable analogy with many types of documentary filmmaking practice. A more critical look at ethnography and the issues of representing others in appropriate written forms occurs in James Clifford and George Marcus, eds., *Writing Culture: Poetics and Politics of Ethnography* (Berkeley: University of California Press, 1986). It has relevance for documentary and ethnographic film. Two other books on Jean Rouch, Mick Eaton, *Anthropology, Reality, Cinema: The Films of Jean Rouch* (London: British Film Institute, 1979), and Joram ten Brink, ed., *Building Bridges: The Cinema of Jean Rouch* (New York: Wall-flower Press, 2007), explore issues of participatory filmmaking as they arise in relation to the work of one of the key founders of this mode.

Reflexive documentary work receives frequent consideration in the collected interviews with Trinh T. Minh-ha, *Framer Framed* (New York: Routledge Press, 1992), and her *Cinema Interval* (New York: Rout-ledge, 1999); these books include scripts and sketches from her films, which reveal the high degree of conscious fabrication she employs. Annette Michelson, *Kino-Eye: The Writings of Dziga Vertov* (Berkeley: University of California Press, 1984), gives us the original essays and manifestos by this pioneering Soviet filmmaker who is often cited as an early practitioner of reflexive documentary. Valuable contextual readings include Bertolt Brecht's theories of theater as presented in John Willet, ed., *Brecht on Theatre* (New York: Hill and Wang, 1992), and Victor Shklovsky's theories of estrangement or ostranenie in literature, especially in his essay "Art as Technique," found in Lee Lemon and Marion Reis, eds., *Russian Formalist Criticism: Four Essays* (Lincoln: University of Nebraska Press, 1965).

Contextual readings for performative documentary include two books by Judith Butler, *Gender Trouble* (New York: Routledge, 1990), and *Excitable Speech* (New York: Routledge, 1997). Earlier, J. L. Austin delivered a series of lectures at Harvard University on how words can achieve or perform tangible effects. The published lectures, J. O. Ur-mson and Marina Sbisa, eds., *How to Do Things with Words*, 2nd ed. (New York: Oxford University Press, 1975), explores this phenomenon but, as the text here indicates, it is only indirectly linked to the concept of performative documentary. A chapter in Bill Nichols, *Blurred Bound-aries*, discusses performative documentary in some detail. Aspects of Michael Renov and Erika Suderberg, eds., *Resolution: Contemporary Video Practice* (Minneapolis: University of Minnesota Press, 1996), take up issues of performativity, as well as reflexivity. Ilan Avisar's sen-sitive reading of *Night and Fog* in *Screening the Holocaust: Cinema's Image of the Unimaginable* (Bloomington: Indiana University Press, 1988), suggests ways in which this landmark film could be considered performative even though Avisar does not use that term specifically.

The question of what documentaries generally take up as topics invites reflection on the basic forms of social organization and the types of visible phenomena that accompany them. Useful readings include Peter Berger and Thomas Luckman, *The Social Construction of Reality* (New York: Anchor, 1990); George Lakoff and Mark Johnson, *Metaphors We Live By*; Irving Goffman, *Interaction Ritual: Essays on Face to Face Behaviour* (Chicago: Aldine, 1967), and his *Presentation of Self in Everyday Life* (New York: Doubleday, 1959); Sol Worth, *Through Navajo Eyes: An Exploration in Film Communication and Anthropology* (Bloomington: Indiana University Press, 1973), and his *Studying Visual Communication* (Philadelphia: University of Pennsylvania Press, 1981); and W. J. T. Mitchell, *Iconology: Image, Text, Ideology* (Chicago: University of Chicago Press, 1986), and *Picture Theory: Essays on Verbal and Visual Representation* (Chicago: University of Chicago Press, 1994).

Many books address the question of film and politics. Brian Winston, *Claiming the Real*, is one important revision of documentary history based on an assessment of the political impact of the form. Paula Rabinowitz, *They Must Be Represented*, gives a broad overview to the political issues surrounding documentary representation in the 1930s. William Alexander, *Films on the Left*, recounts the struggles to build a leftist filmmaking community in the United States, while Bill Nichols, *Newsreel: Documentary Filmmaking on the American Left, 1969–1974* (New York: Arno Press, 1980), picks up the story with the attempt by Newsreel to be the filmmaking arm of the New Left. Benedict Anderson, *Imagined Community: Reflections on the Origin and Spread of Nationalism* (New York: Verso, 1991), has stirred controversy with its argument that nation-states are constructs heavily beholden to the work of symbolic representation by such media as journalism, film, and television. Patricia Zimmerman, *States of Emergency: Documentaries, Wars and Democracies* (Minneapolis: University of Minnesota Press, 2000), brings issues of the nation-state and film into the era of the global economy and cybernetic systems. A valuable survey of film's representation of historically traumatic events can be found in Frances Guerin and Roger Hallas, eds., *The Image and the Witness: Trauma, Memory and Visual Culture* (New York: Columbia University Press, 2007).

The consequences of a shifting political climate for an individual artist's career receive illuminating discussion in Thomas Waugh, *Jo-*

ris Ivens and the Evolution of the Radical Documentary, 1926–1946; in Annette Michelson, ed., *Kino-Eye: The Writings of Dziga Vertov;* and in the catalogue for a MoMA exhibition of Rodchenko's work, Magdalena Dabrowski, ed., *Aleksandr Rodchenko* (New York: MoMA, 1998). Rodchenko, a Soviet artist, designer, and photographer, was a contemporary of Eisenstein and Vertov.

The shift from national politics to a more personal sense of politics and of the ramifications of identity politics receives exploration in numerous writings, among them Chris Holmlund and Cynthia Fuchs, eds., *Between the Sheets, In the Streets;* Patricia Zimmerman, *Reel Families: A Social History of Amateur Film* (Bloomington: Indiana University Press, 1995); Michelle Citron, *Home Movies and Other Necessary Fictions* (Minneapolis: University of Minnesota Press, 1998); Diane Waldman and Janet Walker, *Feminism and Documentary;* and Alexandra Juhasz, ed., *Women of Vision: Histories in Feminist Film and Video* (Minneapolis: University of Minnesota Press, 2001). An earlier but helpful discussion of feminist theory and documentary film occurs in E. Ann Kaplan, *Women and Film: Both Sides of the Camera* (New York: Methuen, 1983). Her later book, *Looking for the Other: Feminism, Film and the Imperial Gaze* (New York: Routledge, 1997), explores issues of cross-cultural representation in fiction and nonfiction. Thomas Waugh has given us an excellent history of gay erotica in *Hard to Imagine: Gay Male Eroticism in Photography and Film from Their Beginnings to Stonewall* (New York: Cambridge University Press, 1996); his collected writings, *The Fruit Machine: Twenty Years of Writing on Queer Cinema* (Durham, N.C.: Duke University Press, 2000), focus more pointedly on documentary and fiction film.

Chon A. Noriega, *Shot in America: Television, the State and the Rise of Chicano Cinema* (Minneapolis: University of Minnesota Press, 2000), and Phyllis R. Klotman and Janet K. Cutler, eds., *Struggles for Representation: African American Documentary Film and Video* (Bloomington: Indiana University Press, 1999), both give thoughtful consideration to documentary film as a means of personal but also collective expression in relation to the Chicano and African American communities, respectively.

Chapter 9, on how to write about documentary film, includes numerous references to work on Robert Flaherty. The material cited there is illustrative of what can be found but even more information can be located through additional book and article searches. Peter Wintonik's film *Cinéma Vérité: Defining the Moment* (Montreal: National Film Board of Canada, 1999), for example, is one of many films that include illustrative clips from *Nanook of the North*. *Nanook* itself is available as a film from the Museum of Modern Art and as a DVD, in a remastered version, from the Criterion Collection, a company renowned for its high-quality DVD releases of classic films.

In addition to the chapter devoted to the topic here, several basic reference works are useful for essay writing on documentary film. These include *The Chicago Manual of Style*, 15th ed. (Chicago: University of Chicago Press, 2003); the *MLA Style Manual and Guide to Scholarly Publishing*, 3rd ed. (New York: MLA, 2008); and Kate Turabian, *A Manual for Writers of Term Papers, Theses and Dissertations*, 7th ed. (Chicago: University of Chicago Press, 2007). Timothy Corrigan, *A Short Guide to Writing about Film*, 7th ed. (New York: Longman, 2009), gives many film-specific examples and tips.

Filmography

7 *Plus Seven*, Michael Apted, United Kingdom, 53 min., 1970

7 *Up*, Paul Almond, United Kingdom, 30 min., 1964

16 *in Webster Groves*, Arthur Barron, CBS Special, 46 min., 1966

49 *Up*, Michael Apted, United Kingdom/United States, 135 min., 2005

60 *Minutes*, CBS News TV series, 60 min. each episode, 1968

À *Propos de Nice*, Jean Vigo, France, 18 min., 1930

Abortion Stories: North and South, Gail Singer, National Film Board of Canada, 55 min., 1984

Act of Seeing with One's Own Eyes, The, Stan Brakhage, 32 min., 1971

Afrique, je te plumerai (Africa, I'm Going to Fleece You), Jean-Marie Téno, Cameroon/France, 88 min., 1993

Aileen Wuornos: The Selling of a Serial Killer, Nick Broomfield, 87 min., 1992

Always for Pleasure, Les Blank, 58 min., 1978

America's Most Wanted, Glenn Weiss, TV series, 30 min. each episode, 1988

American Dream, Barbara Kopple, 98 min., 1990

American Family, An, Craig Gilbert, National Educational Television (NET), 12 1-hour episodes, 1972

American Teen, Nanette Burstein, 101 min., 2008

Andalusian Dog, An. See *Un Chien Andalou*

Anderson Platoon, The (La Section Anderson), Pierre Schoendorffer, Vietnam/France, French Broadcasting System, France, 65 min., 1966

Anemic Cinema (Anémic cinéma), Marcel Duchamp, France, 5 min., 1926

Anthem, Marlon Riggs, 9 min., 1991

Antonia: Portrait of a Woman, Jill Godmilow and Judy Collins, 58 min., 1974

Arrival of a Train (Arrivée d'un train), August and Louis Lumière, France, 1 min., 1895

Artie Shaw: Time Is All You've Got, Brigitte Berman, Canada, 114 min., 1985

Australia's Funniest Home Movie Show, Bryan Cockerill, TV series, Australia, 30 min. each episode, 1990–2009

Aventure Malgache, Alfred Hitchcock, British Ministry of Information,

United Kingdom/France, 31 min., 1944

Ax Fight, The, Timothy Asch and Napoleon Chagnon, Yanomamö series, Venezuela/United States, 30 min., 1975

Basic Training, Frederick Wiseman, 90 min., 1971

Battle 360 (Battle 360: Call to Duty), TV series, the History Channel, Flight 33 Productions, 60 min. each episode, 2008–

Battle of Chile, The, Patricio Guzmán, Cuba/Chile/Venezuela, 3 parts at 100 min. each, 1975, 1977, 1979

Battle of Midway, The, John Ford, 18 min., 1942

Battle of San Pietro, The, John Huston, 33 min., 1945

Battleship Potemkin (Bronenosets Potyomkin), Sergei M. Eisenstein, Soviet Union, 75 min., 1925

Before Spring, Joris Ivens, China, 38 min., 1958

Before Stonewall: The Making of a Gay and Lesbian Community, Greta Schiller and Robert Rosenberg, 87 min., 1984

Berkeley in the Sixties, Mark Kitchell, 117 min., 1990

Berlin: Symphony of a Great City (Berlin: Die Sinfonie der Grosstadt), Walter Ruttmann, Germany, 53 min., 1927

Best in Show, Christopher Guest, 90 min., 2000

Bicycle Thieves (a.k.a. *The Bicycle Thief*) (*Ladri di Biciclette*), Vittorio De Sica, Italy, 93 min., 1948

Black Is, Black Ain't (Black Is . . . Black Ain't: A Personal Journey through Black Identity), Marlon T. Riggs, 88 min., 1995

Blair Witch Project, The, Daniel Myrick and Eduardo Sánchez, 80 min., 1999

Blood of the Beasts (La Sang des bêtes), Georges Franju, France, 22 min., 1949

Body Beautiful, The, Ngozi Onwurah, 20 min., 1991

Bon Voyage, Alfred Hitchcock, British Ministry of Information, United Kingdom/France, 26 min., 1944

Bontoc Eulogy, Marlon Fuentes, Philippines/United States, 50 min., 1995

Born into Brothels: Calcutta's Red Light Kids, Ross Kaufman and Zana Briski, Calcutta, India/United States, 83 min., 2004

Bowling for Columbine, Michael Moore, 119 min., 2002

Bridge, The, Joris Ivens, 11 min., 1928

Broken Rainbow, Mario Florio and Victoria Mudd, 70 min., 1985

Bus 174 (Ônibus 174), José Padilha, Brazil, 120 min., 2002

Cabinet of Dr. Caligari, The, Robert Wiene, Germany, 52 min., 1920

Cadillac Desert: Water and the Transformation of Nature, 4 parts (*Mulholland's Dream; An American Nile; The Mercy of Nature; Last Oasis*), Jon Else, 60 min. each, 1997

Cane Toads: An Unnatural History, Mark Lewis, Australia, 46 min., 1987

Cannibal Tours, Dennis O'Rourke, Papua New Guinea/Australia, 70 min., 1988

Capitalism: A Love Story, Michael Moore, 127 min., 2009

Capturing the Friedmans, Andrew Jarecki, Magnolia Pictures present, 108 min., 2003

Chair, The, Drew Associates: Gregory Shukur, Richard Leacock, D. A. Pennebaker, 60 min., 1962

Chile, Obstinate Memory, Patricio Guzmán, Canada/France, 53 min., 1997

Chronicle of a Summer (Chronique d'un eté), Jean Rouch and Edgar Morin, France, 90 min., 1960

Cinema-Eye. See Kino Glaz.

City, The, Ralph Steiner and Willard Van Dyke, 43 min., 1939

Civil War, The, Ken Burns, Public Broadcasting System, 9 parts, 680 min., 1990

Coal Face, Alberto Cavalcanti, Great Britain, 10 min., 1935

Color Adjustment, Marlon T. Riggs, 88 min., 1991

Comedy in Six Unnatural Acts, A, Jan Oxenberg, 41 min., 1975

Common Thread: Stories from the Quilt, Rob Epstein and Jeffrey Friedman, 79 min., 1989

Complaints of a Dutiful Daughter, Deborah Hoffmann, 44 min., 1994

Composition in Blue (Komposition in Blau), Oskar Fischinger, Germany, 4 min., 1935

Contempt (Le Mépris), Jean-Luc Godard, Italy/France, 105 min., 1963

Control Room, Jehane Noujaim, United States/Qatar, 84 min., 2004

Cops, John Langely, TV series, 30 min. each episode, 1989

Corporation, The, Mark Achbar and Jennifer Abbott, Canada, 145 min., 2003

Corpus: A Home Movie for Selena, Lourdes Portillo, 56 min., 1999

Cove, The, Louis Psihoyos, 92 min., 2009

Crazy Ray, The. See Paris Qui Dort

Crisis: Behind a Presidential Commitment, Robert Drew, 53 min., 1963

Crumb, Terry Zwigoff, 119 min., 1994

Daisy: The Story of a Facelift, Michael Rubbo, National Film Board of Canada, 57 min., 1982

Danube Exodus, Péter Forgács, Hungary, 60 min., 1998

Darwin's Nightmare, Hubert Sauper, Australia/Belgium/France, 107 min., 2004

Daughter Rite, Michelle Citron, 55 min., 1978

David Holzman's Diary, Jim McBride and L. M. Kit Carson, 71 min., 1968

Day after Trinity, The (The Day after Trinity: J. Robert Oppenheimer and the Atomic Bomb), Jon Else, 88 min., 1980

Dead Birds, Robert Gardner, West New Guinea/United States, 83 min., 1963

Derrida, Kirby Dick and Amy Ziering Kofman, United States/France, 84 min., 2002

Devil Never Sleeps, The (El Diablo Nunca Duerme), Lourdes Portillo, Mexico/United States, 87 min., 1994

Diagonal Symphony (Symphonie diagonale), Viking Eggeling, Germany, 5 min., 1924

Do the Right Thing, Spike Lee, 120 min., 1989

Dont Look Back, D. A. Pennebaker, Great Britain/United States, 96 min., 1967

Double Indemnity, Billy Wilder, 107 min., 1944

Down and Out in America, Lee Grant, 57 min., 1986

End of St. Petersburg, The (Konyets Sankt-Peterburga), Vsevolod Pudovkin, Soviet Union, 69 min., 1927

Enron: The Smartest Guys in the Room, Alex Gibney, 110 min., 2005

Enthusiasm (Simfoniya Donbassa), Dziga Vertov, Soviet Union, 69 min., 1930

Ethnic Notions, Marlon T. Riggs, 57 min., 1986

Etre et avoir (To Be and to Have), Nicolas Philibert, France, 100 min., 2002

Every Day except Christmas, Lindsay Anderson, Great Britain, 41 min., 1957

Extremely Personal Eros: Love Song 1974 (*Gokushiteki erosu: Renka 1974*), Kazuo Hara, Japan, 92 min., 1974

Eyes on the Prize, Henry Hampton, Public Broadcasting System, 14 1-hour segments, series I: 1987, series II: 1990

Fahrenheit 9/11, Michael Moore, 122 min., 2004

Fall of the Romanov Dynasty, The (*Padeniye dinastii Romanovykh*), Esther Shub, Soviet Union, 90 min., 1927

Family Business, Tom Cohen, Middletown series, Public Broadcasting System, Peter Davis, Producer, 90 min., 1982

Far from Poland, Jill Godmilow, 106 min., 1984

Fast, Cheap and Out of Control, Errol Morris, 80 min., 1997

Feeding the Baby (*Repas de bébé*), Louis Lumière, France, 1 min., 1895

Feeling My Way, Jonathan Hodgson, United Kingdom, 5 min., 1997

Fièvre, Louis Delluc, France, 30 min., 1921

Film about a Woman Who . . , A, Yvonne Rainer, 105 min., 1974

Finding Christa, Camille Billops and James Hatch, 55 min., 1991

Fireworks, Kenneth Anger, 20 min., 1947

First Contact, Robin Anderson and Bob Connelly, Papua New Guinea/Australia, 54 min., 1984

Fog of War: Eleven Lessons from the Life of Robert McNamara, The, Errol Morris, 107 min., 2003

Forest of Bliss, Robert Gardner, India/United States, 91 min., 1985

Forrest Gump, Robert Zemeckis, 142 min., 1994

Four Families, Margaret Mead, Fali Bilimoria, John Buss, Richard Gilbert, and William Novik, National Film Board of Canada, 58 min., 1959

Frantz Fanon: Black Skin, White Mask, Isaac Julien, France, Martinique/Great Britain, 70 min., 1996

Free Fall (*Az Örvény*), Péter Forgács, Hungary, 75 min., 1997

G.I. Jane, Ridley Scott, 125 min., 1997

Gimme Shelter (a.k.a. *The Rolling Stones: Gimme Shelter*), David Maysles, Albert Maysles, and Charlotte Zwerin, 91 min., 1970

Glass (*Glas*), Bert Haanstra, Netherlands, 11 min., 1958

Gleaners and I, The (*Les Glaneurs et la glaneuse*), Agnès Varda, France, 82 min., 2000

Global Assembly Line, The, Lorraine Gray, 58 min., 1986

God Grew Tired of Us: The Lost Boys of Sudan, Christopher Quinn, 86 min., 2005

Grass: A Nation's Battle for Life, Merian C. Cooper and Ernest B. Schoedsack, 70 min., 1925

Great Road, The, Esther Shub, Soviet Union, 1927

Greed, Eric Von Stroheim, 140 min., 1925

Grey Gardens, Albert and David Maysles, 95 min., 1975

Grizzly Man, Werner Herzog, Canada/United States, 104 min., 2005

Growing Up Female: As Six Becomes One, Julia Reichert and Jim Klein, 60 min., 1971

Gunner Palace, Michael Tucker and Petra Epperlein, 85 min., 2004

Hard Metals Disease, Jon Alpert, 57 min., 1987

Harlan County, U.S.A., Barbara Kopple, 103 min., 1977

Harvest of Shame, Edward R. Murrow, CBS News, 60 min., 1960

Heart of Spain, Herbert Kline and Geza Karpathi, Frontier Films, Spain/United States, 30 min., 1937

Hell House, George Ratliff, 85 min., 2001

High School, Frederick Wiseman, 75 min., 1968

His Mother's Voice, Dennis Tupicoff, Australia, 52 min., 1997

History and Memory: For Akiko and Takashige, Rea Tajiri, 33 min., 1991

Hoop Dreams, Steve James, Frederick Marx, and Peter Gilbert, 170 min., 1994

Hospital, Frederick Wiseman, 84 min., 1970

Hotel Terminus: The Life and Times of Klaus Barbie, Marcel Ophuls, France/United States, 267 min., 1988

Hour of the Furnaces, The (*La Hora de los hornos*), Octavio Getino and Fernando E. Solanas, Argentina, 260 min., 1968

Housing Problems, Edgar Anstey and Arthur Elton, United Kingdom, 30 min., 1935

How Yukong Moved the Mountains (*Comment Yukong déplaça les montagnes*), Joris Ivens and Marceline Loridan, France/China, 12 1-hour segments, 1976

Human Behavior Experiments, The, Alex Gibney, 58 min., 2006

Human Remains, Jay Rosenblatt, 30 min., 1998

Hunters, The, John Marshall and Robert Gardner, 72 min., 1957

I Am a Sex Addict, Caveh Zahedi, 99 min., 2005

Imagining Indians, Victor Masayesva Jr., 90 min., 1993

In and Out of Africa, Ilisa Barbash and Lucien Taylor, France/United States, 59 min., 1992

In the Land of the Head Hunters (restored, retitled, and released as *In the Land of the War Canoes*, 1972), Edward S. Curtis, 47 min., 1914

In the Year of the Pig, Emile de Antonio, 101 min., 1969

Inconvenient Truth, An, Davis Guggenheim, 96 min., 2006

Indonesia Calling, Joris Ivens, Australia, 15 min., 1946

Inflation, Hans Richter, Germany, 8 min., 1928

Injury to One, An, Travis Wilkerson, 53 min., 2002

Intimate Stranger, Alan Berliner, 60 min., 1992

Isle of Flowers (*Ilha das Flores*), Jorge Furtado, Brazil, 13 min., 1989

Jane, D. A. Pennebaker, Richard Leacock, and Drew Associates, 54 min., 1962

Janie's Janie, Geri Ashur and Peter Barton, 25 min., 1971

Jazz: The Story of America's Music, Ken Burns, 10-episode TV series, 1,114 min., 2000

Jeanne Dielman, 23 Quai du Commerce, 1080 Bruxelles, Chantal Ackerman, Belgium/France, 201 min., 1975

Jesus Camp, Heidi Ewing and Rachel Grady, 84 min., 2006

JFK, Oliver Stone, France/United States, 189 min., 1991

Journal Inachevé. See *Unfinished Diary*

Joyce at 34, Joyce Chopra and Claudia Weill, 28 min., 1972

Kenya Boran, parts 1 and 2, David McDougall and James Blue, Faces of Change series, 33 min. each, 1974

Kino Glaz (a.k.a. *Cinema-Eye, Kino-Eye*), Dziga Vertov, Soviet Union, 74 min., 1924

Kinopravda (*Cinema Truth*), Dziga Vertov, Soviet Union, 81 min., 1925

Komosol (a.k.a. *Komsomolsk, Song of Heroes*), Joris Ivens, Soviet Union, 50 min., 1932

Koyaanisqatsi, Godfrey Reggio, 87 min., 1983

Kurt and Courtney, Nick Broomfield, 95 min., 1998

L'Affiche (*The Poster*), Jean Epstein, France, 73 min., 1924

L'Age d'or (*The Golden Age*), Luis Buñuel, France, 60 min., 1930

L'Avventura, Michelangelo Antonioni, Italy, 142 min., 1960

L'Etoile de Mer (*The Starfish*), Man Ray, France, 15 min., 1928

La Roue (*The Wheel*), Abel Gance, France, 130 min., 1923

La Terra Trema (*The Earth Trembles*), Luchino Visconti, Italy, 160 min., 1948

Ladri di Biciclette. See *Bicycle Thieves*

Land without Bread (*Terre sans Pain* or *Las Hurdes*), Luis Buñuel, Spain, 27 min., 1932

Las Madres de la Plaza de Mayo, Susana Muñoz and Lourdes Portillo, Argentina/United States, 64 min., 1985

Last Days, The, James Moll, Hungary/United States, 87 min., 1998

Last Waltz, The, Martin Scorsese, 117 min., 1978

Le Retour à la Raison (*Return to Reason*), Man Ray, France, 3 min., 1923

Les Maîtres Fous, Jean Rouch, France, 30 min., 1955

Les Racquetteurs, Gilles Groulx and Michel Brault, National Film Board of Canada, 15 min., 1958

Lessons of Darkness (*Lektionen in Finsternis*), Werner Herzog, Germany/France/United Kingdom, 50 min., 1992

Letter to Jane, Jean-Luc Godard and Jean-Pierre Gorin, France, 45 min., 1972

Letter without Words, Lisa Lewenz, 62 min., 1998

Letters from China. See *Before Spring*

Life and Debt, Stephanie Black, 80 min., 2001

Life and Times of Rosie the Riveter, The, Connie Field, 65 min., 1980

Listen to Britain, Humphrey Jennings and Stewart McAllister, Great Britain, 21 min., 1941

Loneliness of the Long-Distance Runner, The, Tony Richardson, Great Britain, 104 min., 1962

Lonely Boy, Roman Kroiter and Wolf Koenig, National Film Board of Canada, 27 min., 1962

Looking for Langston, Isaac Julien, Great Britain, 55 min., 1988

Lost Boys of Sudan, Megan Mylan and Jon Shenk, 87 min., 2003

Louisiana Story, Robert Flaherty, 75 min., 1948

Maelstrom, The (*The Maelstrom: A Family Chronicle*), Péter Forgács, Netherlands, 60 min., 1997

Man Bites Dog (*C'est arrivé près de chez vous*), Rémy Belvaux, André Bonzel, and Benoît Poelvoorde, Belgium/France, 95 min., 1992

Man on Wire, James Marsh, United Kingdom/United States, 94 min., 2008

Man with a Movie Camera, The (*Chelovek s kinoapparatom*), Dziga Vertov, Soviet Union, 103 min., 1929

Maquilapolis (*Maquilapolis: City of Factories*), Vicki Funari and Sergio de la Torre, Mexico/United States, 68 min., 2006

March of the Penguins, Luc Jaquet, France, 80 min., 2005

Married Couple, A, Allan King, Canada, 90 min., 1970

Meat, Frederick Wiseman, 112 min., 1976

Memorandum, Donald Brittain and John Spotton, National Film Board of Canada, 58 min., 1965

Ménilmontant, Dimitri Kirsanoff, France, 35 min., 1926

Metallica: Some Kind of Monster, Joe Berlinger and Bruce Sinofsky, 134 min., 2004

Metropolis, Fritz Lang, Germany, 115 min., 1927

Midnight Movies: From the Margin to the Mainstream, Stuart Samuels, Canada/United States, 86 min., 2005

Milk, Gus Van Sant, 127 min., 2008

Misère au Borinage, Joris Ivens and Henri Storck, Belgium, 36 min., 1934

Moana: A Romance of the South Seas, Robert J. Flaherty, Samoa/United States, 26 min., 1927

Model, Frederick Wiseman, 129 min., 1980

Momma Don't Allow, Karel Reis and Tony Richardson, Great Britain, 22 min., 1956

Mondo Cane (It's a Dog's World), Gualtiero Jacopetti and Franco E. Prosperi, Italy, 105 min., 1962

Monster, Patty Jenkins, United States/Germany, 109 min., 2003

Monster Kid Home Movies, Robert Tinnell, 120 min., 2005

Monterey Pop, D. A. Pennebaker, 82 min., 1968

Murderball, Henry Alex Rubin and Dana Adam Shapiro, 88 min., 2005

My Architect: A Son's Journey, Nathaniel Khan, 116 min., 2003

N!ai: The Story of a !Kung Woman, John Marshall, Odyssey series/PBS, Kalahari Desert (Nambia, Angolia)/United States, 58 min., 1980

Nanook of the North, Robert Flaherty, Canada/United States, 55 min., 1922

Night and Fog (Nuit et brouillard), Alain Resnais, Poland/France, 31 min., 1955

Night Mail, Harry Watt and Basil Wright, 30 min., 1936

Nitrate Kisses, Barbara Hammer, 67 min., 1992

No Lies, Mitchell W. Block, 16 min., 1973

Nobody's Business, Alan Berliner, 60 min., 1996

Nosferatu, F. W. Murnau, Germany, 63 min., 1922

Not a Love Story: A Film about Pornography, Bonnie Sherr Klein, National Film Board of Canada, 68 min., 1981

Nuer, The, Hilary Harris, George Breidenbach, and Robert Gardner, Ethiopia/United States, 75 min., 1970

N.Y., N.Y., Francis Thompson, 15 min., 1957

Obedience, Stanley Milgram, 45 min., 1965

October (Ten Days That Shook the World), Sergei M. Eisenstein, Soviet Union, 104 min., 1927

Old and the New, The (The General Line), Sergei M. Eisenstein and Grigori Aleksandrov, Soviet Union, 70 min., 1929

Operation Abolition, House Un-American Activities Committee with Washington Video Productions, 45 min., 1960

Operation Correction, American Civil Liberties Union, 47 min., 1961

Pacific 231, Jean Mitry, 10 min., 1949

Paradise Lost: The Child Murders at Robin Hood Hills, Joe Berlinger and Bruce Sinofsky, 150 min., 1996

Paris Is Burning, Jennie Livingston, 71 min., 1990

Paris Qui Dort (The Crazy Ray), René Clair, France, 36 min., 1924

People's Century, The, WGBH-Boston/PBS, 26 1-hour episodes, 1998

Play of Light: Black, White, Grey (Zeigt ein Lichtspiel: Schwarz, weiss, grau), Laszlo Moholy-Nagy, Germany, 6 min., 1930

Plow That Broke the Plains, The, Pare Lorentz, U.S. Resettlement Administration, 25 min., 1936

Portrait of Jason, Shirley Clarke, 105 min., 1967

Power of Nightmares: The Rise of the Politics of Fear, The, Adam Curtis, United Kingdom, 180 min., 2004

Prelude to War, first of the seven *Why We Fight* films, Frank Capra, United States War Department, 54 min., 1941

Primary, Drew Associates: Robert Drew, D. A. Pennebaker, and Richard Leacock, with Terence Macartney-Filgate and Albert Maysles, 60 min., 1960

Prince Is Back, The, Marina Goldovskaya, Russia, 59 min., 1999

Rabbit in the Moon, Emiko Omori, 85 min., 1999

Radio Bikini, Robert Stone, 56 min., 1987

Rain (Regen), Joris Ivens, Holland, 14 min., 1929

Real Sex, Patti Kaplan, Home Box Office series, approximately 27 50-min. episodes, 1992–2001

Reassemblage, Trinh T. Minh-ha, Senegal/United States, 40 min., 1982

Report from the Aleutians, John Huston, U.S. Army Signal Corps, 47 min., 1943

Revolution Will Not Be Televised, The (a.k.a. *Chavez: Inside the Coup*), Kim Bartley and Donnacha O'Briain, Ireland/Netherlands/United States, 74 min., 2002

Rhythmus 23, Hans Richter, Germany, 4 min., 1923

Rien que les Heures, Alberto Cavalcanti, France, 45 min., 1926

River, The, Pare Lorentz, Farm Security Administration, 31 min., 1937

Road to Guantanamo, The, Mat Whitecross and Michael Winterbottom, United Kingdom, 95 min., 2006

Roger and Me, Michael Moore, 87 min., 1989

Rome, Open City (Roma, città aperta), Roberto Rossellini, Italy, 100 min., 1945

Roses in December, Ana Carringan and Bernard Stone, El Salvador/United States, 56 min., 1982

Roy Cohn/Jack Smith, Jill Godmilow, 90 min., 1994

Russia of Nicholas II and Leo Tolstoy, The, Esther Shub, Soviet Union, 60 min., 1928

Ryan, Chris Landreth, Canada, 14 min., 2004

S 21: The Khmer Rouge Killing Machine (S-21: La machine de mort Khmère rouge), Rithy Panh, 101 min., 2003

Sad Song of Yellow Skin, Michael Rubbo, National Film Board of Canada, South Vietnam/Canada, 58 min., 1970

Salesman, Albert Maysles, David Maysles, and Charlotte Zwerin, 90 min., 1969

Salt for Svanetia (Sol Svanetii), Mikhail Kalatozov, Soviet Union, 53 min., 1930

Salt of the Earth, Herbert J. Biberman, 94 min., 1954

Sans Soleil, Chris Marker, France, 100 min., 1982

Saturday Night and Sunday Morning, Karel Reisz, United Kingdom, 89 min., 1960

Saving Private Ryan, Steven Spielberg, 170 min, 1998

Schindler's List, Steven Spielberg, 196 min., 1993

Scorpio Rising, Kenneth Anger, 30 min., 1964

Sea Horse, The (L'hippocampe), Jean Painlevé, France, 14 min., 1934

Selling of the Pentagon, The, Peter Davis, CBS News, 52 min., 1971

Seven Days in September (7 Days in September), Steven Rosenbaum, 94 min., 2002

Seventeenth Parallel, The (Le 17e Parallèle: La guerre du peuple), Joris Ivens, Vietnam/France, 113 min., 1968

Shadows, John Cassavetes, 87 min., 1960

Sherman's March, Ross McElwee, 155 min., 1985

Shoah, Claude Lanzman, Poland/France, part 1, 273 min.; part 2, 290 min., 1985

Sicko, Michael Moore, 123 min., 2007

Silence, Orly Yadin and Sylvie Bringas, United Kingdom, 10 min., 1998

Silverlake Life: The View from Here, Tom Joslin, Mark Massi, and Peter Friedman, 99 min., 1993

Smiling Madame Beudet, The (La souriante Madame Beudet), Germaine Dulac, France, 54 min., 1922

Smoke Menace, John Taylor, Great Britain, 14 min., 1937

Soldier Girls, Joan Churchill and Nick Broomfield, 87 min., 1980

Solovky Power (Solovetsky vlast), Marina Goldovskaya, Soviet Union, 90 min., 1988

Song of Ceylon, Basil Wright, Ceylon/Great Britain, 40 min., 1934

Song of the Rivers (Des Lied der Ströme), Joris Ivens and Joop Huisken, East Germany, 100 min., 1954

Sorrow and the Pity, The (La Chagrin et le Pitié), Marcel Ophuls, France, 260 min., 1970

Spanish Earth, The, Joris Ivens, 52 min., 1937

Speak Body, Kay Armatage, Canada, 20 min., 1987

Standard Operating Procedure, Errol Morris, 116 min., 2008

Star Wars (Star Wars Episode IV: A New Hope), George Lucas, 122 min., 1977

Statue of Liberty, The, Ken Burns, Paramount Home Entertainment, 60 min., 1985

Strange Fruit, Joel Katz, 57 min., 2002

Strange Victory, Leo Hurwitz, 80 min., 1948

Stranger with a Camera, Elizabeth Barret, 58 min., 1999

Strike, Sergei M. Eisenstein, Soviet Union, 82 min., 1925

Super Size Me, Morgan Spurlock, 100 min., 2004

Surname Viet Given Name Nam, Trinh T. Minh-ha, 108 min., 1989

Survivor, Charlie Parsons, TV series, 60 min. each episode, 2000–2009

Takeover, David and Judith MacDougall, 90 min., Australia, 1981

Tale of the Wind (Une histoire de vent), Joris Ivens, France, 80 min., 1988

Tarnation, Jonathan Caouette, 88 min., 2003

Taxi to the Dark Side, Alex Gibney, United States/Iran, 106 min., 2007

Terre sans Pain. See Land without Bread

Thin Blue Line, The, Errol Morris, American Playhouse/PBS, 115 min., 1988

Thin Red Line, The, Terrence Malick, 170 min., 1998

Things I Cannot Change, The, Tanya Ballantyne, National Film Board of Canada, 58 min., 1966

This Film is Not Yet Rated, Kirby Dick, 97 min., 2005

This Is Spinal Tap, Rob Reiner, 82 min., 1984

This Sporting Life, Lindsay Anderson, United Kingdom, 134 min., 1963

Three Songs of Lenin (Tri pesni o Lenine), Dziga Vertov, Soviet Union, 62 min., 1934

Ties That Bind, The, Su Friedrich, 55 min., 1984

Times of Harvey Milk, The, Robert Epstein and Richard Schmiechen, 87 min., 1984

Tongues Untied, Marlon Riggs, 45 min., 1989

Train Leaving a Station. See Arrival of a Train

Trance and Dance in Bali, Gregory Bateson and Margaret Mead, Character Formation in Different Culture series, Bali/United States, 20 min., based on fieldwork in 1936–1938, released in 1952

Tribulation 99: Alien Anomalies Under America, Craig Baldwin, 48 min., 1991

Trip to the Moon, A (Voyage dans la lune), Georges Méliès, France, 14 min., 1902

Triumph of the Will (Triumph des Willens), Leni Riefenstahl, Germany, 107 min., 1935

Trouble the Water, Carl Deal and Tia Lessin, 94 min., 2008

Truman Show, The, Peter Weir, 103 min., 1998

Turksib, Victor A. Turin, Soviet Union, 57 min., 1929

TV Nation, Michael Moore, TV series, 1994

Two Laws, Carolyn Strachan and Alessandro Cavadini with the Borrolola community, 130 min., 1981

Two Spirits: Sexuality, Gender and the Murder of Fred Martinez, Lydia Nibley, 65 min., 2009

Un Chant d'amour (A Song of Love), Jean Genet, France, 77 min., 1950

Un Chien Andalou (An Andalusian Dog), Luis Buñuel and Salvador Dali, France, 16 min., 1929

Unfinished Diary (Journal Inachevé), Marilu Mallet, Canada, 55 min., 1983

Union Maids, Jim Klein, Miles Mogulescu, and Julia Reichert, 51 min., 1976

Up the Yangtze, Yung Chang, Canada, 93 min., 2007

Vent d'est, Jean-Luc Godard, 92 min., 1970

Vernon, FL, Errol Morris, 56 min., 1981

Victory at Sea, Henry Salomon and Isaac Kleinerman, NBC Television, 26 30-minute episodes, 1952–1953

Waltz with Bashir (Vals Im Bashir), Ari Folman, Israel/Germany/France/United States/Finland/Switzerland/Belgium/Australia, 87 min., 2008

War, The, Ken Burns and Lynn Novick, 7-part PBS TV series, 840 min. total, 2007

War Comes to America, Frank Capra and Anatole Litvak, U.S. War Dept., part 7 of the Why We Fight series, 70 min., 1945

War Game, The, Peter Watkins, Great Britain, 45 min., 1966

War Room, The, Chris Hegedus and D. A. Pennebaker, Pennebaker Associates, 96 min., 1993

Watering the Gardener (a.k.a. The Waterer Watered) (L'Arroseur arrosé), Louis Lumière, France, 1 min., 1895

Watsonville on Strike, Jon Silver, 70 min., 1989

Ways of Seeing, with John Berger, BBC, Great Britain, 4 30-minute episodes, 1974

We Are the Lambeth Boys, Karel Reisz, Great Britain, 52 min., 1958

Wedding Camels, David and Judith MacDougall, Turkana Conversations

Trilogy, Kenya/Australia, 108 min., 1980

Wheel, The. See *La Roue*

When the Levees Broke: A Requiem in Four Acts, Spike Lee, 240 min., 2006

When We Were Kings, Leon Gast, 88 min., 1996

Who Killed Vincent Chin? Renee Tajima-Peña and Christine Choy, 87 min., 1988

Why Vietnam? U.S. Department of Defense, Vietnam/United States, 32 min., 1965

Why We Fight, Eugene Jarecki, United States/France/United Kingdom/Canada/Denmark, 99 min., 2005

Why We Fight series, Frank Capra and Anatole Litvak, United States War Department, 7-part film series, 1942–1945

Wild Parrots of Telegraph Hill, Judy Irving, 83 min., 2004

Wild Safari 3D: A South African Adventure, Ben Stassen, an Image Maximum (IMAX) film, Belgium, 45 min., 2005

Wind from the East. See *Vent d'est*

With Babies and Banners: The Story of the Women's Emergency Brigade, Lorraine Gray, Anne Bohlen, and Lynn Goldfarb, 45 min., 1979

Woman's Film, The, S.F. Newsreel Women's Caucus, 40 min., 1971

Wonderful, Horrible Life of Leni Riefenstahl, The, Ray Müller, Germany, 180 min., 1993

Word Is Out, Mariposa collective: Nancy Adair, Peter Adair, Andrew Brown, Robert Epstein, Lucy Massie Phenix, and Veronica Silver, 130 min., 1977

Workers Leaving the Lumière Factory (La Sortie des usines Lumière), Louis Lumière, France, 1 min., 1895

Yanomamö series. 22-part film series. See *The Ax Fight*

Yidl in the Middle: Growing Up Jewish in Iowa, Marlene Booth, 58 min., 1998

Yosemite: The Fate of Heaven, Jon Else, 58 min., 1988

Zvenigora, Alexander Dovzhenko, Soviet Union, 90 min., 1928

List of Distributors, Internet Distribution Venues, Internet Search Engines, and International Distributors

This list is considerably expanded from the one in the first edition. Independent Media Publications has recently published *The Independent's Guide to Film Distribution*, a comprehensive guide to distribution for the filmmaker working outside the studio system in fiction and nonfiction. The book covers self-distribution, on-line distribution, deal-making tips, and preparing a film for distribution.

The World Wide Web has proven a very rich resource for information and viewing and several sites are listed below, both under "Distributors" and "Internet Distribution Venues." What is on the web changes frequently; new resources can often be found by doing a web search for a film title, director, or other topic. Representative topics or titles are listed here. Check distributor websites for up-to-date information on their holdings.

DISTRIBUTORS

7th Art Releasing

1614 N. Fairfax Ave.
Los Angeles, CA 90046
Phone: (323) 845-1455

Fax: (323) 845-4717
Website: www.7thart.com
Contact: seventhart@7thart.com

Among its documentary titles are *The Long Way Home; Afghan Story; Gender Trouble; Eyewitness; The Last Jewish Town; Always a Bridesmaid; Why We Wax;* and *American Pimp.*

Agee Films

James Agee Film Project
P.O. Box 73
Riverdale, MD 20738
Phone: (301) 277-3880
Website: www.ageefilms.org
Contact: jagee@cstone.net

Their documentaries include *Appalachia: A History of Mountains and People; Tell about the South: Voices in Black & White; The Story of Modern Southern Literature; Long Shadows; Agee;* and *Toni Morrison's Nobel Prize Acceptance Speech.*

Alive Mind Media

56 West 45th St., Suite 805
New York, NY 10036
Phone: (212) 398-3112
Fax: (212) 398-3275
Website: www.alivemindmedia.com

Alive Mind carries programming such as *Hair: Let the Sun Shine In*; *Fierce Light*; *The Tibetan Book of the Dead*; *Ernesto "Che" Guevara: The Bolivian Diary*; *Through the Eastern Gate*; and *Arab Labor*.

Anchor Bay Entertainment

70 The Esplanade, Suite 300
Toronto, Ontario, Canada M5E 1R2
Phone: (416) 862-1700
Website: www.anchorbayentertain
ment.com
Contact: questions@anchorbayent
.com

Their documentary titles include *Ladies or Gentlemen*; *Seven Days in September*; *Bloodsucking Cinema*; *Larry Flynt: The Right to Be Left Alone*; *Manufacturing Dissent*; and *Midnight Movies: From the Margin to the Mainstream*.

Argot Pictures

484 7th St., Apartment 2
Brooklyn, NY 11215
Phone: (718) 369-1180
Website: www.argotpictures.com
Contact: jim@argotpictures.com

Argot carries such documentaries as *Fire Under the Snow*; *American Casino*; *Throw Down Your Heart*; and *Secrecy*.

Arthouse Films

c/o Hastens
80 Greene St.
New York, NY 10012
Phone: (212) 966-1760
Fax: (212) 202-3538
Website: www.arthousefilmsonline
.com
Contact: info@arthousefilmsonline
.com

Arthouse carries documentary titles such as *A Walk into the Sea*; *Milton*

Glaser; *Joan Mitchell: Portrait of an Abstract Painter*; *Jack Smith & The Destruction of Atlantis*; and *Harry Smith's Old Weird America*.

Balcony Releasing

26 Mill Lane
Amherst, MA 01002
Phone: (413) 253-6783
Fax: (413) 253-6782
Website: www.balconyfilm.com
Contact: greg@balconyfilm.com

Balcony Releasing has released such films as *Kurt Cobain: About a Son*; *Dr. Bronner's Magic Soapbox*; *The Same River Twice*; *Al Franken: God Spoke*; *Enlighten Up*; and *Pray the Devil Back to Hell*.

Berkeley Media, LLC

2600 Tenth St., Suite 626
Berkeley, CA 94710
Phone: (510) 486-9900
Fax: (510) 486-9944
Website: www.berkeleymedia.com
Contact: info@berkeleymedia.com

Their collection includes titles such as *In and Out of Africa*; *Sexism in Language: Thief of Honor, Shaper of Lies*; *You Don't Know Dick*; *Beyond Our Boundaries*; and *Birdsong and Coffee: A Wake Up Call*.

Bullfrog Films

P.O. Box 149
Oley, PA 19547
Phone: (610) 779-8226
Website: www.bullfrogfilms.com
Contact: info@bullfrogfilms.com

Examples of recent titles include *All in This Tea*; *Homo Toxicus*; *Crips and Bloods: Made in America*; and *Milking the Rhino*.

California Newsreel

500 Third St., Suite 505
San Francisco, CA 94107
Phone: (415) 284-7800
Fax: (415) 284-7801
Website: www.newsreel.org
Contact: contact@newsreel.org

California Newsreel carries some of
the classic Newsreel titles such as *Black
Panther* and *San Francisco State: On
Strike*, many more recent films on
Africa. Their documentary titles in-
clude *Black Is, Black Ain't*; *Big Mama*;
Liberia: An Uncivil War; *Frantz Fanon:
Black Skin, White Mask*; *Banished*;
Color Adjustment; and *Herskovits at the
Heart of Blackness*.

Cambridge Documentary

P.O. Box 390385
Cambridge, MA 02139
Phone: (617) 484-3993
Fax: (617) 484-0754
Website: www.cambridge
documentaryfilms.org
Contact: mail@cambridge
documentaryfilms.org

This distributor carries titles such as
Rape Is . . . ; *The Strength to Resist: The
Media's Impact on Women and Girls*;
Defending Our Lives; *Pink Triangles*;
and *Choosing Children*.

Canadian Film Distribution Center

Canadian Studies at SUNY
Plattsburgh
101 Broad St.
Plattsburgh, NY 12901
Phone: (518) 564-2226
Fax: (518) 564-2300
Website: www.plattsburgh.edu/
academics/canadianstudies/
filmandvideo.php
Contact: mark.richard@plattsburgh
.edu

The nonprofit center distributes many
National Film Board of Canada films
and other Canadian films such as *Acid
Rain: Requiem or Recovery*.

Canadian Filmmakers Distribution Centre

401 Richmond St. W., Suite 119
Toronto, Ontario, Canada MV5 3A8
Phone: (416) 588-0725
Fax: (416) 588-7956
Website: www.cfmdc.org
Contact: members@cfmd.org

This distribution center represents
about 550 filmmakers worldwide and
over 2,600 films ranging from the 1950s
to the present. Some of their documentary film titles include *Becoming Susan*;
Class Queers; *Digital Nudes in Oil*; and
Fragments de Corps.

Canyon Cinema

145 Ninth St., Suite 260
San Francisco, CA 94103
Phone: (415) 626-2255
Website: www.canyoncinema.com
Contact: dominic@canyoncinema
.com

Canyon Cinema's list runs from the
complete works of Kenneth Anger and
Bruce Conner to radical 1960s Newsreel titles like *Off the Pig* and *People's
Park*, as well as newer work by independent filmmakers. Their collection
includes over 3,500 film titles following
the experimental movement from the
1930s to the present.

Castle Hill Productions

36 West 25th St., 2nd Floor
New York, NY 10010
Phone: (212) 242-1500
Fax: (212) 414-5737
Website: www.castlehillproductions
.com
Contact: mm@castlehillproductions
.com

Their list includes titles such as Orson Welles's *Othello*; John Cassavetes's *A Woman Under the Influence*; John Ford's *Stagecoach*; *The Lives of Lillian Hellman*; *JFK: Years of Lightning, Day of Drums*; *A Great Day In Harlem*; and *Elia Kazan: A Director's Journey*.

The Center for Independent Documentary

Their titles include *Before Homosexuals*; *After Stonewall*; *94 Years and One Nursing Home Later*; *Frank: A Vietnam Veteran*; *Murder at Harvard*; *Mysticism and Monotheism*; and *She's a Boy*.

Choices, Inc.

369 S. Doheny Dr., PMB 1105
Beverly Hills, CA 90211
Phone: (888) 570-5400
Fax: (310) 839-1511
Website: www.choicesvideo.net
Contact: getinfo@choicesvideo.net

Choices is a distributor with many documentary titles from around the world. Their titles include *Dateline Afghanistan: Reporting the Forgotten War*; *Missing, Presumed Dead: The Search for America's POWs*; and *Radiation: A Slow Death*.

Cinema Epoch

10940 Wilshire Blvd., 16th Floor
Los Angeles, CA 90024
Phone: (310) 443-4244
Website: www.cinemaepoch.com
Contact: info@cinemaepoch.com

Cinema Epoch's catalogue includes the documentary titles *Prostitution Pornography U.S.A.*; *Little Shaolin Monks*; *American Carny: True Tales from the Circus Sideshow*; and *The Man You Had in Mind*.

Cinema Guild

115 West 30th St., Suite 800
New York, NY 10001
Toll Free: (800) 723-5522
Phone: (212) 685-6242
Fax: (212) 685-4717
Website: www.cinemaguild.com
Contact: info@cinemaguild.com

Over the last 30 years the Cinema Guild has come to be one of the leading distributors of documentary and fiction films and videos in markets including theatrical, television, cable, internet, and home video. They carry a wide array of contemporary documentaries in an extensive list of categories including African studies, art history, death and dying, disabilities, religious studies, shorts, women's studies, and gay and lesbian studies. Their list of movies includes such documentaries as *Out of Sight*; *Secuestro: A Story of a Kidnapping*; *South Africa: Beyond a Miracle*; *Valley of Tears*; and many other titles focusing on social change. The collection also includes a large number of Latin American, Caribbean, Middle Eastern, and African titles, such as *Maquila: A Tale of Two Mexicos*; *Lanfanmi Selavi*; *Hanan Ashrawi: A Woman of Her Time*; and *The Man Who Drove Mandela*.

Davidson Films

735 Tank Farm Rd., Suite 210
San Luis Obispo, CA 93401
Toll Free: (888) 437-4200
Phone: (805) 594-0422
Fax: (805) 594-0532
Website: www.davidsonfilmstore.com
Contact: dfi@davidsonfilms.com

Specializing in educational films, Davidson has been working to produce and distribute films for such institutions as the National Science Foundation, Macmillan, and the Encyclopedia

Britannica since their start-up in 1955. Their catalogue includes such films as *Three Films on Infancy and Toddlerhood; Morality: The Process of Moral Development; Performance Assessment: A Teacher's Way of Knowing*; and *Human Brain Development: Nature and Nurture.*

Direct Cinema Limited

P.O. Box 10003
Santa Monica, CA 90410-1003
Phone: (310) 636-8200
Fax: (310) 636-8228
Website: www.directcinema.com
Contact: orders@directcinema
limited.com

Direct Cinema carries both short and feature-length documentaries in subject areas such as the Holocaust (*Angels of Vengeance; The Hunt for Adolf Eichman*), Jewish life and culture (*Half the Kingdom; Intermarriage: When Love Meets Tradition*), history (*Primary; Vietnam Requiem; Four Little Girls*), dance and opera (*Sing Faster: The Stagehand's Ring Cycle; Suzanne Farrell: Elusive Muse*), and anthropology (*The Amish and Us; Cannibal Tours*).

Documentary Educational Resources

101 Morse St.
Watertown, MA 02472
Phone: (617) 926-0491
Fax: (617) 926-9519
Website: www.der.org
Contact: docued@der.org

DER specializes in ethnographic, documentary, and nonfiction films from around the world. The Yanomamo, Bushmen, and !Kung series are represented, as well as such newer works as *How the Myth Was Made; Movement ®evolution Africa; Breaking the Cycle; When Medicine Got It Wrong*; and *Postcards from Tora Bora.*

Docurama Films

902 Broadway, 9th Floor
New York, NY 10010
Phone: (212) 206-8600
Fax: (212) 206-9001
Website: www.docurama.com
Contact: info@newvideo.com

Docurama's collection includes such documentary films as *Dont Look Back; The Brandon Teena Story; Hacking Democracy; Murder on a Sunday Morning; Operation Homecoming: Writing the Wartime Experience*; and *Maya Lin: A Strong Clear Vision.*

Downtown Community Television Center

87 Lafayette St.
New York, NY 10013
Phone: (212) 966-4510
Fax: (212) 226-3053
Website: www.dctvny.org
Contact: info@dctvny.org

DCTV has helped artists to broadcast work via cable television, the internet and their Cybercar, a production vehicle with a giant video wall mounted on the side. Their documentary list includes *Afghanistan: From Ground Zero to Ground Zero; High on Crack Street: Lost Lives in Lowell; Hunger in the Suburbs*; and *Main Street USA.*

Echo Bridge Entertainment

3089 Airport Rd.
La Crosse, WI 54603
Phone: (608) 784-6620
Fax: (608) 784-6635
Website: www.echobridge
entertainment.com
Contact: sales@echobridgehe.com

Their documentary section includes such films as *America's Shield; The Boneyard; The Six Degrees of Helter Skelter; Going Hollywood: The 30s*; and *The Forgotten Coast.*

Electronic Arts Intermix

535 West 22nd St., 5th Floor
New York, NY 10011
Phone: (212) 337-0680
Fax: (212) 337-0679
Website: www.eai.org
Contact: info@eai.org

EAI was founded in 1971 and its collection ranges from historical works of the 1960s to the present and all titles can be ordered from its website. Arranged by artist, EAI carries the work of Phyllis Baldino, Jean-Luc Godard, Terry Fox, John Cage, Chris Marker, Paper Rad, and Andy Warhol, among many others.

Elephant Eye Films

27 W. 20th St., Suite 607
New York, NY 10011
Phone: (212) 488-8877
Website: www.elephanteyefilms.com
Contact: info@elephanteyefilms.com

Among their films are some documentary features such as *Billy the Kid*; *Planet B-Boy*; *Fidel's Last Dance*; and *Audience of One*.

Em Gee

6924 Canby Ave., Suite 103
Reseda, CA 91335
Phone: (818) 881-8110
Fax: (818) 981-5506
Website: www.emgee.freeyellow.com
Contact: Murray713@hotmail.com

Em Gee specializes in early cinema, with more than 6,000 American and international titles in distribution. Some titles of interest include *Rescued by Rover* and *La Jetée*.

Facets Multimedia, Inc.

1517 W. Fullerton Ave.
Chicago, IL 60614
Phone: (800) 331-6197
Fax: (773) 929-5437
Website: www.facets.org

Facets carries an unusually diverse array of quality films on DVD and videotape, including some rare, out-of-print, and hard-to-find titles. Their documentary titles include *Nanook of the North*; *The Battle of San Pietro*; *The 11th Hour*; *21 Days to Baghdad*; *Two Laws*; the *Up* series; *Shoah*; and *Mr. Death: The Rise and Fall of Fred A. Leuchter, Jr.*

Fanlight Productions

c/o Icarus Films
32 Court St.
Brooklyn, NY 11201
Toll Free: (800) 937-4113
Phone: (617) 469-4999
Fax: (617) 469-3379
Website: www.fanlight.com
Contact: info@fanlight.com

Fanlight carries titles such as *The Chemo Ate My Homework*; *A Family Disrupted*; *Four Films on Grief and Bereavement*; *Grey, Black and Blue: Nursing Home Violence*; and *Positive Images of Aging*.

The Film Desk

Brooklyn, New York
Website: www.thefilmdesk.com
Contact: info@thefilmdesk.com

The Film Desk primarily releases new 35mm prints of international classics such as Charlie Chaplin's *Monsieur Verdoux*, François Truffaut's *The Wild Child*, and new American documentaries (Alexander Olch's *The Windmill Movie*). They have also acquired the rights to Susan Sontag's 1974 documentary *Promised Lands*, for 2010 release.

Film Ideas, Inc.

308 North Wolf Rd.
Wheeling, IL 60090
Toll Free: (800) 475-3456
Phone: (847) 419-0255
Fax: (847) 419-8933

Website: www.filmideas.com
Contact: mikec@filmideas.com

Their titles include *The Faces of AIDS*; *Historic Milestones: 24 Global Events*; *Blood vs. Germs: News You Can Use*; *Picky Eaters: Mealtime Tips for Parents*; and *I Do: Do-It-Yourself Wedding Planning*.

Film Movement

109 West 27th St., Suite 9B
New York, NY 10001
Phone: (866) 937-3456
Website: www.filmmovement.com
Contact: info@filmmovement.com

Their catalogue can be searched by genre, and their documentary titles include *Her Name Is Sabine*; *Anytown, USA*; *Let the Church Say Amen*; *Mine*; and documentary shorts including *Motorcycle*; *Holland Tunnel*; and *Hold Up*.

Filmakers Library

124 East 40th St.
New York, NY 10016
Phone: (212) 808-4980
Website: www.filmakers.com
Contact: info@filmakers.com

Filmakers Library offers a very strong selection of documentary titles on an array of topics such as labor (*Battle of the Titans*; *Children of the Silver Mountain*), health and disability (*Sex, Drugs and Middle Age*; *Who Lives, Who Dies: Rationing Health Care*; *The Cyborg Revolution*), immigration (*Blue Collar & Buddha*; *Chinatown Files*), environment (*American Thirst, Canadian Water*; *The Chemical Kids*), gay, lesbian, and gender issues (*Adventures in the Gender Trade*; *Just Married: The Epic Battle Over Gay Marriage*), and religion (*Get the Fire! Young Mormon Missionaries Abroad*; *Be a Patriot, Kill a Priest*).

Films Media Group

200 American Metro Blvd., Suite 124
Hamilton, NJ 08619
Toll Free: (800) 257-5126
Phone: (609) 671-1000
Fax: (609) 671-0266
Website: www.ffh.films.com
Contact: custserv@films.com

Formerly known as Films for the Humanities and Sciences, this distributor carries more than 12,000 titles focusing on educational video and multimedia programs for schools, colleges, libraries, and the medical community. The company's films include such titles as *Drugs: The Straight Facts*; *Breaking the Facts*; *In Darwin's Garden: Evolutionary Theory and Nature's Laboratory*; *The Secret Life of Your Body Clock*; *Bill Moyers Journal: Robert Wright on the Evolution of God/Obama and Environmentalists*; *The Era of American Dominance Is Over: A Debate*; and *High Anxieties: The Mathematics of Chaos*.

Films Transit International, Inc.

166 Second Ave.
New York, NY 10001
Phone and Fax: (212) 614-2808
Website: www.filmstransit.com
Contact: dianaholtzberg@films transit.com

Their expansive catalogue of documentary films includes such classic titles as *Crumb*; *Grass*; *The Times of Harvey Milk*; and *The Wonderful, Horrible Life of Leni Riefenstahl*, as well as categories such as current affairs, politics, and history with titles including *Belfast Girls*; *China's Sexual Revolution*; and *Atomic Café*.

First Independent Pictures

2999 Overland Ave., Suite 218
Los Angeles, CA 90064
Phone: (310) 838-6555

Fax: (310) 838-9972
Website: www.firstindependent
pictures.com
Contact: aan@firstindependent
pictures.com

First Independent distributes a small number of documentary titles such as *Arthur "Killer" Kane* and *America the Beautiful*.

First Run Features

The Film Center Building
630 Ninth Ave., Suite 1213
New York, NY 10036
Phone: (212) 243-0600
Fax: (212) 989-7649
Website: www.firstrunfeatures.com
Contact: infor@firstrunfeatures.com

Founded by a group of young filmmakers in 1979, First Run has come to specialize in the distribution of independent, foreign, and documentary films. Their titles include *After Stonewall*; *Before Stonewall*; *Inside the Koran*; the *Up* series; and *Born in Flames*.

Flower Films

10341 San Pablo Ave.
El Cerrito, CA 94530
Toll Free: (800) 572-7618
Phone: (510) 525-0942
Fax: (510) 525-1204
Website: www.lesblank.com
Contact: Blankfilm@aol.com

Les Blank's distribution company carries all his own films including *All in This Tea*; *Always for Pleasure*; *Garlic Is as Good as Ten Mothers*; *Werner Herzog Eats His Shoe*; and *Burden of Dreams*. Flower Films also distributes other films such as *Cajun Visits*; *In the Land of the Owl Turds*; *"N" Is a Number*; *Wild Wheels*; and *The Story of Anna O: A Study on Hysteria*.

Frameline

145 Ninth St., Suite 300
San Francisco, CA 94103
Phone: (415) 703-8650
Fax: (415) 861-1404
Website: www.frameline.org
Contact: info@frameline.org

Founded in 1977, Frameline's strength lies in gay, lesbian, bisexual, and transgender films. They carry titles such as *Asian Queer Shorts*; *Call Me Troy*; *Tongues Untied*; *Just Call Me Kade*; *A Union in Wait*; and *Is It Really So Strange?*

Gigantic Pictures

59 Franklin St., Ground Floor
New York, NY 10013
Phone: (212) 925-5075
Fax: (212) 925-5061
Website: www.giganticpictures.com
Contact: info@giganticpictures.com

Gigantic's titles include *Girls and Dolls*; *The Smile of Isaac*; *Real Sex #27: Slippery When Wet*; *Goodbye Solo*; *Plastic Bag*; and *The First Seven Years*.

HBO Entertainment

Phone: (212) 512-1208
Website: www.hbo.com/docs
Contact: http://www.hbo.com/apps/
submitinfo/contactus/submit

As part of Home Box Office, Inc., HBO's Documentary Films is responsible for the production and distribution of a wide array of HBO films. Their titles include *A Boy's Life*; *A Father . . . a Son . . .* ; *Once upon a Time in Hollywood*; *Addiction*; *Aileen: Life and Death of a Serial Killer*; *Alive Day Memories: Home from Iraq*; *Along Came a Spider*; *Bus 174*; *Cannibal: The Real Hannibal Lecters*; and *Born Rich*.

IFC Films

11 Penn Plaza
New York, NY 10001
Website: www.ifcfilms.com
Contact: maboxer@ifcfilms.com or kghowe@ifcfilms.com

This arm of the Independent Film Channel network has been involved in theatrical film distribution since 2000. Their documentary titles include *Indie Sex*; *At the Death House Door*; *Heavy Load*; *My Winnipeg*; and *The New York Times Portrait of Kore-Eda Hirokazu*.

Icarus Films

32 Court St., 21st Floor
Brooklyn, NY 11201
Phone: (718) 488-8900
Fax: (718) 488-8642
Website: www.icarusfilms.com
Contact: mail@icarusfilms.com

Icarus Films began in 1978 and caries such titles as *War and Love in Kabul*; *The World's Next Supermodel*; *In Search of Memory*; *Seeds of Hunger*; and *Amateur Photographer*. The company also carries a large number of Latin American (*The Comrade: Life of Luiz Carlos Prestes*; *Chile*; *Obstinate Memory*), Asian (*Sunrise Over Tiananmen Square*; *From Opium to Chrysanthemums*), and African titles (*Chronicle of a Genocide Foretold*).

Indican Pictures

8424A Santa Monica Blvd., #752
West Hollywood, CA 90069
Phone: (323) 650-0832
Fax: (323) 650-6832
Website: www.indicanpictures.com

Their documentaries include *The Wonder of It All*; *A Lawyer Walks into a Bar . . .*; *The Black List*; *Dare Not Walk Alone*; *God & Gays: Bridging the Gap*; and *Fatboy*.

Insight Media

2162 Broadway
New York, NY 10024-0621
Toll Free: (800) 233-9910
Phone: (212) 721-6316
Fax: (212) 799-5309
Website: www.insight-media.com
Contact: custserv@insight-media.com

With over 14,000 titles, its subject areas include communication and film studies (*Gender and Communication: How Men and Women Communicate Differently*; *Body Language: Cultural Differences*; *A Movie Lover's Guide to Film Language: Classic Scenes from Timeless Films*), religion and philosophy (*Spirituality*; *No God but God*; *Islam and Its Five Pillars*), and many other subjects.

Janus Films

215 Park Ave. S., 5th Floor
New York, NY 10003
Website: www.janusfilms.com

Janus has been the distributor for many titles now part of the Criterion Collection.

Kino International

333 W. 39th St., Suite 503
New York, NY 10018
Toll Free: (800) 562-3330
Phone: (212) 629-6880
Fax: (212) 714-0871
Website: www.kino.com
Contact: contact@kino.com

Kino distributes contemporary world cinema, American independents, and documentaries. Its documentary titles include *Back to Normandy*; *Billy Wilder Speaks*; and *Off to War*.

Koch Lorber Films

22 Harbor Park Dr.
Port Washington, NY 11050

Phone: (516) 484-1000
Fax: (516) 484-4746
Website: www.kochlorberfilms.com
Contact: videoacquisitions@kochent.com

Their documentary titles include Eric Steel's *The Bridge*; *Lipstick & Dynamite: The First Ladies of Wrestling*; *Our Brand Is Crisis*; *9 Star Hotel*; *Imaginary Witness*; and *Glass: A Portrait of Philip in Twelve Parts*.

Laemmle/Zeller Films

11523 Santa Monica Blvd.
Los Angeles, CA 90025
Phone: (310) 478-1041
Fax: (310) 478-4452
Website: www.laemmlezellerfilms.com

A full-service virtual distribution company, Leammle/Zeller offers independent documentary films such as David Vyorst's *The First Basket*.

Las Américas Film Network

Phone: (504) 919-1078
Fax: (801) 340-7462
Website: www.lasamericasfilms.org
Contact: info@lasamericasfilms.org

Their documentary films include *90 Miles, and the March Continues!*; *Estadio Nacional (National Stadium)*; *Gay Cuba*; *El Immigrante*; and *Judios en Chile, emigrantes en el tiempo (Jews in Chile: Immigrants through Time)*.

Lonely Seal Releasing

1680 N. Vine St.
Hollywood, CA 90028
Phone: (323) 465-7325
Fax: (323) 465-0504
Website: www.lonelyseal.com
Contact: john@lonelyseal.com

Lonely carries feature films, specialty programming, and documentaries,
which include such titles as *Artists off The Grid: The Road to Wonder Valley*; *Whaledreamers*; *Evita: The Truth Behind the Myth*; and *Shades of Gray*.

Magnolia Pictures

115 West 27th St., 7th Floor
New York, NY 10001
Phone: (212) 924-6701
Fax: (212) 924-6742
Website: www.magpictures.com
Contact: nblock@magpictures.com

Magnolia's releases have included *Enron: The Smartest Guys in the Room*; *Capturing the Friedmans*; *Bubble*; *Bukowski: Born into This*; *Gonzo: The Life and Work of Dr. Hunter S. Thompson*; *Man on Wire*; and *Mr. Untouchable*.

Maya Releasing

1201 W. 5th St., Suite T-210
Los Angeles, CA 90017
Phone: (213) 542-4420
Website: www.mayareleasing.com
Contact: marye@maya entertainmentgroup.com

Maya focuses on the U.S. Latino market. Their theatrical releases and home entertainment titles change frequently; current lists of new releases are available on their website.

Maysles Films

343 Lenox Ave.
New York, NY 10027
Phone: (212) 582-6050
Fax: (212) 586-2057
Website: www.mayslesfilms.com
Contact: info@mayslesfilms.com

Maysles Films markets the work of Albert Maysles and his late brother David Maysles to the home entertainment market. The collection includes some of their best-known works such as *Gimme Shelter* and *Muhammad and Larry*, as well as other classic titles including *Psychiatry in Russia; Showman; Orson Welles in Spain; What's Happening! The Beatles in the USA; Salesman;* and *Meet Marlon Brando.*

Microcinema International

1636 Bush St., Suite 2
San Francisco, CA 94109
Phone: (415) 447-9750
Fax: (509) 351-1530
Website: www.microcinemadvd.com
Contact: infor@microcinema.com

Their documentaries include *Divine Horsemen: The Living Gods of Haiti; The End of Suburbia; From the Ground Up; Last Bolshevik;* and *The Art Guys.*

Monarch Films, Inc.

368 Danforth Ave.
Jersey City, NJ 07305
Phone: (201) 451-3770
Fax: (201) 451-3877
Website: www.mfilms.com
Contact: monarchfilms@aol.com

Monarch's documentary titles include *Bounty Hunters: Dead or Alive; Children of the Red Cross; Incest; Tankboy;* and *Lee: Beyond the Battles.* Also available on this site are downloads to be watched online.

Movies Unlimited

3015 Darnell Rd.
Philadelphia, PA 19154
Phone: (800) 668-4344
Fax: (215) 637-2350
Website: www.moviesunlimited.com
Contact: status@moviesunlimited
.com

The documentary collection includes works by Emilio De Antonio, Ken Burns, Barbara Kopple, Errol Morris, Les Blank, and Robert Flaherty. The documentary section also includes

series such as A&E *Biography* and films focusing on human sexuality such as *Liberty in Restraint; Loving and Cheating; Kinsey* (documentary); *Zoo;* and *Paris Is Burning.*

The Museum of Modern Art

Circulating Film and Video Library
11 West 53rd St.
New York, NY 10019
Phone: (212) 708-9400
Website: www.moma.org
Contact: www.moma.org/about/info/

MoMA has a selective repertoire of classic documentary titles within its collection, including the Lumière brothers' *Feeding the Baby* in black-and-white 35mm film format, Maya Deren's *Meshes of the Afternoon* in black-and-white 16mm format, Robert Flaherty's *Nanook of the North* in black-and-white 35mm format, Cao Fei's *i.Mirror by China Tracy (AKA: Cao Fei) Second Life Documentary Film,* Pare Lorentz's *The River;* and Luis Buñuel's *L' Age d'or,* among others.

NAATA Distribution

346 9th St., 2nd Floor
San Francisco, CA 94103
Phone: (415) 863-0814
Fax: (415) 863-7428
Website: www.asianamericanmedia
.org
Contact: www.naata.visualnet.com/
mail.html

The National Asian American Telecommunications Association collection includes over 200 films such as *Passing Through; Not Black or White; Citizen Hong Kong; First Person Plural; Regret to Inform; Unwanted Soldier;* and *We Served with Pride: The Chinese American Experience in WWII.*

National Black Programming Consortium

68 East 131st St., 7th Floor
New York, NY 10037
Phone: (212) 234-8200
Fax: (212) 234-7032
Website: www.nbpc.tv
Contact: info@nbpc.tv

Since 1979, the NBPC has distributed stories of the black experience. Their documentaries include such titles as *Free to Dance* and the *AfroPop* series.

National Film Board of Canada

Norman-McLaren Building
3155, Côte-de-Liesse Rd.
Saint-Laurent, Quebec, Canada
H4N 2N4
Toll Free: (800) 267-7710
Phone: (514) 283-9000
Fax: (514) 283-7564
Website: www.nfb.ca
Contact: www.nfb.ca/about/
contact-us/

NFB is a public agency that was created in 1939 to produce and distribute Canadian films. The NFB distributes more than 13,000 films and strives to add new titles weekly. They carry most of the well-known NFB titles, such as *Sad Song of Yellow Skin*, and newer releases such as *Everybody's Children; Chroniques Afghans;* and *A Dream for Kabul.*

The New American Cinema Group Inc./Film-Makers' Cooperative

475 Park Ave. South, 6th Floor
New York, NY 10016
Phone: (212) 267-5665
Fax: (212) 267-5666
Website: www.film-makerscoop.com
Contact: filmmakerscoop@gmail
.com

The Film-Makers' Cooperative began in 1962 and currently has more than 5,000 films and videotapes in its collection. The co-op carries the work of Maya Deren, George Kuchar, Stan Brakhage, Michael Snow, Emily Breer, and Nestor Almendros, among others.

New Day Films

190 Route 17M
P.O. Box 1084
Harriman, NY 10926
Toll Free: (888) 367-9154
Phone: (845) 774-7051
Fax: (845) 774-2945
Website: www.newday.com

New Day Films is a documentary filmmakers' cooperative democratically run by over a hundred filmmakers since 1971. With a catalogue of about 150 titles, their films cover a diverse range of social issues with titles such as *At Home in Utopia; Children of the Left; Miles from the Border; Men Are Human, Women Are Buffalo;* and newer titles such as *34x25x36; Bachelorette 34;* and *Straightlaced—How Gender's Got Us All Tied Up.*

NTIS National Audiovisual Center

U.S. Department of Commerce
National Technical Information Service
Alexandria, VA 22312
Phone: (703) 605-6000
Website: www.ntis.gov

NAC is a federal clearinghouse for audio-visual materials. It carries films made under the auspices of government agencies, from *The Plow That Broke the Plains* and the *Why We Fight* series to *Red Nightmare* and *Why Vietnam?*

Oscilloscope Pictures

511 Canal St., #5E
New York, NY 10013
Phone: (212) 219-4029
Fax: (212) 219-9538
Website: www.oscilloscope.net
Contact: www.oscilloscope.net/film/contact

Oscilloscope Pictures distributes a number of independently produced films including such documentaries as *The Thorn in the Heart* (*L'epine dans le Coeur*); *Unmistaken Child*; *The Garden*; *Frontrunners*; *Flow*; and *Treeless Mountain*.

Outcast Films

P.O. Box 260
New York, NY 10032
Phone: (917) 520-7392
Fax: (845) 774-2945
Website: www.outcast-films.com
Contact: info@outcast-films.com

Outcast addresses lesbian, gay, bisexual, and transgender issues. Their documentary features include titles such as *Sex in an Epidemic*; *Act Up: Oral History Project*; *Cruel and Unusual*; and films by the well-known filmmaker Su Friedrich including *The Ties That Bind* and *Hide and Seek*.

Palm Pictures

76 Ninth Ave., Suite 1110
New York, NY 10011
Phone: (212) 320-3600
Website: www.palmpictures.com
Contact: cindy.banach@palmpictures.com

Their documentary titles include *Gunner Palace*; *Talking Heads: Stop Making Sense*; *Scratch*; *Paperboys*; and the works of directors such as Chris Cunningham, Spike Jonze, and Michel Gondry.

Paper Tiger Television

339 Lafayette St., 3rd Floor
New York, NY 10012
Phone: (212) 420-9045
Website: www.papertiger.org
Contact: info@papertiger.org

With a mission toward works that will "challenge and expose the corporate control of mainstream media," Paper Tiger has been producing and distributing since 1981 and was built on a belief in free speech and equality in access to communication and media. About 520 programs are also available and include *Urban Environmentalism: DIY Living Green*; *Love Me, Love My Avatar*; *Infiltrating the Underground: The Corporatization of Radical Culture*; *Homecoming Queens*; *Who Wants to Be America's Next Top President?*; and *Rock, Paper, Missiles*.

Passion River Films

416 Main St., 2nd Floor
Metuchen, NJ 08840
Phone: (732) 321-0711
Fax: (732) 321-4105
Website: www.passionriver.com

Their genres include health films, thrillers, instructional films, foreign films, films on film movements, and documentaries, among more. Their documentary list includes works such as *Astronaut Pam: Countdown to Commander*; *His Highness Hollywood*; *Day in the Lyfe*; *Dying to Live: The Journey into a Man's Open Heart*; and *The Sandwich Kid*.

PBS Video

1320 Braddock Place
Alexandria, VA 22314-1698
Phone: (800) 344-3337
Fax: (703) 739-5269
Website: www.pbs.org

PBS carries material produced for the Public Broadcasting System including many titles by Ken Burns such as his *Jazz, The Civil War*, and *National Parks* series of programs; the *American Experience* series; the *Frontline* series; and the *P.O.V.* series.

Regent Releasing

10990 Wilshire Blvd., Penthouse
Los Angeles, CA 90024
Phone: (310) 806-4288
Fax: (310) 806-4268
Website: www.regentreleasing.com
Contact: info@regentreleasing.com

With award-winning documentaries such as *Showbusiness: The Road to Broadway*, Regent carries a number of titles that cover the genre of documentary, world and cultural issues, and includes works dealing with gay and lesbian topics.

Select Media

270 Lafayette St., Suite 809
New York, NY 10012
Phone: (800) 343-5540
Phone: (800) 707-6334
Fax: (845) 774-2945
Website: www.selectmedia.org
Contact: sophie@selectmedia.org

Select Media's titles include *The Hard Way; The Subject Is: HIV; The Truth about Sex*; the *AIDS Film Series*; and *In Due Time*.

Skylight Pictures

330 West 42nd St., 24th Floor
New York, NY 10036
Phone: (212) 947-5333
Fax: (212) 643-1208
Website: www.skylightpictures.com

Skylight has such titles as *The Reckoning; Living Broke in Boom Times; When the Mountains Tremble; Poverty Outlaw*; and *Takeover*.

Solid Entertainment

15840 Ventura Blvd., Suite 306
Encino, CA 91436
Phone: (818) 990-4300
Website: www.solidentertainment.com
Contact: info@solidpgms.com

Their titles include *St. Bernard's Parish: After the Flood; American Pit Bull; Food Hunter; Uncorked! Wine Made Simple; With a Right to Kill*; and *Inside the Britannic*.

Swank Motion Pictures, Inc.

10795 Watson Rd.
Saint Louis, MO 63127
Phone: (800) 876-5577
Website: www.swank.com
Email: swank.com/contact.html

Swank represents distribution for such producers as Walt Disney Pictures, Paramount Pictures, Warner Brothers, Dreamworks Pictures, Lionsgate, Tri Star Pictures, HBO, and several other major and independent studios. Its documentary titles include *When We Were Kings; Roger and Me*; and *Baraka*.

Telling Pictures

10 Arkansas St., Suite F
San Francisco, CA 94107
Website: www.tellingpix.com
Contact: info@tellingpictures.com

Telling Pictures distributes films produced by Jeffrey Freidman and Rob Epstein, including *Sex in '69: The Sexual Revolution in America; Paragraph 175; The Times of Harvey Milk*; and *The Celluloid Closet*.

Third World Newsreel

545 Eighth Ave., 10th Floor
New York, NY 10018
Phone: (212) 947-9277
Fax: (212) 594-6417
Website: www.twn.org

Third World Newsreel carries many classic Newsreel titles such as *Wilmington; People's War;* and *Columbia Revolt,* as well as more recent work addressing issues for people of color in the United States, such as *Cuban Roots/Bronx Stories; Kabul, Kabul; Borne in War;* and *Imagining Place.* Third World also carries a large number of Latin American titles.

TVF International

375 City Rd.
London EC1V 1NB, England
Phone: 44 0 20 7837 3000
Fax: 44 0 20 7278 8833
Website: www.tvfinternational.com
Contact: int@tvf.co.uk

Their extensive collection includes films under such subjects as biography, arts, people and culture, health and family, wildlife and natural history, sex and relationships, travel and adventure, crime, world affairs, and religion and philosophy, among others.

Video Data Bank

112 S. Michigan Ave.
Chicago, IL 60603
Phone: (312) 345-3550
Fax: (312) 541-8073
Website: www.vdb.org
Contact: info@vdb.org

Founded in 1976 at the inception of the video arts movement in the United States, the Video Data Bank is one of the largest providers of alternative and art-based video by and about contemporary artists. It carries over 1,200 titles by 260 artists including George Kuchar, Sherry Millner, Jem Cohen, Jeanne C. Finley, Terry Fox, and Nelson Henricks.

Wolfe Video

P.O. Box 64
New Almaden, CA 95042

Phone: (408) 268-6782
Fax: (408) 268-9449
Website: www.wolfevideo.com

Wolfe Video is one of the largest exclusive distributors of gay and lesbian films. Its collection includes both fiction and documentary; documentary titles include *Tongues Untied; Trantasia; Beyond Hatred; Before Stonewall; Gay Sex in the 70s; For the Love of Dolly;* and *Yves Saint Laurent.*

Women Make Movies

462 Broadway, Suite 500WS
New York, NY 10013
Phone: (212) 925-0606
Fax: (212) 925-2052
Website: www.wmm.com
Contact: info@wmm.com

WMM was established in 1972 as an answer to the under-representation and misrepresentation of women in the media industry. Their catalogue includes many important documentaries such as *A Boy Named Sue; Surname Viet Given Name Nam; Reconstruction; Love & Diane;* and *Daughter Rite.*

Zeitgeist Films Ltd.

247 Centre St.
New York, NY 10013
Phone: (212) 274-1989
Fax: (212) 274-1644
Website: www.zeitgeistfilms.com
Contact: mail@zeitgeistfilms.com

Their catalogue includes award-winning independent and international films, including well-known documentaries such as *Into Great Silence; The Corporation; Ballets Russes; The Gleaners and I;* and *Manufacturing Consent: Noam Chomsky and the Media.*

Zipporah Films, Inc.

One Richdale Ave., Unit #4
Cambridge, MA 02140

Phone: (617) 576-3603
Fax: (617) 864-8006
Website: www.zipporah.com
Contact: info@zipporah.com

Zipporah distributes the films of Frederick Wiseman, including such award-winning and renowned titles as *Meat*; *Zoo*; *High School*; *Primate*; *Public Housing*; *Domestic Violence*; and *La Danse—Le Ballet de l'Opéra de Paris*.

INTERNET DISTRIBUTION VENUES

Ambrose Video 2.0

www.ambrosedigital.com

Ambrose Digital is the video-streaming website, focusing its work on educational films. It is possible to play entire titles that are set up in shorter concept clips, which make it easy to use them in the classroom. Their on-line index of films includes the BBC's *Complete Works of Shakespeare* series; *Connections*; *The Ascent of Man* series; *Core Astronomy*; *Classical European Composers* series; and many other titles in many different subject areas.

DOC ALLIANCE.COM

www.docalliancefilms.com

This website arose from the cooperative efforts of five different documentary film festivals in Europe. The on-line portal of Doc Alliance for Video on Demand offers permanent access to 250 outstanding documentaries selected by the five partner festivals. Twenty new films are added monthly and these can be acquired through streaming or download.

EZTakes

www.eztakes.com

EZTakes offers a catalogue of over 5,000 film titles for downloading. Their documentary titles include *Little Shoalin Monks*; *King: Man of Peace in a Time of War*; *Czech Dream*; and *Bob Dylan—1966 World Tour: The Home Movies*.

Films on Demand Digital Education Video

http://ffh.films.com/digitallanding.aspx

Films on Demand is a web-based digital video service that streams videos from the Films Media Group company.

GrapeFlix

www.grapeflix.com

Grapeflix is an extensive on-line distribution venue. With categories including live performances, anime and animation, shorts, LGBT, science fiction, fantasy, and horror, it also offers a collection of documentaries from different theatrical distributors. The documentary titles include *Drowned Out*; *Disfigured*; *McLibel*; *Dying to Have Known*; and *Beautiful Truth*.

HungryFlix

www.hungryflix.com

HungryFlix provides downloads of feature films, short films, how-to video, music videos, sports, documentary, and television series and music. Their documentary downloads include *Amazing Thailand*; *The Alpha and Omega Code*; *Tsunami*; and *Twenty Years without Justice: The Bhopal Chemical Disaster*.

IFC Films

www.ifcfilms.com/dvd-digital-download

Not only does the Independent Film Channel offer releases to purchase on DVD, they also offer films and mini-web-series for digital download.

IndiePix

www.indiepixfilms.com/download

IndiePix offers DVDs for sale and also sell download-to-own, which features such documentaries as *A Life among Whales*; *A Triple Affair*; *Committing Poetry in Times of War*; *India and Free Trade: A Closer Look at Bhopal*; and *Facing the Habit*.

Jaman

www.jaman.com

Their online library is sectioned by genre and includes an extensive documentary section and also American independent films, extreme horror, kids and family, gay and lesbian, cult, comedy, Bollywood, classics, Spanish language, and Hollywood, among others, and a world map of movies to choose from by country.

MovieFlix

www.movieflix.com

Movieflix offers viewing choices in features and films in the subject areas of black culture, action, comedy, family, classics and classic television, film noir, foreign films, literature, "indie," and documentary, among others.

National Film Board of Canada

www.nbpc.tv

NFB is a public agency that was created in 1939 to produce and distribute Canadian films and has since adapted itself to the digital era, offering over 700 full-length films, trailers, and clips for free on their website.

Netflix

www.netflix.com

Netflix is the well-known on-line video store that has revolutionized home video entertainment. They offer an extensive, revolving library of movies on demand and for rental through the mail.

Penn State Media Sales

http://www.mediasales.psu.edu/

This venue carries mainly educational films for institutional use, including the extraordinary investigation into whether humans will defer to authority even if it means putting another life at risk: *Obedience*. Titles can be viewed on-line or purchased.

Reframe Collection

www.reframecollection.com

Reframe's titles are divided by collections, filmmakers, genres, and subjects, allowing easy search access.

Rick Prelinger Archives

www.archive.org/details/prelinger

Prelinger Archives was founded in 1983 by Rick Prelinger in New York City. Over the next 20 years, it grew into a collection of over 60,000 advertising, educational, industrial, and amateur films. This site is dedicated to the entire archive of Prelinger's works and stock footage with many titles available for on-line viewing.

Si Mi

www.si-mi/com

Si Mi is a website dedicated to allowing its users to sell and share media works including videos, music, podcasts, animation, ebooks, and games.

UbuWeb

www.ubu.com

UbuWeb offers hundreds of avant-garde and experimental shorts for noncommercial and educational purposes only.

INTERNET SEARCH ENGINES: PRODUCTION, POSTPRODUCTION, AND DISTRIBUTION SUPPORT AND INFORMATION

Docuseek.com is useful for locating distributors of many social issue and educational documentaries. It currently searches the catalogues of Bullfrog Films, First Run/Icarus Films, New Day Films, Fanlight Productions, and Frameline.

Imdb.com (Internet Movie Database) provides film reviews and lists of casts and crews of well-known fiction and documentary films. It searches amazon.com for title availability on VHS and DVD.

A&E IndieFilms

www.aetv.com/indiefilms

A&E IndieFilms has commissioned, acquired, and provided finishing funds for such documentaries as *American Teen*; *Murderball*; *Jesus Camp*; and *My Kid Could Paint That*.

Environmental Media Stock Footage

www.envmedia.com/stock
Contact: bpendergraft@envmedia
.com
Phone: (843) 474-0147

Environmental Media has accumulated unique documentary raw stock footage of people, plants, animals, and landscapes and thousands of film and digital photographs, which they license to filmmakers.

Getty Images

www.gettyimages.com

Getty Images was created with the idea of bringing fragmented stock footage and photography into the digital age. This site offers dozens of interesting, fragmented clips in sections on creative footage and editorial footage.

New Love Films

www.newlovefilms.com

New Love's website offers very helpful tips and information regarding the filming processes of preproduction, production, exhibition, distribution, and more.

Thought Equity Motion

www.thoughtequity.com

Thought Equity provides a massive collection of film clips in DVD and HD. It does not include complete films but focuses on clips and footage.

INTERNATIONAL DISTRIBUTORS

AUSTRALIA

AIATSIS Film Unit

Australian Institute of Aboriginal and Torres Strait Islander Studies
GPO Box 553
Canberra, A.C.T. 2601, Australia
Phone: 62 2 6246 1111
Fax: 62 2 6261 4285
Website: www.aiatsis.gov.au
Contact: executive@aiatsis.gov.au

AIATSIS is an independent Commonwealth Government statutory authority devoted to Aboriginal and Torres Strait Islander studies. The AIATSIS Audiovisual Archives hold the world's largest collection of film and video materials relating to Australian Aboriginal and Torres Strait Islander studies.

Australian Film Institute

236 Dorcas St.
South Melbourne, Victoria 3205,
Australia
Phone: 613 9696 1844
Fax: 613 9696 7972
Website: www.afi.org.au
Contact: info@afi.org.au

The AFI was established in 1958 and is Australia's major distributor of Australian documentaries, short fiction, and animation. It operates the AFI Library, which holds Australia's most comprehensive collection of film and television literature.

Ronin Films

P.O. Box 1005
Civic Square
Canberra, ACT 2608, Australia
Phone: 02 6248 0851
Fax: 02 6249 1640
Website: www.roninfilms.com.au

Ronin distributes educational films and videos in the territories of Australia and around the world. Its documentary subject areas include Aboriginal Australians, docu-dramas, East Timor, environment, health, history, gender and sexuality, France, Russia, war, and women's issues. Titles include *Aboriginal Rules*; *About Baghdad*; *Agent Orange*; and *Saving Xavier*.

AUSTRIA

Austrian Film Commission

Stiftgasse 6
A-1070 Vienna, Austria
Phone: 43 1 526 33 23-0
Fax: 43 1 526 68 01

Website: www.afc.at
Contact: office@afc.at

Although not a film distributor, the Austrian Film Commission acts as an information clearinghouse for Austrian fiction and documentary films.

Sixpackfilm

Neubaugasse 45/13
P.O. Box 197
A-1071 Wein, Austria
Phone: 43 1 526 09 90 0
Fax: 43 1 526 09 92
Website: www.sixpackfilm.com
contact: office@sixpackfilm.com

Sixpackfilm distributes European avant-garde films, many with a documentary import.

CANADA

Canada Groupe Intervention Video

4001 Berri #105
Montreal, Quebec H2L 4H2,
Canada
Phone: (514) 271-5506
Fax: (514) 271-6980
Website: www.givideo.org
Contact: info@givideo.org

GIV distributes films and videos by women directors from Canada, the United States, and Latin America. Its documentary titles include *Boy, Girl*; *Breast Feeding: Who Loses, Who Wins*; *A Cancer Video*; and *Black Women of Brazil*.

Vivo Media/Video Out

1965 Main St.
Vancouver BC V5T 3C1, Canada
Phone: (604) 872-8337
Website: www.videoinstudios.com/
www.videoout.ca
Contact: info@vivomediaarts.com

As an artist-owned production, exhibition, and distribution center, Vivo has become a fully operating film facility. It is connected to Video Out Distribution, which is a nonprofit, nonexclusive distributor of media art and video to galleries, festivals, and educational institutions.

DENMARK

Danish Film Institute

Det Danske Filminstitut/Danish Filminstitute
Gothersgade 55
1123 Copenhagen K, Denmark
Phone: 45 33 74 34 00
Fax: 45 33 74 34 01
Website: www.dfi.dk
Contact: dfi@dfi.dk

The Danish Film Institute is a national agency responsible for supporting and encouraging film and cinema culture in Denmark. The DFI develops, produces, and distributes fiction films and documentaries.

FRANCE

Light Cone

12 Rue des Vignoles
75020 Paris, France
Phone: 33 1 46590153
Fax: 33 1 46590312
Website: www.lightcone.org
Contact: www.lightcone.org/en/contact

Light Cone distributes experimental films and videos by Stan Brakhage, Caroline Avery, Pip Chodorov, Abigail Child, Maya Deren, Jonas Mekas, Jennifer Burford, Hans Richter, and Bill Morrison, among many others. Many films in their collection have a documentary and experimental film import.

Pathé International

Paris, France & London, United Kingdom
Phone: Paris: 33 1 71 72 33 05
London: 44 2 074 624 427
Website: www.patheinternational.com

Pathé International distributes feature films and documentaries in France as well as internationally in such themes as science fiction, musicals, westerns, literature adaptation, history, and horror.

Play Film Distribution

14 Rue du Moulin Joly
75011 Paris, France
Phone: 33 1 44 07 56 85
Website: www.playfilm.fr
Contact: playfilm@playfilm.fr

Play Film Distribution produces and distributes documentary films on such topics as ethnography (with a particular focus on the Iranian experience), the arts, cinema, history, biography, and current affairs. Its titles include *Atomic Alert*; *The Time of Turning Inward*; *7 Women*; *The Other Way*; and *And There Was Creation*.

GERMANY

A.G. Dok

Im Deutschen Filmmuseum
Schweizer Straße 6
D-60594 Frankfurt Am Main, Germany
Phone: 49 69 6237 00
Fax: 49 69142 966424
Website: www.agdok.de

A.G. Dok is the distribution arm of the German Documentary Filmmaker's Association. It represents many important German documentarians who produce films on varied topics, including women's issues, war and peace, human rights, the arts, German reunification, music, and sexuality.

INDIA

Reliance MediaWorks, Ltd.

Film City Complex, Goregaon-East
Mumbai 400 065, Maharashtra,
India
Phone: 91 22 2842 3333
Fax: 91 22 2843 1685
Website: www.adlabsfilms.com

As one of the largest entertainment media groups in India, Reliance Media-Works is well known for its distribution services in India.

UTV Software Communications Ltd.

1181-1182, 8th Floor, Solitaire Corporate Park
Guru Hargovindji Marg,
Chakala, Andheri
Mumbai 400 093, India
Phone: 91 22 40981400
Fax: 91 22 40981650
Website: www.utvnet.com

UTV is India's first integrated global media and entertainment company carrying films and videos in various genres and for multiple distribution platforms.

UNITED KINGDOM

British Film Institute Collections

21 Stephen St.
London W1T 1LN, England
Phone: 0207 255 1444
Website: www.bfi.org.uk
Contact: www.bfi.org/uk/help/contact/53

British Film Institute Collections contains the largest collection of films and television titles in Europe and includes the National Film and Television Archive. Its documentary holdings range from early historical newsreels to important contemporary documentaries.

Cinenova

40 Rosebery Ave.
London EC1R 4RX, England
Phone: 0181 981 68 28
Fax: 0181 983 44 41
Website: www.cinenova.org.uk
Comcast: info@cinenova.org.uk

Cinenova is the United Kingdom's only film and video distributor specializing in work directed by women. Its catalogue includes films from Europe, Canada, and the United States and covers issues that range from female sexuality to cultural identity and oral history. Its titles include *Great Dykes of Holland*; *Woman: Who Is Me?*; *Voices from Iraq*; and *Rape Culture*.

Dogwoof Pictures

Studio 311
Panther House
38 Mount Pleasant
London WC1X0AN, England
Phone: 44(0) 20 7833 3599
Fax: 44(0) 70 7900 3270
Website: www.dogwoof.com
Contact: info@dogwoof.com

Dogwoof is a distributor of social issue independent films, world cinema, and documentaries in the United Kingdom. Their documentary titles include *Black Gold*; *Don't Move*; *The Age of Stupid*; *Disarm*; and *How to Cook Your Life*.

Index

Page numbers in *italics* indicate photo captions and tables.

À Propos de Nice (1930), 137
aboriginal people, 53, *185*, 205. *See also* indigenous people; *Nanook of the North* (1922); Native American culture
Abortion Stories: North and South (1984), 68
abstract concepts, 99–101
Abu Ghraib, 55, 89, 108
Academy of Motion Picture Arts and Sciences, 2–4, 13, 19, 37, 232, 243
Ackerman, Chantal, 229–30
The Act of Seeing with One's Own Eyes (1971), 32
activism. *See also* social issues documentary: and collaboration, 225; and gay rights, 3; labor activism, 70, 213–14, 232; and minority groups, 236; and Newsreel, 228; and voice of documentary, 70–71
actors, 45
adult movies, 128
advertising, 146
advocacy: and citizenship, 141; and classification of documentary films, 150, 154; and environmental issues, 168; and Free Cinema, 29; and

rhetoric, 86; and Soviet Cinema, 141, 216; and voice of documentary, 72–73; and war mobilization, 157
A&E Biography series, 159
aesthetic responses, 255–56
affective goals, 203
Aileen Wuornos: The Selling of a Serial Killer (1992), *11*, 12
Al Jazeera, 88
alienation, 199
Allakariallak, 13, 269–70
allegory, 7–8, 11–12, 14, 68, 132, 142
Allende, Salvador, 240, 241
Alpert, Jon, 184
alternative values, 103
Always for Pleasure (1978), 18, 166
ambiguity of issues, 86–87, 88
ambush interviews, 182
American Dream (1990), 4
An American Family (1972), 46, 108
American Idol (television), xii
American Institute of City Planners, 22
American Teen (2008), 39, 40, 46
America's Most Wanted, 167
Amsterdam International Documentary Film Festival, 19
An Andalusian Dog (1929), 129, 165
Anderson, Lindsay, 28, 29
The Anderson Platoon (1966), 110

Anemic Cinema (1926), 129
Anger, Kenneth, 166, 236
animated documentary, 110–11, *112*.
    See also Waltz with Bashir (2008)
Anka, Paul, 108
Anthem (1991), *234*, 236
anthropology, 65, *152*, 154, 156, 181,
    189. *See also* ethnographic film
apparent proof, 82–83
archival film: and documentary con-
    ventions, 27; and mixed modes of
    documentary, 32; and movements in
    documentary, 30; and the participa-
    tory mode, 31, *193*; and persuasive
    role of documentary, 112–13, *114*;
    and voice of documentary, 72, 73
Aristotle, 78–79, 86
arrangement in documentaries, 85–89
Arrival of a Train (1895), 121, 163
Artie Shaw: Time Is All You've Got
    (1985), 3
artificial proofs, 78–79
artistic proofs, 78–79
Ashur, Geri, 229
assumptions about documentary, 33–34
Auden, W. H., 154
audience of documentaries: and as-
    sumptions about documentary, 33–
    34; and classification of documentary
    films, 142; and epistephilia, 40–41;
    and ethical issues, 57–58; and expec-
    tations, 38–41; and indexical quality
    of images, 34–38; and interpretation,
    96–97; and relationship between ele-
    ments of documentary, 59–66; and
    sponsored films, 146
audio recording, 61, 111. *See also* sound
    recording; voice-over commentary
Austin, J. L., 203
Australia's Funniest Home Movie Show
    (television), 127–28
authenticity, xiii–xiv, 121
authoritative commentary, 85
autobiographical films, 107, *153*,
    181–82
avant-garde film, 94, 129, 130–31
Aventure Malgache (1944), 221
The Ax Fight (1975), 32

Barbie, Klaus, 4
Barnouw, Erik, 72, 148
Barton, Peter, 229
Basic Training (1971), 62
Battle 360 series, 32
The Battle of Chile (1975, 1977, 1979),
    241
The Battle of Midway (1942), 221
The Battle of San Pietro (1945), 38, 100,
    109, 221
Battleship Potemkin (1925), 9, 140, 217
Bazin, André, 122, 133
Before Spring (1958), 224
*Before Stonewall: The Making of a Gay
    and Lesbian Community* (1984), 232
behavioral experimentation, 54–55
Berger, John, 167
Berkeley in the Sixties (1990), 4
Berlin: Symphony of a Great City (1927),
    75, 130, *131*, 138
Berliner, Alan, 60, 65, 80, 169, 244–45
Berlinger, Joe, 176
Bernardi, Daniel, 264
Best in Show (2000), 33
Bicycle Thieves (1948), 9, 15, 133, *135*
biography, *153*, 159, 181–82. *See also*
    autobiographical films
The Birth of Whiteness (Bernardi), 264
Black, Stephanie, 213
Black Is, Black Ain't (1995), 109
The Blair Witch Project (1999), xii, 17,
    33, 196
Block, Mitchell, 56–58, 57, 115–16
Blood of the Beasts (1949), 63, 84, 167
The Body Beautiful (1991), 80, 116–18,
    118, 202, 206
Bohlen, Anne, 230
Bomba, Abraham, 92
Bon Voyage (1944), 221
Bontoc Eulogy (1995), 73, 80, 92, 195,
    202
Booth, Marlene, 65
Born into Brothels (2004), 5, 132, 167,
    248
Boston Blackie, 76
Bowling for Columbine (2002), 60,
    182–83
Brecht, Bertolt, 199

The Bridge (1928), 31, 129, 130, 224
Bringas, Sylvie, 164
Briski, Zana, 5, 167, 248
Britain, 17, 28–29, 123, 141, 212, 219–20
British Film Institute, 19
Brittain, Donald, 35
Broken Rainbow (1985), 3
Broomfield, Nick, 12, 62, 188
Buñuel, Luis, 28, 48–50, 129, 165, 197, 226
Burns, Ken, 3, 170–71
Burstein, Nanette, 39, 46
Bus 174 (2002), 117
Butler, Judith, 235

The Cabinet of Dr. Caligari (1920), 133
cable television, 2
Cadillac Desert (1997), *193*
camcorder technology, xii
The Camera and I (Ivens), 225
camera techniques, 23, 254, 267
Canada, 124, 220
Cane Toads (1987), 84
Cannibal Tours (1988), 40
canon of documentary works, xv–xvi
Caouette, Jonathan, 5, 65, 80, 93, 202, 206
Capitalism: A Love Story (2009), 60
Capra, Frank, 170, 221
Capturing the Friedmans (2003), 40, 86–87, 117–18
case history, 189
Cassavetes, John, xii
categorization of documentary films, 143–45, *145*, 154
Cavadini, Alessandro, 53, *53*
Cavalcanti, Alberto, 28, 129–30, 222–23
Cayrol, Jean, 206, *207*
CBS News, 43
Central Intelligence Agency (CIA), 55
The Chair (1962), 173
character development, 254
charismatic documentary subjects, 58–59, 93
Chavez: Inside the Coup (2002), 98–99
Chile, 240–41

Chile, Obstinate Memory (1997), 32, *149*, *152*, 154, 241–42
Chin, Vincent, 4, *5*
Chopra, Joyce, 229
Choy, Christine, 4, 202
Chronicle of a Summer (1960): and identity politics, 240; and modes of documentary, 31; and the observational mode, 173; and the participatory mode, 182, 184, 185–87; and personal portraiture, 246; and role of documentary filmmakers, 20
chronology, 72, 98–99, 254
Churchill, Joan, 62
Cicero, 77
cinema of attractions, 126–27, 129, 136, 137
cinéma vérité, 184, 218
cinematic codes, 148
cinematic techniques, 148. *See also* camera techniques
cinématographe, 127
The City (1939): and documentary conventions, 21–22, *24*; and ethical issues, 52; and the expository mode, 167; and national identity, 221; and persuasive role of documentary, 105; and speaker/audience relationship, 64
The Civil War (1990), 159
Clair, René, 129
Clark, Dick, 182
Clarke, Shirley, 67–68, 245–46
class issues: and depiction of workers, 212–13; and identity politics, 238; and national identity, 215, 227; and persuasive role of documentary, 112–13, *114*; and Workers' Film and Photo Leagues, 223–24
classic oration, 86
classification of documentary films. *See* modes of documentary films
Clinton, Bill, 88
Coal Face (1935), 215, 222
Cohn, Roy, *179*
collaboration: and Ivens, 224–25; and the observational mode, 178; and participant-observation style, 181,

268; and the participatory mode, 185, 187; and voice of documentary, 69–70
Color Adjustment (1991), 229, 235
A Comedy in Six Unnatural Acts (1975), 236
"coming of age" narratives, 37
commemorative rhetoric, 107–108
Common Threads: Stories from the Quilt (1989), 4
communication, triangle of, 94–99
Communist Party, 223–24
community, 215–16
compilation films, 157, 193
Complaints of a Dutiful Daughter (1994), 80, 110, 184
complexity of issues, 86–87
Composition in Blue (1935), 163–64
composition of shots, 72. See also camera techniques
computer technology, 180
confessions, 182
Connie, Field, 161
consent, 53–56, 175
Constructivism, 137–41, 216, 219
"Constructivism in the Cinema" (Gan), 138
Contempt (1963), 96–97
contested concepts, 101–102
continuity editing, 23–24, 39, 132
Control Room (2004), 88
Cooper, Merian C., 136, 137, 137
Cops (television), xii, 32, 127
Corporation for Public Broadcasting, 19
Corpus: A Home Movie for Selena (1999), 201
The Cove (2009), 22–23
creativity, 6–7, 14, 36
credibility, 81, 84, 248
criminal acts, 57–58
Crisis: Behind a Presidential Commitment (1963), 160
critical rhetoric, 107–108
cross cutting, 39
Crumb (1994), 86, 189
cultural identity, 97, 103, 110, 115. See also ethnographic film; identity politics

Cultural Revolution, 224
Curse of the Blair Witch (television), xii
Curtis, Adam, 243
Curtis, Edward S., 136

Daisy: The Story of a Facelift (1982), 43, 44, 44–45, 54
Dali, Salvador, 129, 165
Dani tribe, 114
Danube Exodus (1998), 166, 180
Darwin's Nightmare (2004), 87–88
Daughter Rite (1978), 195, 196
David Holzman's Diary (1968), 196
The Day after Trinity (1980), 161
De Antonio, Emile, 30
De la Torre, Sergio, 231, 231–32
De Sica, Vittorio, 15, 133, 135
Dead Birds (1963), 40, 114, 167, 226
Deal, Carl, 244, 245
deception, 55–56, 56–58, 57, 90
defining documentary film, 1–41; and audience of documentaries, 33–41; changes in definitions, 15–16; and classification of documentary, 142–43; common characteristics, 6–14; and community of documentary practitioners, 19–20; and conventions, 20–28; and the Golden Age of documentary, 1–6; and institutional frameworks, 16–19; and modes of documentary, 30–33; and movements in documentary filmmaking, 28–30; working definition, 14
deliberative rhetoric, 105
Delluc, Louis, 129
democracy, 43
demonstrative expression, 138
demonstrative proofs, 82–83
Depression-era films, 30
The Devil Never Sleeps (1994), 191, 192
Diagonal Symphony (1924), 129
dialogue, 254
diaries, 181–82
diary films, 107, 153
dictatorship, 107
digital media: and future of documentary, 2; and image fidelity, xii–xiv;

and modes of documentary, 159; and voice of documentary, 159
direct address, 76, 76, 92, 154–55
discourses of sobriety, 36–37
Discovery, 18
discrimination, 236
distribution, 2, 18
Do the Right Thing (1989), 7
docudramas, 145
Documentary: A History of the Non-fiction Film (Barnouw), 72, 148
Documentary Film Classics (Rothman), 263, 264
Documentary (journal), 19
documentary modes. See modes of documentary films
Documenting the Documentary (Grant and Sloniowski, eds.), 264
Donovan, Jean, 203–204
Dont Look Back (1967), 21, 173–74
Dos Passos, John, 224
Double Indemnity (1944), 87
Dovzhenko, Alexander, 129, 219
Down and Out in America (1986), 4
Dox (journal), 19
Drew, Richard, 29
Drew, Robert, 160, 178
Drew Associates, 29
Duchamp, Marcel, 129
Dulac, Germaine, 129
Durran, Carman, 232
DVDs: and future of documentary, 2, 18–19; and modes of documentary, 33; and the participatory mode, 180; special advantages of, 87; and voice-over commentary, 58
Dylan, Bob, 21, 174

early documentary, 61. See also origin of documentary film
economic issues, 4, 30, 213–14
editing: and continuity, 23–24, 39, 132; and critical rhetoric, 107; and demonstrative proofs, 82; evidentiary, 25–26, 35, 132, 169; the observational mode, 172, 176–77; and poetic expression, 130; and representation of concepts, 100; and rhetorical ora-

tory, 138–39; and voice of documentary, 72; and writing about documentary film, 254
Eggeling, Viking, 129
Eisenstein, Sergei, xii, 133, 139–40, 216–17, 219
El Diablo Nunca Duerme (1994), 191, 192
electrification, 22, 156
elements of documentary, relationship between, 59–66
eloquence, 93
Else, Jon, xiv, 161, 168
embodied knowledge, 201
emotional appeals, 88, 134, 135, 255–56
Empire Marketing Board, 220
empiricism, 102, 125, 130, 134–35
The End of St. Petersburg (1927), 133
Engel, Wendy, 51
Enron: The Smartest Guys in the Room (2005), 14, 31, 55, 154–55, 215
Enthusiasm (1930), 29
epistephilia, 40–41
Epstein, Jean, 129, 130
Epstein, Rob, 232
Eskimo culture, 266–71, See also Nanook of the North (1922)
essay films, 107
ethical issues of documentary-making, 42–66; and classification of documentary films, 157; and filmmaker/subject relationship, 116; and the observational mode, 174–76; and the participatory mode, 182; purpose of ethics, 50–59; representations of people, 45–50; and satire, 50; speaker/subject/audience relationship, 59–66; and voice of documentary, 69–70; and writing about documentary film, 268–69
Ethnic Notions (1986), 235
ethnicity and race, 227, 238, 240. See also ethnographic film
ethnographic film. See also Nanook of the North (1922): and Ackerman, 230; and Blank, 18; and classification of documentary films, 152; and Gardner, 114; and the performative

mode, 205–206; and the reflexive mode, 197, 200; and writing about documentary film, 268
ethos, 79
Etre et avoir (2002), 48
European documentary, 28, 131. See also *specific countries*
European Documentary Film Institute, 19
events portrayed in documentary, 10–14, 99–101
Every Day except Christmas (1957), 28
everyday life, 123
evidentiary editing, 25–26, 35, 132, 169
exhibitionism, 126, 128
expectations of audiences, 38–41
experimentation, 121
experts, 80
explanatory role of documentary, 251–52
exploitation of subjects, 52
"Exploration as construction: Robert Flaherty and *Nanook of the North*" (Sherrill), 264–65
exploration films, *151*, 154
expository mode: and classification of documentary films, *149*, 154–55, 156–57, 167–71; described, 31; and DVD, 33; and ethical issues, 54; and the performative mode, 206–207; and persuasive role of documentary, 116; qualities of, *210–11*; and voice of documentary, 73, 159, 167–71
expressionist techniques, 133
Extremely Personal Eros: Love Song 1974 (1974), 188
Eyes on the Prize (1987, 1990), 3, 4, 106, 159, 190

Facebook, xiv–xv, 2
Facets, 19
factual appeals, 88. See also *evidentiary editing*
Fahrenheit 9/11 (2004), 5, 60, 93, 167, 191
faith, 126
The Fall of the Romanov Dynasty (1927), 112–13, *114*, 118, 140, 191

familiarity of documentary, 42
Family Business (1982), 40
family dynamics, 46–47, 116–17
Fanon, Frantz, 202
Far from Poland (1984), 106, 113, *115*, 195, *197*
Farm Security Administration, 222
fashion photography, *118*
Fast, Cheap and Out of Control (1997), 86
Feeding the Baby (1895), 121
Feeling My Way (1997), 164
feminism, 229–30
fetishism, 126
Fever (1921), 129
FIAF database, 265
fictional film: contrasted with documentary, xi–xii; and modes of documentary, 143–45, *145*; and origins of documentary film, 121–22; and stereotypes, 39; and voice of documentary, 69
fidelity of imagery, xii–xiii. See also *indexical quality of documentary*
Field, Connie, 24–25, 192, 230
Fièvre (Fever) (1921), 129
A Film about a Woman Who . . . (1974), 229, *230*
Film and Photo Leagues, 213
film festivals, 19
Finding Christa (1991), 65, 110, 184
Fireworks (1947), 236
First Contact (1984), 40
first-person essays, *152–53*
Fischer, Becky, 46, 47, 58–59, 88
Fischinger, Oskar, 163–64
Five-Year Plan, 74
Flaherty, Robert: and classification of documentary films, 154; and ethical issues, 49; indexical quality of documentary, 125; and national identity, 219–20, 222; and origins of documentary film, 123, 130, 224; and personal portrait films, 244; and rhetorical oratory, 136; and rules of documentary, 12–13; and sponsorship of films, 43, 146–47; and voice of documentary, 69–70, 71; and writ-

ing about documentary film, xviii, 253–54, 255, 257–59, 260, 262–63, 264–71

flashbacks, 130

fluidity of documentary genre, 20–21, 155

The Fog of War: Eleven Lessons from the Life of Robert McNamara (2003), 31, 243, 246

Folman, Ari, 80, 111, *112*, 202, 204

Forest of Bliss (1985), 202

Forgács, Péter: and new forms of identity, 234; and the participatory mode, 180; and the performative mode, 207–209, *208*; and personal portrait films, 244; and the poetic mode, 166

Forrest Gump (1994), xii

Foucault, Michel, 190

Foundation for Independent Film and Video, 19

Four Families (1959), 116

Fourth World, 229

Franju, Georges, 63

Frantz Fanon: Black Skin, White Mask (1996), 202

Free Cinema, 28, 29

Free Fall (1997), 166, 208, 234, 244

Freud, Sigmund, 104

Friedman, Arnold, 86–87

Friedman, David, 87

Friedman, Elaine, 87

Friedman, Jesse, 86–87

Friedman, Peter, 246

Friedrich, Su, 80, 169

Frontier Films, 224

Fuentes, Marlon, 73, 80, 92, 202

Funari, Vicki, *231*, 231–32

Gan, Alexei, 138

Gance, Abel, 129, 130, 163

Gardner, Robert, 114, 202

Gast, Leon, 191

Gates, William, 37

gay and lesbian culture, 192, 232–33, 238

gender issues, 44, 198–99, 235, 239–40

Gender Trouble (Butler), 235

Genet, Jean, 236

Geneva Conventions, 243–44

G.I. Jane (1997), 62

Gibney, Alex, 54–55, 243

Gilbert, Craig, 46

Gilbert, Peter, 37, 237

Gimme Shelter (1970), 173

Ginsburg, Faye, 263

Glass (1958), 166

The Gleaners and I (2000), 80, 102, 202

The Global Assembly Line (1986), 231

global warming, 77

God Grew Tired of Us: The Lost Boys of Sudan (2005), 239

Godard, Jean-Luc, 96, 185, 194

Godmilow, Jill: and the expository mode, 169; and the observational mode, *178*, *179*; and persuasive role of documentary, 106, 113, *115*; and the reflexive mode, 195

Goffmann, Erving, 8–9

Golden Age of documentary film, 1–6

Goldfarb, Lynn, 230

Goldovskaya, Marina, 89, 90, 91, *139*, *140*

Gore, Al, 77

Government Post Office (G.P.O.), 220, 222

governmental policy, 79–80

government-sponsored documentaries: and classification of documentary films, 157; and institutional frameworks, 17; and modes of documentary, 147; and national identity, 219–22; and origins of documentary film, 123; and public policy, 22

Grady, Rachel, 46, 58–59

graphic design, *137*

Grass: A Nation's Battle for Life (1925), 136, 137, *137*, 258

Great Britain. *See* Britain

Great Depression, 141

The Great Road (1927), 140

Greed (1925), xii

"green" communities, 21–22

Grey Gardens (1975), 174–75

Grierson, John: and the British Documentary movement, 28; and definitions of documentary, 6–7, 12, 13, 16,

17; and movements in documentary, 28–29; and national identity, 219–21, 222–23, 226; and origins of documentary film, 123–24, 224; and persuasive role of documentary, 94; and rhetorical oratory, 141; and social/political issues, 213, 221–22

Griffith, D. W., 132

Grizzly Man (2005), 35, 46, 93, 117, 183

group profile films, 153

Growing Up Female (1971), 198, 229

Gulags, 89

Gulf War, 82

Gunner Palace (2004), 110

Gunning, Tom, 126

Guzmán, Patricio, 169, 241–42

Haanstra, Bert, 166

Hammer, Barbara, 233, 234

hand-held cameras, 30, 56–57

Hara, Kazuo, 188

Hard Metals Disease (1987), 184

Harlan County, U.S.A. (1977), 191, 213

The Harvest of Shame (1960), 12, 40, 60, 231

Hauka tribesmen, 51, 97

Heart of Spain (1937), 224

Hell House (2001), 88

Hellman, Lillian, 224

Hemingway, Ernest, 167, 224

hero worship, 95

Herzog, Werner, 46, 183

hierarchical patterns, 70

High School (1968), 28, 31, 40, 173, 175

His Mother's Voice (1997), 111, 113, 204

historical representation: and classification of documentary films, 150; and metaphorical representation, 117; and rhetorical oratory, 105–106, 136; and voice of documentary, 80

historiography, 12

History and Memory (1991), 32, 80, 81, 202, 246

History Channel, 32–33

history essays, 181–82

Hitchcock, Alfred, 221

Hitler, Adolf, 22, 50, 94–95

Holliday, Billie, 249

Holocaust, 106, 164

home movies, 207–209, 208

homophobia, 246–48

Hoop Dreams (1994), 4, 21, 37, 56, 237

Hospital (1970), 100, 102

Hot Springs Documentary Film Festival, 19

Hotel Terminus (1988), 4

The Hour of the Furnaces (1968), 40

House Un-American Activities Committee (HUAC), 98

Housing Problems (1935), 40, 212–15, 222, 229

How to Do Things with Words (Austin), 203

How Yukong Moved the Mountains (1976), 224

Hughes, Langston, 202, 206

The Human Behavior Experiments (2006), 55

Human Remains (1998), 107

Humanities Full Text database, 264

Humphrey, Hubert, 35

The Hunters (1957), 226

Hurdanos, 49–50

Hurricane Katrina, 102, 244, 245, 248

Hurwitz, Leo, 224, 226–27

Huston, John, 100, 221

Huston, Walter, 243

I Am a Sex Addict (2005), 198

identity politics, 228–29

Imagining Indians (1993), 229

immigrant communities, 239–40

implicit representation, 74

impressionism, 130, 133. *See also* poetic mode

In and Out of Africa (1992), 49, 51

In Media Res, 19

In the Land of the Head Hunters (1914), 136

In the Land of the War Canoes (1927), 136

In the Year of the Pig (1969), 30, 190

inartistic proofs, 78

An Inconvenient Truth (2006), 77, 105

independence movements, 227
indexical quality of documentary: and audience, 34–36; and classification of documentary films, 147, 157; and narrative storytelling, 133–34; and origins of documentary film, 124–25, 128; and the participatory mode, 183; and "rayograms," 129; and rhetorical oratory, 135–36, 137; and writing about documentary film, 271
indigenous people, 53, 65, 185, 205, 266–68
indirect address, 76, 77, 92
individual profile films, 153
Indonesia Calling (1946), 227
industrial films, 146, 146
Inflation (1928), 129
informational film, 101, 147
informed consent, 53–56
informing logic of documentary, 21–22, 40–41, 69
institutional framework of documentary: and audience of documentaries, 33; and classification of documentary films, 142–43; and definition of documentary, 16–19; and "discourses of sobriety," 36–37; institutional discourses, 62; and origins of documentary film, 123–24, 125
instructional films, 101
International Documentary Association, 19
International Federation of Film Archives, 265
International Monetary Fund (IMF), 213–14
Internet Movie Database (IMDB), 224, 261–62
Internet resources, 2, 260–63
interpretation, 96–97
interviews, 31, 76, 91, 155, 189
Intimate Stranger (1992), 65, 80, 244–45
Inuit culture, 12–13, 43, 266–71
invention, rhetorical, 78–85
investigative reporting, 149, 187–88. See also television journalism
irony, 85

Isle of Flowers (1989), 84
Italian neo-realist films, 45, 133, 135
Ivens, Joris: and contesting the nation-state, 224–25, 227; and the expository mode, 167, 170, 171; and labor issues, 213; and origins of documentary film, 129, 130, 224; and the participatory mode, 185; and the poetic mode, 162, 165; and Workers' Film and Photo Leagues, 224

Jacopetti, Gualtiero, 49, 127
Jane (1962), 174
Janie's Janie (1971), 229
Jarecki, Eugene, 40, 100
Jazz (2000), 60, 191
Jeanne Dielmann, 23 Quai du Commerce, 1080 Bruxelles (1975), 229
Jennings, Humphrey, 28, 223
Jesus Camp (2006), 46, 47, 58–59, 88, 98
JFK (1991), 7, 146
Joslin, Tom, 246
journal films, 153
journalism: and the expository mode, 168–69; and institutional frameworks, 16; and modes of documentary, 31, 146, 147; and movements in documentary, 28, 29; and social/political issues, 212; and voice of documentary, 82–84, 158, 159
Joyce at 34 (1972), 198, 229
judicial rhetoric, 105–106
Julien, Isaac, 202
juxtaposition, 75–76

Kalatazov, Mikhail, 28
Kaufman, Ross, 167
Kayapo Indians, 65, 205
Kennedy, John F., 35, 146, 160
Kenya Boran (1974), 177
King, Allan, 109
King, Rodney, 61, 88
King Kong, 136
Kino Glaz (a.k.a. Kino-Eye: 1924), 217–18
kino-eye, 29, 138–39, 217–18, 223

Kino-Eye: The Writings of Dziga Vertov
(Michelson), 217
kinopravda (film truth), 184, 217–18
Kirsanoff, Dimitri, 129
"kitchen sink" feature films, 29
Klein, Bonnie, 187
Klein, Jim, 229, 230
Komosol (1932), 224
Kopple, Barbara, 4, 158, 191, 213
Koyaanisqatsi (1983), 21, 31, 74–75
Kurt and Courtney (1998), 188

La Danse (2009), 28
La Roue (The Wheel) (1923), 129, 130,
163
La Terra Trema (1948), 133
Labyrinth Project, 180
L'Affiche (The Poster) (1924), 129
L'Age d'or (1930), 165
Land without Bread (1932): and artistic
proofs, 84; and credibility of docu-
mentary, 8; and documentary con-
ventions, 21, 28; and ethical issues,
48–50, 49, 59; and the expository
mode, 169; and modes of documen-
tary, 32; and national identity, 226;
and the performative mode, 203; and
the reflexive mode, 197
language of documentary makers, 20
Lanzmann, Claude, 35, 184
Las Hurdes, Spain. *See Land without
Bread* (1932)
Las Madres de la Plaza de Mayo (1985),
3, 190, 203
The Last Days (1998), 35
Latin American documentary, 28
L'Avventura (1960), 87
Le Retour à la Raison (1923), 129
Leacock, Richard, 29, 178, 265–66
Les Maîtres Fous (1955), 31, 51, 97, 226
Les Racquetteurs (1958), 20, 173
Lessons of Darkness (1992), 75
L'Etoile de Mer (1928), 130
Letter to Jane (1972), 194
Letter without Words (1998), 65
library resources, 259–60, 263, 264
Life and Debt (2001), 213–14

The Life and Times of Rosie the Riveter
(1980), 24–26, 27, 30, 76, 161, 192,
230
Listen to Britain (1941), 31, 204
Livingston, Jennie, 205, 236
location filming, xiv, *xiv*, 125, *135*
logic, 77–79, 103
*The Loneliness of the Long Distance
Runner* (1962), 29
Lonely Boy (1962), 108
Looking for Langston (1988), 202
Lorentz, Pare, 123, 220, 221, *221*
Loridan, Marcelline, 185–87
Lost Boys of Sudan (2003), 239
Louisiana Story (1948), 130, 146–47,
267
Lujan, Lourdes, 232
Lumière Brothers (August and Louis):
and early cinema, xvii; and origins of
documentary film, 121, *123*, 125, 127,
128, 224; and the poetic mode, 163

MacDougall, David, 176, 177, *185*, *200*
MacDougall, Judith, *185*, *200*
Mallet, Marilu, 80, 188, 240–41
Man Bites Dog (1992), 57
Man on Wire (2008), 12
Man with a Movie Camera (1929): and
documentary conventions, 20–21;
and modes of documentary, 32, 156;
and movements in documentary, 29;
and narrative storytelling, 133; and
national identity, 217; and origins of
documentary film, 130–31; and the
participatory mode, 184; and the re-
flexive mode, 195, 197
Maquilapolis (2006), 231, *231*–32
Mariposa collective, 192–94, 232
Marker, Chris, 28, 158, 166, 197–98,
239
A Married Couple (1970), 109, 110
Marsalis, Wynton, 60
Martinez, Fred, 246–48, *247*
masked interview, 177
Mayles brothers, 174
McElwee, Ross, 50–51, 54, 184, *186*
McNamara, Robert, 243, 246

Mead, Margaret, 116, 117
Meat (1976), 63
Media Worlds (Ginsburg), 263
medical imaging, xv
Meeropol, Abel, 249
Méliès, Georges, 122
Memorandum (1965), 35
memory, 90–92
Menchú, Rigoberta, 235
Ménilmontant (1926), 129
"mere footage" term, 75, 146, 146
Metallica: Some Kind of Monster
    (2004), 31
metaphorical representation, 83–84,
    108–119
metonymy, 83–84
Metropolis (1927), 133
Metz, Christian, 121
Milgram, Stanley, 54, 55
military coups, 98–99
military-industrial complex, 100
Milk, Harvey, 232
Milk (2008), 2, 234
Misère au Borinage (1934), 213, 224–25
Mitry, Jean, 162, 163
Moana (1926), 137
mobility, 30
mockumentaries, 8, 16–17, 85, 142, 145
Model (1980), 176
modes of documentary films, 142–71,
    172–211. See also expository mode;
    observational mode; participatory
    mode; performative mode; poetic
    mode; reflexive mode; and cinéma
    vérité, 218; and classification of docu-
    mentary films, 143, 147–57, 149–53;
    described, 30–33, 147–57; examples
    of, 149–53; and forms of persuasion,
    103–104; and models for documen-
    tary, 147–57, 149–53; relationship to
    other film forms, 144–47; and social
    issues, 242–43; and voice of docu-
    mentary, 72, 158–62; and writing
    about documentary film, 255
Moholy-Nagy, Laszlo, 162
Momma Don't Allow (1956), 28–29
Mondo Cane (1962), 49, 127, 127

"mondo" films, 127, 127–28
Monster (2003), 10, 11
Monster Kid Home Movies (2005), 128
montage, 130, 133, 138–41
Monterey Pop (1968), 174
Moore, Michael: and box office suc-
    cesses, 4; and classification of
    documentary films, 142; and ethical
    issues, 43, 51, 56; and the expository
    mode, 167, 169; and filmmaker as
    character, 60; and modes of docu-
    mentary, 155; and the participatory
    mode, 182–83, 191; and persuasive
    role of documentary, 5, 98; and
    speaker-audience relationship, 61
Morin, Edgar, 184, 187, 218, 246
Morris, Errol: and arrangement of
    documentaries, 86, 89; box office
    successes, 4; and critical rhetoric,
    107–108; and ethical issues, 47–48,
    55; and the participatory mode, 191;
    and personal portraiture, 243; and
    speaker-audience relationship, 60;
    and staged events, 125; and voice of
    documentary, 76, 92
movements and documentary style, 29
MoveOn.org, 228
Müller, Ray, 191
Murrow, Edward R., 12, 231
mythical origins of documentary,
    120–21, 121–24

N!ai: Story of a !Kung Woman (1980),
    108
Nanook of the North (1922): and clas-
    sification of documentary films,
    154; and definition of documentary,
    12–13, 15; and documentary conven-
    tions, 20; and ethical issues, 43, 44,
    46, 49; and indexical quality of im-
    ages, 125; and national identity, 226;
    and origins of documentary film,
    123; and personal portrait films, 244;
    and persuasive role of documentary,
    108; and the reflexive mode, 200;
    and rhetorical oratory, 136; and
    speaker-audience relationship, 61;

and voice of documentary, 69–70;
and writing about documentary film,
xviii, 253–71
Nanook Revisited (1998), 269
narrative, 77, 103, 128, 131–35
National Basketball Association, 56
National Film Board of Canada, 220
National Socialist Party, 50
nationalism and national identity, 141,
215–23, 225–26, 242
Native American culture, 246–48, 247.
See also Nanook of the North (1922)
Navajo culture, 246–48
Nazi Party, 22, 50, 94–95, 177–78
neo-realism: and classification of docu-
mentary films, 144–45, 145; Italian
neo-realist films, 45, 133, 135; and
narrative storytelling, 133, 135; and
the observational mode, 174
Netflix, 19
neutrality of documentary filmmakers,
59
New Day Films, 19
New Deal, 141, 221
New Iranian cinema, 45
New York Times, 266
news broadcasting, 82–83
Newsreel (group), 227–28, 231
newsreels, 24, 138, 146
Night and Fog (1955), 31, 35, 110, 142,
206–207, 207
Night Mail (1936), 16, 60, 74, 125, 154
Nitrate Kisses (1992), 233, 234
No Lies (1973), 33, 56–58, 57, 59,
115–16, 196
Nobody's Business (1996): and filmmaker as character, 60; and metaphorical
representation, 110; and the participatory mode, 181; and personal
portraiture, 244–45; and speaker-
audience relationship, 65; and voice
of documentary, 80
nonartificial proofs, 78
nonfiction films, 143–45, 145, 148–49,
149–53
noninterventionist approach to documentary, 28
nonverbal communication, 92

North American documentary, 28
Nosferatu (1922), 133
Not a Love Story (1981), 187
The Nuer (1970), 97
Nuremberg rally, 52, 95, 96, 170, 171,
177–78
N.Y., N.Y. (1957), 164

Obedience (1965), 40, 54, 55
objectivity, 84–85, 125
observational mode: and classification
of documentary films, 144, 150,
154, 157; described, 31, 172–79; and
movements in documentary, 30; and
narrative storytelling, 133; origins of,
160; qualities of, 210–11; and voice of
documentary, 73, 76
October (1927), 133, 140, 217
Odets, Clifford, 224
The Odyssey (Homer), 96–97
The Old and the New (1929), 140, 217
Omori, Emiko, 80, 83, 188
online resources, 33
Onwurah, Ngozi, 80, 116–17, 118, 202,
206
Operation Abolition (1960), 98
Operation Correction (1961), 98
Ophuls, Marcel, 187
Oppenheimer, Robert J., 161
oration. See also voice-over commentary: classical, 86, 88; and delivery,
92; and early documentary, 128; and
persuasion, 104–105; and voice of
documentary, 77–78
organization, 100
origin of documentary film, 120–41;
and convergence of factors, 124–28;
and myth, 120–21; and narrative
story telling, 131–35; and the 1920s,
128–31; and realism, 121–24; and
rhetorical oratory, 135–41
Oscar-winning documentaries, 2–4, 13,
232, 243
ostranenie, 199

Pacific Film Archive, 260
Pacific 231 (1949), 162–63, 163
Painlevé, Jean, 146

Palace of Delights (1982), *xiv*
Panh, Rithy, 99
Paradise Lost (1996), 176
Paris Is Burning (1990), 108, 205, 236
Paris Qui Dort (The Crazy Ray) (1924), 129
participatory citizenship, 141
participatory mode: described, 31, 157, 179–94; examples of, *151*; participant-observation style, 181, 268; qualities of, *210–11*; and voice of documentary, 70–71
pathos, 79
Pennebaker, D. A., 29, 142, 178
The People's Century (1998), 159
performative mode: and classification of documentary films, *152*, 157; described, 32, 199–209; and ethical issues, 45–46; and gay and lesbian biography, 235–37; and new forms of
· identity, 235–37; and persuasive role of documentary, 116–17; qualities of, *210–11*; and social issue documentaries, 246; and voice of documentary, 158–59
periods of documentary style, 28–30
personal portrait documentary, 244, *250–51*, 253
persuasion, 26, 68, 103–108, 168. *See also* expository mode
Petit, Philippe, 12
Peto, Gyorgy, 166, 209
Philibert, Nicolas, 48
photogénie, 130, 133, 141
photographic images: and origins of documentary film, 122, 124–25; and realism, 134; and representation of concepts, 99–100; scientific uses of, 127; shortcomings of, 42–43
photography, documentary compared to, 121
photomontage, *131*
physical realism, 134–35
Play of Light: Black, White, Grey (1930), 162
plot, 132
The Plow That Broke the Plains (1936), 22, 31, 40, 169, 221

poetic mode: and classification of documentary films, *150*, 154, 157, 162–66; described, 31; and Forgács, *208*; Gan on, 138; and Ivens, *165*; and origins of documentary film, 128, 129–31; and the performative mode, 206; and persuasive role of documentary, 103, 116–17; poetic experimentation, 129–31; and political subjects, 214–15; qualities of, *210–11*; and rhetorical oratory, 137; and speaker-audience relationship, 60; and voice of documentary, 74, 77, 162–66
point-of-view shots, 39
political issues, 212–52; and anthropological filmmaking, 65; and arrangement of documentaries, 87–88; and contesting the nation state, 223–28; and documentary conventions, 27; and ethical issues, 43, 50; and gay and lesbian biography, 236; and identity politics, 238–42; and the major media, 1; and national identity, 215–23; and new forms of identity, 228–38; and Newsreel films, 228; and the participatory mode, 182, 190; and people as victims/agents, 212–15; and personal portraiture, 242–49; and persuasive role of documentary, 94–95, 98; and the politics of identity, 238–42; and rhetoric, 79–80, 141
popular memory, 91
popularity of documentary, 4, 143
Portillo, Lourdes, 3, 190, *191, 192, 201*
Portrait of Jason (1967), 67, 245–46
postcolonial studies, 70
postproduction, 172. *See also* editing
The Power of Nightmares: The Rise of the Politics of Fear (2004), 243
Prelude to War (1941), 222
The Presentation of Self in Everyday Life (1959), 8–9
Primary (1960), 20, 31, 35, 133, 173
primary source material, 259
The Prince Is Back (1999), 139, *140*
problem/solution structure: and *Always for Pleasure*, 18; and *An Inconvenient Truth*, 77; and arrangement of docu-

mentaries, 85–86; and *The City*, 25; and conventions in documentary, 21–23; and rhetoric, 63; and voice of documentary, 59–60
pro-filmic events, 34
propaganda, xv, 89, 90
psychological realism, 134
public opinion, 44, 222
public policy, 79–80
publicity, xii
Pudovkin, Vsevolod, 133, 219

Quintilian, 86

Rabbit in the Moon (1999), 80, 83, 188
race issues, 227, 238, 240
radio, 181
Radio Bikini (1987), 4
Rain (1929), 75, 129, 157, 162, *165*, 224
Rainer, Yvonne, 229–30
Ray, Man, 129, 130
"rayograms," 129
Real World (television), 9
realism: and Constructivism, 139–40; and Ivens, 225; neo-realism, 45, 133, *135*, 144–45, *145*, 174; and origins of documentary film, 121–24; and photographic images, 134; psychological, 134; reality television, xii, 32, 126, *127*, 159, 212–13; and the reflexive mode, 195–97; reproductions of reality, 13; Socialist Realism, 138, 219
Reassemblage (1982), 32, 156, 194, 195
reconstructions, 125, 269. *See also* reenactment
recurring topics, 101–103, 108
Red Scare, 98
reenactment: and classification of documentary films, *145*; and definition of documentary, 13; and persuasive role of documentary, 106, *115*, 116–17; and speaker-audience relationship, 66; and writing about documentary film, 269–70
reflexive mode: and animated elements, 33; and classification of documentary films, *151*, 155–56; described, 31–32, 194–99; and identity politics, 239;

and origins of documentary film, 130–31; and persuasive role of documentary, 113, 115–16; qualities of, *210–11*; and voice of documentary, 158–59
Reichert, Julia, 229, 230
Reisz, Karel, 28, 29
Report from the Aleutians (1943), 221
reporting. *See* journalism
representative quality of documentary, 68
reproductions of reality, 13
research, 258–59
Resnais, Alain, 35, 206, 207
responsibility of documentary filmmakers. *See* ethical issues of documentary-making
retrospection, 91–92
Revillon Freres, 43, 268, 269
The Revolution Will Not Be Televised (2002), 98–99
rhetoric: and arrangement, 85–89; and definition of documentary, 141; deliberative, 105; and delivery, 92–93; frameworks of, 86; and invention, 78–85; and memory, 90–92; and origins of documentary film, 128, 135–41; and persuasive role of documentary, 104–105, 118; and social issue documentaries, 248–49; and speaker-audience relationship, 63; and style, 89–90; and voice of documentary, 77–78; and writing about documentary film, 255
Rhetoric (Aristotle), 79
Rhythmus 23 (1923), 129
Riefenstahl, Leni: and camera techniques, *96*; and choreography, 95; and ethical issues, 50, *52*; and the expository mode, *170*, *171*; and the observational mode, 177–78; and the participatory mode, 191–92; and persuasive role of documentary, 94; and problem/solution style, 22
Rien que les Heures (1926), 129–30
Riggs, Marlon: and metaphorical representation, 109; and new forms of identity, *234*, 235, 236; and the

performative mode, 202, 204; and personal portrait films, 244; and speaker-audience relationship, 65–66

The River (1937): and classification of documentary films, 156; and government sponsorship, 22; and narrative storytelling, 132; and national identity, 220, 221, *221*, 222; and speaker-audience relationship, 64

The Road to Guantanamo (2006), xii

Roberts, Scott, 102, 244, *245*, 248

Rodchenko, Aleksandr, 138

Roger and Me (1989): box office success, 4; and documentary conventions, 21; and ethical issues, 43, 51, 56; and filmmaker as character, 60; and identity politics, 240; and the participatory mode, 183; and voice-over commentary, 60

Romanov family, 112–13, See also *The Fall of the Romanov Dynasty* (1927)

Rome, Open City (1945), xii, 133

Rony, Fatimah Tobing, 264, 269–70

Rosenblatt, Jay, 107

Roses in December (1982), 203–204

Rossellini, Roberto, xii, 133

Rotha, Paul, 28

Rouch, Jean, 51, 184, 187, 218, 246

Roy Cohn/Jack Smith (1994), *178*, *179*

Rubbo, Michael: and ethical issues, 43, *44*, 54; and identity politics, 241; and the participatory mode, 188; and speaker-audience relationship, 61; and voice of documentary, 80

Russia, 131, 140–41, 216. See also Soviet cinema

The Russia of Nicholas II and Leo Tolstoy (1928), 140–41

Ruttmann, Walter, 130, *131*

Ryan (2004), 204

S 21: The Khmer Rouge Killing Machine (2003), 99

Sad Song of Yellow Skin (1970), 188

safari films, 128

Salesman (1969), 31, 133

Salt for Svanetia (1930), 74, 203

Salt of the Earth (1954), 9

salvage ethnography, 269

Sans Soleil (1982), 28, 166, 197–98, 239

satire, 50. *See also* mockumentaries

Saturday Night and Sunday Morning (1960), 29

Saving Private Ryan (1998), 38

Schindler's List (1993), 7, 11

Schoedsack, Ernest B., *136–37*, 137

science: and "cinema of attractions," 127; and modes of documentary, 143; and origins of documentary film, 124; proof vs. persuasion, 77; scientific evidence, 146; scientific films, 147; scientific imaging, 129

Sci-Fi Channel, xii

Scorpio Rising (1964), 166

The Sea Horse (1934), 146

secondary source material, 259, 262–63

self-presentation, 9

The Selling of the Pentagon (1971), 43, 44, 60, 167

The Seventeenth Parallel (1968), 224

sexual identity, 229, 232–36, *233*, *234*

Shadows (1960), xii, 9

shared values, 85

Shell Oil, 147

Sherman's March (1985): and ethical issues, 50–51, 54; and metaphorical representation, 110; and the participatory mode, 184, *186*; and voice-over commentary, 60

Shoah (1985): and indexical quality of images, 35; and modes of documentary, 31; and the participatory mode, 184, 191; and persuasive role of documentary, 106; and voice of documentary, 67–68

shortcomings of photographic images, 42–43

Shub, Esther: and movements in documentary, 28; and national identity, 218–19; and origins of documentary film, 224; and the participatory mode, 191; and persuasive role of documentary, 112–13, *114*; and rhetorical oratory, 140; and voice of documentary, 158

Sicko (2007), 5, 60, 154–55, 215

Sight and Sound magazine, 29
Silence (1998), 164
Silver, Jon, 70–71, *71*, 184
Silverlake Life: The View from Here (1993), 110, 117, 246
Simpson, O. J., 63
Sinofsky, Bruce, 176
16 in Webster Groves (1966), 167, 169
16mm cameras, 172
60 Minutes, 16, 182
Slouching toward Las Vegas (Thompson), 61
The Smiling Madame Beudet (1922), 129
Smoke Menace (1937), 105, 215
social issues documentary, 212–52; characteristics of, *250–51*; and contesting the nation state, 223–28; and context, 95; and conventions of documentary, xiv; documentary's role in, 2, 4; and metaphorical representation, 109; and movements in documentary, 30; and national identity, 215–23; and new forms of identity, 228–38; and people as victims/agents, 212–15; and personal portraiture, 242–49; and persuasive role of documentary, 103, 105; and the politics of identity, 238–42; and role of documentary filmmakers, 19–20; and social actors, 45–46; and social agendas, 141; and social institutions, 103; and social policy films, 221–22; and voice of documentary, 80
social sciences, 181
Socialist Realism, 138, 219
sociology, *152*, 189
Soldier Girls (1980), 40, 62
Solidarity movement, 106, 113
Solovky Power (1988), 31, 89, 90, *91*
Song of Ceylon (1934), 31, 60, 74, 166
Song of the Rivers (1954), 224
The Sorrow and the Pity (1970), 187
sound recording, 72
sound track, 26–28, 111
source material, 259–64
Soviet cinema: and film theory, 130; and movements in documentary, 28;

and national identity, 216–19, 222; and origins of documentary film, 123–24, 133, 137–41
Spanish Civil War, 224
The Spanish Earth (1937), 31, 109, 167, 170, *171*, 224
Speak Body (1987), 68
speaker/subject/audience relationship, 59–66, 94
spectacle, 124, 126–27
speech, 67, 254. *See also* oration; voice-over commentary
Spielberg, Steven, 11, 38
sponsorship of documentary, 22, *146*, 146–47, 268–69. *See also* government-sponsored documentaries
Spurlock, Morgan, 5
staged events, 73, 117, *118*, *123*, 125
"Stand Up! Stand Up!" (Anderson), 29
Standard Operating Procedure (2008), 55, 89, 108
Stanford prison experiment, 54–55
Star Wars, 95
The Statue of Liberty (1985), 3
Steiner, Ralph, 21–22, *24*
stereotypes, 39, 46, 50, 156, 199
Stone, Oliver, 146
Stonewall riots, 192
Storck, Henri, 213, 224–25
storytelling, 137
Strachan, Carolyn, 53, *53*
Strange Fruit (2002), 249
Strange Victory (1948), 226–27
Stranger with a Camera (1999), 154, 156
Strike (1925), xii, 140, 217
Stroheim, Eric von, xii
Studies in Documentary Film (journal), 19
stylistic choices, 63, 70–71, 89–90, 132
subjectivity, 32, 81, *113*
subjects of documentary, 7–8, 8–10, 10–14, 101
summarizing documentaries, 256–58
Super Size Me (2004), 5, 142
Surname Viet Given Name Nam (1989), 195, *196*, *197*, *198*, 239–40, *241*
surrealism, *102*, 129

surveillance footage, 146, 147
Survivor (television), xii, 9, 127
suspension of disbelief, 126
synthetic portrait, 138

Tajima-Peña, Renee, 4, 202
Tajiri, Rea, 80, 81, 202
Takeover (1981), 185
Tale of the Wind (1988), 224
talking points, 90
tangible representations, 109–110
Tarnation (2003): and metaphorical representation, 117–18; and new forms of identity, 236; and the participatory mode, 181; and the performative mode, 202; and speaker-audience relationship, 65; and voice of documentary, 80, 93
Taxi to the Dark Side (2007), 243–44
"Taxidermy and Romantic Ethnography: Robert Flaherty's Nanook of the North," 264
technological innovation, 159, 172, 179–80
television journalism: and the expository mode, 168–69; and modes of documentary, 31, 146, 147; and social/political issues, 212–13; and voice of documentary, 82–84, 158, 159
Tennessee Valley Authority, 22, 156, 220, 222
tertiary source material, 259–62
testimonial, 151
The Crazy Ray (1924), 129
The Poster (1924), 129
The Wheel (1923), 129, 130, 163
theater of the absurd, 102
thesis statements, 257–58
The Thin Blue Line (1988): and arrangement of documentaries, 87; box office success, 4; and ethical issues, 47–48; and filmmaker as character, 60; and the participatory mode, 191; and persuasive role of documentary, 106; and staged events, 125; and voice of documentary, 75–76, 92

The Thin Red Line (1998), 38
The Things I Cannot Change (1966), 51–52
The Third Eye: Race, Cinema and Ethnographic Spectacle (Rony), 264
third person perspective, 61–62
Third World Newsreel, 19
This Is Spinal Tap (1984), 16–17, 85
This Sporting Life (1963), 29
Three Songs of Lenin (1934), 204
The Ties That Bind (1984), 80
The Times of Harvey Milk (1984), 2, 3, 232, 236
titles and intertitles, 76
To Be and to Have (2002), 48
Tongues Untied (1989): and metaphorical representation, 117; and modes of documentary, 32; and new forms of identity, 235, 236; and the performative mode, 202, 204, 206; and personal portraiture, 244, 246; and speaker-audience relationship, 65–66
torture, 243–44
traditions of documentary filmmaking, 120–21
Trance and Dance in Bali (1952), 31, 226
travelogues, 128, 151
Treadwell, Timothy, 35, 46, 93, 183
Treaty of Versailles, 22
triangle of communication, 94–99
Trinh T. Minh Ha: and the expository mode, 169; and identity politics, 239–40, 241; and the reflexive mode, 194, 195, 196, 197
A Trip to the Moon (1902), 122
Triumph of the Will (1935): and camera techniques, 96; and contesting the nation-state, 225; and ethical issues, 50, 52; and the expository mode, 170, 171; and the observational mode, 177–78; and origins of documentary film, 128; and persuasive role of documentary, 94–95; and problem/solution style, 22; and Star Wars, 95
Trouble the Water (2008), 102, 215, 244, 245, 248
The Truman Show (1998), xii

trust, 69–70
Tupicoff, Dennis, 111, *113*
Turin, Victor A., 28, 137
Turksib (1929), 137, 203
TV Guide, xii
TV Nation (1994), 60
Two Laws (1981), 53, *53*, 175
Two Spirits: Sexuality, Gender and the Murder of Fred Martinez (2009), 246–48, *247*
types of documentary, 15. *See also* modes of documentary films

Un Chant d'amour (1950), 236
Un Chien Andalou (An Andalusian Dog) (1929), 129, 165
Unfinished Diary (1983), 80, 188, 240–41
Union Maids (1976), 30, 230
United Nations Educational, and Scientific Organization (UNESCO), 220
United Nations (UN), 220
University of California at Berkeley (UCB), 260
University of California at Los Angeles (UCLA) Library, 260

values and beliefs, 79–80
Van Dyke, Willard, 21–22, *24*
Varda, Agnès, 80, 102, 202
Vawter, Ron, *178*, *179*
Venezuela, 98–99
Vernon, FL (1981), 108
Vertov, Dziga: and classification of documentary films, 156; and Grierson, 223; and Ivens, 224; and movements in documentary, 28, 29; and narrative storytelling, 133; and national identity, 216, 217–19, 221; and Newsreel films, 228; and origins of documentary film, 123–24, 130–31, 224; and the participatory mode, 184; and the reflexive mode, 195, 197; and rhetorical oratory, 138–39
Victory at Sea (television), 110, 167
Vietnam, 30, 239–40, 243

Vigo, Jean, 137
Visconti, Luchino, 133
visual anthropology, *152. See also* anthropology; ethnographic film
voice of documentary, 67–93. *See also* voice-over commentary; and arrangement, 85–89; categories of voice, 72–77; and classification of documentary films, 147, 158–62; and delivery, 92–93; described, 120; and the expository mode, 167, *168*, 169; and indexical quality of documentary, 125; and invention, 78–85; and memory, 90–92; and modes of documentary, 158–62; and orator's voice, 77–78; and poetic expression, 129–31; qualities of voice, 67–72; and social issues vs. personal portraits, *250–51*; and style, 89–90; Voice of Authority, 76
voice-over commentary. *See also* voice of documentary: and definition of documentary, 15; and documentary conventions, xiv; and ethical issues, 48–49, 51, 58; and institutional frameworks, 17; and metaphorical representation, 116; and mixed modes of documentary, 32; and 1930s period films, 30; and the participatory mode, *183*; and persuasive role of documentary, 100; relationship among elements of documentary, 59–66; and *The River* (1934), 220; "voice-of-God" commentary, 59–60, 74, 76, 160–61, 167, *168*, 169

Waltz with Bashir (2008): and definition of documentary, 13–14; and metaphorical representation, 111; and modes of documentary, 32; and performative mode, 202, 204; and persuasive role of documentary, *112*; and voice of documentary, 80
The War (2007), 159
The War Game (1966), 32
The War Room (1993), 31, 88
The War (series), 171

Watering the Gardener (1895), 121

Watsonville on Strike (1989), 70–71, *71*, 184, 225

Waugh, Tom, 235

Ways of Seeing (1974), 167

"WE: Variant of a Manifesto," 29

We Are the Lambeth Boys (1958), 29

Wedding Camels (1980), 40, 110, 176, 200

Weill, Claudia, 229

When the Levees Broke (2006), 244

When We Were Kings (1996), 191

Who Killed Vincent Chin? (1988), 4, *5*, 202, 246

Why We Fight (2005), 40, 100, *221*, 222

Why We Fight (series): and audience expectations, 40; and classification of documentary films, 157; and the expository mode, 167, 170; and modes of documentary, 150; and national identity, 221–22; and the performative mode, 208; and personal portraiture, 243

Wikipedia, 261–62

Wilkerson, Travis, 169

Winston, Brian, 212–13, 214, 222, 228

Wiseman, Frederick: and movements in documentary, 28, 29; and the observational mode, 175, 176, 178; and persuasive role of documentary, 100, 102; and speaker-audience relationship, 62, 63; and voice of documentary, 158

With Babies and Banners (1979), 30, 230

The Woman's Film (1971), 198, 228–29

Women Make Movies, 19

The Wonderful, Horrible Life of Leni Riefenstahl (1993), 191

Word Is Out (1977), 67–68, 182, 192, 232, 234

Workers' Film and Photo Leagues, 223–24, 226

Workers Leaving the Lumière Factory (1895), xvii, 121–22, *123*

World War II. *See also* *Triumph of the Will* (1935); *Why We Fight* (series): and audience of documentaries, 40; and expository films, 171; and government-sponsored documentary, 27; and indexical quality of images, 35; and modes of documentary, 32; and movements in documentary, 30; and personal portraiture, 243

World Wide Web, 259

Wright, Basil, 28, 166, 223

writing about documentary, 253–71; preparation, 253–57; research, 259–65; sample essays, 265–67, 268–70, 270–71; thesis development, 257–59

Wuornos, Aileen, *10*, *11*, 11–12

Yadim, Orly, 164

Yamagata Documentary Film Festival, 19

Yidl in the Middle (1998), 65

Yosemite: The Fate of Heaven (1988), 168

YouTube, xiv–xv, 2, 19

Zahedi, Caveh, 198

Zapruder, Abraham, 7, 146

Zvenigora (1928), 129

Zwigoff, Terry, 86, *189*

BILL NICHOLS edited *Movies and Methods*, vols. 1 and 2, works that helped establish film studies as an academic discipline. His *Representing Reality* (IUP, 1991) launched the contemporary study of documentary film, and the first edition of *Introduction to Documentary* (IUP, 2001) has become the most widely used introductory textbook in the field. His general introduction to film, *Engaging Cinema*, was published in 2010. It is the first introduction to film studies that integrates a study of film's formal qualities with its enormous significance as a medium of social representation and personal expression.

CPSIA information can be obtained
at www.ICGtesting.com
Printed in the USA
BVHW01s1429111217
502490BV00013B/380/P